Mimesis, Desire, and the Novel

Studies in Violence, Mimesis, and Culture

Mimesis, Desire, and the Novel

RENÉ GIRARD AND LITERARY CRITICISM

Edited by Pierpaolo Antonello
and Heather Webb

Michigan State University Press · *East Lansing*

Copyright © 2015 by Michigan State University

♾ The paper used in this publication meets the minimum requirements of ANSI/NISO Z39.48-1992 (R 1997) (Permanence of Paper).

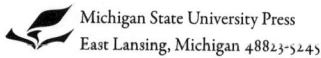 Michigan State University Press
East Lansing, Michigan 48823-5245

Printed and bound in the United States of America.

21 20 19 18 17 16 15   1 2 3 4 5 6 7 8 9 10

LIBRARY OF CONGRESS CONTROL NUMBER: 2015930557
ISBN: 978-1-61186-165-5 (pbk.)
ISBN: 978-1-60917-452-1 (ebook: PDF)
ISBN: 978-1-62895-173-8 (ebook: ePub)
ISBN: 978-1-62896-173-7 (ebook: Kindle)

Book design by Charlie Sharp, Sharp Des!gns, Lansing, Michigan
Cover design by David Drummond, Salamander Design, www.salamanderhill.com
Cover image is Paolo and Francesca by Jean-Auguste-Dominique Ingres (1819) © Musées d'Angers, photo P. David. Used with permission.

g **green press INITIATIVE** Michigan State University Press is a member of the Green Press Initiative and is committed to developing and encouraging ecologically responsible publishing practices. For more information about the Green Press Initiative and the use of recycled paper in book publishing, please visit *www.greenpressinitiative.org*.

Visit Michigan State University Press at *www.msupress.org*

Contents

Acknowledgments

This book gathers essays that were developed from a selection of papers presented at a series of conferences held in 2011 to celebrate the fiftieth anniversary of the publication of René Girard's first book, *Mensonge romantique et verité romanesque*. We would like to thank *Imitatio: Integrating the Human Sciences* and in particular Lindy Fishburne and Jimmy Kaltraider for their financial support. We are very grateful to the participants and chairs at the conferences held at Stanford University (April 2011), University of Cambridge (May 2011), Institute for Cultural Inquiry, Berlin (June 2011), and Yale University (September 2011) for their contributions and the stimulating dialogue that emerged on each of those occasions. Our warmest thanks go to the local co-organizers of the conferences: Robert Harrison (Stanford), Alex Houen (Cambridge), Manuele Gragnolati and Christoph Holzhey (Berlin), and Pericles Lewis and Barry McCrea (Yale) for hosting, co-funding, and above all, fostering intense and critical discussion. Many thanks to Bill Johnsen, who enthusiastically subscribed to this project and helped with the editing process. Finally, we would like to thank René and Martha Girard for their kindness and support, and for granting us the permission to republish the essay "Literature and Christianity" at the end of this volume.

Introduction

The year 2015 marks the fiftieth anniversary of the publication of the English translation of René Girard's first book: *Mensonge romantique et verité romanesque,* which was originally published in 1961 in his native France by Grassett. Translated by Yvonne Freccero, it was titled *Deceit, Desire, and the Novel: Self and Others in Literary Structures.* This was quite a remarkable achievement for a novice in the field of literary studies, also considering that Girard was a historian by formation. He studied at the École de Chartes in Paris, where he graduated in 1947, and received a PhD in history from the University of Indiana at Bloomington in 1953. The book was widely reviewed, and it is still regarded as one of the classics of literary criticism, not only for its insights into some of the canonical novels of European modernity, but also because it proposed a comprehensive theory of desire and the intersubjective constitution of human identity that has triggered a wider interest outside the field of literary studies. *Deceit, Desire, and the Novel* has gained the status of one of those *livres de chevet* cherished by many readers and critics of different generations, while the notion of "triangular desire" has become a sort of buzzword among students and literary scholars, "one of the many bits of heavy theoretical artillery that one was expected to be able to deploy" as part of literary training.[1] For this reason, in this introduction we will not provide a summary or overview of Girard's theory. We expect that the basic tenets of Girard's thought are known to the reader; this volume will instead highlight the literary, social, and historical complexity that can emerge from those deceptively simple central concepts such as "triangular desire."

Girard's book had quite an unusual destiny: it represents the seed, the genetic starting point, for what would become one of the most encompassing, challenging, and far-reaching theories ever conceived in the humanities in the last century. The later academic (and commercial) success of books such as *Violence and the Sacred* (1972) and *Things Hidden Since the Foundation of the World* (1978) overshadowed Girard's first work, however, diverting the attention of his readers away from the hermeneutic potential of the mimetic dynamics applied to literary texts.

Moreover, the intensity of its focus on a certain set of issues, as well as its evident religious undercurrent, made this book, and Girard's work in general, something of a "stumbling block" in the field of literary studies. While scholars were obliged to admire the original hermeneutic acumen of the analysis, as well as the broad critical and historical vision that the book provides, they often critiqued a sort of "reductionism" of the mimetic lens, and were suspicious toward any religious tones that might threaten the "critical correctness" that dominated literary studies. The book was thus somewhat marginalized; it was frequently read, but only rarely did scholars fully engage with its arguments. With the present volume, however, reception history is not our primary focus; we offer, instead, a discussion forum in which new generations of scholars and critics reassess, challenge, and expand the theoretical and hermeneutical reach of this fundamental book, taking into consideration Girard's later theorization, but also engaging with criticism of his work. It is our belief that an open critical discussion is to be preferred to forms of exclusionary criticism. As Cirian Morón-Arroyo admitted, Girard's books and theory often elicit a "hypercritical, conflictual desire to expose the apparent weakness of the theory,"[2] to the point that a few oversights in the formulation of such a wide-ranging theoretical perspective have been deployed to dismiss his theory altogether.[3]

It is true that *Deceit, Desire, and the Novel*, in spite of its imaginativeness and boldness, is an imperfect book, because it holds unanswered questions and underdeveloped points that have been only partially addressed with a sort of retrospective gaze by Girard (or his followers), in the light of his later theorization. The apparent theoretical single-mindedness of the analysis in *Deceit, Desire, and the Novel*, if closely scrutinized, already bears the traces of the potential ramifications of the literary, historical, philosophical, and even theological implications of Girard's theory, stretching far beyond the horizons of his textual analysis. All the essays collected in this volume in fact work to bring back some of the richness that Girard inevitably had to expel in order to make his argument clear and methodologically compelling. A form of reductionism was the necessary first step to see the bigger picture in a clearer form, in order to go back to the textual sources with a more competent eye, and with a different and extended form of insight. This volume hence offers a mixture of sympathetic and critical voices that provides a balanced account (far from being exhaustive, though) of the richness and the exegetical and critical potentiality that *Deceit, Desire, and the Novel* still has for contemporary readers.

The volume is divided into two parts. The first part is devoted to the discussion of some theoretical issues outlined by *Deceit, Desire, and the Novel*, and addresses criticism of some key points. The second part collects a series of case studies—in the form of analyses of specific novels and authors—that are organized in chronological order so as to demonstrate Girard's understanding of the historical evolution of the relationship between mimesis and desire, particularly within the long history of the novel.

Literary Knowledge

The first part of our volume focuses on the cognitive and epistemological potentiality of the novel from the point of view of mimetic theory. In this respect, *Deceit, Desire, and the Novel* could be seen as a productive stumbling block in literary studies because, on the one hand, it compels us to wrestle with the referential pole of literature and its cognitive and ethical dimension, and on the other, because of its "centrifugal pull," it forces contemporary readers to spell out what remains important and relevant in literature and literary studies today. It is the complexity of the interrelation between the referential grounding and effectiveness of literary texts and the open-endedness and instability of their reception that makes literature and critical literary analysis more relevant and essential for our understanding of social reality.

The spirit that informed Girard's critical effort in *Deceit, Desire, and the Novel* was not the idea of elaborating a general theory of culture to be super-imposed on the texts in a rigid manner, but to interrogate a series of texts (a sort of minimal canon of European novels) in order to see what they have to say about human relationships.[4] As he claims in his book on Dostoyevsky: "It is not the disincarnate thought that interests us but the thought embodied in the novels."[5] Robert Doran rephrases the notion, by saying that "imaginative text can be as 'critical' as the critical text, and can even usurp it. . . . what Girard offers us is not a theory of literature or a theory that makes use of literature for some other end, but literature as theory."[6] According to Girard, our best novelists are then also our best critics, because they "apprehend intuitively and concretely, through the medium of their art, if not formally, the system in which they were first imprisoned together with their contemporaries. Literary interpretation must be systematic because it is the continuation of literature."[7] The greatness of modern authors, according to Girard, would be measured by their ability to show, with phenomenological insight, the fabric of human relationships, dominated and shaped by intersubjective drives and forces (chiefly driven by competitive imitation), and the reality of modern (pseudo)individualism, wrestling with a social world that has been divested of any form of religious transcendence, but desperately trying to recuperate some substitute forms by investing other individuals with a power that can be called at the same time transcendental and metaphysical.

We could say that Girard anticipated, in his own terms and with his own vocabulary, the shift that occurred in contemporary philosophy, by authors such as Martha Nussbaum, Richard Rorty, Charles Taylor, or Jacques Der-rida,[8] who underscored the relevance of "narrative thinking," or the truths about the human condition that literature can unfold and reveal better than any other discursive form. As he puts it: "literature accurately described human relationships long before psychology, anthropology and sociology were established as academic disciplines."[9] If Girard's approach to literature is somehow "eccentric" in respect to other thinkers it is because Girard's insight was not an "adaptation" of specific philosophical premises for given texts,[10] but stemmed from the novelistic knowledge that is intrinsic to the literary genius. It is true that Girard did not remain fully faithful to these methodological premises, as his hermeneutical approach eventually took the shape of a "theory" in its own right, which inevitably filtered the texts for what was immediately useful to its corroboration; nonetheless, it offers to literary criticism the kind of historical and cognitive potential that is intrinsic to literature and literary analysis, showing how much the critical exercise at the core of the humanities could become a form of knowledge, in proper scientific terms.

As far as literary criticism is concerned, Girard's approach maintains a level of partiality because of the systematic and comparative nature of his approach, which tends to focus on similarities rather than divergences. A typical objection in this regard—expressed in this volume by Alessia Ricciardi and David Quint—is that most novels—most literature worthy of the name—have an "advantage over the critic, . . . of offering more than one point of view." The same understanding is shared by Maria DiBattista in her chapter, "Jealousy and Novelistic Knowledge." According to her, Girard gives us a compelling "but nonetheless incomplete conception of the kind of particularized knowledge . . . the novel can disclose." Novelistic knowledge in fact reflects and entertains a more dynamic notion of the relations between the desiring Self and the desired Other, a relation in which, for instance, "jealousy plays a dominant and not always negative role," as Girard argues in *Deceit, Desire, and the Novel.* Imitative desire "can metamorphose into a jealous zeal not merely to possess but to know the beloved." Jealousy is a figure of "transport and transition" that disposes us "to acknowledge the separate and uncontrollable existence of the Other."

As a matter of fact, desire in general is often associated with knowledge and the search for one's identity. As Jacques Lacan observed, patients often cling to their desires because they give a sense of purpose in life and shape their identity. The pain that desire inflicts on the subject puts her on a quest for understanding, which leads to self-knowledge and self-improvement, as symbolically represented, for instance, by the *quête* of the knight in medieval courtly literature, or by the tradition of the bildungsroman.[11] The same applies to Girard, for knowledge emerges as the realization on the part of the protagonists of the deceptive nature of desire, because of its unstable and fundamentally "inauthentic" mimetic fluctuations. However, this implies that there is an intrinsic epistemic obliquity in novelistic knowledge, for it always wrestles with the deceptive nature of the very knowledge we acquire from the metamorphoses of desire, because of our intrinsic need to think in terms of differences, which are mythical projections ("the business of the mythical subject is the construction of differences," De Lauretis argues),[12] rather than similarities, which represent our realities.

Desire, in Theory

In his article "Theories of Desire," Jay Clayton argues that desire is intrinsic to both representation and social reality, as it drives and shapes narrative on one hand, but also pushes the boundaries of representation by constantly addressing the referential pole of literature. This has a particular resonance at the theoretical level, for the hope of moving beyond formalism is one of the things that unites a quite diverse group of literary theorists who have explored the role of desire in literature, including, among many others, Peter Brooks, Leo Bersani, Teresa de Lauretis, Luce Irigaray, Julia Kristeva, Eve Kosofsky Sedgwick, Linda Kauffman, and, of course, René Girard.[13]

Somehow it is typical of scholars working on Girard to stress his exceptionalism in respect to coeval theoretical thinking. Such emphasis is prompted also by his constant contention with thinkers who were actually particularly perceptive (and therefore very close and instrumental to Girard's intuitions) in reference to the discussion of concepts such as desire, imitation, or sacrifice (Freud and Nietzsche are probably the most interesting cases).[14] However, as this volume testifies, Girard's thought actually resonates more deeply and thoroughly if connected with other thinkers or critics, as is done here in reference, for instance, to Erich Auerbach, Robert Alter, Simone Weil, Roland Barthes, Gilles Deleuze, Slavoj Žižek, and Franco Moretti, who may corroborate some of Girard's claims, but also give more subtle readings in areas where Girard lacked systematicity or nuance.

An example is Ricciardi's chapter, the second in our volume, where she flags the "molecular intensity" of Proust, which resists any "molar" grip, to use Gilles Deleuze's terminology, and points to apparent "uncategorizable singularities." By insisting on triangulation as a first principle, Ricciardi argues, Girard does not succeed in accounting for the multiple and rhizomatic aspects of desire in Proust. One of the most typical objections to Girard's model of desire refers to the plethora of models in modern times:

"Beginning with Proust, the mediator may literally be anyone at all and he may pop up anywhere."[15] This in fact resists the possibility of a complete and coherent mapping of any person's behavior according to a strict triangular logic and structure, since the modeling of one's behavior could be the result of the amalgamation of different suggestions and tensions, where models could be internalized as well as actively present in the social surrounding. The "net" result could take the form of what appear to be "singularities." On this score, one may refer to what Rosa Mucignat writes in her account of the "topology" of novels (in her chapter titled "For a Comparative Topography of Desire"): we should not look for any hierarchical structuring of desire, or for a causal chain in the theory of imitative desires, that may lead to a *primus motor*, an "unmoved mover." We should rather talk of "a multitude of triangular force fields that divert, accelerate, or reverse [the subject's] trajectory." What the novel permits is the experimental "isolation," the microscopic examination, as if in a *Gedankenexperiment*, of the behavioral strategies of a few characters that act as probes in the structural social fabric of our desires.

To make Girard's thinking more convergent, one can also read it in genealogical terms as part of a more complex network of influences and dialogues. A critical and theoretical question that is only partially addressed by this volume is the genealogical understanding of Girard's mimetic theory, which presents the imprints of different influences. The first obvious one is Hegel through the reading of Alexander Kojève, who left an indelible mark on a whole generation of French thinkers (Jacques Lacan, Raymond Aron, Jean-Paul Sartre, Georges Bataille, Maurice Merleau-Ponty), and also reached Girard and his contemporaries (like Foucault and Derrida). In the first pages of Kojève's *Introduction to the Reading of Hegel*, we can see how much Girard's formulation of mimetic desire is in debt to Kojève's: "Desire directed toward a natural object is human only to the extent that it is 'mediated' by the Desire of another directed toward the same object: it is human to desire what others desire, because they desire it."[16] Kojève's formulation is paradigmatic for Girard also when he explores the Hegelian dimension of "recognition," which informs Girard's reading of authors such as Stendhal, Proust, or Nietzsche ("all human, anthropogenetic Desire—the Desire that generates Self-Consciousness, the human reality—is, finally, a function of the desire of 'recognition'"),[17] which leads to the latent or manifest conflict ("their meeting can only be a fight to the death") of the Hegelian relationship between master and slave.[18]

In this respect, Girard could be also inscribed in the coeval philosophical perspectives that deconstructed the modern ideal of individual autonomy and authenticity, by underscoring the intersubjective and dynamic elements of any form of identity, distancing himself also from any philosophy of subjectivity or existentialism. In this light one could read, for instance, Girard's take on Simone de Beauvoir and Jean-Paul Sartre, in essays published at the time of *Deceit, Desire, and the Novel*.[19] In the theoretical part of his essay in this volume, Christoph Holzhey also asks whether Girard's conception of desire should be grounded "in lack or excess, or also to privilege desire or pleasure as a theoretical category,"[20] which may entail a possible constructive dialogue with Jacques Lacan on the one hand, and with Georges Bataille on the other.[21] Clément Rosset, for instance, situates Girard in a French tradition of modern writers and philosophers who have associated desire with lack (Baudelaire, Mallarmé, Bataille, Lacan, and Derrida), although, as already suggested, we should keep in mind that desire is a dynamic notion in Girard, and excess could be seen as an overcompensatory "rebound" of lack. The "hollow man" is, by definition, "insatiable."

Such considerations would require a more in-depth discussion of the relationship between Girard's theory of desire and psychoanalysis, also considering the fact that when investigating desire in literary representations, critics tend to make an almost automatic reference to psychoanalysis, and Freudianism in particular, under the assumption that it provides a more supple reading and understanding of the dynamics of desire (inside and outside the text).[22] For various theoretical reasons that we cannot discuss in the space of this introduction, Girard has been soundly critical of Freud and psychoanalysis in general. Due to the way Girard tried to distance himself from Freud, there have been relatively few studies on the possible convergence of Girard with psychoanalytic thinking.[23] A refreshing formulation about what is at stake in the potential dialogue between mimetic theory and psychoanalysis comes from Scott Garrels. According to Garrels, mimetic theory emphasizes the collective nature of nonconscious behavior based on immediate imitation, as contrasted with any notion of a personal unconscious or internal world of past experiences. On the one hand, Girard understood before contemporary cognitive neurosciences that imitation is the scaffolding from which the human mind is constructed. It is the very vehicle from which internal representation is established. However, on the other hand, Girard never posits the fundamental distinction between an "immediate" and a "deferred" imitation. Mimetic theory, Garrels argues, might benefit from a clearer understanding of how deferred imitation actually functions in the mind of the adult, since it does not explain on what basis humans might imitate old affect-laden schema (be they good or bad), which are represented in the form of memory in the presence of contrary imitative models.[24]

What also would be important to underscore in Girard's contention with psychoanalysis, above all from the point of literary theory, is the critique of any hypostatization of "mythical" structures, like the Oedipus complex in the Freudian narrative, which is indeed only a "fiction." Besides the fact that the Oedipus story for Girard is simply one of the many mythical accounts of persecutory mechanisms,[25] in psychological terms the Oedipus story could be defined simply as a metaphor, the literary description of specific mimetic patterns that may have personal or historical salience but cannot be hypostatized. Besides appetites, which are biological preconditions, only imitation is assumed by Girard as the hardwired scaffolding of our behavior, while desire can only be defined in cultural, social, and historical terms.[26] The Oedipus story may have simply a purely descriptive value with reference to specific cases, both real or literary, but cannot be assumed in any general or substantial terms. As Girard suggested, for instance, in reference to Proust's *Recherche*, Marcel's childhood was not imprinted by his father's presence, but rather by his mother's ambivalence.[27] Another modernist writer like Italo Svevo, in his psychological masterpiece *Zeno's Conscience* (1923), explicitly challenges Freud's Oedipal narrative by revealing the more fundamental, horizontal, fraternal, mimetic structure of rivalry that dominates the protagonist's intentions, dreams, and behavior.[28] If one feels a particular cognitive or epistemological attachment to narratives like the Oedipal one, she should also refer to other classical figures like Cronus, Laius, Electra, Narcissus, Cain, Proteus, Telemachus, to express different metaphorical or "mythical" articulations of mimetic relational dynamics and their "pathologies."[29] All these images and figures may find a more subtle and nuanced articulation and understanding from the point of view of mimetic theory than from Freudianism. It would also help to understand how and why writers use different patterns or archetypical structures to represent mimetic dynamics and power struc-tures.[30] In this sense novelists may have a deeper insight into the structure of identity and desire than philosophers, critics, or analysts.

Sex, No Thanks

To a contemporary critical reader interested in theories of desire it is quite striking that in *Deceit, Desire, and the Novel* there are no preoccupations with sexuality. Holzhey in his chapter, for instance, argues that "pleasure and pain play in fact an important role [in Girard] that is surprisingly undertheorized." As mentioned previously, this was partially due to the deliberate avoidance in *Deceit, Desire, and the Novel* of psychoanalysis and in particular of Freud's "pansexualism," a "conscious strategy on Girard's part to avoid being lumped in with the mass commentators of psychoanalysis."[31] The most interesting point in Girard's argument, however, is the downward-spiraling dynamic of sexual pleasure in respect to desire, for there is an intrinsic instability in their association. For Girard, in fact, "the 'physical' and the 'metaphysical' in desire always fluctuate at the expense of each other. This law . . . explains for example the progressive disappearance of sexual pleasure in the most advanced stages of ontological sickness."[32] As Yue Zhuo phrases it in her contribution to this volume, "it is the metaphysical desire that is insatiable" in the masochist, not its sexual epiphenomenal manifestation.

   In the mimetic dynamics represented in literature, pleasure, and sexual pleasure in particular, also manifest an asymptotic component, akin to Girard's understanding of the relationship between mediation and desire. Roland Barthes argued that the deferral of sexual encounter and sexual plea-sure is a deliberate textual strategy that allows the reader to engage with "the pleasure of the text."[33] However, this cannot be solely confined to the textual and literary domain, for it mirrors a more deep-seated kernel of the dynamic of our desires. In the paradigmatic epistolary novel *Les liaisons dangereuses* (1782) by Pierre de Laclos, for instance, the protagonists locate pleasure less in physical favors than in the knowledge of the other's desire. Sex ends seduc-tion, as it were, for pleasure is not given by the sexual experience but the control of the desire one exerts on another human being.[34] In discussing the Roman erotic elegy, a genre certainly not belonging to romantic modernity,

Joy Connolly sees the genre as "the search for ways to defer bliss and thus its own ending: to extend the space in which its discourse operates by deforming the erotic discourse itself."[35]

Girard's reading on this score may be also interpreted within a historical and philosophical framework, where the "pleasure principle" may be characterized by an "entropic degeneration" due to historical circumstances related to the increase of the internal mediation proper to the processes of democratization. As Elena Pulcini argues in her book, *L'individuo senza passioni* [*The Passionless Individual*] (through the rereading of Montaigne, Rousseau, and Tocqueville), the so-called *homo democraticus* has been growing increasingly weak, socially indifferent, and pathologically narcissistic,[36] which leads to a restructuring of the notion of pleasure that may have or may not have an explicit link to sex. Narcissism could be in fact clinically linked to both forms of hyper- and hypo-sexualization, and it is actually sexual "anorexia," this modern form of mystical asceticism, which Girard finds the most interesting to analyze.[37] That would also help to read examples and representations of "ascetic Don Juanism," as in the case of Mikhail Lermontov's *A Hero of Our Time* (1841), later adapted for the screen by Claude Sautet in *A Heart in Winter* (1992), rendered as an insightful case of a competitive love triangle. On the other hand, and moving to the opposite side of the pendulum, the discussion of the representation of sexual desire from the point of view of mimetic theory would be an interesting case study because of its link to violence. As Leo Bersani expresses it, "desire is intrinsically violent" and there is a "complicity between narrativity and violence."[38] Narrative sexuality is characterized in particular, according to Bersani and Dutoit in their analysis of Sade, by a linear movement toward explosive climaxes, a movement aided by the "isolation and imprisonment of the object of desire" and crowned by a violent act.[39] Far from being the realm of pleasure, the "frontal" representation of sexuality in novels often involves its Dionysiac underpinning, that is, the ritualistic connection to sacred violence and murder (as Georges Bataille intuited). As Jay Clayton rephrases it in Girardian terms, narrative and art represent a realm where violence could be experienced ritualistically, in safe "homeopathic" terms.[40] Sexuality would be then one of the forms in which the transgressions and the undifferentiations proper to the Dionysiac and the carnivalesque manifest themselves, always bordering with violence.

Queering Girard

Deceit, Desire, and the Novel is a book that was published before structuralism and poststructuralism, before gender and queer studies; Girard felt no
pressure to discuss the thematization of female or homosexual desire in modern European novels. This has spurred criticism that is justified at some level,
but at times has been used to brush off Girard's perspective too quickly.[41] If
Deceit, Desire, and the Novel seems confined to the description of a male-
dominated society, where women mainly act as symbolic tokens, this may be
just a reflection of the canonical authors that Girard considers (all inscribed,
for obvious historical reasons, in patriarchal structures). However, there is
now a growing body of critical analysis of the representation of female desire
in literature from the perspective of mimetic theory, in which the female
subject is in full transition through the various poles of the mimetic triangulation (subject, object, mediator, rival, scapegoat, etc.),[42] expressing all the
particular declensions of mimetic female desire.[43]

Girard's "heterosexual normativity" is another point of contention in
the discussion of his theory of desire (as critically exposed here by Ricciardi
in her chapter), which defines homosexuality as a "deviation" from "normal
Don Juanism," and considered sexual differences only in the terms of triangular desire: "just as heterosexual desire entails a mediator of the same sex,
homosexual desire entails a mediator of the other sex."[44] The propensity for
thinking in structural terms, and his insistence on rivalrous dynamics, may
have somehow blocked Girard's thinking on this regard: "One of the advan-
tages of conceiving of this genesis [of desire] in rivalry is that it occurs in an
absolutely symmetrical way in both sexes. In other words, any form of sexual
rivalry is homosexual in structure, with women as well as with men."[45]

It should be stated, though, that far from giving a fixed and totally prescriptive account of the dynamics of triangular desire, Girard writes that the
triangle is just "a model of a sort, or rather a whole family of models. . . . They
always allude to the mystery, transparent yet opaque, of human relations,"[46]
manifesting a theoretical hesitation in discussing at length all the potential
ramifications and reach of his theory in relation to sexual desire and sexual
identity. This is also highlighted by the different emphasis and (problematic) formulations given by Girard in *Deceit, Desire, and the Novel*, in *Things*

Hidden, and later in *A Theater of Envy*. A more supple discussion on the subject from the perspective of mimetic theory would surely be required, first of all because it is not clear whether sexual identity should be considered as grounded on a ontological base or purely performative. As Girard expresses it in *A Theater of Envy*, it seems more the latter, where sexuality presents a continuum of expressions according to the mimetic dynamics it may be historically subjected to ("Sexual differences are mobile, variable, and inessential, whereas the triangular structure is permanent and essential").[47] However, in *Deceit, Desire, and the Novel* Girard claims that only "*some* forms of homosexuality"[48] can be described from the point of view of a "performative" dynamics, suggesting the integration with a more essentialist perspective. On this regard, one may wish to look to discussions like Eve Kosofsky Sedgwick's, who claims that the debate between a "constructivist" and "essentialist" understanding of homosexuality is a "conceptual impasse" from the point of view of queer theory.[49] This may be also a limited approach to a mimetic understanding of the subject matter. There are in fact "many and thorough asymmetries between the sexual continuums of women and men, between female and male sexuality and homosociality"[50] that need to be taken into account from the perspective of (a queered) mimetic theory. What it would also be required, from the point of view of literary criticism, are more analytical case studies where the dynamics of LGBT sexual desire and identity are discussed and analyzed with reference to literary, cinematic, or theatrical representations.[51]

Positive and Negative Mimesis

One of the problems with *Deceit, Desire, and the Novel* is that it retains the polemical tone, that reactive moralism, typical of the early Girard, which went against coeval trends of literary criticism, and, in general, against the current interpretation of desire in the constitution of modern subjectivity. This led him to adopt a sort of theoretical "Manichaeism" in his early formulations, which posits an intrinsic polarity between the "positive" mediation of desire by God, and the "negative," idolatrous mediation wielded by the others:

> Choice always involves choosing a model, and true freedom lies in the basic
> choice between a human or a divine model. The impulse of the soul toward
> God is inseparable from a retreat into the Self. Inversely the turning in on
> itself of pride is inseparable from a movement of panic toward the Other.[52]

His insistence on the negative and rivalrous side of mimesis intended to address the lack of attention to these fundamental aspects of human behavior in philosophical and critical discourse.[53] This initial "strategic" gesture, however, became crystalized in a restrictive take on the full mimetic dimension of human subjectivity, overlooking the emancipatory and positive aspects of internal mediation, or "intimate mediation," as Benoît Chantre called it in the recent conversation with Girard, *Battling to the End*.[54] Another reason for this oversight, Martha Reineke has argued, was Girard's increasing inattentiveness to phenomenology, and in particular to Merleau-Ponty's writing, which was crucial in the gestational years of *Deceit, Desire, and the Novel*. In that book, for instance, "Girard argues that affective memory and sensory experience are the 'source of the true and the sacred' and the 'salvation' of Marcel Proust. Understanding that mimetic desire runs through the body, Girard finds in sensory experience the mechanism of spiritual conversion." Moreover, Girard suggests that Proust's references to "habit, sensation, idea, or feelings" allude to an incipient phenomenology within the pages of *In Search of Lost Time*. Indeed, Girard asserts that "the most fruitful intuitions of phenomenological and structural analysis are already present in Proust." Therefore, Reineke argues, "When Girard set aside his early phenomenological explorations, he eliminated from mimetic theory the means by which humans move from acquisitive mimesis and its violent manifestations toward our true end: mutuality and connection with others. When we reconsider embodied practices of mimesis and desire, we can hold to the course from which Girard diverged and retrieve for mimetic theory insights that remain vital to it."[55]

For this and other reasons, many of the essays of this volume are compelled to recuperate the *pars construens* of mimetic desire. Internal mediation does not necessarily end in rivalry and antagonism, but can form the basis of our education, affective coordination, mutual understanding, empathy, and love. Luca Di Blasi, for instance, asks why Girard in *Deceit, Desire, and the Novel* "constantly focused on negative interpretations of mimetic desire," while acknowledging in principle the existence of the "passionate person," as in the case of Fabrice del Dongo, who is defined in the text by his "emotional autonomy, by the spontaneity of his desires, by his absolute indifference to the opinion of Others."[56] "Before Girard described much later mimetic desire as ambivalent and even as intrinsically good," Di Blasi argues, "we find in *Deceit, Desire, and the Novel* a notion of mimetic desire that was in a double sense devalued." Di Blasi's interpretation is that Girard needed to underplay or "hide" any form of spontaneity and autonomy in name of the totalizing nature of mimetic desire for political reasons: to avoid a potential interpretation of his theory as elitist, aristocratic, and hierarchical. Girard's conversion actually testifies to this movement: "the acknowledgment of his own entanglement in mimetic desire," Di Blasi argues, allowed Girard "to understand the self as deeply connected with the other and permitted a positive revaluation of equality, democracy, and, in consequence, also mimetic desire as 'intrinsically good.' On this basis, Girard could blame modern elitist individualism for not recognizing the mimetic character of desire."

Holzhey also aptly points out that Girard's theory is "paradoxical" in the sense of being antinomic, because it rejects any form of dualism. Holzhey underscores that in *To Double Business Bound* (1978) Girard acknowledges that "everything we call our 'self,' our 'ego,' our 'identity,' our 'superiority'" must be seen as ambivalent and paradoxical: "both the ultimate prize we are trying to win . . . and a most frightful burden."[57] If Girard's early formulation may have led us to believe that desire would inevitably spiral toward death and a hellish condition, we should account also for "systems with positive feedback," for a desire that is indeed ascending and that creates pleasure, as in the positive transfer of loving relationships.

Not surprisingly, one of the most interesting representations of a form of positive or redemptive mimesis comes actually from literature, and from Dante's *Comedy* in particular. As Manuele Gragnolati and Heather Webb argue in their essay in this volume, "In his discussion of the mimetic nature of desire, Girard has put almost exclusive emphasis on its conflictual and antagonistic aspects (envy, jealousy, rivalry, resentment, blaming, scapegoating, violence, sacrifice), leaving aside the positive and constructive ones (empathy, the pedagogical modeling of desire, reciprocal positive mirroring, nonconflictual love, and the emancipatory role of art)." Dante's *Commedia*, in particular the *Purgatorio*, "provides what we could call a medieval version of therapy, an approach that intends to heal the individual of the dangerous aspects and involutional dynamics of desire, and that intends to direct her from the mechanisms of rivalry and self-referential compulsions typical of the *Inferno*, through a difficult and painful redirection and re-modeling of desire in Purgatory, to the complete openness of desire in Paradise."

Mimetic Reading

Umberto Eco argues that we are so fascinated by Dante's *Inferno* and cannot really empathize with his *Paradiso* and its characters, because the latter is no longer a place of our imagination and our understanding.[58] With modernity, we have expelled the idea of a possible "paradise," as we live in a constant state of crisis, of impending doom, haunted by "the sense of an ending," to quote Frank Kermode.[59]

For modern readers, who seem more interested in tales of falls rather than in tales of redemptions, the positive side of mimesis and its representation might be less appealing than the negative. One of the unexpressed and underlying arguments that might be present in *Deceit, Desire, and the Novel* pertains in fact to the position of the reader and the problem of reception, something that in general has been overlooked by Girard in his critical writing. The problem of reception is central for instance to Karen Feldman's chapter in this volume. Feldman discusses the particular notion of "realism" implicit in Girard's approach, which involves what might be called "textual effectivity," the possibility for a text to intervene in the world. Feldman's point is that in order to assert the effectivity of texts like the Bible or the novel, Girard had to restrict the range of effects to one trajectory alone: the revelation of truth, discounting the "ungovernability of effects" of any text, which is "the hallmark of a literary approach."[60]

To the question posited by Feldman, "What is the guarantee of [the Bible] being understood, and not, for instance, misused?" one may answer that in fact in history the Bible has been (mis)used to legitimize reciprocal violence: "the agency of the Bible in the world cannot, it seems, be guaranteed; its proper reception also not; and its effectivity is—and has been—wayward, violent, and persecutory. These might be effects of misreading, misappropriations, and perversions of the revelation of Scripture, but they nonetheless belong to the history of the Scripture." The emphasis on history is here important, as Girard's theory is not a Gnostic theory, as some have argued,[61] because it does not establish a form of revelation based on pure knowledge. The Scriptures per se do not provide any shield to our traumatic and conflictual drives, to our disposition to persecution. The revelation that we find in the Gospels is realized in history, through a historical process of progressive revelation and emancipation, through the increased figural salience of unjust persecutions and violence.

Another point to emphasize is the way we read, understand, and empathize with the protagonists of the novel. In an acute essay on an "Enlightenment" rereading of the religious undercurrents of *Deceit, Desire, and the Novel*, Stefano Brugnolo argues that there is very little sympathy on the part of Girard for the novelistic characters he discusses in his book: "to interpret Don Quixote, Emma Bovary, Anna Karenina only as anti-models, as illustrations of the danger of mimetic desire, prevents us from grasping that their power and greatness rely also on their very 'innocent' mimetic meandering, which is common to everybody."[62] These heroes somehow are the victims of the increased freedoms that are given to modern men and women, who are compelled to venture the uncharted territory of metaphysical desire in order to achieve a form of revelation, which is utterly novelistic. Brugnolo thus proposes a less "Manicheistic" description of novelistic knowledge and its dynamics that cannot be reduced to a "moral tale":

> To claim that all the adventures of Don Quixote fall under the sign of the "ontological sickness," and that the only truth about those adventures would amount to their final repudiation, would mean mutilating the meaning of the novel, an act opposite and complementary to that carried out by the romantics when only extolled the sublime and heroic side of the hidalgo. We can surely claim that Cervantes wished to represent a sort of mimetic delirium, but it is hard not to see in Quixote's meandering an attempt of emancipation from his poor life, a path of freedom, experimentation, self-determination. . . . The novelistic conversion forgives, understands, and includes, not excludes or rejects as Girard clearly believes.[63]

The process of recognition (and eventually of epiphany and spiritual metamorphosis) on the part of the reader is first of all based on the process of identification, of compassionate or empathetic identification with novel-istic characters. The mimetic impulse is a mechanism for learning through "embodied simulations," as a contemporary neuroscientist would phrase it.[64] And literature is in fact a process to re-creating these experiences. Mimesis, as *imitatio*, implies both representation, recognition, and identification.

Moreover, in Girardian terms, as both Leo Bersani and Daniele Giglioli suggested, in order to criticize the protagonist for being under the mesmeriz-ing spell of his or her mediator, the novelist ought to make the protagonist an object of interest and fascination, that is, "both a *mediator* and a *scapegoat*."[65] In *A Future for Astyanax* Bersani argues in fact that "the hero of realistic fiction supports a novelistic structure which includes his expulsion from the viable structures of fiction and of life. The novelist glamorizes a figure who exposes the factitious nature of the social and esthetic orders in the name of which the novelist will sacrifice that figure."[66] By "reading for the plot," we identify and empathize both with forms of abjection, of persecu-tion, of expulsion, of discrimination, and with figures of self-abjection and self-expulsion, along with their insufficient self-mastery in reference to the oscillations of mimetic desire.

As Girard suggested in a conversation with Nadine Dormoy Savage, the writers may stage in their novels the dynamics of persecution and victimiza-tion that they themselves suffered, and that they interiorized sometimes in pathological terms.[67] The novel in this sense would also bring into light not only the deceptive nature of desire and its autonomy, but also the sacrificial and scapegoating dynamics of modern society, where writing may have a "therapeutic" or "political" value for the artists themselves, signaling the coming to terms with figures, structures, zones, and experience of abjection (and their revelation). This is an element that Girard was not able to develop in his first book, lacking the complete anthropological theory he developed in later works, but also because he shied away, until recently, from a discus-sion of the dynamic of social cohesion and the role of sacrifice in the modern context. All the masterpieces examined by Girard in *Deceit, Desire, and the Novel*, and the history of the modern novel in general, could in fact be reread and rediscussed under the light of the notions and dynamics of sacrifice and scapegoating, highlighting those victimary mechanisms that the meta-morphosis of desire, and the waves of passions such as resentment and envy, produce in modern societies. The theme of victimization and persecution, including the growing plague of anti-Semitism, for instance, is central to Proust's *Recherche*, where even the narrator is "complicit with the great collective lynching that is renewed every day to consolidate the community."[68] The same could be applied to Dostoyevsky,[69] as well as to modernist writing, where structures of contagion and sacrifice abound (see in this regard essays by Jan-Melissa Schramm and Brian Sudlow in this volume).

Myth, History, and Reality

The subtitle of the English edition of *Mensonge romantique et verité romanesque* signals the sort of critical pigeonholing to which the book was subjected. To be listed under the critical rubric of structuralism was in fact an obvious choice, given the cultural climate of the period, during which structuralism was quickly and massively entering into the critical vocabulary of European and American scholars and intellectuals. Girard's comparative and systematic method was able to isolate veritable "structures" of desire as represented in modern fiction. However, those structures were not described in a purely synchronic perspective, typical of the structuralist analysis, but suggested a historical progression, with an intrinsic sociocultural and political relation between desire, modernity, and the process of democratization.

Girard's book implies a historical understanding of the role of literature in Western European modernity as well as its social referent, which has prompted critics to see in it an Hegelian undercurrent in the way he approaches literary, cultural, and social forms and phenomena. However, Girard's structure of thinking is more antinomical than strictly dialectical, as it does not provide any sort of *Aufhebung*. His perspective could be inscribed in the tradition of the *longue durée* approach, which he shares with books like Auerbach's *Mimesis* or Frye's *Anatomy of Criticism*. Because of its time frame, *Deceit, Desire, and the Novel* essentially could be regarded as a book that explores how "internal mediation" became dominant in modern Western cultures, as well as the etiology of "deviated transcendence," as expressed and thematized by modern European novels: from the external mediation of chivalric epic in *Don Quixote*, to the underground interpersonal apocalypticism of Dostoyevsky's novels.

What is at stake in the implicit trajectory delineated by Girard in *Deceit, Desire, and the Novel* is the process of a progressive "disenchantment" of the world, a process of de-idealization, which concerns not only religion (particularly Christianity in the Western context) in the first instance, but all substitutive, immanent forms of religiosity (literature, elitism, snobbism, glamour, capitalism, romantic love, etc.). In this sense, the polarization between *mensonge* (lie) and *verité* (truth) in the original French title is, as said, tinted by moral overtones, and by the polemic character of Girard's book in respect to coeval literary criticism, but also by the partial elaboration of mimetic theory in its historical dimension. Having, in fact, in mind the further development and refinement of the theory brought forward by subsequent books, the possible polarity which is at the core of *Deceit, Desire, and the Novel* could be rather defined as between "myth" and "reality"; between the mythical "transfiguration of the desired objects," which according to Girard constitutes the unity of internal and external mediation, and the realism of the novels, which is the unmasking of the mythical character of "metaphysical desire."[70]

Taken in a broader historical terms, the increasing spread of internal mediation as represented in the modern novel could be seen not only in negative terms (as suggested by Quint in his chapter in this volume), but as the inevitable and, from a political and ethical standpoint, welcome result of the democratic transformation of traditional social structures based on radical social separations, aristocratic elitism, patriarchy, slavery, tribal identity, and so on. Human beings have always been "idolatrous" in their history, but Western modernity has been characterized by the progressive moving away from "mythical thinking" toward a more realistic, immanent, democratic understanding of social, cultural, political, and psychological forces and realities, even at the price of being thrown, in the most pathological cases, into the abyss of the internal mediation and deviated transcendence. If modern individualism is, according to Girard, a by-product of Christianity, deviated transcendence may also be seen as the way through which humankind explores both material and social reality, as well as the vast field of their existential possibilities—many of which may lead to the "Dostoyevskian Apocalypse," but that stem from the freedom of choice that is intrinsic to Christian ethics.

The chronological organization of the second part of the volume reflects the historical focus and transformative tension that is implicit in *Deceit,*

Desire, and the Novel, adding a further historical depth through the discussion of texts that fall outside the modern, historical brackets put forward by Girard in his first book.

A Premodern Perspective on Imitation, Influence, and Its Anxieties

The increasingly pressing interest in matters anthropological and scriptural that have characterized Girard's intellectual trajectory from *Deceit, Desire, and the Novel* to *Violence and the Sacred* and *Things Hidden* made him lose sight of the function, role, and focus of premodern literature in probing this complex historical process. Apart from a short essay on Dante[71] and the reference to Guillaume de Machaut's *Jugement dou Roy de Navarre,* employed as an entry point for his anthropological discussion in *The Scapegoat,* Girard's interest in Western literature ventured only as far back as Cervantes and Shakespeare, at the threshold of European modernity.

However, by looking back at the classical, medieval, or early modern contexts, one can highlight the historical continuity and the complexity of the mimetic understanding of cultural and social forms. This would allow us to bypass the aporias that inevitably were present in the early formulation of *Deceit, Desire, and the Novel.* As Marco Formisano underscores in his contribution to this volume, "Greek and Latin texts . . . offer an unexpected interpretive wealth." In particular, "Within the Greek and Latin textual tradition, as is well known, the concept of imitation is absolutely central not only as aesthetic but also as ethical criterion." In premodern cultures and texts, for instance, imitation, far from being hidden, is actually praised and glorified; it is the basic mechanism that defines cultural transmission, identity construction, and art production. As Robert Doran similarly writes in his essay "Imitation and Originality": "just as modern societies cannot tolerate too much imitation, premodern societies cannot tolerate too much originality."[72] Worth noticing also is that "the dialectic between admiration and rivalrous destruction (*eris,* strife) is the essence of the creative drive."[73] "The very core of ancient literary aesthetics," Formisano writes, "is based on competition with exemplary models; behind an apparently slavish admiration is concealed a sense of rivalry and a drive to overcome the model." This also flags the intrinsic self-reflexive element of literature: imitation and the "anxiety of influence" is at the core of the trade, as Dante, for instance, epitomizes in choosing Virgil as his guide in the *Commedia*.

The first section of Part 2 is therefore devoted to a discussion of some premodern texts, from the classical and medieval period. Formisano focuses on the analysis of one of the central literary genres of Roman imperial literature: the panegyric, that is, speech in praise of Roman emperors. He explains that the notion of admiration was one of the rhetorical modalities of mimetic dynamics in classical literature, where the emperor, the writer, and the text constitute a force field that defines a particular original form of mimetic tension: "the desire of the panegyrist is directed to the emperor but also to the text itself, which produces competition with the preceding textual tradition." In the panegyric, "The triangulation is constituted by the one who praises, the one who is praised, and the literary tradition—in particular the epic and historiographic genres with which the panegyrist establishes a sort of competition. Precisely this textuality assumes the role of the mediator, as Girard argues in the case of Don Quixote and chivalric romance."

However, as Robert Doran rightly underscores: "Classical aesthetics was inextricable from anthropological concerns."[74] Formisano in fact highlights that: "modern Western readers are accustomed to conceiving a speech written in order to celebrate established power as an act of submission, flattery, and adulation and to seeing such a speech as self-serving, lying, hypocritical"; while recently scholars have tried "to reestablish some positive political values the panegyrical texts may have had." In particular, the panegyric warns the emperor of the danger of adulation itself, from any form of "enthusiasm," which etymologically refers to the founding murder at the base of royal institutions. By referring to Girard's reading of Shakespeare's *Julius Caesar*, and the sacrificial origins of royal authority as discussed in *Things Hidden*, Formisano emphasizes that "admiration and the speech genre that most represents it, panegyric, are inevitably and fatally linked with murder."

This intrinsic connection between the aesthetic and the anthropological becomes evident also in Bill Burgwinkle's essay on "medieval sanctity," and in particular in his analysis of the oldest known saint's life in Occitan, the *Cancó de Santa Fe*, dated to the second half of the eleventh century. Burgwinkle underscores the "unique power that Girard attributes to the literary text to bear witness to the sort of institutionalized scapegoating that underlies mythmaking, and, in bearing such witness, to demystify it." A retrospective reading of *Deceit, Desire, and the Novel* would allow us to in fact reestablish the link between novelistic truth and scapegoating, which are also intrinsic to the revelatory power of literature (Auerbach's *Mimesis* could be actually read consistently in this direction).

Burgwinkle's essay also challenges and complexifies Girard's theory, for it clearly shows that the important distinction to be made is not between "horizontal" or "vertical" transcendence, between the mediation by others, and the mediation by God, but rather and simply between positive and negative mediation. The "Christian saint" that Girard accounts as one of the greatest moral examples at the end of *Deceit, Desire, and the Novel*[75] is far from being exempted by the negative sways of mimetic desire. Vertical transcendence does not protect us from rivalry and competition, as God could be turned into a model-rival to be outdone in terms of performative sacrifice. That is the principle of devilish temptation: to rival the divine, to establish an antagonistic relationship with Christ, in a pre-Nietzschean sense:[76] "the devil essentially imitates this primordial desire to be desired—a taste acquired from God—as he works endlessly to circumvent this flow of desire and adoration and redirect it toward himself." Therefore, in the medieval scenario discussed by Burgwinkle, "the young saint's imitation of Christ's martyrdom leads not to a cessation of violence through her sacrifice but to another more deadly cycle of violence that will soon thereafter spin out of control."

A too "zealous" imitation (the etymology of "jealousy," as DiBattista points out in her chapter), can also induce forms of religious and confessional rivalries, as indicated by Burgwinkle in the attitude of some medieval saints, who fought the pagans with rivalrous forms of self-sacrificial asceticism: "The two religions emerge in this example as *'frères ennemis,'* insufficiently differentiated and bound in a pact of ritual sacrifice and murder. All that Faith can do to distinguish herself from these self-denying pagans is to perform her ascetic practices in an even more single-minded and obsessive way, and cleave to the model of Christ."

At the pinnacle of medieval poetry and thought we then find Dante's *Divine Comedy*, to which Girard referred tangentially in several instances (including his text in this volume), and which was the subject of a short essay on the episode of Paolo and Francesca in Canto V of *Inferno*, seen as a form of bovarism and *"mensonge romantique" avant la lettre.*[77] As Manuele

Gragnolati and Heather Webb explain in their chapter in this volume, Girard's interpretation was surely pertinent and insightful but again partial, because it deals with the infernal dispositions of mimetic desire, overlooking the fact that Dante is interested in a journey of redemption and salvation: "Dante illustrates a theory of desire that not only prefigures some of Girard's points about the novelistic revelation of the mechanisms of imitative desire, but also considers a greater variety of aspects of these mechanisms than does Girard. Most importantly, perhaps, Dante illustrates a range of modes of mimetic desire that include positive and even salvific modes, while Girard's articulation of mimetic desire sees the mechanism as fundamentally negative." What becomes clear, for instance, from *Purgatorio* is that the process of purgatory "does not seem to aim at eradicating interpersonal desire from the subject, but at correcting and transforming it." Desire is intrinsically good and may be expressed in a positive, nonrivalrous way, both vertically and horizontally.

Dante, as a Christian thinker, would never subscribe to some of Girard's tenets in *Deceit, Desire, and the Novel* ("Christianity directs existence toward a vanishing point, either toward God or toward the Other. Choice always involves choosing a model, and the true freedom lies in the basic choice between a human or a divine model"[78]). His theological and poetic construction reveal the fundamental and inescapable role played by human models, both real and literary. In fact Dante describes purgatorial souls meditating upon positive and negative examples taken from the Bible and classical mythology. We are born within a human world and we are nurtured and directed by human models. For this reason, parental symbolism is always invoked by Dante when he refers to either Virgil or Beatrice, his two guides through his journey of salvation (examples of both external and internal, or intimate, mediation). Hell on the contrary is the place of isolation, narcissism, and, above all, pride, the ultimate and fundamental sin for Dante: "everyone thinks he alone is condemned to hell, and that is what makes it hell."[79] It is not by chance that Francesca does not address a single word to her "beloved" Paolo in the episode recounted by Dante.

In Dante, Gragnolati and Webb argue, there is also a more positive understanding of desire as a joy in itself rather than a lack that needs to be satiated: "the spiritual motion of desire continues to be active as long as the beloved object makes the enamoured soul rejoice." For Dante, "humankind makes the mistake of directing its affection and desires toward those goods that are diminished by sharing. . . . It is only through the love of God that redirects desire upward, to heavenly goods that are infinitely shareable, and in fact, increased by sharing, that this infernal pattern of rivalry and envy may be avoided." This could also be linked, anthropologically and cognitively, to Ann Cale Kruger's recent discussion of the notion of "communion" through the lens of Girard's mimetic theory. She explains that cognitive psychologists "describe a distinctively human propensity to share psychological states (or intentions) with others." The human desire to share intimate thought, feeling, and intentions is anthropologically constitutive of our species from infancy.[80]

Topologies of Modernity

There has always been plenty of scope for conflict, envy, and rivalry, in history for models are part of the way the human being constructs his or her own identity. What is constitutively modern is "deviated transcendence":[81] the investment of the Other with divinity, and the metaphysical sickness that derives from it: "it is in internal mediation that the profoundest meaning of the *modern* is found."[82]

This deviated form of transcendency and its "spiritual pandemic," which had a horizontal rather than vertical outlook, produced some interesting effects in respect to novelistic representation—the novel as a veritable probe, a seismograph that detects the mimetic fluctuations of the modern social fabric. Rosa Mucignat's essay in this volume is in this sense an interesting analysis of the topography of mediated desire, which also helps to bridge modern and postmodern considerations. Mucignat's argument is in fact twofold. First she maps the progressive implosion of the "cartography" of desire in the novels of the European tradition Girard considered in *Deceit, Desire, and the Novel,* from the picaresque meandering in a region like La Mancha in *Quixote,* to the network of cities and villages of *The Red and the Black*, to the magnetic field of Paris as the center of the world in Flaubert's *Sentimental Education,* to the closed elitist circles of Proust's and Dostoevsky's novels. A world divested of God's authority produced a centripetal implosion, the concentric looping around the black hole of the symbolic attractive center of the social order, eventually collapsing in the limited space of an individual psyche (with modernism).

Mucignat's essay then considers the opposite movement, that is, the outreaching trajectory of mimetic desire, which after the implosion into the individual fragmented consciousness reaches out and "stretches beyond national boundaries and annexes, countries, races, and continents, in the heart of a universe where technical progress is wiping away one by one the differences between men."[83] Mucignat tangentially touches upon an understanding of modernity that Girard was reluctant to flesh out for quite some time and eventually made an attempt at conceptualization in *Battling to the End* (2007), in the last chapter of *Evolution and Conversion* (2007), and in his dialogues with Gianni Vattimo (2010).

However, Mucignat sets aside these totalizing questions, and through Franco Moretti's perspectives on the "cartography of novels" asks if mimetic theory could also be employed in the description of "relations of admiration, imitation, and antagonism that exist between cultures." Peripheral literatures, according to Moretti, in fact "borrow" and "imitate" the more prestigious and fashionable forms from the center of Western culture, Europe and North America—a perspective fully discussed, from the point of view of mimetic theory and with reference to Latin America, by João Cezar de Castro Rocha in his book *¿Culturas shakespearianas?*[84] Through an analysis of Omar Pamuk's *Snow*, Mucignat shows how the novel expresses and articulates the form of envy and resentment between cultures in the fully interconnected and globalized world we are living in, zooming in on the complex renegotiation of identities at the individual level, but which also resonates and reflects what has also become evident at the macro-political one. As Mucignat writes poignantly: "The new triangle resembles the shapes of fractal geometry, where the same pattern is reproduced in an infinitely small and infinitely large scale. The space in which it is inscribed is no longer the nation-state or the metropolis. The entire planet is divided into a center and an extended periphery, which in turn are fragmented into smaller, relative centers and peripheries, until we reach the inner world of the individual's consciousness, also composed of multiple, constantly shifting centripetal and centrifugal tensions."

In his chapter in this collection David Quint then brings the discussion back to the center of the social matrix in which the novel was born and developed "when a nascent capitalism expanded the opportunities for men and women in fact to be other somebodies . . . novels have a history and came into being to depict and reflect upon a newfound social mobility." In this regard, Quint argues that "Girard's is a top-down social view of the novel," where the snobbery and inauthenticity that are afflicting the aristocracy "gradually spread to the lower layers of that society."[85] However, the novel, being a realist genre, is essentially a view of society from the bottom. "Girard makes this history of the genre possible by his jumping chronologically from Cervantes to Stendhal, leaving out the entire eighteenth-century novel and its various versions of the rise of a sometimes virtuous bourgeoisie." The kind of universalization of mimetic desire that we see in *Deceit, Desire, and the Novel* is the reduction of its vast dynamic to pride.[86] The novelistic intelligence is not only linked to his veridical charge in respect the metamorphosis of desire, but in the way it represents the range of human possibilities that these metamorphoses allow. Dickens's characters, for instance, present a spectrum of existential possibilities charged by mimetic dynamics (whether characterized by resentment, envy, or positive reconciliation with the character's own place and role in society) within the new modern forms of social mobility. Girard warns that "if we consider all the heroes individually we shall be tempted to take seriously the excuses they give of their desires. We run the risk of missing the metaphysical meaning of that desire."[87] Those excuses might have something to do, Quint argues, "with inequitable circumstances that would require social action."

Miss Wade's autobiographical account in Dickens's *Little Dorrit* (1855–57) is, for instance, "a textbook case and confirmation of Girard's model of mimetic desire, of identification with and hatred of the mediating Other, and it bears more than passing resemblance to Girard's own textbook case, the more pathological hero of *Notes from the Underground*." British society never experienced the extremes of the French Revolution; it remained more structured in social layers that had a marginal permeability, while social exclusion remained part of the social fabric and vocabulary. This social exclusion is interiorized and made part of Miss Wade's identity, which is in fact defined by her contempt and resentment. According to Quint, this class resentment may expresses not only the bad conscience of the novel, as Girard argues, but also "its social conscience and realism." Girard is an acute theorist of ressentiment, Quint concludes, "which he sees turning upon and poisoning the self in a kind of short circuit. But *ressentiment* or a human response very much akin to it can go under the name of *indignation*, with a more altruistic valence and less blaming of society's victims. Indignation describes both the feelings of persons whose dignity has been taken away from them *and* the feelings that move others—readers of novels among them—on their behalf: and it contains the awareness that dignity, pride if you will, can be a human and social good."

In "'Let Us Carve Him as a Feast Fit for the Gods': Girard and Unjust Execution in Nineteenth-Century Narrative," Jan-Melissa Schramm also interrogates Charles Dickens's novels, in particular *A Tale of Two Cities* (1859), starting from where Quint's essay concludes, by analyzing the different, contradictory pulls of the modern democratic process in England. She underscores the "epistemological crisis" suffered by nineteenth-century British society, which was "in urgent need of democratic reform but hop[ed] to avoid the bloodshed of another French Revolution." Schramm considers a different focalization, by integrating the perspectives put forward by *Deceit, Desire, and the Novel* with the sacrificial dynamic fleshed out by Girard in his later works, and that found a literary focalization in Shakespeare, an author who combined a deep insight on the mimetic dynamic of desire, with the foundational political role of sacrificial violence, particularly in his historical dramas. More than the revulsion of mimetic desire, Schramm is in fact interested in the role of sacrifice in modern cultures: sacrifice, martyrdom, and undeserved death became prominent motifs of nineteenth-century writing. The novel's history is coincident with the rise of individualism and what Joseph Slaughter has called "the birth pains of . . . democratic citizen-subjectivity."[88] "Yet, culturally, the Victorians could not escape the traction of Evangelical self-sacrifice."

> Realist fiction with morally improving intentions thus placed itself in an awkward position, denouncing physical violence (particularly Chartist agitation), yet advocating self-sacrifice in the interests of a greater good. . . . Victorian fiction is extraordinarily attentive to the costs involved in such transactions, giving voice to the suffering individuals who will potentially be excluded from wider benefit, yet at the same time affirming that self-interest must be sacrificed to the greater good.

In the genealogy of modern resentment and metaphysical sickness described in *Deceit, Desire, and the Novel*, Dostoyevsky's novels represent the pinnacle of this historical trajectory, where the "corrosive disease" of the internal mediation "exerts its dissolving power at every level of existence, reaching a degree that is not seen in the French novelists." That is perhaps why, shortly after the publication of *Mensonge romantique* in 1961, Girard moved further to the "underground" and devoted an entire book to Dostoyevsky, *Du double à l'unité* (1963), translated into English only in 1997 under the title of *Resurrection from the Underground*.[89] Yue Zhuo explores the connections between these two books and the complex "metaphysical theater" of Dostoyevsky's novels, while underscoring the reader's fascination with the split self and chaos so pervasive in Dostoyevsky. Our fascination with Dostoyevsky's characters, Zhuo argues, comes from the fact that "the underground man's drama, compared to that of the snob, is purer and more 'authentic,' because it is a lonely metaphysical one freed from concerns of material gain and social advantage." The underground man is in fact a romantic and antimodern person who rejects rationalist values such as pragmatism and utilitarianism, and therefore has a heroic if not mystic quality and allure. The underground man's obsessions seem both "pathological" and "metaphysical" to us. They belong to "the world of the psychiatrist or philosopher." In this sense the masochist, "the manifestation of the romantic underground man in the modern world," is a philosophical and literary figure because the masochist "perceives the *necessary* relation between unhappiness and metaphysical desire."

Modernism: Deviated Transcendence and Death

Girard observes that metaphysical desire is animated by a mortal dynamism that tends toward "disintegration and death": "to perceive the meta-physical structure of desire is to foresee its catastrophic conclusion."[90] This seems particularly true with modernist writing, where death seems to function as a black hole toward which everything is—sooner or later—drawn: "it is the inevitable termination of that ever more effective negation of life and spirit, deviated transcendence. The affirmation of the self ends in the negation of the self. The will to make oneself God is a will to self-destruction that is gradually realized."[91] Not dissimilarly, Erich Auerbach, in *Mimesis*, argued that in modernist texts, we sense an atmosphere of universal doom: James Joyce's *Ulysses*, Virginia Woolf's *To the Lighthouse*,[92] and other novels "which employ multiple reflection of consciousness . . . leave the reader with an impression of hopelessness . . . a turning away from their practical will to live . . . hatred of culture and civilization have developed, and often a radical and fanatical urge to destroy."[93] What seems to emerge in central figures of literary and philosophical modernism is in particular a distinctive "polymorphism" as a result of the collapse of bourgeois values.[94] As Nidesh Lawtoo shows in his book *The Phantom of the Ego*, "Protean forms of psychic dispossession take place in a widening number, with increasing speed and power of infection."[95]

The authors discussed by Wittman, Sudlow, and Welge in their respective chapters in this volume seem to provide different strategies in the wrestling with the maelstrom of self-deception, nihilism, and death in which their modern(ist) heroes were sucked—though, the result of their bad faith is quite similar, being death (Bernanos), nihilism (Pirandello), or defeat (Arlt). Coincidently, there is a whole Dostoyevskian matrix that seems to characterize this type of literary modernism, where many of these authors clearly recognized in the Russian novelist the most insightful and powerful description of the underground condition that seems so ubiquitous in their contemporary world.

In Bernanos's short stories, for instance, according to Sudlow, there is a clear emphasis on death as the ultimate stage of the progress of mimetic desire and violence: "in Bernanos's imagination one must go to death's door to find any hope of salvation." What becomes visible in this process of "descent to hell" is that "there are no rites left to evacuate conflict. None of the death scenarios in these stories rehearse the catharsis that ritualization of hostility might afford." Everything lies "under the sign of deception": Bernanos's characters explicitly choose to love through bad faith and delusion, as the only viable existential strategy. "There is arguably no classic Girardian conversion in any of these three short stories. Nevertheless, there are moments of awareness or illumination that suggest where deliverance is to be found: in the recognition of the disaster that imitative desire can lead to, or the acknowledgment of the Christian solution to the dilemmas that immoderate mimetic desire can produce."

In the play *Lazzaro*, analyzed by Laura Wittman, Pirandello mocks the idea of resurrection, where neither science nor religion seem able to provide any form of real understanding or theological or existential salience of the modern, biologically motivated occurrences of this event. Pirandello's aim is to stage the contention between two ideological doubles, by unmasking the rivalrous emulation that exists between the apparently opposed discourses of science and religion: "In *Lazzaro*, such a refusal yields a religious interpretation that is unaware of mimicking scientific models; but it can also yield its complementary opposite, a resentful, militantly secular view that is unaware of its metaphysical resentment." Eventually, "the skeptic Pirandello recognizing that a religious myth that is familiar to people may be preferable to no myth at all," while the final "resurrection" is achieved through bad faith rather from any form of revelation. What is in fact revealed is the nothingness behind identity and behind life and death.

In discussing the work of the Argentinian writer Roberto Arlt, Welge explores, through the idea of "performative mimesis," what seems to be the prelude of the avant-gardist and postmodern idea of mimetic identity. This is magnified by Arlt's peripheral position in respect to the European cultural center, for emulation and parody are characteristic of the literatures of "Shakespearean countries," as Castro Rocha has called them. In a very Dostoyevskian way, the Arltian individual strives to transcend his low social standing, through "imaginary greatness," which end "invariably and inevitably in defeat." However, in contrast to Dostoyevsky or Cervantes, Arlt's heroes do not lead toward a "conversion." Arlt's novelistic and dramatic protagonists are somehow beyond any notion of truth or falseness, for they achieve presence to the extent that they perform a preconceived image or type. In Arlt's novel there is a "dispersal of any notion of organic unity and subjectivity, as well as any 'romantic' notion of individual artistic originality," which is substituted by a "theatrical conception of personhood": "the character's search for self-identity is bound up with a kind of metaliterary and metatheatrical chain, in which every mask hides yet another mask." Biblical scriptures also features in the encyclopedia of Arlt's characters, although it does not provide any form of "deliverance" or "revelation," but is presented as a fictional narrative like any other, subject to any possible divergent interpretation. Accordingly, Arlt's protagonists choose a form of fictional self-mythization through literature and cinema as phantasmagoric strategy against the failure of mimetic desire. One of the characters "stresses that he aims to invent a new image of a god for the masses hungry for miracles, making use of the sensationalist press, photography, and cinematography," "creating the image of a pseudo-Christ figure whose physiognomy would be a cross 'between Krishnamurti and Rudolph Valentino.'" In this sense,

"Arlt's paradoxical staging of mimetic desire demonstrates the aporias of a specifically modernist situation in which the false romanticism of desire is dramatically heightened, and it can no longer be renounced, as Girard would have it, but rather is the collective sign of a social and psychological utopia."

A Sense of Recognition? Reading and Writing after Girard

Within the vast postmodern repertoire of images, topoi, citations, typological structures, and their more or less parodic reusage, one may wonder if the notion of triangular desire, or the scapegoat representational template, may have become common currency in world literature. They are tropes with superabundant presence, not only in literature but also in cinema, art, and television.[96]

There would be an entire monograph to be written on Girard's influence on contemporary authors, who may have stumbled on *Deceit, Desire, and the Novel*, or other Girardian texts, finding useful hints, thematic focalization, representational saliency. Milan Kundera is surely the most eloquent and obvious example, as investigated by Trevor Cribben Merrill in his book *The Book of Imitation and Desire*.[97] Daniel Pennac in his series "La Saga Malaussène" (1985–99), Christa Wolf in *Medea* (1996), J. M. Coetzee in *Disgrace* (1999) and *Elizabeth Costello* (2003), and Alberto Garlini in *Futbol bailado* (2004) are other examples of contemporary writers who explicitly took inspiration from Girard's theory of violence.[98] One may also wonder if V. S. Naipaul in *The Mimic Men* (1967), Philip Roth in *The Professor of Desire* (1977), or Peter Shaffer in his plays may have exploited Girard's intuitions. This would widen the kind of influence Girardian theory may have had outside the field of literary criticism, which inevitably has (meta)consequences on the critical level: Can a literary theory inspire creative production? Is this borrowing further evidence of both the anthropological and literary saliency of Girard's theory? What is the added or residual cognitive and cultural value of these literary forms from the perspective of mimetic theory, besides its further corroboration?

In the final section of the book Christoph Holzhey, Trevor Merrill, and Robert Buch analyze novels that were written after the publication of

Deceit, Desire, and the Novel and *Violence and the Sacred*, and that could be inscribed in a cluster of texts where a particular consonance, or an increased sense of recognition, or a direct influence with Girard's theorization could be detected.

The most difficult case to assess—but also a fascinating one from the point of view of mimetic theory—is Pier Paolo Pasolini, an author and director who was literally haunted by (self)sacrificial and Christian imagery, and who, starting from the 1960s, became interested in the history and anthropology of religion.[99] The influence of Dante's *Commedia* was also critical to accord Pasolini's works (in this specific case, his posthumous novel *Petrolio*), to Girard's perspectives. *Petrolio* (1975) in fact, according to Holzhey, is "centrally concerned with mimetic desire and exhibits many of its vicissitudes analyzed by Girard"; however, "it is also more attuned to the ambivalence of mimetic desire and allows for alternative developments." Through Dante, Pasolini makes clear, for instance, how much "the past was ruled by models, which are therefore not considered as negative per se but rather as necessary for a happiness anchored in what Pasolini calls 'Reality' and endows with a sense of the sacred." In Pasolini, mimetic desire is somehow "taken for granted," and "what is deplored is the absence of desires capable of eliciting desire." Holzhey then picks up from Girard the possibility of thematizing a sort of "post-mimetic desire."[100] By attacking any form of bourgeois snobbism and the coquetterie displayed by heterosexual couples ("their utter self-sufficiency and total lack of interest"), Pasolini "imposes a different reading, namely that what is denounced is a love so insincere that it is unreal, devoid of any desire or interest whatsoever and therefore incapable of eliciting desire or interest" in others. On the opposite side of the spectrum, Pasolini struggles with his own tragic sense of the radical loss of a "real" object of desire: the urban subproletariat, and the archaic Italian peasants: "Pasolini's desire does not change in its aim, but it can no longer find objects." However, this is one of the points where the real and the mythical implode in Pasolini, as the loss of any object of desire points to a narcissistic image of reality where transformation and change is seen as a form of loss, of departure from a mythical Eden, historically and socially situated in his youth. Pasolini, though, "holds onto desire in a thoroughly fragmented, confusing, self-splitting, and self-shattering text," while he produces a "ruthless satire on the conformist, corrupted behavior of the formerly cherished others." In a truly modernist fashion, Holzhey eventually sees Pasolini as an example of Baudelaire's recognition of "a truly superior laughter, the one that welcomes its own downfall."[101]

Trevor Merrill then discusses Jonathan Franzen's novelistic "conversion," mapped through the transition from his earlier novel, *Strong Motion* (1992), to his most accomplished work to date, *The Corrections* (2001).[102] "According to Girard's conception of how great novels are written, the novelist has to write his (or her) novel twice: the first time around, the outcome of his creative efforts is fundamentally self-serving. . . . The second version of his book is born of that eye-opening realization, which leads to him handing over some version of his own delusion to the protagonist. The character in turn becomes the bearer of and believer in the lie, even as he marches slowly through the narrative toward truth." The "corrections" in the case of Franzen are both existential but also literary. There is constantly a self-reflexive element in the novel, as a form of *Künstleroman*. As René Girard observes: "One should not compare the author's successive works to the musical exercises by which musicians gradually increase their virtuosity. What is essential lies elsewhere."[103] Great literature, writes Girard, "requires a victory over pride itself."[104] In Franzen's own words, *The Corrections* came into being through an act of retrospective self-demystification, which also resonates with the notion of "de-creation" that Wolfgang Palaver discusses in his contribution to this volume. Franzen had to overcome his "wish to be all intellect, all worldly expertise, so as to avoid the messy business of [his] private life," which amounted to "to repress *shame*." By doing so, he creates a hero who is "more than just the victim of his own undisciplined impulses and depressive tendencies. He is also a hero who matures into an adult by the novel's conclusion."

Jonathan Littell's *The Kindly Ones* (2006) finally could be seen as one of most ambitious literary projects to incorporate and expand some of Girard's ideas on mimetism and violence, albeit integrated with a vast repertoire of other theoretical and historical sources. Girard is in fact one of the many voices of a very cognate intertextual matrix, where Bataille, Kristeva, Agamben, and others converge in this dissonant contemporary image of a personal and collective historical apocalypse, sought to capture both the "pathology" and the "banality" of evil, epitomized by Maximilien Aue, the protagonist of Littell's novel, a SS officer who helped to carry out the Holocaust.

The point of Buch's discussion is not genetic, but rather structural: "Girardian tropes are prominently at work in the novel and cast light on some of its most intractable enigmas." Aue's desire, for instance, is mimetic, almost in a literal sense, for it is not triangular, but dyadic, and ultimately narcissistic: "Aue's desire springs from a painful and violent cut: The separation from his twin sister Una. . . . Aue's main fantasy is to recover this blissful sense of wholeness." The prelapsarian condition he mourns seems to be closer to the psychoanalytic notion of Chora, as expressed by Kristeva for instance, a phase in child development that was never touched by Girard's interest. Aue could also be seen as an "abject figure, an outcast, a kind of *homo sacer*, or in Girard's parlance, a scapegoat, bearer of the accursed share."[105] With a perfect Nietzschean inversion between Dionysus and Christ, Aue presents himself "in the guise of the ultimate scapegoat, the supreme victim: *Ecce homo*." Doubles also abound in the novel, not only at the individual level, but at the collective and ideological ones, which seems to foresee the kind of perspective Girard exposes in *Battling to the End*. As Buch phrases it, "The Nazi fantasy of racial supremacy is in essence a replication of Jewish exceptionalism"; "the attempt to obliterate sameness and to restore and consolidate difference compounds the issue, resulting in more likeness rather than less, endowing the Germans with a monstrous singularity."

What is also interesting from Buch's analysis and Littell's novel is its constant address to the reader: "Hypocrite lecteur, mon semblable, mon frère." Key to the reader address is the idea of "aggressively antagonizing the audience while by the same token insisting on the shared humanity of reader and narrator, the shared reservoir of ambition and anxiety, pettiness and magnanimity, cruelty and compassion," which somehow recognizes our own implication in the long history of human persecution, being private or collective, which is also one of the most challenging and discomforting implications of Girard's theory.

The Religious (Un)conscious

The volume closes by giving Girard the last word on the subject, in the form of one of his last talks on literary matters, dominated by the religious dimension of his critical approach and by the meaning of his own conversion. It is a conclusive remark that also points to a genetic moment, because it takes us back to the gestational period in the composition of *Deceit, Desire, and the Novel*.[106] In *Deceit, Desire, and the Novel* Girard explains that the novelist experiences a process of "conversion," or spiritual and cognitive metamorphosis, which takes the shape of a full self-awareness in relation to his or her individual autonomy, which also triggers the creative process at the base of the novel, and its power of demystification. As Girard writes: "The Christian form seems to be present in Western literature whenever the hero-creator is saved from an idolatrous world by a spiritual metamorphosis which makes him able to describe his former condition. The work records its own genesis, in the form of a fall and redemption."[107]

The confessional and religious inspiration of *Deceit, Desire, and the Novel* is surely one of the least "palatable" aspects of Girard's book and theory for mainstream literary criticism. The idea to inscribe the "truth" of the novel, its intrinsic intention, in the notion of "conversion" is surely an effect of existential focalization by Girard, who came to a personal religious conversion while writing this book. Some critics, sympathetic with the Girardian perspective, but also anxious to provide a "politically correct" version of his take, have noted that the hermeneutic power of Girard's theory holds its validity in spite of the confessional position of its author.[108] If this is true up to a certain point, the issues at stake from a historical and hermeneutic standpoint are actually more complex. We may wish to step outside the limits of a confessional dynamics; however, the theme and the structure of conversion remains of fundamental relevance, when one thinks not only of the novel, but criticism itself being influenced by its religious "subconscious," or rather by the linguistic and semantic structures, conceptual parameters and symbolic forms, we still borrow inadvertently from biblical and religious exegesis. As Northrop Frye phrased it in *The Great Code*: "Many issues in critical theory today had their origin in the hermeneutic study of the Bible; many contemporary approaches to criticism are obscurely motivated by a God-is-dead syndrome that also developed out of Biblical criticism."[109] One can read Wolfgang Palaver's essay in this direction. Palaver analyzes Girard's perspective through the lens of Simone Weil's concept of "creative renunciation" as a way to overcome "idolatry." The effectiveness of the work of art is not achieved through forms of narcissistic self-glorification or self-divinization on the part of the writer, because great art ultimately "stems from renunciation and self-loss" that imitates "God's way of creation that consists primarily in renunciation."

What needs to be discussed is not so much or not only the religious underpinning of Girard's theory, but rather the contours of the religious (and Christian in particular) subtexts that survive within modern Western culture, and in literature in particular.[110] The dissolution of medieval theocentrism, and the emergence of modern humanism and individualism, cannot simply be equated with the disappearance of the religious, but with its metamorphosis. The language and codes with which reality has been read survived, albeit converted into different forms. The history of the novel can be conceptualized in various ways: on one hand, it is the expression of the need for self-representation of a particular social class, the bourgeoisie, which, in its radical reshuffling of the class system in Europe, contributed to the exasperation of the dynamics of internal mediation; on the other hand, being the literary form that "absorbed" the social, cultural, and aesthetic functions performed by the Bible, assuming the role of secularized scriptures, as Wolfgang Iser argued,[111] it maintains an aesthetic "energy" that, according to Girard, stems from its revelatory power and its demystifying force.

As Girard writes, "the resort to Christian symbolism . . . has no religious significance" personally for some writers, as in the case of the agnostic Proust, but symbolism belongs to the novelistic form, the "archetype" of which is Saint Augustine's *Confessions*, "the first work whose genesis is truly inscribed in its form."[112] Religious symbolism, broadly intended, is also intrinsic to the novel as a formal entity and mechanism that allows us to experience a sense of "totality." As Frank Kermode would say, the "time of the novelist" is what makes *chronos* become *kairos*, "historical moments of intemporal significance."[113] In this sense we might share Cesáreo Bandera's and Stefano Brugnolo's suggestions that a way to describe the history of the novel, from a Girardian point of view, would be through an analysis of the way the transposition-translation of the thick imagery of Western religious traditions has been diluted into a secular and rational language, a process that is still occurring even in a postmodern context:

> Many of these images retain a strong evocative power, many translations
> have proved disappointing, or were not able to exhaust the potential of
> meaning of those images. It happens then that those images, having lost

their substantial and normative value, have acquired an utopian one: they present themselves as challenges to secular thought, as an endless task of desecration. Of this kind seem to me the religious symbols (grace, conversion, redemption, etc.), that, according to Girard, inspired the novelistic modern vision. They were inherited by tradition but after being creatively remotivated.[114]

A task for the scholarship, then would be to return to an understanding, shared by thinkers and critics like Frye, Gadamer, Ricoeur, Ong, Kermode, Agamben, and Girard, among others, to fully understand how terms like "sacrifice," "epiphany," "divinity," "apocalypse," "sublime," "grace," "conversion," "fall and redemption," and so on, were resemantized or remotivated within the history of modern literature and how they are still present in our ways of understanding and analyzing literary texts.

Notes

1. Elisabeth Ladenson, "Girard's Proust," paper delivered at the conference *"Deceit, Desire, and the Novel* Fifty Years Later," Yale University, October 14, 2011.

2. Ciriaco Morón-Arroyo, "Cooperative Mimesis: Don Quixote and Sancho Panza," *Diacritics* 8.1 (1978): 83.

3. Two examples are Hayden White, "Ethnological 'Lie' and Mythical 'Truth,'" *Diacritics* 8.1 (1978): 2–9; Toril Moi, "The Missing Mother: The Oedipal Rivalries of René Girard," *Diacritics* 12.2 (1982): 21–31.

4. "Theorie du roman e théorie de l'homme sont, pour Girard, corrélatives et ne peuvent s'exposer qu'ensemble." Jean Cohen, "La Théorie du roman de René Girard," *Annales. Histoire, Sciences Sociales* 20.3 (1965): 465.

5. René Girard, *Resurrection from the Underground: Feodor Dostoevsky*, ed. and trans. James G. Williams (New York: Crossroad Publishing Company, 1997), 20.

6. Robert Doran, "Introduction: Literature as Theory," in *Mimesis and Theory: Essays on Literature and Criticism, 1953–2005*, by René Girard, ed. R. Doran (Stanford: Stanford University Press, 2008), xiv.

7. René Girard, *Deceit, Desire, and the Novel: Self and Other in Literary Structure*, trans. Yvonne Freccero (Baltimore: Johns Hopkins University Press, 1965), 3.

8. See, for instance, Martha Nussbaum, *Love's Knowledge: Essays on Philosophy and Literature* (Oxford: Oxford University Press, 1990); Nussbaum, *Poetic Justice: The Literary Imagination in Public Life* (Boston: Beacon Press, 1996); Richard Rorty, "Heidegger, Kundera and Dickens," in *Essays on Heidegger and Others* (Cambridge: Cambridge University Press, 1991).

9. René Girard, *Evolution and Conversion: Dialogues on the Origin of Culture*, with Pierpaolo Antonello and João Cezar de Castro Rocha (New York: Continuum, 2007), 173.

10. At some point he stated candidly that "it was my good fortune at the time that I knew nothing of 'critical theory.' I did not realize that critics were supposed to look for differences, singularities, and not for similarities, in the work they studied. Similarities were and still are frowned upon." Rebecca Adams, "Violence, Difference, Sacrifice: A Conversation with René Girard," *Religion and Literature* 25.2 (1993): 12.

11. For a discussion in the light of Girard's perspective see Wulf Koepke, "Quest, Illusion, Creativity, Maturity and Resignation: The Questionable Journey of the Protagonist of the Bildungroman," *Helios* 17.1 (1990): 129–43.

12. Teresa De Lauretis, *Alice Doesn't: Feminism, Semiotics, Cinema* (Bloomington: Indiana University Press, 1984), 120.

13. Jay Clayton, "Narrative and Theories of Desire," *Critical Inquiry* 16.1 (1989): 34.

14. "His enemies are mirror images of himself"; White, "Ethnological Lie," 7.

15. Girard, *Deceit, Desire, and the Novel*, 92.

16. Alexandre Kojève, *Introduction to the Reading of Hegel: Lectures on the "Phenomenology of Spirit,"* trans. H. J. Nichols, reprint edition (Ithaca, NY: Cornell University Press, 1980), 6.

17. Kojève, *Introduction to Hegel*, 7. For a general discussion on this matter, see George Erving, "René Girard and the Legacy of Alexandre Kojeve," *Contagion* 10.1 (2003): 111–25.

18. Girard, *Deceit, Desire, and the Novel*, 96ff.

19. Girard, *Mimesis and Theory*, 50–55, 134–59. For Girard, while de Beauvoir remains trapped in her naive belief in her freedom and genuine spontaneity, Sartre seems to move in the direction of a possible "novelistic conversion." *Le parole* seems to bring to fulfillment, at the level of aesthetic intuition, the awareness of the failure of the heroic project of *Being and Nothingness*. In the Oedipal analysis of the structures of his childhood, Sartre is in fact partially coming to terms with his dependence on the Other. However, he turns into an antihero who is only the negative image of the same autonomy prior professed and that ends in the regressive process of *Nausea*.

20. See especially Deleuze and Guattari, *L'Anti-Œdipe* (Paris: Les éditions de Minuit, 1972) and Gilles Deleuze, "Plaisir et désir," *Magazine littéraire* 325 (1994): 57–65.

21. These connections are explored, for instance, by Bo Earle, "Performance of Negation, Negation of Performance: Death and Desire in Kojève, Bataille, and Girard," *Comparative Literature Studies* 39.1 (2002): 48–67; Giuseppe Fornari, *Storicità radicale: Filosofia e morte di Dio* (Massa: Transeuropa, 2013); Fornari, *A God Torn to Pieces: The Nietzsche Case* (East Lansing: Michigan State University Press, 2013).

22. See, for instance, Peter Brooks: "Through study of the work accomplished by fictions we may be able to reconnect literary criticism to human concern. In our attempt to move beyond strict formalism . . . psychoanalysis promises, and requires, that . . . we engage the dynamic of memory and the history of desire as they work to shape the creation of meaning within time." Peter Brooks, *Reading for the Plot: Design and Intention in Narrative* (Cambridge: Harvard University Press, 1992), xvi.

23. Exceptions are Eugene Webb, *The Self Between: From Freud to the New Social Psychology of France* (Seattle: University of Washington Press, 1993); and Martha Reineke, *Sacrificed Lives: Kristeva on Women and Violence* (Bloomington: Indiana University Press, 1997).

24. See Scott R. Garrels, "Imitation, Mirror Neurons, and Mimetic Desire: Convergence between the Mimetic Theory of René Girard and Empirical Research on Imitation," *Contagion* 12–13

(2005–6): 47–86; Scott R. Garrels, ed., *Mimesis and Science: Empirical Research on Imitation and the Mimetic Theory of Culture and Religion* (East Lansing: Michigan State University Press, 2012).

25. See René Girard, *Oedipus Unbound: Selected Writings on Rivalry and Desire*, ed. Mark Anspach (Stanford: Stanford University Press, 2004).

26. As Girard explains, desire is eminently human: "If desire is so fixed, it means that there isn't much difference between desire and instincts. In order to have *mobility* of desire—in relation to both appetites and instincts from one side and the social milieu from the other—the relevant difference is *imitation*, that is, the presence of the *model* or models, since everybody has one or more. Only mimetic desire can be *free*, can be *genuine* desire, human desire, because it *must* choose a model more than the object itself. Mimetic desire is what makes us human, what make possible for us the breakout from routinely animalistic appetites, and constructs our own, albeit inevitably unstable, identities. It is this very mobility of desire, its mimetic nature, and this very instability of our identities, that makes us capable of *adaptation*, that gives the possibility to learn and to *evolve*" (Girard, *Evolution and Conversion*, 58).

27. Girard, *Deceit, Desire, and the Novel*, 35.

28. Cf. P. Antonello, "Rivalità, risentimento, apocalisse: Svevo e i suoi doppi," in *Identità e desiderio: La teoria mimetica e la letteratura italiana*, ed. P. Antonello and G. Fornari (Massa: Transeuropa, 2009), 143–63.

29. For theoretical and clinical discussions, see, for instance, Iris Levy, "The Laius Complex: From Myth to Psychoanalysis," *International Forum of Psychoanalysis* 20.4 (2011): 222–28; Rachel Bowlby, *Freudian Mythologies* (Oxford: Oxford University Press, 2009); Massimo Recalcati, *Il complesso di Telemaco: Genitori e figli dopo il tramonto del padre* (Milan: Feltrinelli, 2013); John W. Crandall, "The Cronus Complex," *Clinical Social Work Journal* 12.2 (1984): 108–17; Domenica Mazzu, ed., *Politiques de Caïn: En dialogue avec René Girard* (Paris: Desclée de Brouwer, 2004).

30. It is the case, for instance, of Pier Paolo Pasolini, who adopted both the Oedipus and the Laius "complexes" in his works, in particular in *Oedipus Rex* (1967) and *Affabulazione* (1969). Sylvia Plath in "Daddy" (1962) makes reference to the Electra complex, while E. L. Doctorow in *Loon Lake* (1980) presents a parody on the legendry "Ulysses-Telemachus" theme that has its origin in Tennyson's "Ulysses."

31. Doran, "Introduction: Literature as Theory," in Girard, *Mimesis and Theory*, xvii. .

32. Girard, *Deceit, Desire, and the Novel*, 87.

33. Roland Barthes, *The Pleasure of the Text*, trans. Richard Miller (New York, 1975).

34. Dawn Marlan, "The Seducer as Friend: The Disappearance of Sex as a Sign of Conquest in *Les liaisons dangereuses*," *PMLA* 116.2 (2001): 314–28.

35. Joy Connolly, "Asymptotes of Pleasure: Thoughts on the Nature of Roman Erotic Elegy," *Arethusa* 33.1 (2000): 71–98.

36. Elena Pulcini, *L'individuo senza passioni: Individualismo moderno e perdita del legame sociale* (Turin: Bollati Boringhieri, 2001).

37. See, for instance, René Girard, *Anorexia and Mimetic Desire*, trans. Mark R. Anspach (East Lansing: Michigan State University Press, 2013).

38. Leo Bersani and Ulysse Dutoit, *The Forms of Violence: Narrative in Assyrian Art and Modern Culture* (New York: Schocken Books, 1985), v.

39. Bersani and Dutoit, *The Forms of Violence*, 40.

40. Clayton, "Narrative and Theories of Desire," 44–45.

41. Toril Moi argues that Girard "cannot account for feminine desire," essentially because he does not take into account the preoedipal stage, and the period of the child's development "when all its desires take her [the mother] as their object." Moi, "The Missing Mother," 27. Moi's argument, however, is partially at fault here. First of all, because there is not any Oedipal stage in Girard's account of identity formation. Second because, at the early stage of infancy we cannot speak in terms of desire, which involves more socially and culturally driven dynamics. In infancy, we are mainly in the realm of physical need and demands, to use Lacanian terminology.

42. See, for instance, Laura Gorfkle and Amy R. Williamsen, "Mimetic Desire and the Narcissistic (Wo)man in 'La ilustre fregona' and the Persiles: Strategies for Reinterpretation," *Hispania* 77.1 (1994): 11–22; Diane Chambers, "Triangular Desire and the Sororal Bond: The 'Deceased Wife's Sister Bill,'" *Mosaic* 29.1 (1996): 19–36; Lahoucine Ouzgane, "Desire, Emulation, and Envy in *The Portrait of a Lady*," *Contagion* 8.1 (2001): 114–34; Matthew Taylor, "What Persuasion Really Means in *Persuasion*: A Mimetic Reading of Jane Austen," *Contagion* 11.1 (2004): 105–23; Simon De Keukelaere, "What Is Deviated Transcendency? Woolf's *The Waves* as a Textbook Case," *Contagion* 12–13.1 (2005): 195–218; Katharine Bubel, "Transcending the Triangle of Desire: Eros and the 'Fulfillment of Love' in *Middlemarch* and *Jane Eyre*," *Renascence* 60.4 (2008): 295–308; Anne McTaggart, "What Women Want? Mimesis and Gender in Chaucer's Wife of Bath's Prologue and Tale," *Contagion* 19.1 (2012): 41–67.

43. Following Freud, Teresa De Lauretis argues that women are capable of identifying with various characters at various times and of alternating between different kinds of identifications. The "power of female desire" is chacterized by "its duplicity and ambivalence." De Lauretis, *Alice Doesn't*, 156.

44. René Girard, *A Theater of Envy: William Shakespeare* (Oxford: Oxford University Press, 1991), 260.

45. René Girard, *Things Hidden Since the Foundation of the World*, research undertaken in collaboration with Jean-Michel Oughourlian and Guy Lefort, trans. by Stephen Nann and Michael Metteer (Stanford: Stanford University Press, 1987), 337.

46. Girard, *Deceit, Desire, and the Novel*, 2–3.

47. Girard, *A Theater of Envy*, 260.

48. Girard, *Deceit, Desire, and the Novel*, 47.

49. Eve Kosofsky Sedgwick, *Between Men: English Literature and Male Homosocial Desire* (New York: Columbia University Press, 1985), 22.

50. Sedgwick, *Between Men*, 22.

51. See on this score D. S. Neff, "Two into Three Won't Go: Mimetic Desire and the Dream of Androgyny in *Dancing in the Dark*," *Modern Fiction Studies* 34.3 (1988): 387–403; Mario Klarer, "David Leavitt's 'Territory': René Girard's Homoerotic 'Trigonometry' and Julia Kristeva's 'Semiotic Chora,'" *Studies in Short Fiction* 28.1 (1991): 63–76; Serena Anderlini-D'Onofrio, "Plural Happiness: Bi and Poly Triangulations in Balasko's *French Twist*," *Journal of Bisexuality* 9.3–4 (2009): 343–61; Ann-Sofie Lönngren, "Triangular, Homosocial, Lesbian: A Queer Approach to Desire in August Strindberg's Novel *A Madman's Manifesto*," *Contagion* 19.1 (2012): 205–29.

52. Girard, *Deceit, Desire, and the Novel*, 58.

53. Girard, *Evolution and Conversion*, 76.

54. René Girard, *Achever Clausewitz* (Paris: Carnets Nord, 2007), 370ff. On the notion of positive internal mediation see also G. Fornari, *La bellezza e il nulla: L'antropologia cristiana di Leonardo da Vinci* (Milan: Marietti, 2005); Petra Steinmair-Pösel, "Original Sin, Grace, and Positive Mimesis," *Contagion* 14 (2007): 1–12; Vern Neufeld Redekop and Thomas Ryba, eds., *René Girard and Creative Mimesis* (Lanham, MD: Lexington Books, 2013).

55. Martha Reineke, "After the Scapegoat: René Girard's Apocalyptic Vision and the Legacy of Mimetic Theory," *Philosophy Today* 56.2 (2012): 141–53.

56. Girard, *Deceit, Desire, and the Novel*, 19.

57. René Girard, *"To Double Business Bound": Essays on Literature, Mimesis, and Anthropology* (Baltimore: Johns Hopkins University Press, 1978), 130.

58. Umberto Eco, *On Literature* (Orlando, FL: Harcourt Books, 2004), 16–22.

59. Frank Kermode, *The Sense of an Ending: Studies in the Theory of Fiction*, 2nd ed. (Oxford: Oxford University Press, 2000).

60. However, the comparative lens of Girard's analysis did not scrutinize the biblical text as a whole, but those kernels, those "texts of persecution," expressing the injust and arbitrary suffering of the victim, which are at the core of its revelatory power.

61. Girard, *Evolution and Conversion*, 218–19. See, for instance, P. Valadier, "Violenza del sacro e non violenza del cristianesimo nel pensiero di René Girard," *La Civiltà Cattolica* (1983), 370.

62. S. Brugnolo, "La visione romanzesca e la visione cristiana: Una rilettura illuministica di *Menzogna romantica e verità romanzesca*," *Nuova corrente* 137 (2006): 24–25.

63. Brugnolo, "La visione romanzesca," 23.

64. See V. Gallese, "The Two Sides of Mimesis: Girard's Mimetic Theory, Embodied Simulation and Social Identification," *Journal of Consciousness Studies* 16.4 (2009): 21–44.

65. S. Giglioli, "René Girard e la teoria letteraria: Un caso ancora aperto," in Antonello and Fornari, *Identità e desiderio*, 5–13 (10).

66. Leo Bersani, *A Future for Astyanax: Character and Desire in Literature* (Boston: Little, Brown, 1976), 69–70.

67. Nadine Dormoy Savage, "Conversation avec René Girard," *French Review* 56.5 (1983): 711–19: "[Dostoyevsky's epilepsy and Proust's asthma] are two psychosomatic illnesses, and those are diseases that could be seen as the representation of persecution, of sustained violence. It's extraordinary. But I do not want to make a cause. It is a symptom. Proust is not a normal asthmatic, and Dostoyevsky is not an ordinary epileptic. At the same time, I think it is a revelation of the intensity with which people like them live the role of the victim that they have both certainly experienced, even with threats of paranoia. They have succumbed neither one nor the other, making them true art. You could say that being a great artist, in human relationships, in the novel, is not to succumb to paranoia in circumstances that favor it" (715).

68. Alberto Beretta Anguissola, "Marcel Proust e René Girard: Un triplice confronto," in Antonello and Fornari, *Identità e desiderio*, 22.

69. See, for instance, in *The Brothers Karamazov*, Ivan recounting his story of "The Grand Inquisitor": "Imagine that you are creating a fabric of human destiny with the object of making men happy in the end, giving them peace and rest at last, but that it was essential and inevitable to torture to death only one tiny creature—that baby beating its breast with its fist, for instance—and to found

that edifice on its unavenged tears, would you consent to be the architect on those conditions?"; F. Dostoyevsky, *The Brothers Karamazov*, trans. Constance Garnett (New York: Vintage, 1950), 291.

70. One way to look at this problem is to consider some of the issues discussed by Girard with Gianni Vattimo in their book *Christianity, Truth and Weakening Faith* (2010), in which they express their common belief that Christianity, through its desacralizing force, acted as "the religion of the exit from religion," and that democracy, civil rights, individual freedoms, laicism, have all been, if not precisely invented in the absolute sense, "facilitated" in their development and expression by the Christian cultures. Secularization in its various cultural aspects is a Christian by-product, as it were, and the novel, one of the "seismographers" of these transformations. Cf. G. Vattimo and R. Girard, *Christianity, Truth, and Weakening Faith: A Dialogue*, ed. P. Antonello (New York: Columbia University Press, 2010); in particular the introduction and the first chapter: "Christianity and Modernity."

71. Girard, *"To Double Business Bound,"* 1–8.

72. Robert Doran, "Imitation and Originality: Thinking Creative Mimesis in Longinus, Kant, and Girard," in Redekop and Ryba, *Girard and Creative Mimesis*, 111.

73. Doran, "Imitation and Originality," 116.

74. Doran, "Introduction: Literature as Theory," in Girard, *Mimesis and Theory*, xxv.

75. Girard, *Deceit, Desire, and the Novel*, 272.

76. Girard, *Evolution and Conversion*, 236.

77. Girard, *"To Double Business Bound,"* 1–8.

78. Girard, *Deceit, Desire, and the Novel*, 58.

79. Girard, *Deceit, Desire, and the Novel*, 57.

80. Ann Cale Kruger, "Imitation, Communion, and Culture," in Garrells, *Mimesis and Science*, 113.

81. Girard, *Deceit, Desire, and the Novel*, 77.

82. Girard, *Deceit, Desire, and the Novel*, 92.

83. Girard, *Deceit, Desire, and the Novel*, 138.

84. João Cezar de Castro Rocha, *¿Culturas shakespearianas? Teoría Mimética y América Latina*, Cátedra Eusebio Francisco Kino (Guadalajara: ITESO/Universidad Iberoamericana, 2013).

85. Girard, *Deceit, Desire, and the Novel*, 227.

86. Girard, *Deceit, Desire, and the Novel*, 56–59.

87. Girard, *Deceit, Desire, and the Novel*, 55.

88. Joseph Slaughter, *Human Rights, Inc.: The World Novel, Narrative Form, and International Law* (New York: Fordham University Press, 2007), 57.

89. René Girard, *Dostoïevski: Du double à l'unité* (Paris: Plon, 1963), translated into English under the title of *Resurrection from the Underground: Feodor Dostoevsky*, ed. and trans. James G. Williams (New York: Crossroad, 1997). A new edition of the English translation under the same title was recently published by Michigan State University Press (2012).

90. Girard, *Deceit, Desire, and the Novel*, 288.

91. Girard, *Deceit, Desire, and the Novel*, 287.

92. In this genealogy, one could also include Italo Svevo's *La coscienza di Zeno*; see Antonello, "Rivalità, risentimento, apocalisse," 143–63.

93. Erich Auerbach, *Mimesis: The Representation of Reality in Western Literature*, trans. Willard R. Trask, Fiftieth Anniversary Edition (Princeton, NJ: Princeton University Press, 2003), 551.

94. Girard, *Deceit, Desire, and the Novel*, 258.

95. Nidesh Lawtoo, *The Phantom of the Ego: Modernism and the Mimetic Unconscious* (East Lansing: Michigan State University Press, 2013), 281. A thoughtful study of modernist writing from the point of view of mimetic theory is William A. Johnsen, *Violence and Modernism: Ibsen, Joyce, and Woolf* (Gainesville: University Press of Florida, 2003).

96. There is an increasing number of publications that analyze the representation of sacrifice that appears so pervasive and dominant in modern and contemporary cinema. See for instance Robert Casillo, "School for Skandalon: Scorsese and Girard at Cape Fear," *Italian Americana* 12.2 (1994): 201–25; E. Arens, "Dead Man Walking: On the Cinematic Treatment of Licensed Public Killing," *Contagion* 5 (1998): 14–29; D. Culbertson, "The Body and the Blood: Sacrificial Expulsion in *Au Revoir Les Enfants*," *Contagion* 5 (1998): 46–56; G. Larcher, F. Grabner, and C. Wesseley, eds., *Visible Violence: Sichtbare und verschleirte Gewart im Film* (Münster: Lit, 1998), 93–98; Paul Graham, "Revisiting Violence in *The Godfather*: The Ambiguous Space of the Victimage Model," *Journal of Religion and Film* 9.2 (2005); A. McKenna, "Fellini's Crowds and the Remains of Religion," *Contagion* 12–13 (2005–6): 159–82; P. Antonello and E. Bujatti, eds., *La violenza allo specchio: Passione e sacrificio nel cinema contemporaneo* (Massa: Transeuropa, 2009); Stephen Teo, "The Aesthetics of Mythical Violence in Hong Kong Action Films," *New Cinemas* 8.3 (2010): 155–67; David Humbert, "Hitchcock and the Scapegoat: Violence and Victimization in *The Wrong Man*," *Journal of Religion and Film* 16.2 (2012); Nicholas Bott, "How Can Satan Cast Out Satan? Violence and the Birth of the Sacred in Christopher Nolan's *The Dark Knight*," *Contagion* 20.1 (2013): 239–51.

97. Trevor Cribben Merrill, *The Book of Imitation and Desire: Reading Milan Kundera with René Girard* (New York: Continuum, 2013).

98. Cf. Andy Lamey, "Sympathy and Scapegoating," in *J. M. Coetzee and Ethics: Philosophical Perspectives on Literature*, ed. A. Leist and P. Singer (New York: Columbia University Press, 2010), 171–93; P. Antonello, "Narratives of Sacrifice: Pasolini and Moro," in *Imagining Terrorism: The Rhetoric and Representation of Political Violence in Italy 1969–2009*, ed. P. Antonello and A. O'Leary (London: Legenda-Maney, 2009), 30–47.

99. Cf. S. Rohdie, *The Passion of Pier Paolo Pasolini* (Bloomington: Indiana University Press, 1996); G. Pozzetto, *Lo cerco dappertutto: Cristo nei film di Pasolini* (Milan: Ancora, 2007); S. Rimini, *La ferita e l'assenza: Performance del sacrificio nella drammaturgia di Pasolini* (Rome: Bonanno, 2007); Stefania Benini, "Per una lettura girardiana di *Teorema*: dall'espulsione al sacrificio," in in Antonello and Fornari, *Identità e desiderio*, 165–82.

100. Girard, *Mimesis and Theory*, 264.

101. Girard, *"To Double Business Bound,"* 130.

102. Robert Doran remarks that literary conversion is not a form of religious experience; essentially it is "the recognition of the failure of desire—the failure of selffulfillment through desire" (Girard, *Mimesis and Theory*, xxiii). However, one cannot separate this existential manifestation and experience from its religious connotations, in the same way "deviated transcendence," as a pivotal manifestation of modern individualism, can be fully understood and articulated only from a religious perspective.

103. Girard, *Deceit, Desire, and the Novel*, 3.

104. Girard, *Deceit, Desire, and the Novel*, 72.

105. For a discussion of the connection between Girard and Agamben see Christopher A. Fox, "Sacrificial Pasts and Messianic Futures: Religion as a Political Prospect in René Girard and Giorgio Agamben," *Philosophy Social Criticism* 33 (2007): 563–95; Frederiek Depoortere, "Reading Giorgio Agamben's *Homo Sacer* with René Girard," *Philosophy Today* 56.2 (2012): 108–17.

106. As Anstell and Jackson suggested, *Deceit, Desire, and the Novel* can be described through the lens of one of his inspirational sources, St. Augustine's *Confessions*. Cf. Ann W. Astell and J. A. Jackson, "*Deceit, Desire, and the Novel* Fifty Years Later: The Religious Dimension. An Introduction to the Forum," *Religion and Literature* 43.3 (2011): 138.

107. Girard, *Mimesis and Theory*, 69.

108. See Doran, "Introduction."

109. Northrop Frye, *The Great Code: The Bible and Literature* (London: Ark, 1982), xvii.

110. There are still scholars, Frye maintains, that "in discussing cultural issues originally raised by the Bible and still largely informed by it, proceed as though the Bible did not exist." Frye, *The Great Code*, xvii.

111. Wolfgang Iser, *Prospecting: From Reader Response to Literary Anthropology* (Baltimore: Johns Hopkins University Press, 1993), 132.

112. Girard, *"To Double Business Bound,"* 5.

113. Kermode, *Sense of an Ending*, 46–47.

114. Brugnolo, "La visione romanzesca," 17. For a thorough discussion of the relationship between Christianity, secularization, and modern fiction see Cesáreo Bandera, *The Sacred Game: The Role of the Sacred in the Genesis of Modern Literary Fiction* (University Park: Pennsylvania State University Press, 1994).

PART ONE

Theoretical Considerations

Jealousy and Novelistic Knowledge

Maria DiBattista

I n the repertoire of emotions that fascinate, when they do not dismay, René Girard, jealousy occupies a preeminent and ultimately fateful place. In *Deceit, Desire, and the Novel* Girard identifies jealousy as one of the "vices" of internal mediation and seconds Stendhal's warning against jealousy as one of the distinctly "*modern* emotions."[1] As this formulation suggests, jealousy for Girard is less a moral failing than a symptom of an ontological sickness endemic to the spiritual culture of modernity. According to his diagnosis, the jealous lover disguises the true nature of his affliction by attributing all his sufferings to a possessive "temperament" rather than to the more fundamental spiritual disorder that is its actual source.

This is one of the primary deceits Girard sets out to expose and cauterize, as it were, at its ontological root in mediated desire. Girard discredits the jealous lover's sustaining belief that his desire is spontaneous and that the cause of his sufferings exists outside rather than within him. Just the opposite is the case, Girard insists: the lover desires only what the Rival, in his hidden but actual role as Model and Mediator, desires. The torments of jealousy originate in the lover's unacknowledged and helpless enthrallment to the Rival, an enthrallment that itself conceals an even deeper desire to possess what the Rival possesses so that one might become the Rival. Only thus, according to the terrible and delusional logic of mediated desire, does the jealous subject believe he can be cured of his desire and attain that fullness of being that is he has been yearning for all along.

Girard's diagnosis does not stop here, however. He goes on to claim that this spiritual malady is endemic to times and cultures when the distance between the desiring subject and the mediator begins to contract, thereby allowing "these two spheres to penetrate each other more or less profoundly." We come full circle in arriving at the one of the central and perhaps the grandest claim advanced by *Deceit, Desire, and the Novel*—that "it is in internal mediation that the profoundest meaning of the *modern* is found."[2]

Both when it is used to describe a particular emotion and when it is evoked to characterize a cultural epoch (the age of the novel), the word *modern* acquires an imposing but essentially negative prestige. Girard's attitude toward the modern is one of the most striking features of his work, but it is also one of the most confounding. To take the immediate case in point: In what sense can jealousy be regarded as a modern emotion? Modern seems a term ill-suited to describe an emotion that most would regard as a perennial presence rather than a recent arrival in the annals of human desire. This was my first, admittedly intuitive response to Girard's depiction of the modern emotions, but in its wake came another, more enduring perplexity that quickly hardened into a concrete question: how does, indeed how could the idea of the modern, a distinctly temporal term, comport with Girard's account of the geometric structure of desire whose value, not to mention whose truth, consists in giving us fairly accurate measurements of the movements within and between immaterial, atemporal spiritual states?

Girard himself insists at the outset of his magnificent study that triangular desire is not a gestalt, but rather constitutes "a systematic metaphor" that "has no reality whatever": "The real structures," he writes, "are inter-subjective. They cannot be localized anywhere."[3] Girard seems to anticipate and subsequently answer objections like mine in arguing that triangular desire represents a radical change in the way human beings understand and experience their own selfhood. Imitative or mediated desire emerges and flourishes, he asserts, within a culture where God is either dead or denied or so removed from the horizon of the human world that his reality only declares itself as an absence that can never be compelled to make its presence known, much less felt. Understandably, the Self feels cut off from the divine inheritance, with its promise of plenitude of being. The denial or absence of God does not eliminate transcendency, however, "but diverts it from the *au-delà* to the *en-deçà*."[4] The Self, in an act compounded of pride and desperation, looks to find in the Other what is so grievously missing in itself. The Self finds the divinity it is looking for, although not in its original or genuine form. In Girard's arresting phrase, the Other is taken for a god; that is, the Other appears to be a self-sufficient and blessed being who enjoys all the benefits of what Proust calls, with how much irony it is not easy and perhaps not even wise to decide, "a real existence."

It is in the distressed and impoverished inner landscapes of a world from which the gods may have fled (but not the need for them) that jealousy as a modern emotion begins to germinate. Jealousy, like envy and impotent hatred, is a primary sign and symptom of the deviated transcendency[5] that invests the Other with divinity. Yet unlike envy and impotent hatred, which are self-consuming passions spawned by *ressentiment*, jealousy offers an opportunity to become more outward looking in a more curious and a potentially more self-enlightening way. Jealousy conduces to a knowledge uniquely available to it—novelistic knowledge, let us call it, a concrete knowledge of the "real" and distinct and, most importantly, independent existence of other people. Jealousy does not impress or even interest Girard in this capacity. Girard's Truth is as invariable as it is transcendent. For Girard, "desire is one"; "the exceptions to the rule of desire are never more than apparent,"[6] he insists. We will not find this rule expounded in any modern treatise on the afflictions of the soul and heart. It belongs to the novel, whose rise coincides with the spiritual pandemic of deviated transcendency, to reveal the secret of our desire, a secret that only the novel can at once harbor, disguise, and expose.

For Girard, then, the novel offers us the most complete as well as most profound record of modern desire and its vicissitudes. This record always and inevitably attests to the same essential Truth: that our desire is never spontaneous, but is determined by the Mediator who, once chosen, is blindly and slavishly imitated. Any competing or ancillary knowledge of the Other—or even of oneself—that does not confirm this truth would not be knowledge such as Girard pursues, values, and understands it. Girard gives us, then, a compelling, spiritually demanding and exalted but nonetheless incomplete conception of the kind of particularized knowledge (as distinguished, however finely and painfully, from essential Truth) the novel can disclose.

For novelistic knowledge reflects and entertains a dynamic notion of the relations between the desiring Self and the desired Other, a relation in which jealousy plays a dominant and not always negative role. Even its etymology declares its fittingness for the double offices Jealousy can perform in monitoring the life and conduct of the beloved. Jealousy derives from the Greek *zelos*, or zeal, a word that conveys both the idea of jealousy but also of emulation or rivalry. Girardian mediation, it would seem, is latent within this classical understanding of jealous zeal. Here is how the classicist Carl Buck parses this ur-Girardian word: "Most of the words for 'envy' . . . had from the outset a hostile force, based on 'look at' (with malice), 'not love,' etc. Conversely, most of those which became distinctive terms for 'jealousy' were originally used also in a good sense, 'zeal, emulation.'"[7] I cite Buck because he alerts us to an older, but still active and more positive meaning lurking in jealousy—jealousy as zeal in a "good" sense. Jealousy is not, after all, an emotion of uniform consistency. It is composed of various, sometimes discontinuous states of feeling, not all of them degrading to the dignity or intellect. Imitative desire can metamorphose into a jealous zeal not merely to possess but to know the beloved. Girardian accounts of novelistic desire overlook this potential and positive transformation. This strikes me as a significant oversight. "Positive" jealousy has the potential to realize one of the fundamental moral goods of the novel—the concrete, if not disinterested knowledge of the Other as a separate existence.

This is a potential explored with great sympathy (as well as cunning) in Roland Barthes's *A Lover's Discourse*, which also assigns jealousy a prominent place in his inventory of amorous feelings. In reflecting on the sorrowful case of Goethe's Young Werther (who is for Barthes the paradigmatic amorous subject), Barthes remarks that Werther "shows himself to be anything but jealous."[8] Only when Werther's epistolary account of his ecstatic sorrows yields to the fully dramatized narrative of the book's final panel does the rivalry between Werther and Albert, Charlotte's fiancé, become acute and acrimonious. Barthes seems to ratify here the Girardian law of mediated desire: it is the rival who activates desire.

Yet for Barthes, the same cause yields different effects and results in a somewhat different kind of movement. It is, Barthes proposes, "as if jealousy appeared in the simple transition from I to he, from an imaginary discourse (saturated by the other) to a discourse of the other—of which Narrative is the statutory voice." Barthes treats jealousy as a figure of transport and transition. Jealousy for him is that heightened charge of feeling that conveys the lover out of his self-insulating, compulsively circular discourse, which, although it contains a great deal of the fictive, stubbornly resists the objectifying details that bring novelistic fiction into the sphere of actual life. Jealousy is zealous in its desire to possess and know the most trivial facts as well as the defining life circumstances of the Other (the primary object of novelistic discourse), not just the physical body of the loved one (the primary object of the lover's discourse).

Barthes plays on this etymological cognate of jealousy in rebelling against the Freudian dogma that all lovers think themselves unique, thus making jealousy a "normal" rather than exalted or transgressive state. Jealousy, he insists, "is ugly, is bourgeois: it is an unworthy fuss, a zeal—and it is this *zeal* which I reject."[9] In this rejection, Barthes shows himself to be a remarkable lover, but no novelist. Nonetheless, Barthes helps us see that jealousy not only masks the craving to become another by possessing what the mediator/rival possesses; it also disposes us to acknowledge the separate and uncontrollable existence of the Other. Jealousy is the statutory voice of narrative not just because it expresses the inevitable theme of novelistic or mediated desire, but also because its zealous pursuit of the Other is the route to novelistic knowledge, which is the knowledge of the inalienably separate existence of Other people.

The statutory voice of narrative is embodied in the Proustian narrator, who has little in common with Werther: "Is he even a lover?" asks Barthes, and then decides, "He is merely jealous."[10] Marcel might claim the opposite, that he was merely a lover until he became jealous. Only then can he begin the emotional travail and obsessive researches whose end will be his beginning as a novelist of his own life. Jealous desire activates a quest whose goal is not complete possession, but total knowledge of the beloved. George Eliot, one of Proust's early and beloved tutors in novelistic desire, anticipates this Proustian insight in contending that "Jealousy is never satisfied with anything short of an omniscience that would detect the subtlest fold of the heart."[11] Proust's researches into lost time aspire to such omniscience and for this reason, the jealous man—Swann in particular—is a primary figure of identification for the Proustian narrator.

That novelistic knowledge results from jealous researches rather than more impersonal and detached investigations into the lives of characters should not be deemed a moral detriment to the novel's objective representation of life. Quite the contrary. In his zealous investigations of the daily habits, the inner motives, the hidden dreams, and the practiced deceptions of his characters' lives, the novelist is not content with telling us all we need to know (a purely utilitarian knowledge of other people). The "true" novelist will only be satisfied in relating all we can and indeed must know—the subtlest fold of the heart. Marcel comes to understand this emotional dynamic in his jealous love for Albertine: "It is one of the faculties of jealousy to reveal to us the extent to which the reality of external facts and the sentiments of the heart are an unknown element which lends itself to endless suppositions. We imagine that we know exactly what things are and what people think for the simple reason that we do not care about them. But as soon as we have a desire to know, as the jealous man has, then it becomes a dizzy kaleidoscope in which we can no longer distinguish anything."[12] Proust acknowledges that omniscience is the inducement with which jealousy lures the lover into endless suppositions about the external facts and inner life of the loved one. These suppositions, in which love aspires to gain complete knowledge of the Other, are doomed to frustration. But the opposite is also true. The novelist who does not display any jealous interest in his characters may present us with a narrative that purports to represent what people think and feel, but such an account is in danger of devolving into a parody of realism, since what it recounts is not so much who people are but how little we care to know about them.

For Proust, jealousy is inherently novelistic because it counteracts our habitual indifference toward others and makes us at once curious and mystified by the sights, events, and persons that previously had seemed either transparent or too trivial to attract our notice. The power of jealousy to arouse our emotional interest and stimulate our curiosity is revealed, with that amazing casualness with which Proust typically introduces his most essential discoveries, during one of the narrator's last conversations with Swann at an afternoon reception hosted by the Princess of Guermantes. The narrator seeks to ascertain the truth of a rumor that Gilbert, Prince of Guermantes, has repudiated Swann. Swann, who knows he is dying, appears more amused at the falseness of the story than concerned for his social reputation, and so instead of answering Marcel directly, responds with a digression expatiating on his own temperamental incuriosity: "People are very inquisitive," he observes. "I've never been inquisitive, except when I was in love and when I was jealous. And for all that that taught me! Are you jealous?" The narrator replies that he has never experienced jealousy and therefore does not know what it is. To which Swann replies:

> Well, I congratulate you! [*je vous en félicité*]. When you are a little bit jealous it is not altogether unpleasant, from two points of view. For one thing, because it enables people who are not inquisitive to take an interest [*s'interresser*] in the lives of others, or at least of one other person. And then, it gives you quite a sense of the sweetness of possession [*la doceur de posséder*], of getting into a carriage with a woman, of not allowing her to go off alone. But that is only in the very early stages of the disease, or when the cure is almost complete. In between it is the most frightful of tortures [*le plus affreux des supplices*].[13]

Swann is not being wholly ironical when he describes the sweet and pleasurable sensations that marked the early stages of his amorous disease. For the story of Swann's love has confirmed that both in its initial and final stages, jealousy, which sickens, can also be a revitalizing and even rejuvenating affliction. Thus we should only give partial credit to Swann's claim that jealousy taught him very little and then only what was painful. The narrative tells a different story. Jealousy temporarily "cures" Swann of his spiritually debilitating habits; his caddishness as an impulsive and inconstant lover; his disinclination toward sustained mental reflection; the cultivated superficiality of his social persona, exemplified in his inveterate tendency to enclose any serious thought in ironic quotation marks. Jealousy disrupts the narcissism, indifference, and laziness that regulates Swann's social existence and in fact determines so much of our social relations, an indifference and laziness that confine our knowledge of what people think and feel to the vagaries of rumor, the questionable testimony of anecdote, and the distortions of gossip. Jealousy awakens our curiosity at the expense of our indifference—and of course jeopardizes our immunity to the contagious fascination of the Other. Curiosity is zealous and as Swann notes, acquisitive, where indifference is complacent and indolent.

Yet it is not the moralist, but the psychologist in Proust who understands jealousy as an intellectual obsession to seek out the very truth that may deliver a fatal blow to our narcissism in confirming a suspicion that gratifies our desire to know at the expense of our illusion that we are loved. Proust's analysis of jealousy is in many ways confirmed, but by no means superseded, by Sigmund Freud's 1922 essay, "Certain Neurotic Mechanisms in Jealousy, Paranoia, and Homosexuality." It was Harold Bloom who first alerted me to the importance of this essay for understanding Proustian jealousy—indeed jealousy as the novelistic emotion par excellence. Sexual jealousy, he proclaims, "is the most novelistic of circumstances, just as incest, according to Shelley, is the most poetical of circumstances."[14] Bloom further alerted me to the novelistic implications of Freud's distinction between three kinds or phases of jealousy: normal or competitive jealousy, projected jealousy, and delusional jealousy.[15] These phases map out the passage from the lover's enraptured discourse (the self-enclosed object of Barthesian study) to the novel's more inclusive and wide-ranging discursiveness about the lives of Others. Interestingly, normal or competitive jealousy does not interest Freud especially, for it yields him little in the way of analytic material. Yet that does not mean it is deficient in novelistic material. Freud in fact observes that it is "easy to see" that normal or competitive jealousy is activated by the thought of losing the loved one, a feeling abetted by the ego's tendency to hold itself accountable for its own failures and losses. The irrational component in jealousy derives from the archaic memories of the child's affective life, a kind of involuntary and painful memory of those oedipal rivalries that were supposedly settled by the normal developmental outcome of the Oedipus complex. So described, normal, competitive jealousy seems to be an ur-form of the quintessential novelistic desire as Girard represents it. Translated into Girardian terms, competitive jealousy masks ontological identification with the rival. It inspires a desire to become Another rather than to know Someone else.

Projected jealousy, which, like normal competitive jealousy, Freud takes to be universal, originates in an internal fantasy of infidelity rather than in a fear of, or attraction to, a rival. Freud praises social conventions for recognizing this common libidinal impulse to search out new objects, and in a striking moment of *savoir faire* that one might find reckless, unfeeling, or amusing, depending on one's own experience in these matters, commends the wisdom of society in tolerating the potentially divisive feelings aroused by "these little excursions in the direction of unfaithfulness." Freud maintains that the desire sublimated in harmless acts of flirtation, coquetry and infidelity will eventually "find satisfaction in some kind of return to the faithfulness to the original object." A jealous person, however, cannot rest with such assurances, because, Freud explains, "he does not believe in any such thing as a halt or a turning-back once the path has been trodden, nor that a flirtation may be a safeguard against actual infidelity."[16] The jealous person projects his own fantasy of infidelity as a path that must be followed, that admits, once one undertakes to follow it, of no direct or even circuitous return (the Joycean circuit of desire in *Ulysses*). What projected jealousy projects is a kind of narrative fatefulness whose emotional itinerary Proust found *a côté de chez Swann*, an itinerary named in honor of the man, notoriously impulsive, faithless, and often caddish until the great affair of his life, who first followed its path.

Delusional jealousy lies at the outermost limits of that path. Delusional jealousy also involves a projection of repressed fantasies of infidelity but takes as its object one's own sex. I do not have space to pursue this dimension of Swann's love and the delusional jealousy it activates, except to remark that possible confirmation of this unconscious identification with the male rival may account for the curious dream that concludes *Swann's Way* and signals the end of Swann's love for Odette. Swann manifests not only Girardian longings for the rival-mediator whose being he jealously covets, but also the intrinsic bisexuality of human nature in a dream passage of enormous interest and high comedy, which contains, as its most startling, ambiguous, and yet telling detail, the dream-metamorphosis of Madame Verdurin into an androgynous male with elongated nose and freshly sprouted moustache.

Let me conclude by meditating on a deservedly famous scene that dramatizes and collapses the normal, projected, and delusional manifestations of jealousy into one compact and—let us admit it—modern emotion: Swann's vigil under Odette's window. His tormented feelings at this early stage of his jealous desire are oddly compounded of anguish at the thought of Odette's being with Forcheville and relief that he is now receiving confirmation, however painful, that Odette's independent existence, of what the narrator calls her "other life," was "now within his grasp, fully illuminated by the lamp" (*il la tenait là, éclairée en plein par la lampe*). At this moment Swann is seized by the strangely energizing belief that Odette's life is not only within his grasp, but within his power, since she is now "an unwitting prisoner in that room into which, when he chose, he could go to surprise and to capture" (*prisonnière sans le savoir dans cette chambre où, quand il le voudrait, il entrerait la surprendre et la capturer*). That we can seize any life, even unawares, is one of the narcissistic delusions that the Girardian novel exposes as a vain and harmful belief. But that doesn't mean that Swann's jealous and painful awareness of Odette's "other life" yields nothing but more torment and futile longing. It revives Swann's passion for truth, dormant since youth. Only now the object of truth is not a historical fact, a moral idea, or an aesthetic object but "Odette's actions, her relationships, her plans, her past"—in other words, Odette's life, novelistically observed and rendered.

Swann's jealousy, which leads him to do something he has never thought to do before—attend to "the smallest occupations of this woman's life"—is a model of the novelistic conversion of the indifferent observer to the passionate investigator (the novelist as lover). Thus it is, the narrator informs us, that Swann, the man who believed that the activities of another person could engage only the lowest, most commonplace part of his mind, begins to engage in "all manner of actions that would have shamed him up to now, such as spying, tonight, outside a window, tomorrow perhaps, for all he knew, cleverly inducing neutral people (*les indifférents*) to speak, bribing servants, listening at doors, now seemed to him to be, fully as much as were the deciphering of manuscripts, the weighing of evidence, and the interpretation of old monuments, merely methods of scientific investigations with a real intellectual value and appropriate to a search for the truth."[17] Swann is at the wrong window, so that his insistence that his jealous researches are precisely on a level with the aesthete's and historian's scholarly researches strike a fine irony.

A fine but not a damning irony. We should not feel too secure in our knowledge of how things "really" are. The jealous lover's suspicions may in most instances, as in this farcical episode, be dismissed as what Freud calls "delusions of reference," but without such delusional and potentially endless suppositions, the Proustian novel could not be written, nor its epic researches pursued and concluded. Freud, on the basis of clinical evidence, observed that delusions of reference are in fact not lacking in truth, for nothing is projected "where there is nothing of the sort already."[18] The novelist, I would claim, engages in similar acts of sustained attention to the commonplace acts through which the unconscious or hidden life of Others reveals itself. Once more Swann leads the way to this recognition:

> He knew that the reality of certain circumstances which he would have given his life to reconstruct accurately could be read behind that window striated with light, as within the gold-illuminated cover of one of those precious manuscripts to whose artistic richness itself the scholar who consults them cannot remain indifferent [*ce ne peu rester indifférent*]. He felt a delicious pleasure in learning [*volupté de connaître*] the truth that so impassioned him in this unique, ephemeral, and precious transcript, made of a translucid substance so warm and so beautiful.[19]

The truth Swann discovers is unique and ephemeral, but enlivened by the all the warmth of individualized life. It is jealousy that arrives at this uniquely novelistic truth in which the reality of other people is reconstructed with such zealous accuracy.

For Proust novelistic knowledge is arrived at through a jealous reading of others, a reading that proceeds from within and through ourselves. Such is the import of Iago's last line, "Demand me nothing. What you know, you know" (act 5, scene 2). The author of Othello's jealousy anticipates the final tautology of novelistic knowledge. What we know, we know. And we only know, or at least we know best, what excites our jealous desire. The destiny of jealous desire need not always be fatal, however. Freud concludes his speculative essay on the links between homosexuality and jealous paranoia by returning to the "normal" jealousies of childhood. The child's (the boy's, always the boy for Freud) hostile and aggressive attitude toward his brothers, rivals for the attention and love of the mother, is subdued "under the influence of upbringing" and soon yields to a repression in which the former rivals become "the first homosexual love-objects." But then Freud adds, most interestingly for our case, that the transformation of the child's jealous feelings

> represents too an exaggeration of the process which, according to my view, lead to the birth of social instincts in the individual. In both processes there is first the presence of jealous and hostile impulses which cannot achieve

satisfaction; and both the affectionate and the social feelings of identification arise as reactive formations against the repressed aggressive impulses.[20]

Thus jealousy may actually, surprisingly, and actively assist in the birth of the
social instincts, in which the life of others becomes increasingly entwined
with our sense of our own existence.

In his essay on reading, Proust maintains that the life of the book culminates "in what for the author could be called Conclusions but which for
the reader are Provocations": "We can feel that our wisdom begins where the
author's ends, and we want him to give us answers when all he can do is give
us desires."[21] A very Girardian conclusion. The novel's name for this linger-
ing provocation is jealousy, that *volupté de connaître* that will be gratified by
nothing less than an omniscience that can detect the subtlest folds of the
heart, a heart that, if Girard is right—and I believe he is—proves as necessary
to us as our own.

Notes

1. René Girard, *Deceit, Desire, and the Novel: Self and Others in Literary Structures*, trans. Yvonne
   Freccero (Baltimore: Johns Hopkins University Press, 1965), 14.

2. Girard, *Deceit, Desire, and the Novel*, 92.

3. Girard, *Deceit, Desire, and the Novel*, 2.

4. Girard, *Deceit, Desire, and the Novel*, 59.

5. Girard, *Deceit, Desire, and the Novel*, 77.

6. Girard, *Deceit, Desire, and the Novel*, 34.

7. Carl Buck, *Dictionary of Selected Synonyms in the Principal Indo-European Languages* (Chicago:
   University of Chicago Press, 1949), 1138–39.

8. Roland Barthes, *A Lover's Discourse*, trans. Richard Howard (New York: Hill and Wang 2010),
   144.

9. Barthes, *A Lover's Discourse*, 146.

10. Barthes, *A Lover's Discourse*, 44.

11. George Eliot, *The Mill on the Floss* (New York: Empire, 2010), 290.

12. Marcel Proust, *The Fugitive*, in *Remembrance of Things Past*, 3 vols., trans. C. K. Scott Moncrieff
    and Terence Kilmartin (New York: Vintage, 1982), 3:529.

13. Marcel Proust, *Sodom and Gomorra*, trans. John Sturrock (New York: Viking, 2011), 106–7.

14. Harold Bloom, *Harold Bloom's Critical Views: Marcel Proust* (Philadelphia: Chelsea, 2004), 1.

15. Sigmund Freud, "Certain Neurotic Mechanisms in Jealousy, Paranoia, and Homosexuality" (1922), in *Standard Edition*, ed. James Strachey, 24 vols. (London: Hogarth, 1975), 18:223.

16. Freud, "Certain Neurotic Mechanisms," 224.

17. Marcel Proust, *Swann's Way*, trans. Lydia Davis (New York: Viking, 2003), 180.

18. Freud, "Certain Neurotic Mechanisms," 266.

19. Proust, *Swann's Way*, 180.

20. Freud, "Certain Neurotic Mechanisms," 231.

21. Marcel Proust, *On Reading* (London: Hesperus, 2010), 23.

Desiring Proust

Girard against Deleuze

Alessia Ricciardi

I f we consider the different ways of reading Proust, we might well regard them as making up a continuum in which Gilles Deleuze and René Girard can be said to occupy opposite poles. Deleuze favors approaches that resist dialectical metabolization, for example when he privileges the notion of "disjunctive synthesis," which he introduces in *The Logic of Sense* in order to name a process of thought that does not entail a return to the identity of the same, but rather the disjunctive divergence of multiple ramifications. On the other hand, Girard is, according to his own self-description, a dialectician. One of Girard's many achievements is to have reinvented dialectic from the point of view of the novel. Unlike the classical Hegelian variety, this novelistic mode of dialectic for the most part eschews logical deduction or reconciliation. Moreover, in order to give a concrete account of the anxious dialogue between the self and others, novelistic dialectic must synthesize the two most important themes of the *Phenomenology of Mind*, as Girard points out in *Deceit, Desire, and the Novel*, namely "the unhappy consciousness" and "the dialectic of master and slave."[1] For Girard, triangular desire must be recognized as the basis of "the novelistic novel" that is a work of genius and its critique of the Romantic lie regarding the primacy of spontaneous desire.[2]

Whereas what is at stake for Girard is the structuring, dialectical role of mimetic desire and its movement toward a unifying synthesis of the self and the other, what is at stake for Deleuze is the productive potential of desire, which will result not in unity but rather a "transversal dimension."[3] Girard sees the truth of the novel as inhering in the recovery of "transcendency" from a debased, secularized modernity. Deleuze, instead, regards the transversal dimension as not transcendent, but rather an immanent production of the artistic machine. It would be easy to conclude, with respect to Proust, that these two critical modes must remain largely juxtaposed and in contrast to one another like the Méséglise way and the Guermantes way, which are "unknowable to each other, in sealed vessels and without communication between them of different afternoons."[4]

Yet, as the example of Gilberte in *À la recherche du temps perdu* suggests, perhaps there may be a point of connection after all. Girard's and Deleuze's styles of interpretation certainly share a strong belief in the strategic value of literature. In a celebrated essay, Deleuze praises the achievements of Sade and Masoch in giving imaginative life to our pathologies as instances of "the efficiency of literature."[5] Indeed, one might say that for both Girard and Deleuze literature is always efficient in this sense. Far from functioning as a weakened form of philosophy or religion—as a sort of illustrative accoutrement for their theoretical positions—literature in their work actively structures and shapes their philosophical beliefs. How, then, may we describe the originality and specificity of their engagements with literature? And does their shared conviction of the importance of the work of literature, when examined more closely, ultimately support a contrasting view of their interpretations of Proust or a more complicated picture?

For Girard, the novel offers hope of a corrective to the shocks inflicted on Western society by the secularization of religious belief in the modern era. In the second chapter of *Deceit, Desire, and the Novel*, he summarizes the spiritual dilemma dramatized in the writings of some of the most eminent masters of nineteenth- and early twentieth-century fiction, namely Dostoyevsky, Stendhal, Flaubert, and Proust: "God is dead, man must take his place" (56). However, as human beings we can overcome neither our longing for the infinite nor our fear of the emptiness, against which Ecclesiastes warns us: "each individual . . . believes that he alone is excluded from the divine inheritance and takes pains to hide this misfortune" (57). As a result, the individual subject ascribes to the mediator possession of the divine inheritance, which in turn leads to the bleak prospect that "nothing separates him from divinity, nothing but the mediator himself, whose rival desire is the obstacle to his own desire" (58). In this way, "the imitation of Christ becomes the imitation of one's neighbor," as Girard puts it, and the mediator is turned into "the god with a human face" (59, 61). Literature represents a potential antidote to this "poisoned" state of mind (80) because all novels of genius function for Girard as a sort of bildungsroman. These narratives fulfill such a role not in the Goethean sense of chronicling the hero's moral education, but rather insofar as they confront us with the necessity of a conversion experience that leads to renunciation of the traps of metaphysical desire, thus transforming the "deviated transcendency" of triangular desire into the final "vertical transcendency" associated with resurrection (292, 313). Good literature, in other words, is a sobering conduit to faith, not the Romantic expression of conflict between self and the other.

For Deleuze, literature represents a more joyful force, a process that is driven by an irrepressibly productive desire. Jean-François Lalouette maintains in his essay "De la littérature en générale et de Beckett en particulier, selon Deleuze" that the task of literature in this sense is not the creation of forms but rather "the unceasing genesis of a flow of life, an expression of desire."[6] In both Deleuze's and Girard's theories, however, the most exemplary works of literature seem to achieve a condition of impersonality that thwarts the customary focus of readers on the problematic of "the self" with respect to either the novel's protagonist or author. For both thinkers, desire is a "threat" to the autonomy of the individual, to quote Girard. In Deleuze's case, the writing of desire tends to encourage the emergence of singularity, a concept that appears to resist the claims of psychology or personality. In Girard's, the impersonal condition that he ascribes to the literary representation of desire has to do with his relentless focus on the spiritual dimension of human nature. For him, desire is always imitative, the triumph of suggestion. For Deleuze, desire manifests itself in "singular" assemblages and haecceities, directly defying a Romantic view of the subject. Indeed, there is a fundamental sense in which for Girard as well as for Deleuze desire is never spontaneous or natural, as the Romantics want us to believe, but rather always an assemblage or *agencement*. In Girard's thought, of course, this assemblage takes the shape of the primal triangulation between the desiring subject, the mediator, and the desired object. Although such a schema may be too overtly dialectical or structural for Deleuze, the strategy still aligns with one of the fundamental tenets of his philosophy.

When it comes to reading a text, we might say that the most important question for Girard is "what does it mean?" whereas for Deleuze it is "how does it work?"[7] As Jean-Jacques Lecercle observes in *Badiou and Deleuze Read Literature* (2010), the difference between the two attitudes amounts to a distinction between what might be called reading for meaning and reading for intensity. The latter approach seeks to establish the speed of the literary work, its bifurcations, proliferations, and the affects involved, as if the text were an "electric circuit," to borrow Lecercle's phrase, "as the circulation of intensities and affects is what . . . [it] is about."[8] Deleuze concerns himself chiefly with elaborating the logic of sense, to cite the title of one of his most famous books. Girard sets out on nothing less than a search for the truth. However, the ultimate effect of both undertakings is closer to a forceful intervention than to a respectful close reading.[9] This interpolation is in both instances provocative, counterintuitive, stubborn, and, at times, problematic—and, in this regard, Girard's hermeneutic struggles with Proust in *Deceit, Desire, and the Novel* are especially pertinent—even for the author. Reflecting specifically on Proust, we might indeed ask: do these critical negotiations stifle his text or do they succeed in unleashing its potential? And why does Proust play such a crucial role in the respective economies of their thought?[10]

Proust's importance to Deleuze must be measured across the philosopher's entire oeuvre; indeed, it may be said that, more than a literary object, what Deleuze found in Proust was an entire philosophical and methodological paradigm of productive desire. We ought to recall on this score that Proust's work supplied Deleuze with the concept of the time-image, which is to say the notion of emancipated time that animates the second volume of his magisterial study of the cinema.[11] It thus should come as no surprise that the entry for Proust comprises the longest list in the concordance to Deleuze's writings and includes citations in all of the philosopher's books from *Proust and Signs* to *Essays Critical and Clinical*, as Lecercle reminds us.[12] In fact, the English version of *Proust and Signs* itself may be said to represent a sort of palimpsest of the various stages of Deleuze's relation to Proust at least through the late 1970s, as the anthology covers a span ranging from the first French edition of 1964 to the inclusion of a second section, "The Literary Machine," for a reissue in 1970 and finally the addition of a new conclusion, "Presence and Function of Madness: The Spider," for the third edition in 1977. Although Deleuze in the earliest material elucidates Proust's writing in quasi-structuralist terms by focusing on the semiotics of worldliness, love, and art in the *Recherche*, the philosopher increasingly moves away in his essays of the 1970s from straightforward interpretation to more open-ended and challenging lines of questioning. In doing so, he comes to avoid strictly dialectical explanations of Proust, whom he instead begins to praise for calling attention to the importance of the illogical, disjunctive claims of our faculties. As he argues in *Proust and Signs*, truth for Proust reveals itself not through the process of analytic explanation but rather, as the narrator of the *Recherche* observes, in the individual's "rush of blood to the face" or a speaker's "sudden silence."[13] What Girard finds discomforting, as we will see, in Proust's sprawling and unstable narrative offers Deleuze a glimpse of an entirely new perspective on the literary work of art and what it exposes of our subjective, inner life: "One would look in vain in Proust for platitudes about the work of art as organic totality . . . it is in the meanders and rings of an anti-logos style that it makes the requisite detours in order to gather up the ultimate fragments, to sweep along at different speed all pieces, each one of which refers to a different whole, to no whole at all, or to no other whole than that of style."[14]

For Girard as well, Proust seems to play a privileged role in the economy of his thought. Along with Cervantes, Stendhal, Dostoyevsky, Flaubert, and Madame de Lafayette, Proust emerges in *Deceit, Desire, and the Novel* as a writer who illuminates the concept of metaphysical desire, enabling the critic to gauge "how much literary substance it really embraces" (3). Whereas Cervantes and Stendhal inaugurate this principle, Proust, as the last author in the series, faces the task of verifying the limits of the doctrine in its fullest and most complicated manifestations. For example, Girard credits Proust with making the role of the mediator in the triangular play of desire "more obvious than ever," whereas he regards Stendhal as having left the process "more or less implicit" in his fiction (23–24). Indeed, on the evidence of the two chapters that he dedicates to Proust, "The Worlds of Proust" and "Technical Problems in Proust and Dostoyevsky," he may as well have given to the conclusion of *Deceit, Desire, and the Novel*, in which he observes that "Proust's aesthetics . . . are indissolubly united with the escape from metaphysical desire" (297–98), the title "My Struggle with Proust." Already in the second chapter of his treatise he has to admit that the metaphysical significance of desire in the *Recherche* is relegated to "meager and isolated sentences," as, unlike Dostoyevsky, Proust "seems to adopt a solipsistic theory of desire which completely falsifies the experience of his characters," at least insofar as we accept Girard's mimetic theory as the truth (76–77).

It is telling in this regard that, in order to demonstrate Proust's align-ment with his own view of desire as a frustrated response to the secularism of modernity, Girard must cite no less than at three different points the same passage on Bergotte from *Le temps retrouvé* in which the narrator declares that "every person who makes us suffer we can associate with a divinity, of which that person is only a fragmentary reflexion."[15] Having rendered his judgment in the third chapter that Proust makes the role of the mediator "obvious" to an unprecedented degree, the critic is able to remark without any apparent hesitancy that "Proust described the fall of the mediator with an extraordinary wealth of detail."[16] If, as Girard contends, the snobs of the *Recherche* suffer even more than the "vaniteux" of Stendahl's *Le rouge et le noir*, the social position to which Proust's characters aspire, in the wake of the aristocracy's historical obsolescence, finally has become "imperceptible,"[17] a very Deleuzian concept indeed.

In an essay entitled "Marcel Proust" that first appeared in 1962, a year after the publication in France of *Mensonge romantique et vérité romanesque*, Girard yet more bluntly advances the claim that Proust belongs to the nov-elistic and philosophical tradition of the metaphysicians of desire, which he notes is best exemplified by Nietzsche and Dostoyevsky. Dismissing all doubt, the critic declares that there is no fundamental difference between Proust and Dostoyevsky when it comes to the inclination to project onto others the attributes of divinity.[18] Although he admits that, unlike Dos-toyevsky, Proust in his ostensible reliance on the terms of classical psychol-ogy renders metaphysical desire imperceptible, Girard insists throughout the essay on what might be called the "molar" similarity of the two novelists, to use a Deleuzian term for the macroscopic or aggregate condition of complex bodies. This insistence clearly aligns with the theoretical position set forth in *Deceit, Desire, and the Novel* that the ultimate purpose of the novel is to bring to light, and thereby allow us to overcome, the "deviated transcendency" of the triangular relationship between subject, mediator, and object. In other words, Girard's argument in the essay reinforces a circular tendency to regard literature itself as nothing other than the philosophical proving ground of his own theory of desire, an impulse that appears to be oblivious to considerations such as tone, structure, style, cultural and historical milieux, or ethical and political meaning.

Nabokov, who hated Dostoyevsky and loved Proust, would certainly have found Girard's view to be incomprehensible in its indifference to matters of form and style. In the essay on Proust, Girard stresses an image of the author that is both conventional in sentiment and disconcerting in its one-dimensionality. By painting him as the paradigm of the suffering artist who, through the attempt to give voice to his own metaphysical desire, in the end reconciles truth and beauty, the critic concludes that Proust is first and foremost a Christian writer.[19] One might well reply that this pronouncement completely ignores the novelist's modernity as a relentless problematizer of the multifariousness of his characters' desires. More than many other writers, Proust seems to accommodate a wide array of interpretations. While it may be valid to note an important Christian dimension to his achievement, it would be myopic to privilege this aspect of the author over others of at least equal importance such as his concern with the aristocracy, class affiliation, and snobbery, his fascination with the rites of lesbian and gay desire, his interest in family relationships and generational differences, or his ceaseless attention to questions of art and aesthetics. Consequently, it is hard to sympathize with an interpretation that pretends to have the last word about Proust without taking into account his gift for what we might call poetic "transversality," to invoke once again the name that Deleuze gives in *Proust and Signs* to "time, the dimension of the narrator, which has the power to be the whole *of* these parts without totalizing them, the unity *of* these parts without unifying them."[20] This is a gift that indeed might be said to represent the opposite of any metaphysics of desire or logic of rivalry in much the same sense that immanence represents the opposite of transcendence.

In this light, we would do well to observe that, as it progresses, Girard's handling of Proust in *Deceit, Desire, and the Novel* loses what a Deleuzian would call its "molar" grip and surrenders to "molecular" intensity, which is to say that it retreats from a strict adherence to categorical principles and begins to respond to the questions raised by uncategorizable singularities: "As the mediator draws nearer, unity is broken up into multiplicity. . . . Beginning with Proust, the mediator may literally be anyone at all and he may pop up anywhere."[21] The paragraph that follows in *Deceit, Desire, and the Novel* makes clear that Girard is thinking here of the unlikely prestige enjoyed in Balbec by the "little band" of *jeunes filles en fleur* of which Albertine is a member.

Another important difference between Girard and Deleuze revolves around how they each respond to the awareness that their conceptions of desire are incompatible with pleasure. By the time that we encounter the *Recherche* in the history of the novel, according to Girard, the only moment of pleasure to which Proust can grant plausibility is the scene in which the narrator gazes at Albertine while she is asleep.[22] However, this sharp dichotomy between desire and pleasure, which for Girard is a consequence of the triumph of metaphysical desire, is for Deleuze a healthy sign of our readiness to admit the unimaginative character of pleasure. In an essay titled "Desire and Pleasure," in which he attempts to identify the fundamental differences between his and Foucault's philosophies, Deleuze reminds the reader that Foucault could not bear the word "desire" and adds:

> For my part, I can scarcely tolerate the world pleasure. But why? For me, desire implies no lack; neither is it a natural given. It is an *agencement* of heterogeneous elements that function, it is a process as opposed to structure or genesis; it is affect as opposed to sentiment; it is "haecceity" (the individuality of a day, a season, a life) as opposed to subjectivity. . . . I cannot give any positive value to pleasure because pleasure seems to me to interrupt the immanent process of desire.[23]

One can scarcely imagine any suggestion more antithetical to Girard's way of thinking than Deleuze's view that desire neither implies lack nor represents a natural given. On this score, we may find it useful to reexamine the case of Girard's attack on Deleuze and Guattari's *Anti-Oedipus* and defense of his own ideas in the essay "Delirium as System."[24] By espousing the notion that, insofar as it is productive and constructed, desire is divorced from lack, Deleuze and Guattari's landmark philosophical opus could only succeed in irritating Girard, who demands acknowledgment of the primacy and irreparability of the absence of God in order for his theory of metaphysical desire to make any sense.

"Delirium as System" is more illuminating with respect to what it reveals of Girard's own theory than in virtue of its sarcastic and often gratuitous broadsides against Deleuze and Guattari.[25] According to the essay's argument, Deleuze and Guattari avoid any concrete problematic of desire and certainly do not offer a "unified theory of desire," something which Girard instead claims to be able to do through the shibboleth of mimetic desire, which at one point he compares to a postulate capable of engendering a logical development that unveils at the same time a true historical process.[26] While waging a battle in favor of the principle of identity over difference, he seems thoroughly unaware of Deleuze's fundamental exploration of related ground in *Difference and Repetition*, which was published in 1968, some four years before *Anti-Oedipus*, and established the foundation of Deleuze's critique of philosophical attempts to subsume difference under the notion of identity.

In "Delirium as System," Girard thus signals less interest in providing careful scholarly reflection on Deleuze and Guattari's arguments than in reasserting the value of his own thought. At one point, he confesses to sharing Deleuze and Guattari's love of Proust, who, as he observes, is the only writer to play a significant role in *Anti-Oedipus*, but vehemently rejects their reading of the famous scene in which the narrator kisses Albertine. Without considering Deleuze and Guattari's suggestive interpretation of the scene as a paradigm of "molecular" desire, which is to say a desire that is already on its way to what the two philosophers will describe in *A Thousand Plateaus* as "becoming imperceptible," Girard concludes simply that, in this episode of the *Recherche*, Proust is just portraying the collapse of desire.[27]

The essay is remarkable, among other reasons, for Girard's effort to historicize his theory by arguing that, before the triumph of individualism in the modern era, imitation was encouraged in literature, education, and religious practice.[28] As he sees it, the advent of modernity unhappily brought about a firm entrenchment of the dogma of originality and with it the banishment of mimesis. In spite of this state of things, mimesis apparently manages to survive into the present, albeit in disguised forms that Girard succinctly evokes with the casually brilliant remark that "capitalism demands mimetic free play."[29] Yet the galvanizing challenge that Deleuze and Guattari mount to capitalism's displacement of social repression in the oedipal complex ultimately seems for Girard to insinuate the doubt that, as he puts it, the very project of *The Anti-Oedipus* may be the sign of an "aggravated cultural crisis" in which the absence of the divinity is no longer visible and the slow progress of mimetic desire may be corroding the symbolic order.[30] When Girard concludes his censure of Deleuze and Guattari with the reproach that "here is the philosophy truly suited to the anonymity of contemporary urban relations," he at once gives full-throated voice to the claim of moral victory over his rivals and irrevocable testimony to the reality of his own historical and theoretical defeat.[31]

We might surmise nonetheless that Deleuze and Girard at least agree on the apparently transcendental role of jealousy in stimulating desire. Like Girard, Deleuze greets with skepticism the signifiers of love because, as he and Félix Guattari put it in *A Thousand Plateaus*, such signifiers always entail a certain "amateurism," "an entire mechanism of signifiance, with its referral of interpretations" that inevitably lapses into jealousy and erotomania (as in Swann's case) and so must be recognized as "rotten from the start, made of signifiance and jealousy."[32] Yet we must remember as well that Deleuze and Guattari in the same work reject the suggestion that the narrator's love for Albertine in the *Recherche* recapitulates that of Swann for Odette. Whereas the latter episode may correspond in certain respects with Girard's model, the former is a far more elusive and molecular affair that ultimately manifests nothing less than the fluidity of the protagonists' sexual identities and refuses to be contained within a generalizable definition of desire. "Jealousy," as Deleuze and Guattari aptly note, "is different in Swann and the narrator too, as is the perception of music."[33] The narrator's love for Albertine indeed is congruent with a poetics of haecceities, moments of individuation that have nothing to do with subjectivity. The group of girls of which Albertine is a part first and foremost represents "pure relations of speeds and slownesses."[34] By way of contrast, because he thinks in the mechanically aesthetic terms of forms, resemblances, and subjects, and thus is moved by his jealousy for Odette to unveil her secrets, to become a detective, and to reterritorialize his desire, Swann cannot be viewed as a true precursor of the narrator. In the case of Albertine's liaison with the narrator, she confronts him with lies that seem devoid of content and enact what Deleuze and Guattari define as an "emission" of particles, a "proximity" that the narrator has no choice but to endure like a headache or a flash of involuntary memory: "It is as though Swann's desperate efforts to reterritorialize the flow of things . . . were replaced by the sped-up movements of deterritorialization."[35]

We may find it useful at this point to reflect briefly on Deleuze's and Girard's respective notions of masochism, as well as the resonances and asymmetries between them. Masochism, according to Deleuze in "Coldness and Cruelty," avoids a dialectical relationship to sadism insofar as the two tendencies in fact are not counterparts, respond to different motivating principles, and give rise to very different aesthetics: "Their techniques differ, and their problems, their concerns and their intentions are entirely dissimilar."[36] In his eyes, masochism represents yet another potential battleground in the revolt against the disciplinary agenda of psychoanalysis. What distinguishes it from related impulses, in essence, is certainly not the enjoyment of pain but rather the suspension of belief, the aestheticized space of waiting and fantasy. The disavowal of sexuality in masochism implies not so much a negation of feeling for Deleuze as a dreamed-of eroticism that can be freed from the shackles of pleasure.[37] Or, to put it another way: "To make suffering—the simple result of desire, or, in masochism, its preliminary condition—the actual *object* of that desire is a particularly revealing mistake."[38] This is Girard speaking in *Deceit, Desire, and the Novel*, not Deleuze, but in Girard's thought as well the masochist enjoys an epistemological privilege, because every metaphysical desire tends toward masochism, and sadism is merely imitative (180). In Girard's philosophy, the masochist is the master who has become blasé. The masochist discerns the necessary relation between unhappiness and metaphysical desire, but does not renounce this desire (176–77). Unlike Deleuze, Girard identifies Marcel as the representative of "unquestionable masochism" in the *Recherche* as the character that represents in his eyes the narrative embodiment of masochism (181). Whereas for Deleuze the masochist's desire is the index of a sense of creativity or fantasy that is unencumbered by the teleology of pleasure, masochism for Girard provides an emblem of the external, even traumatic genesis of our desire and thus becomes a conduit to transcendence, not immanence. This scenario is not unlike what happens in Leo Bersani's work. In the wake of Jean Laplanche's theory of seduction, Bersani increasingly has emphasized the ineluctable masochism of sexuality and proposes recurring to aesthetics to find a more benign way of relating to the world.[39]

In *Deceit, Desire, and the Novel*, Girard also contends that Proust makes clear how, in some situations, the mediator personifies "an essential wickedness" insofar as certain characters in the *Recherche* are endowed with a cruelty that is not a response to another's real or threatened aggression but rather an

a priori state of being (190). Yet the critic views such episodes with dissatisfaction, concluding that while they may accurately "reflect" sadomasochistic
behavior, they do not adequately explain or "reveal" the reasons behind such
conduct (190). He then reaches a rather startling conclusion: "Novelistic
genius is based on the ability to transcend and reveal the metaphysical desire
but some dark corners remain, certain obsessions resist the novel's insight.
. . . There is always a critical zone in the extreme areas of metaphysical desire
explored by the novelist. In Proust, some of the aspects of homosexual desires
belong in this zone which novelistic revelation is rather slow to penetrate
and in which it cannot always definitively assert itself" (191). One may
argue that what Girard censures as the "dark corners" of Proust's genius are
examples simply of the ways in which the *Recherche* resists and subverts not
only the normative rules of psychoanalysis as a discipline, but also in certain
cases those of Girard's theory of desire. In this instance, it becomes clear that
one of the basic limitations of this theory is its presumption of heterosexual
normativity:

> Nothing is gained by reducing triangular desire to a homosexuality which
> is necessarily opaque to the heterosexual. If one turned the explanation
> around, the results would be much more interesting. An attempt should be
> made to understand at least some forms of homosexuality from the stand-
> point of triangular desire. Proustian homosexuality, for example, can be
> defined as a gradual transferring to the mediator of an erotic value which in
> "normal" Don Juanism remains attached to the object itself.[40]

Although Girard prudently isolates the adjective "normal" by means of scare
quotes, it is difficult to escape the impression that same-sex desire and the
"novelistic genius" that consists in transcending and revealing the logic of
metaphysical desire ultimately are incompatible.

Of interest in this regard is the way that Girard in the essay "Marcel
Proust" characterizes Mlle Vinteuil as a woman "whose abnormal relationship with a woman friend turns the life of her father, the great musician
Vinteuil, into a horrible martyrdom."[41] Although it may seem impertinent
to look back on the words of a critic written fifty years ago through the lens
of today's so-called political correctness, it is still striking that the one adjective that he fixes on and admittedly reappropriates from the narrator's long,

mesmerizing rehearsal of Mlle Vinteuil's story in the novel is the clinically judgmental adjective: "abnormal."[42] We indeed may conclude that for Girard the difficulty of Proust's novel is to be found not only in its open fascination with Mlle Vinteuil's supposedly aberrant passion, but even more evidently in its relish for the disorienting interactions between the narrator, Albertine, and *les jeune filles en fleur*.

In *A Theater of Envy: William Shakespeare* (1991), almost three decades after *Deceit, Desire, and the Novel*, Girard once again revisits the question of the relationship between homosexual and mimetic desire only to reaffirm the transcendental primacy of the principle of triangulation, which he maintains is indifferent to sexual preference: "Sexual differences are mobile, variable, and inessential, whereas the triangular structure is permanent and essential."[43] The title that the critic gives to an essay dedicated to verifying Joyce's recognition in *Ulysses* of the importance of mimetic desire in Shakespeare's plays aptly sums up the challenge to the totalizing claims of theory posed by the unstable libidinal amalgam of the ménage à trois, which Girard only appears able to name by means of a self-conscious euphemism: "Do You Believe Your Own Theory? 'French Triangles' in the Shakespeare of James Joyce." In answer to this challenge, and perhaps in denial of the very intuition that prompts him three sentences later to acknowledge that sexual idiosyncrasies are "mobile, variable, and inessential," Girard attempts to impose a stark logical order on the asymmetry of triangular liaisons by claiming prescriptively that "just as heterosexual desire entails a mediator of the same sex, homosexual desire entails a mediator of the other sex."[44] Yet his gambit here to reinscribe same-sex desire in the theory of mimetic triangulation is undermined and, in the end, overturned by the transformative erotic impulses that animate Proust's characters. Indeed, in the saga of the narrator and Albertine's ill-fated romance, which one might argue constitutes the fundamental story line of the *Recherche*, the narrator in his ostensibly straight desire for his lover repeatedly confronts and is frustrated by a mediator of the other sex, meaning a female rival such as Andrée, thus defying Girard's "law." Clearly, both the object and the mediator of desire in the Albertine narrative belong to the same sex, a circumstance for which there appears to be no room in Girard's theory, which is structured to reassert in compulsive fashion a "latent heterosexuality" that divides the mediator from the object of homosexual desire.[45]

When it comes to the two cases on which the critic dwells at greatest length, that is, Helena and Hermia in a *A Midsummer Night's Dream* and Shakespeare and his "rivals" in Joyce's *Ulysses*, Girard seems to interpret "homosexuality," unlike heterosexuality, as a consequence of the deviation of mimetic desire and not as a seriously conceivable point of departure. In a revealingly self-referential moment of his treatment of *A Midsummer Night's Dream*, he cites his own verdict from *Desire, Deceit, and the Novel*, which we have already encountered, that gay desire in Proust amounts to a redirection of the erotic investment of "'normal' Don Juanism" from the object to the mediator, continuing on in this case to the final sentence of the original paragraph: "Certain passages in [Dostoyevsky's] *The Eternal Husband* clearly show the beginning of an erotic deviation toward the fascinating rival."[46] In this pronouncement, Girard unmistakably brandishes a rhetoric that presumes a heteronormative point of view. Reflecting on the limits of a sexual ethos that defines itself in the space between the antipodes of "normal Don Juanism" and the "deviation" of homosexuality, we can only conclude that the critic does not succeed in accounting for the multiplicity and rhizomatic aspects of desire in Proust when he insists on triangulation as a first principle. Just as Albertine does, the narrator notoriously desires the group of "jeune filles." There are too many mediators in Proust's world to leave any triangle standing on its vertex.[47] If Girard's theory seems to work a little better with respect to Swann and Odette, this is small consolation. As Deleuze and Guattari observe in *A Thousand Plateaus*, the narrator's virtue is not to be in any way an avatar of Swann, whom they define as a more "arborescent" or totalizing type of character. Finally, the idea that desire should be less modern, less explosive, less multivalent than the Ovidian metamorphoses of Proust's novel may begin to look, in our perhaps "barbarous times," like a truly quaint proposition.[48]

In this sense, Deleuze's concepts of deterritorialization, lines of flight, the rhizome, becoming woman, becoming intense, becoming imperceptible, and so on offer a more supple and wide-ranging assortment of vantage points from which to map the affective plateaus of Proust's fiction. Already in the later editions of *Proust and Signs*, Deleuze distinguishes three "levels" of sexuality at work in the *Recherche*. He defines the first as "the entity of heterosexual loves in their contrasts and repetitions,"[49] which performs the juridical act of love as "a declaration of imaginary innocence extended

between two certitudes of guilt."[50] The second level, which "decomposes" the
entity of the first, encompasses the "Gomorrah" of same-sex desire between
women and the "Sodom" of same-sex desire between men.[51] Deleuze notes
that Proust ascribes to both of these levels "no more than a statistical value,"
meaning that on both of these levels "guilt is experienced socially rather than
morally or internally" and thus reinforces an externalized, behavioristic, and
prescriptive understanding of sexuality.[52] It is only on the third level that
we encounter "the agitations of single particles, of each of the selves that
constitute the throng or army," where we recognize that "an individual of
a given sex . . . bears within itself the other sex with which it cannot communicate directly."[53] The third level Deleuze defines as "transexual," citing a
remark from the narrator that this transexual level "is very wrongly called
homosexuality" and explaining that it "transcends the individual as well as
the entity: it designates in the individual the coexistence of fragments of
both sexes, *partial objects* that do not communicate. . . . An aberrant communication occurs in a transversal dimension between partitioned sexes."[54]
Deleuze maintains that transexuality and transversality in the *Recherche* are
contiguous and necessitate each other. More specifically, he suggests that
Proust's chief interest is to explore a homosexuality that is no longer "aggregate and specific" in the sense of being confined within the rules of same-sex
desire but in fact has become "local and nonspecific" in imagining as well
the possibilities of a man who pursues "what is masculine" in a woman and a
woman who pursues "what is feminine" in a man.[55] However, in response to
this conclusion, it may be fair to ask whether readers such as Eve Kosofsky
Sedgwick and Michal Lucey have not done an even more comprehensive job
of assessing the emergence of same-sex desire as a focus of the *Recherche*.[57]

    We should not fail to notice, however, that in his confrontations with
Proust, Girard was one of the first critics to recognize the plurality of Proust's
worlds, as the title of the ninth chapter of *Deceit, Desire, and the Novel* makes
clear ("The Worlds of Proust"). Before the teleological movement of the revelation of metaphysical desire is completed in *Le temps retrouvé*, according
to Girard, Proust articulates a vision of our existence consisting in separate
"small closed worlds" from Combray to the Verdurins' salon, in "neutral
particles which have no action on each other."[56] These particles bear a strong
resemblance to the "cells," "sealed vessels," "fragments," and "particles" that
Deleuze in *Proust and Signs* emphasizes by way of deconstructing the myth

of the *Recherche* as an organic unity.[58] Girard nevertheless takes pains in *Deceit, Desire, and the Novel* to identify the moral and spiritual heart of the *Recherche* with the church in Combray and its own architectural focal point of the steeple of Saint-Hilary: "The greater the distance from the mystic center, the more painful, frenzied, and futile becomes the agitation, until we arrive at *The Past Recaptured*, which reverses this movement."[59] Although Deleuze's charting of the Proustian search for lost time is not as teleologically definitive as Girard's exposition of the place of the *Recherche* in revealing "the structure of experience," Deleuze surely would have agreed with Girard that, more than being fascinated with the transfiguration of the object by desire, the novelist was fascinated principally with the very "process of transfiguration" itself.[60]

Of course, Girard by his own admission is a dialectical thinker, if no Hegelian, whereas Deleuze most certainly was the least dialectical thinker of his generation. As a result, the two thinkers diverge importantly in their approaches to Proust and their evaluations of his achievement in the *Recherche*. At the end of *Deceit, Desire, and the Novel*, Girard praises Proust for his final escape from metaphysical desire in the last volume of the *Recherche*. In the critic's opinion, the fragmentary multiplicities of "Selves" and "Worlds" that the novel sets in motion in its previous volumes thus are reharmonized at the end. Girard observes in his third chapter that Proust defines these selves as "the 'worlds' projected by successive mediators," which are consigned to an alienated state of independence from one another that prohibits them from "recalling . . . former Selves or anticipating future Selves" (90–91). In the conclusion, however, Girard claims that Proust's aesthetics aim at a "break with the mediator" that leads to a renunciation of the very problematic of metaphysical desire, thus making it possible for the narrator to "recapture past desires" (298). The multiplicities of Selves in the *Recherche* make place at the end for a universal "profound self" in accordance with Proust's effort, according to Girard, "to reconcile the particular and the universal" (298).

Girard openly acknowledges Proust's resistance to this interpretative model when he concedes that the novelist "occasionally gives up his attempt at reconciliation [of Self and Others]" and in certain passages of *Le temps retrouvé*, which the critic dismisses as "clichés of twentieth-century Romanticism," even identifies the task of the work of art with the pursuit of our "differences" and "originality." Girard ascribes such lapses from the higher aesthetic imperative of affirming our communion in the "symbolism of vertical transcendency" with which we commemorate the death and resurrection of the author himself to Proust's "lack of a theoretical vocabulary." A few pages later, the critic characterizes as "surprising" the fact that "Proust never broached the theme of novelistic unity in his own conclusion."[61] It is somewhat unsettling to Girard, in other words, that Proust himself never articulates any explicit link between the classical novelistic conclusion in which the narrator renounces metaphysical desire and his successful recapturing of the past.

In an attempt to locate just such a link, Girard calls our attention to an article that Proust wrote for *Le Figaro* in 1907 entitled "Filial Sentiments of a Parricide," in which he recounts the story of Henri Van Blarenberghe, who committed suicide after killing his mother. In Girard's view, Van Blarenberghe's suicide symbolizes the moment in which "the parricide recovers his lucidity in the course of expiating [his] crime"[62] and thus fascinates the novelist because it represents an enactment of belated moral insight that is missing from the end of the *Recherche*. What is interesting is that, like Deleuze, Girard nevertheless concludes that the theme of affective memory does not play a central role in the novel, because it was necessary for Proust to remain silent about the contributions of his novelistic precursors to the development of this theme in order to sustain the "idolatry" of his own quest for "originality." In other words, if the unity of novelistic conclusion exemplifies what is essential to Western civilization, which is to say the reconciliation between the individual and the world, Proust's insistence on the involuntary character of memory would have "limited," if not in fact violated, the universality of the novel's development for the purposes of theoretical consistency. Proust "was aware of the connection between *The Past Recaptured* and the classical novelistic conclusions," Girard surmises, but deliberately refused to expound on this connection out of an overriding fear of "seeming ridiculous by repeating universally accepted truths."[63]

It may be said, then, that in Girard's eyes Proust ultimately commits the sin of being a snob insofar as he cultivates a mythical, not to say delusional, sense of his own superiority as a means of excusing himself from the vulgar moral obligation of helping to restore historical order to the world. At the same time, there is no doubt that by denying the radical challenge that *la mémoire involontaire* poses in the *Recherche* to the redemptive promise of

Christian teleology or even to the immanence of the transversal, both Girard and Deleuze expose themselves in turn to potential accusations of critical snobbery. (It is helpful to remember in this connection that Deleuze gives to the fifth chapter of *Proust and Signs* the title "The Secondary Role of Memory.") From yet another angle, however, their respective forms of willfulness paradoxically may be regarded as essential to their strong interpretations of the literary text, which they each reveal to be "efficient" in yielding the most difficult, exciting, and provocative philosophical insights. Seen in this light, two of the most productive architects of contemporary thought may be recognized as deriving crucial inspiration for many of their own ideas from the sprawling memory palace of Proust's book, which the narrator himself famously likens to a cathedral. In the volatile and problematic triangulation between Girard, Deleuze, and Proust, the winner of their imaginary contest is, perhaps almost inevitably, the novelist.

Notes

1. Girard asserts that "Hegelian dialectic rested on physical courage," whereas "the novelistic dialectic rests on hypocrisy." This is due to the fact that Hegelian dialectic is situated in a violent past, unlike the most eminent examples of novelistic dialectic chosen by Girard, which belong to the aftermath of Napoleon's defeat. René Girard, *Deceit, Desire, and the Novel: Self and Others in Literary Structures*, trans. Yvonne Freccero (Baltimore: Johns Hopkins University Press, 1965), 110–12.

2. Girard, *Deceit, Desire, and the Novel*, 52.

3. Gilles Deleuze, *Proust and Signs*, trans. Richard Howard (Minneapolis: University of Minnesota Press, 2000), 168. Originally published in French in 1964.

4. Marcel Proust, *Remembrance of Things Past*, trans. C. K. Scott Moncrieff and Terence Kilmartin (New York: Vintage Books, 1982), 1:135.

5. Gilles Deleuze, "Coldness and Cruelty," in Deleuze and Leopold von Sacher-Masoch, *Masochism* (New York: Zone Books, 1991), 15.

6. As cited in Jean-Jacques Lecercle, *Badiou and Deleuze Read Literature* (Edinburgh: Edinburgh University Press, 2010), 59.

7. On the question of Deleuze's approach to literature as a thought experiment, see Lecercle, *Badiou and Deleuze*, 3. As Lecercle observes, Deleuze characterizes the two ways of reading thus: "There are, you see, two ways of reading a book: you either see it as a box with something inside and start looking for what it signifies, and then if you're even more perverse or depraved you set off after signifiers. . . . Or there's the other way: you see the book as a little non-signifying machine, and the only question is 'Does it work, and how does it work?' How does it work for you." Gilles Deleuze, *Negotiations* (New York: Columbia University Press, 1991), 7–8, as cited in Lecercle, *Badiou and Deleuze*, 44.

8. Lecercle, *Badiou and Deleuze*, 45.

9. See Lecercle, *Badiou and Deleuze*, 61, for a strenuous argument in support of this point à propos of Deleuze's approach to literature.

10. One factor important to both Girard and Deleuze, in my opinion, is the resistance of the *Recherche* to psychoanalysis as a mode of criticism. Of course, I am aware that there are numerous psychoanalytic readings of the novel, including Malcom Bowie's delightful Lacanian endeavor, *Proust among the Stars*. However, more than other canonical novelists, Proust seems to resist entrapment in psychoanalytic formulas because of the sheer complexity of his literary strategies, and, so far as I am aware, Lacan himself carefully avoided any dealing with Proust. On this last question, see Jean-Michel Rabaté, *Jacques Lacan: Psychoanalysis and the Subject of Literature* (New York: Palgrave, 2001).

11. "The direct time-image always gives us access to that Proustian dimension where people and things occupy a place in time which is incommensurable with the one they have in space. Proust indeed speaks in terms of cinema." Gilles Deleuze, *Cinema 2: The Time-Image*, trans. Hugh Tomlison and Robert Galeta (Minneapolis: University of Minnesota Press, 1994), 39.

12. Lecercle, *Badiou and Deleuze*, 68.

13. Deleuze, *Proust and Signs*, 106.

14. Deleuze, *Proust and Signs*, 114.

15. Twice in *Deceit, Desire, and the Novel* on page 77 and again on page 80.

16. Girard, *Deceit, Desire, and the Novel*, 90.

17. Girard, *Deceit, Desire, and the Novel*, 86.

18. René Girard, *Mimesis and Theory: Essays on Literature and Criticism, 1953–2005*, ed. R. Doran (Stanford: Stanford University Press, 2008), 61.

19. Girard, *Deceit, Desire, and the Novel*, 65.

20. Deleuze, *Proust and Signs*, 169.

21. Girard, *Deceit, Desire, and the Novel*, 92.

22. Girard, *Deceit, Desire, and the Novel*, 160–61.

23. Gilles Deleuze, *Foucault and His Interlocutors*, ed. Arnold Davidson (Chicago: University of Chicago Press, 1997), 189–90.

24. René Girard, *"To Double Business Bound": Essays on Literature, Mimesis, and Anthropology* (Baltimore: Johns Hopkins University Press, 1978), 84–120.

25. One paragraph in Girard's diatribe against Deleuze and Guattari stands out: "We might ask if Deleuze and Guattari are not like the man who, when forced to witness his wife's rape, congratulates himself because he has transgressed once or twice the chalk circle that the rapist traced around her and ordered him not to cross." This particularly violent rhetoric might in part be explained by Girard's own mimetic expression of that mimetic violence which he perceives at the heart of desire and in view of which he criticizes the naïveté of the "peaceful coexistence" advocated by Deleuze and Guattari. Girard, *"To Double Business Bound,"* 88, 93–94.

26. Girard, *"To Double Business Bound,"* 89.

27. Girard, *"To Double Business Bound,"* 90.

28. Girard, *"To Double Business Bound,"* 114.

29. Girard, *"To Double Business Bound,"* 89, 115.

30. Girard, *"To Double Business Bound,"* 112, 113.

31. Girard, *"To Double Business Bound,"* 114.

32. Gilles Deleuze and Félix Guattari, *A Thousand Plateaus: Capitalism and Schizophrenia*, trans. Brian Massumi (Minneapolis: University of Minnesota Press, 1987), 185, 186.

33. Deleuze and Guattari, *A Thousand Plateaus*, 271.

34. Deleuze and Guattari, *A Thousand Plateaus*, 271.

35. Deleuze and Guattari, *A Thousand Plateaus*, 272.

36. Deleuze, "Coldness and Cruelty," 13.

37. Deleuze, "Coldness and Cruelty," 70–72.

38. Girard, *Deceit, Desire, and the Novel*, 182–83.

39. Leo Bersani and Ulysse Dutoit, *Caravaggio's Secrets* (Cambridge: MIT Press, 1998).

40. Girard, *Deceit, Desire, and the Novel*, 47.

41. Girard, *Deceit, Desire, and the Novel*, 57.

42. The exact wording of the narrator's reading of Mlle Vinteuil's attitude in the Moncrieff-Kilmartin translation runs as follows: "Perhaps she would not have thought of wickedness as a state so rare, so abnormal, so exotic, one which it was so refreshing to visit, had she been able to distinguish in herself, as in all her fellow men and women, that indifference to the sufferings they cause which, whatever names else be given it, is the one true, terrible and lasting form of cruelty." As cited by Girard in *Deceit, Desire, and the Novel*, 191.

43. René Girard, *A Theater of Envy: William Shakespeare* (Oxford: Oxford University Press), 1991, 260.

44. Girard, *A Theater of Envy*, 260.

45. Girard, *A Theater of Envy*, 260.

46. Girard, *Deceit, Desire, and the Novel*, 47; Girard, *A Theater of Envy*, 44.

47. While he may clearly recognize the fascination of the mediator in Proust, which threatens at times even to obliterate the object, Girard in my opinion fails to acknowledge the effect in the *Recherche* of the ever growing and changing plurality of fascinating mediators. This very plurality is what explodes and overcomes the logic of triangulation.

48. In *Theater of Envy*, Girard contemptuously indicts the present era as "barbarous" for not taking "a balanced and humorous view of questions now so loaded with ideological baggage that almost any mention of them makes us feel as if a ton of bricks had been unloaded on us" (44).

49. Deleuze, *Proust and Signs*, 134.

50. Deleuze, *Proust and Signs*, 133.

51. Deleuze, *Proust and Signs*, 134.

52. Deleuze, *Proust and Signs*, 134.

53. Deleuze, *Proust and Signs*, 135.

54. Deleuze, *Proust and Signs*, 136.

55. Deleuze, *Proust and Signs*, 136–37.

56. Girard, *Deceit, Desire, and the Novel*, 213.

57. On the question of same-sex identities in Proust we might find less Dionysian approaches in Eve Kosofsky Sedgwick's classic study, *Epistemology of the Closet* (Berkeley: University of California Press, 1990), and Michael Lucey's *Never Say I: Sexuality and the First Person in Colette, Gide and Proust* (Durham: Duke University Press, 2006).

58. Deleuze, *Proust and Signs*, 116–35.

59. Girard, *Deceit, Desire, and the Novel*, 215.

60. Girard, *Deceit, Desire, and the Novel*, 219, 314.

61. Girard, *Deceit, Desire, and the Novel*, 298, 299, 302–3, 313.

62. Girard, *Deceit, Desire, and the Novel*, 301.

63. Girard, *Deceit, Desire, and the Novel*, 302, 303–7.

Within and Beyond Mimetic Desire

René Girard does not make it easy to do him justice. His pronounced hermeneutics of suspicion easily mobilizes suspicion against his own writings. He appears sometimes enlightening and even wise, sometimes provocative and single-minded. While the monocausal redundancy of his explanations tempts his readers to underestimate him, the coherence of his work and the striking simplicity and plausibility of many of his explanations command respect and admiration.

It seems to me that at least some of these tensions are consequences of some major contradictions in Girard's work. They refer to his key notion of mimetic desire and its constitutive ambiguity.[1] Is mimetic desire mimetic because we reciprocally imitate the desire of the other, or because there is another, authentic desire that mimetic desire imitates? Is, in other words, desire *always* mimetic, as Girard frequently maintained, or does another "authentic" desire exist besides, as he equally sometimes suggested? And if is the latter: why Girard constantly hesitates to provide clear distinctions, even though he usually didn't avoid plain words? Furthermore (and closely related): Is mimetic desire purely negative and evil, as one might think after having read most of Girard's main writings, or is it even "intrinsically good," as he also claimed in a more recent statement?[2]

In this essay, I analyze these continuous contradictions or at least ambiguities in the work of Girard, and will thereby especially concentrate on his first book, *Deceit, Desire, and the Novel*. What makes this work particularly interesting is the fact that it helped Girard to develop his notion of mimetic desire. Girard started writing his book with a pronounced elitist and antimodern worldview and overcame it in the process of writing. In the course of this, an initial distinction between authentic and mimetic desire was somehow, but not completely replaced, by radicalizing and totalizing the devalued part of it. The contradictions I mentioned in the beginning have to do with the inconsistency of a partial overcoming of the notion of authentic desire, or more precisely: keeping the binary code authentic/mimetic.

Focusing on contradictions might appear as an example of an ungenerous or suspicious reading. Yet, apart from my admiration for Girard's work, I am convinced that persisting contradictions can be the most revealing aspects of a relevant theory. More than everything else, they can provide the possibility to understand a theory and its limits. Or, to put it in Girard's own words: "When one realizes that inconsistency is an invariant, it no longer looks like a mere logical inconsistency, but it turns into a clue."[3]

Negative Understanding of Mimetic Desire

If we look at an essay by Girard, written shortly before *Deceit, Desire, and the Novel*, we cannot miss a pronounced antimodern and antiegalitarian affect. A conservative stance toward modernity is apparent all over the work of Girard, but especially here, this aspect seems much more accentuated.[4] In his paper entitled "Pride and Passion in the Contemporary Novel,"[5] published in 1959, and thus written shortly prior to his conversion and the development of the notion of mimetic desire, we can find a clear refusal of his contemporary world. The essay collects most standard elements of conservative critics against modernity and democracy. Girard criticized here the

1. Anonymity and disintegration of modern society: "a self perpetually threatened with anonymity and disintegration in the new democratic society" (3)

2. Emancipation of women: "The romantic women, however, were not far behind men in their egotistical appetites. . . . As real women began to lose some of their femininity, as they started, in other words, that upward climb which led them to the position of prestige and power we see them 'enjoying' today" (3)
3. Modern individualism and atheism: "modern vanity" (4), the "modern egotist is almost convinced that he is God" (4), "mirage of divine autonomy" (6)
4. Mass culture: "everybody is a carbon copy of everybody else" (6)
5. Homosexuality: the "sociologists confirm that the sexes are becoming more alike. And homosexual obsessions are perhaps a paroxysmal form of this very general disease" (7)
6. "Present exaltation of sex" as "symptom of a spiritual disease which has been steadily worsening since the beginning of romanticism" (8)

We should consider these conservative and elitist elements of Girard's worldview in the time when he was writing *Deceit, Desire, and the Novel*, if we want to understand why the discovery of mimetic desire became so immensely relevant for him.

It was, first of all, the perfect instrument to unify different (allegedly) negative processes in modernity. Many (though not all) of them can be understood through the interconnection between growing equality and growing mimetic desire. Most of the negative developments of modernity appear in *Deceit, Desire, and the Novel* as consequences of the transition from "external" to "internal mediation." Girard described "external mediation" as a triangular form of desire, in which the distance between two spheres (the sphere of the mediator and of the subject) is sufficient to eliminate any contact between them. In internal mediation, this distance is sufficiently reduced to allow these two spheres to penetrate each other more or less completely.[6] Since the subject desires what the mediator desires or possesses, increasing equality necessarily leads to increasing conflicts. The mediator bars the way of the subject; he always has what the subject desires. And the other way round: the mediator starts becoming attached by mimetic desire for the other as well. His desire becomes perverted by the desire of the other, and in consequence, we have a sort of reciprocal contamination of mimetic desire.

This process leads first of all to the annihilation of the real or the object. Girard spoke of a "progressive elimination of reality."[7] As long as the mediator was external and out of reach, subjects could openly admire the mediator and desire what he had or he desired. In the moment, however, when he comes closer, he is transformed into a prompt, blocks the view of the desired object, becomes the subject's rival, and gets more and more of his attention. Finally, the mediator is the message.

This theory appears as an interesting contribution to the discourse on nihilism, started some 150 years earlier, when Friedrich Heinrich Jacobi, as one of the first, used the term "nihilism" in a philosophical sense. According to him, transcendental philosophy and particularly Johann Gottlieb Fichte reached the point of complete nihilism, where the "I" finally had destroyed the belief in anything, transforming it in a mere "non-I." At issue was not only Fichte or transcendental idealism, but the destiny or end point of philosophy as such. And in revealing the inherent destiny of philosophy as nihilism, Jacobi wanted to demonstrate the necessity to believe (*Glauben*) and thereby also of religion. Girard shared with Jacobi a certain rivalry toward philosophy; both took the position of (Christian) belief in order to criticize philosophy and especially German idealism.[8] But there is here an interesting difference as well: while Jacobi's early critique of "nihilist" disappearance of the object is based on a philosophy of consciousness and subjectivity, Girard's theory is developed on the basis of intersubjectivity. Girard's mimetic theory thereby provides the possibility to reformulate a critique of nihilism on the basis of intersubjectivity.

A further radicalization of mimetic desire occurs in the moment of transition to double or reciprocal mediation. The rivals reciprocally desire the desire of the other. To imitate one's lover's desire is to desire oneself, thanks to that lover's desire. Girard spoke here of the vicious circle of double mediation.[9] This development of mimetic desire reaches its climax in what Girard called "masochism." This process is not limited to literature, but applies to social processing as well: "The whole of our contemporary world is permeated by masochism."[10] Here the mediator is selected by how he despises everyone else and it is here that his desire becomes not only reciprocal (and by this somehow self-referential), but *sensu stricto* self-reflexive. One could read the whole story of mimetic desire as a process of increasing self-reflexivity and self-consciousness in a Hegelian sense, but instead of being conceived as a positive movement, it is considered as negative process.[11]

Masochism is not the only climax of mimetic desire. In *Deceit, Desire, and the Novel*, Girard mentions another final stage of desire, which, however, is less prominent or elaborated than masochism, and it is not completely clear whether it belongs, for Girard, to masochism or not: "nondesire."

> Nondesire once more becomes a privilege as it was for the wise man of old or the Christian saint. But the desiring subject recoils in terror before the idea of absolute renunciation. He looks for loopholes. . . . The somnambulist hero of American writers is the "solution" to this problem. Nondesire in this hero has nothing to do with the triumph of the mind over evil forces, nor with the self-discipline extolled by the great religions and higher humanisms. It makes one think rather of a numbing of the senses, of a total or partial loss of vital curiosity.[12]

Girard also used the expression "lucid stupefaction," which constitutes the final romantic pose, and detects here the appearance of the truth of metaphysical desire: death. "It is the inevitable end of the contradiction on which that desire is based."[13] The "somnambulist hero" recalls Giorgio Agamben's variations of similar figures who are evocative of "nondesire," like Melville's antihero Bartleby. The Italian philosopher, however, does not interpret them as end points of an aberration. Instead, they appear much more ambivalent.[14] The same holds for the striking proximity between Girard's notions of the other final stage of mimetic desire, masochism, and Žižek's notion of the death drive. "Drive" is the name for "an uncanny excess of life, for an 'undead' urge which persists beyond the (biological) cycle of life and death, of generation and corruption."[15] This drive transforms failure into triumph. The endless circling around the object is its own satisfaction. For Girard, as well as for Žižek, there is a direct transition from a desire caused by a dividing force (the mediator, the symbolic law, the lost) toward a desire/drive directed toward division, hindrance, loss, only that Girard understands this as final step of an negative escalation of mimetic desire, while Žižek keeps its ambiguity.[16] Girard's exclusively negative understanding of the end points of mimetic desire would correspond to a pure negative understanding of mimetic desire itself, not, however, to the intrinsic ambivalence of mimetic desire, he later admitted. Agamben and Žižek seem therefore, paradoxically, to reflect this ambivalence better than Girard himself, and the question arises why Girard constantly focused on negative interpretations of mimetic desire.

Traces of an Authentic Desire

To tell the truth, Girard's understanding of mimetic desire was initially not ambivalent at all. In *Deceit, Desire, and the Novel*, we cannot find a positive valuation of mimetic desire. On the contrary: Already the term as such suggested a clearly negative meaning of the intrinsic nature of mimetic desire. As mimetic, this desire had to be understood as only derived and secondary. Girard later confirmed such a reading. "Normally the word 'imitation' is reserved to designate what is considered inauthentic."[17]

This, in turn, implies that there is an authentic desire as well. And indeed, we can find different passages in *Deceit, Desire, and the Novel* where Girard, discussing Stendhal, seems to suggest the existence of a strong, aristocratic desire or passion:

> Fabrice del Dongo is the perfect example of the passionate person; he is distinguished by his emotional autonomy, by the spontaneity of his desires, by his absolute indifference to the opinion of Others. The passionate person draws the strength of his desire from within himself and not from others.[18]

At a later point, Girard continued: "the noble being rises above other by the strength of his desire" (113). An authentic passion, Girard suggested, existed in the Renaissance in Italy as well as a sort of "natural" aristocracy and hierarchies. In the course of modernity and democratization, however, passion was replaced by increasing mimetic desire and external by internal mediation.

It may be argued that it is not clear whether Girard was here referring to the standpoint of Stendhal or if he was expressing his own opinion. But, first, I would claim that this tendency to hide his opinion in the moment when an original desire is at stake is typical and is visible again and again. Second, while in this passage Stendhal cannot be clearly distinguished from Girard, there is no trace of a self-distancing from Stendhal as well, and as we know Girard admired Stendhal. Therefore I would read this passage as an affirmation. Most of all, however, Girard expressed a very similar position in the conclusion of his book: "Deception gives way to truth, anguish to remembrance, agitation to repose, hatred to love, humiliation to humility, mediated desire to autonomy [*le désir selon l'Autre au désir selon Soi*], deviated transcendency to vertical transcendency."[19] A distinction between authentic, autonomous, and spontaneous desire or passion and its imitation is thus difficult to deny, and actually, it also fits perfectly with Girard's distinction between external and internal mediation: While at least the desire of the external mediator in hierarchical societies is authentic, in societies ruled by internal mediation mimetic desire becomes ubiquitous.

In other words: before Girard described much later mimetic desire as ambivalent and even as intrinsically good, we find in *Deceit, Desire, and the Novel* a notion of mimetic desire that was in a double sense devalued: because of its negative consequences and because of its nature, because it is secondary and mere imitation and at the same time highly contagious and easily attaches the "good" authentic desire of the models, transforming the good hierarchical relation of admiration into toxic rivalry leading to nihilism, self-destruction, and increasing violence.

But the clear and arguably initial distinction authentic/mimetic desire seems from the start (after his conversion) obscured by Girard himself. Decades after *Deceit, Desire, and the Novel*, he very strangely switched between negating and admitting the very possibility of an authentic desire. In *Evolution and Conversion*, he even switched between two sentences from the claim that "there is no authentic desire and any desire is mediated by others" to the claim that "the distinction between an 'authentic' and 'inauthentic' desire is not always groundless" (45).

The tendency to hide the traces of a strong, authentic desire seems even more visible in another gesture. In the English translation of *Mensonge romantique et verité romanesque*, we can find an interesting change regarding exactly the passage where he openly distinguished between "le désir selon l'Autre au désir selon Soi." Instead of speaking of a "desire according to oneself" (or something like that), the translation avoids the noun "desire" and introduces instead the notion "autonomy." "Autonomy," however, is hardly an adequate translation for "désir selon Soi." And I doubt that the translator introduced such a relevant change without Girard's authorization. What makes this translation even more odd: in replacing "authentic desire" with "autonomy," the English translator introduced (or uncovered) a contradiction of *Deceit, Desire, and the Novel*, since Girard used this term in the same book in order to blame modernity.

> All these dogmas [subjectivisms and objectivisms, romanticisms and realisms, individualisms and scientisms, idealisms and positivisms] are the aesthetic or philosophic translation of world-views peculiar to internal mediation. They all depend directly or indirectly on the lie of spontaneous desire. They all defend the same illusion of autonomy in which modern man is passionately devoted.[20]

How can we understand this contradiction between a "good" and a "bad" autonomy? And why did Girard obviously try to obscure authentic desire, something that is still visible here and there in *Deceit, Desire, and the Novel* and that never completely disappeared from his oeuvre?

Totalizing Mimetic Desire and Its Paradoxes

I think that we can dissolve the contradictions of mimetic desire if we consider a last major aspect of it, its connection to conversion. This notion permitted Girard to overcome (at least partially) the sterility and negativity of his elitist antimodernism. The turning point or step beyond his individualist and aristocratic view was, paradoxically, the disappearance of the alternative by totalizing mimetic desire. Why? Only by acknowledging that there is nothing but mimetic desire we can no longer exclude ourselves from it. In that very moment we have to give up the privileged position that attributes mimetic desire only to the other while we implicitly see ourselves as an exception. In *Evolution and Conversion*, Girard put the point pretty clearly:

> I think that the problematic of authenticity, of existential authenticity, is important. What is authentic and what is inauthentic desire? Inauthentic desire is the desire that is influenced by others. When, for instance, Heidegger thinks of others, he always refers to the crowd. This is a pre-understanding

of mimetic desire, which, however, excludes the self, because the self is always inevitably authentic in opposition to the others. The invention of mimetic desire is, in a way, only the suppression of that distinction: there is no authentic desire and any desire is mediated by others. But this suppression implies the conversion. . . . A conversion in which you accept that you are part of the mimetic mechanism which rules human relationships, in which the observer acknowledges the fact that he himself is implicated in his observation. The distinction between an "authentic" and "inauthentic" desire is not always groundless, but when it coincides with the distinction between myself and the others, I think it is quite suspicious.[21]

We can assume that Girard's conversion (during the process of writing *Deceit, Desire, and the Novel*) had to do with the overcoming of his own previous elitist and individualistic standpoint. He experienced himself what he recognized as the experience of the romanesque hero of the novel as well as the modern individual: the need to give up a "promethean egotism" in order to overcome mimetic or mediated desire: "In renouncing divinity the hero renounces slavery."[22]

The acknowledgment that he himself was attacked or possessed by mimetic desire, even and especially when he discovered it everywhere else, was apparently the turning point. The very same concept of mimetic desire, which allowed for blaming increasing equality as the reason for increasing violence, was transformed in a remedy. That which was used as a means for attacking others, at a certain point turned against him. This acknowledgment changed everything. Girard's mimetic desire is, like Derrida's *pharmakos*, poison and remedy at the same time. Mimetic theory is thus not only "a 'narcissistic wound' . . . for it shows that one's desire isn't as free as modern individualism would like it to be";[23] it also heals the wound.

A first paradox, however, arises from the fact that in admitting one's own involvement in mimetic desire one overcomes it: at least to a certain extent and in consequence, nobody really believes in being (completely) involved in mimetic desire. The modern romantics or "promethean" egoists attribute it to the mass or the weak (e.g., to Christian slave morality), the Girardian Christians to the Gnostic or Promethean egoists and their followers.[24]

On closer inspection, it is exactly this "to a certain extent" that seems to be the problem of Girard's notion of conversion. It remains unclear to what degree the conversion transforms the former condition. Does it lead to a completely new stage? Should it be understood in terms of a return to a former condition? Is it merely the introduction of a sort of second-order perspective, which leaves everything the way it was? Or more precisely: Does conversion lead to a sort of Christian or ascetic renunciation from desire at all? Do we, instead, overcome an internally mediated desire by an externally mediated desire, a bad by a good mimetic desire as a sort of *imitatio Christi*? Or, since Girard kept the notion of an authentic desire: Do we overcome mimetic desire through a sort of recovery of an authentic desire? And if it is the latter: Should authentic desire or at least authenticity be attributed to Jesus's "autonomy,"[25] or (also?) to an independent aristocratic passion?

Girard does not seem very clear here: On one side, he presented an emphatic notion of conversion, understood as a turning point in a process that led to violence, annihilation, and death. At the same time, this new achievement apparently includes restorative aspects:

> Recapturing the past is recapturing the original impression beneath the opinion of others which hides it; it is to recognize that this opinion is not one's own. It is to understand that the process of mediation creates a very vivid impression of autonomy and spontaneity precisely when we are no longer autonomous and spontaneous.[26]

Yet, conversion, even though it has somehow changed everything, leaves at the same time everything as it was before. At least epistemologically, Girard tended sometimes to narrow the distinction between the romanesque (or novelistic) and the romantic to a minimal difference. In the English translation of *Mensonge romantique et vérité romanesque*, he added a footnote, speaking of the "essential, yet elusive, difference between the works that passively reflect and those that actively reveal 'mediated' desire.'"[27]

And such an "essential" difference between "passively reflecting" and "actively revealing" is—indeed—"elusive" because there is a constitutive impossibility of detecting the motivation of an author. How can we ever be certain that someone who doesn't reveal mimetic desire or the presence of the mediator is passively reflecting or instead actively hiding it? In fact, Girard himself is far from being consistent in this point. Already the French title distinguishes a "mensonge romantique" from a "verité romanesque."

"Mensonge," however, is much more than just "passively reflecting" something. It implies bad faith and the act of hiding a truth.

But what is more: how can we ever be certain about such a bad faith? This applies particularly for the field of mimetic desire. Since it is impossible to reveal mimetic desire without revealing oneself as the one who was able to overcome it, one cannot but put oneself forward as an example of the mimetic desire of others. Therefore, the use of categories like deception is anything but safe. By underestimating the possibility that the other might be in a position (in the very tension between being inside and outside mimetic desire) similar to his own, Girard continued an elitist understanding rather than overcoming it.

Within and Beyond Mimetic Desire

At this point we are able to understand Girard's double game of totalizing mimetic desire and keeping an authentic desire, mentioning and hiding authentic desire at the same time. The clear expression of authentic desire would permit everybody to remain in the romantic illusion, maintaining that one's own desire is authentic, while others are embroiled in imitation. For ethical or religious reasons Girard had to underline the inescapability of mimetic desire. And at the same time, by keeping a notion of authentic desire, he preserved the possibility of devaluating mimetic desire after having totalized it.

In other words: Girard could oppose the modern illusionary autonomy and spontaneity in the name of a totalized mimetic desire. At the same time, however, he kept the possibility of devaluing mimetic desire from the standpoint of the (re)discovery of an authentic desire.[28] By obscuring the difference between Christian *imitatio Christi* (or renouncement) and regaining access to an authentic desire, Girard was able to fight against elitist individualism *and* struggles for equality at the same time. Or, to put the paradox as clearly as possible: the acceptance of being part of mimetic desire permits us to overcome an illusionary autonomy and to replace it with a real autonomy, which in turn allows us to overcome mimetic desire.

This paradox has political consequences: it provides the possibility of fighting against an (elitist) individualism and an (egalitarian) mimetic desire.

It was exactly the inescapability of mimetic desire that permitted Girard to maintain a centrist political position, to overcome a right-wing elitist, hierarchical, individualist worldview and to remain skeptical toward all political forms of gathering, including struggles for equal rights.[29] More precisely: The acknowledgment of his own entanglement in mimetic desire (his conversion) allowed him to understand the self as deeply connected with the other and permitted a positive revaluation of equality, democracy, and, in consequence, also mimetic desire as "intrinsically good." On this basis, Girard could blame modern elitist individualism for not recognizing the mimetic character of desire and in consequence intersubjectivity or "interdividuality." This step is politically relevant, because the tendency to limit mimetic desire (or resentment) to the other, especially to the weaker other, is one major source of elitist positions down to the present day.[30]

But in keeping the notion of authentic desire, Girard kept the possibility of a constant devaluation of the intrinsic nature of mimetic desire as well. And here I see the major political problem of his specific notion of mimetic desire. Let's take an example from his late book *I See Satan Fall Like Lightning.*[31] Girard spoke here of a current concern for victims:

> The most powerful anti-Christian movement is the one that takes over and "radicalizes" the concern for victims in order to paganize it. The powers and principalities want to be "revolutionary" now, and they reproach Christianity for not defending victims with enough ardor. In Christian history they see nothing but persecutions, acts of oppression, inquisitions. ... This other totalitarianism presents itself as the liberator of humanity. In trying to usurp the place of Christ, the powers imitate him in the way a mimetic rival imitates his model in order to defeat him.[32]

According to Girard, contemporary movements fighting for rights and recognition are imitating a Christian concern for the victims. This is in line with Nietzsche's interpretation of political movements of his time, such as anarchism, as forms of imitation and radicalization of Christianity. Nietzsche, however, could easily devaluate anarchism and socialism, for instance, because he also devalued Christianity. The difficulty of Girard lies in the attempt to maintain a positive understanding of Christian concern for the victims and at the same time devalue contemporary movements. This imitation of Christianity is not understood as "*imitatio Christi*," but rather as an attempt to usurp the place of Christ. But how could Girard make this distinction? This was only possible on basis of the distinction between a good and a bad imitation of a Christian concern, thus on the basis of the binary opposition authentic/only mimetic. And here, we can clearly see again why the few remainders of authentic desire are so relevant: by keeping the possibility of an authentic or good desire, Girard kept a distinction between a good, authentically "Christian" and a bad, only imitative, "anti-Christian," mimetic desire[33] that allowed him to keep an intermediate position: against a "pagan," elitist Nietzschean critique of Christianity and against leftist, revolutionary tendencies.

An early reviewer of the English translation of *Deceit, Desire, and the Novel* ended with the words:

> To be made uneasy by this thorough analysis is probably one of the consequences of the pervasiveness of the disease, which Girard calls contagious, and a testimony to the psychological and metaphysical acumen of the author of this fascinating book.[34]

The opposite is true: it is exactly Girard's combination of totalizing mimetic desire and gaining/preserving a remainder of an authentic desire, or, more formally, the distinction between a good authenticity and a bad imitation (the very same distinction that became a core issue of Derrida's deconstruction, started only a few years after *Deceit, Desire, and the Novel*), that is significant for his theory.[35] And this combination is, as I have tried to argue, perhaps the most relevant reason for the main theoretical contradictions and both epistemological and political problems of Girard's nevertheless impressive mimetic theory.

Notes

1. Preliminary stages and earlier alternative concepts of mimetic desire were already developed, among others, by Hegel, Nietzsche, Kojève, Lacan, and Sartre. Regarding parallel motives in Kojève, Lacan, and Girard see Mikkel Borch-Jacobsen, *Lacan: The Absolute Master* (Stanford: Stanford University Press, 1991), 254.

2. "Mimetic desire, even when bad, is intrinsically good, in the sense that far from being merely imitative in a small sense, it's the opening out of oneself." René Girard, "Violence, Difference,

Sacrifice: A Conversation with René Girard. Interview by R. Adams," *Religion and Literature* 25.2 (1993): 24.

3. René Girard, *Evolution and Conversion: Dialogues on the Origin of Culture*, with Pierpaolo Antonello and João Cezar de Castro Rocha (New York: Continuum, 2007), 163.

4. His early publications before 1959 do not provide clear evidence for a pointed elitist and antidemocratic worldview and one wonders if political circumstances in that very time had influenced Girard's antiegalitarian escalation. And it is striking that exactly when Girard was describing the French Revolution as the starting point of a demonized egalitarian tendency, a revolution against France was at its peak: the Algerian war for independence. I have no evidence that Girard was influenced by this war, but I wonder what would happen if one applied his notion of mimetic desire, as he developed it in 1959, to the simultaneous process of decolonization. In this case, the colonial power France could easily be understood as "external model" for the colonized subjects, and one could easily blame anticolonialism as a process motivated by mimetic desire, as replacement of the external through an internal mediation, which would necessarily lead to increasing violence. At least, it is difficult to understand how his early notion of mimetic desire could provide support for decolonization.

5. René Girard, "Pride and Passion in the Contemporary Novel," *Yale French Studies* 24 (1959): 3.

6. René Girard, *Deceit, Desire, and the Novel: Self and Other in Literary Structure*, trans. Yvonne Freccero (Baltimore: Johns Hopkins University Press, 1965), 9.

7. Girard, *Deceit, Desire, and the Novel*, 87.

8. Girard's critique of idealism and romanticism is structurally similar to Christian-inspired critique of Gnosticism and attempts to read German idealism and Marxism as new forms of Gnosticism. At the very end of *Deceit, Desire, and the Novel*, for example, Girard claimed: "But the only authentic epoché is never mentioned by modern philosophers; it is always victory over desire, victory over Promethean pride" (300). Regarding attempts to read German idealism as Gnosticism, see Luca Di Blasi, *Der Geist in der Revolte: Der Gnostizismus und seine Wiederkehr in der Postmoderne* (Munich: Fink, 2002).

9. Girard, *Deceit, Desire, and the Novel*, 101–4.

10. Girard, *Deceit, Desire, and the Novel*, 285.

11. N. Luhmann provided a much more positive reading of the increasing reflexivity of desire: "In physical interplay one discovers that, beyond one's own desire and its fulfilment, one also desires the other's desire and thus learns that the other wishes to be desired. This makes it impossible for 'selflessness' to provide a foundation for one's actions and the form they take; rather the strength of one's own wish becomes the measure of what one is able to give." See Niklas Luhmann, *Love as Passion: The Codification of Intimacy* (Cambridge, Massachusetts: Harvard University Press, 1986), 28.

12. Girard, *Deceit, Desire, and the Novel*, 272–73.

13. Girard, *Deceit, Desire, and the Novel*, 273, 282.

14. Giorgio Agamben and Gilles Deleuze, *Bartleby, la formula della creazione* (Macerata: Quodlibet, 1993).

15. Slavoj Žižek, *The Parallax View* (Cambridge: MIT Press, 2006), 62.

16. Luca Di Blasi, "Less Than Nihilism," in *Nihilism and the State of Israel: New Critical Perspectives*, ed. Nitzan Lebovic and Roy Ben-Shai (London: Bloomsbury Academic, 2014), 35–49.

17. Girard, *Evolution and Conversion*, 59.

18. Girard, *Deceit, Desire, and the Novel*, 19.

19. Girard, *Deceit, Desire, and the Novel*, 294.

20. Girard, *Deceit, Desire, and the Novel*, 16. Already in "Pride and Passion in the Contemporary Novel," he criticized the "mirage of divine autonomy": Girard, "Pride and Passion," 6.

21. Girard, *Evolution and Conversion*, 45.

22. Girard, *Deceit, Desire, and the Novel*, 294.

23. Girard, *Evolution and Conversion*, 172.

24. Nietzsche is in many senses the main rival of Girard. Girard's later distinction between Satan and Christ is the perfect inversion of Nietzsche's distinction between Dionysus and the Crucified. See, e.g., René Girard, "Dionysus versus the Crucified," *MLN* 99.4 (1984): 816–35.

25. See Raymund Schwager, *Bekehrung und Authentizität: Bernard Lonergan und René Girard* (Universität Innsbruck, 2000); available from http://www.uibk.ac.at/theol/leseraum/texte/29.html.

26. Girard, *Deceit, Desire, and the Novel*, 38.

27. Girard, *Deceit, Desire, and the Novel*, 17.

28. For a completely different notion of conversion that intensifies a split instead of providing the slightest possibility of a way out see Luca Di Blasi, "One Divided by Another: Split and Conversion in Pasolini's *San Paolo*," in *The Scandal of Self-Contradiction: Pasolini's Multistable Subjectivities, Geographies, and Traditions*, ed. Luca Di Blasi, Manuele Gragnolati, and Christoph Holzhey (Berlin: Turia+Kant, 2012), 189–207.

29. Girard described himself as "centrist" and "anti-crowd." Girard, *Evolution and Conversion*, 23.

30. Peter Sloterdijk is a current example of one holding such an "elitist" position. In his essay on Girard, he missed exactly this point, when he identified mimetic desire with resentment and limited it to the loser. See Peter Sloterdijk, "Erwachen im Reich der Eifersucht. Notiz zu René Girards anthropologischer Sendung," in René Girard, *Ich sah den Satan vom Himmel fallen wie einen Blitz: Eine kritische Apologie des Christentums*, trans. Elisabeth Mainberger-Ruh (Munich: Hanser, 2002), 248. On Slotedijk's misreading of Girard, and more generally, on the peculiar nature of a resentment of the privileged, see also Luca Di Blasi, *Der weiße Mann. Ein Anti-Manifest*, (Bielefeld: transcript, 2013), especially 41–49.

31. René Girard, *I See Satan Fall Like Lightning* (Maryknoll, MD: Orbis, 2001).

32. Girard, *I See Satan Fall*, 180–81.

33. Regarding this positive imitation, see René Girard, *Battling to the End: Conversations with Benoit Chantre* (East Lansing: Michigan State University Press, 2009), especially 109–10. The specificity of Girard's conservative way is more visible if we compare it to poststructuralism: here as well, we find a totalizing gesture, but one that does not permit a way out. In consequence, this "totality" transforms, becomes a "not-all." Thereby, mimetic desire (or immanence) appears no longer as purely negative, but really as ambivalent. At least from a poststructuralist or postmodern view, it is exactly the possibility to get (or recover) an authentic desire beyond mimetic desire that permitted Girard to stop halfway and to maintain a negative understanding of mimetic desire.

34. Ralph Harper, "*Deceit, Desire, and the Novel* by René Girard," *Journal of Religion* 47.1 (1967): 54.

35. See for instance Jacques Derrida, *L'écriture et la différence* (Paris: Éditions du Seuil, 1967).

On Girard's Biblical Realism

René Girard's studies of scapegoating, ritual, and sacrifice claim that Judeo-Christian Scripture demystifies, or reveals to us fully, the violent foundations of human institutions and the centrality of victimage in our history, psychology, and social organization. Although this thesis entails religious and anthropological considerations, it also evokes some of the broadest questions that literary scholars face—namely regarding what a book can do, how reading and criticism operate in the world, and what they have to do with positive transformations of human life on the largest scale. In the following pages I would like to revisit the intersection of Girard's literary and anthropological/religious claims, and in particular his conception of realism, which appears most prominently in *Deceit, Desire, and the Novel* but also play a role in Girard's later treatments of literature and film. At stake are his claims for the effectivity of realism, that is, for a notion of realism that undergirds his readings of Judeo-Christian Scripture and ground his commitment to their potential for understanding and overcoming victimage.

In focusing on Girard's arguments concerning the power of Scripture—or what has been called his epistemology of the Bible—I focus on the part of his corpus that has evoked by far the most controversy.[1] Indeed Girard himself has said that perhaps 99.5 percent of the resistance to his work derives from his use of religion.[2] Considering the stunning scope of Girard's claim for the power of books, and thus for literary scholars, the goal here is to ask whether Girard's claims for the power of Scripture are problematic, not specifically because of his focus on the effectivity of religious texts for overcoming the scapegoat logic that, he argues, has produced so much catastrophe in human history; but instead because he deploys a particular notion of realism. This realism involves what might be called "textual effectivity" and what Girard himself calls "truth."

That is, for Girard, realism seems to be not only a matter of a mimetic reflection of the world in a book, and not only a matter of a literary style. Instead realism verges on what intervenes in the world, for instance in the form of the flesh-and-blood truth of Christ as the bodily, real, actual, end to a sacrificial logic. The fleshly, material aspect of realism is what is here significant. This is not a realist form of representation in a conventional sense; it is a realism that bursts through the representative to the actual. My argument, however, is that Girard's appropriation of this concept of realism in a singular fashion toward the overcoming of sacrifice reflects a literary insufficiency in his reading of the scriptural text, although it provides a distinct anthropological yield for Girard's projects on violence. That is, Girard ascribes to Judeo-Christian Scripture a textual effectivity that in fact has no guarantee; he elides, in other words, the ungovernability of effects, an ungovernability that would be the true hallmark of a literary approach. I will thus suggest that in Girard's monolithic focus on the realism of Scripture regarding mimesis, scapegoating, and a postscapegoating logic, he eclipses other literary elements, which in turn represent other theological, readerly, aesthetic, and even worldly possibilities.

For although Girard claimed in a 1996 interview, "I don't regard myself as a literary critic," his notion of textual effectivity is in his own corpus tied up with a formulation of realism that is inseparable from Girard's literary provenance.[3] And yet literariness is above all a matter of overdetermination, multiple possibilities, and an excess of interpretability; in that way it mimics the overdetermination and multiple possibilities of reality itself. Girard's realism, however, comes up short literarily because it on one hand asserts an effectivity of Scripture but on the other restricts the range of effects to one trajectory alone. In other words, the literary consideration of realism is not literary enough, in tethering realism to one sole effectivity, namely that of salvation. This claim is in one sense not very different from criticisms other literary scholars have made of Girard's teleological reading; my focus, however, on how realism is the site of Girard's deployment of a literary notion toward his religious-anthropological agenda.[4]

Realism

In *Deceit, Desire, and the Novel* Girard formulates a concept of realism that goes beyond the notion of verisimilitude in representation toward a dimension of event and effectivity. In a Heideggerian vein, Girard evokes the notion of an event of disclosure. Indeed what is at stake is precisely the disclosive and eventlike nature of truth—as indicated by the book's French title, *Mensonge romantique et vérité romanesque*. The lie (*mensonge*) to which Girard's title refers is the Romantic notion of individual, spontaneous desire. He argues that the novel, as it unfolds, in effect discloses that this is, in fact, our notion of desire and, moreover, that it is a lie. For Girard, the novelistic truth (*vérité romanesque*) opposed to that lie is the mediated character of desire, the way in which desire is not spontaneous but always mediated and ultimately mimetically conditioned.

The novel is therefore realist insofar as it depicts the truth about desire, but also in another sense, that is, regarding the effectivity of that depiction. That is, for Girard the more important sense of realism pertains to how the novel depicts and thereby unmasks this truth about desire, thereby breaking out of the plane of representation, and critiquing the notion of spontaneous desire that it represents. Hence for Girard novels could be said to engage in what Robert Alter, Frank Kermode, and Chris Fleming call—with respect to biblical texts—"auto-critique."[5] In this mode they are reflective and even active, doing something, namely, unmasking and thus breaking out of the mimetic logic they instantiate. The auto-critical aspect of the novel unmasks the truth of desire, breaching the plane of the page in revealing to us the conditions of our own psychic and worldly lives.

In an article criticizing Erich Auerbach as inadequately theorizing the role of mediation in his concept of mimesis, Girard describes in more detail how realism here means a breaking out of a representational plane and into

the worldly dimension as such in the form of truth. In the context of dis-
agreeing with Auerbach's reading of Peter's betrayal of Jesus in the Gospels,
Girard compares the Gospel story to the masterpieces of European literature
and again refers to the way in which realism breaks into truth. He writes,
"The greatest literary achievements of Western culture—Dante, Shakespeare, Molière, Dostoevsky, Joyce—are not necessarily realistic in the sense
of Balzac, but they are more real or, why not, more true, in their ability to
break out of scapegoat representation."[6] These lines are significant in several
ways for my argument. In Girard's definition, these literary works are not just
realist in their representations of scapegoating, but they are themselves real
or true because they do or perform a breaking out of representation. What is
more, in breaking open the concealment of the mechanisms of scapegoating
in their representations, they engage in auto-critique, which means that they
break through representation and through the division of book and world,
and are thus more than realist; they are real, effective. They make something
happen, they even are a happening. This happening is truth is for Girard,
in accord with both a Hegelian and Heideggerian tradition in which truth
is a matter of the effectivity and unfolding of events rather than of correspondence between language and reality. Realism is therefore not a matter of
mimetic representation, but of exceeding the textual plane of representation
and constituting instead a worldly disclosure, as an event.

In his 1975 review of *Violence and the Sacred*, Hayden White explains
Girard's understanding of the truth of literature, making an accusation
against Girard that echoes Girard's criticism of Auerbach, namely that Girard
neglects the role of mediation. White argues that for Girard, "All the great
literary texts . . . say precisely what they mean. They need no interpretation."[7]
In other words, the novels depict an unmediated truth of the mediated and
displaced career of desire. Literature, in White's portrayal of Girard, therefore "can only speak directly about its true object," in contrast to religion,
which "can never speak directly about its true object, for its power resides
in its concealment of the social function of religion itself."[8] Literature is in
effect free to represent directly the mechanics of desire, because it precisely
does not have the social function that religion does. Insofar as religious ritual
serves as a covert way to channel violence, it cannot show itself as doing so
if the channeling function is to remain effective.[9] In this Girard is a theorist of plot; there is no aesthetic nor stylistic interest here, for the interest is

ultimately anthropological—to unmask the mechanics of desire, as opposed, for instance, to crafting a literary work of language.

What is more, as White explains, Girard's understanding of realism is precisely where his literary criticism fails to reflect on the mediations that complicate its own relationship anthropology. That is, Girard claims both a scientificity and an effectivity in the straightforward revelations by literature of the mechanisms of desire and rivalry. He declares that he has developed a scientific approach to the social implications of his literary study, where such an approach overlooks the interpretive and readerly elements of social science—the mediated quality of scientific knowledge, the way in which it is also formed according to narrative requirements, for instance. Thus White's question in this context becomes whether the discontinuities between literature and society, interpretation and science, and plot and effectivity, are so easily smoothed over in the anthropological yield of Girard's deployment of his concept of literary realism.

Happening and the Book

Girard's later analyses of Judeo-Christian Scripture recapitulate his early insights of *Deceit, Desire, and the Novel* regarding a critical event that takes place in and by means of a book. For Girard, as I have suggested, what happens in great books is the unmasking of a logic, an unmasking that therefore auto-critically disrupts the plane of representation of the book and thus erupts into our worldly events. With regard to the novel it is the mimetic logic of desire that is unmasked. With Scripture, however, it is the unmasking and breaking out of scapegoat logic that is at stake, again producing an exodus from that logic not only within a book but in the world at large. The performative anthropological yield is thus rather more dramatic. The Bible, according to Girard, exposes the violent underpinnings of human relations, and takes the side of the victim, thereby exposing the injustice of scapegoating—and thereby annulling it. That is, in presenting the victim as innocent, and perhaps even more important, as the victim of other human beings—and precisely not a victim of God—Scripture performs the revelation of the sacrificial mechanism. In this procedure of demystification it desacralizes sacrifice and effects a transition to a postsacrificial logic. Although the term "realism" is far less prominent in Girard's discussion of Scripture, the event-like effectivity at issue is the same. The connection between realism and truth is the basis for Girard's claim that the Crucifixion in the Gospels is not above all a depiction of a sacrifice, and not an ultimate sacrifice in order to end all sacrifices, but instead is itself the end of sacrifice.

There is thus a happening at stake that reaches out of the representation on the biblical page. This is the key to the connection between Girard's claims for the realism of French novels and the hopes offered in his biblical studies of violence. The Bible does not just tell us something, it reveals— according to Girard for the first, most important, or most lucidly formulated time—the violence and victimage that underpin our social institutions. It is, to use his earlier term, "realist," in constituting an event and not just a mimetic representation of victimage. For in that revelation and especially in the exodus from sacrifice that the Crucifixion is, it intervenes in the world, in our midst and presence. This is an actual, historical, and, one might even say, material intervention in the world.

The importance of materiality in this respect illuminates a less obvious connection to Erich Auerbach, apart from the concept of mimesis that is central to both of them. In Auerbach's 1944 "Figura" essay he traces the history of the notion of *figura* and lingers over Tertullian's understanding of it in the second century. Auerbach highlights where Tertullian goes against the grain of any allegorical understanding of figura in Scripture. What is significant for Auerbach is that it is not a spiritualizing relationship between Hebrew and Christian Scripture, but a material one, an actual one. Girard's figural reading of Scripture seems at times to operate, in contrast, in a medieval fashion, namely on the basis of allegory. At other times, however, Girard's references seem to evoke the actual, material, historical figura that Auerbach examines in Tertullian. The events of Judah's offering himself in the place of Benjamin and Joseph forgiving all his brothers constitute a figura repeated when Jesus offers himself for all our sakes and the possibility of forgiveness of all our sins. The relation is here not only figural in Auerbach's sense. The events of Judah and Joseph historically make possible the event of Jesus, for Judah becomes the progenitor of Judaism and thus of Jesus himself. The relationships between the two stories are multiple: these are material and historical similarities, they provide a figura/fulfillment schema, and the first events make possible the second events. Girard elides the distinctions between these different relationships in his focus on the model of prefiguration and fulfillment with respect to Hebrew and Christian Scriptures. [10]

What precisely is the nature of the intervention of scripture in the material world, how does a textual effectivity enter the world as such? It seems for Girard on the one hand to be a matter of teaching. In view of the repetitions and imitations that Girard highlights at the biblical the scene of Peter's denial he writes, "The text ... teaches us something about the mimetic nature of desire and of human relations, something no other text ever taught." [11] His point is that the various scriptural representations of the scene show precisely how mimesis among people operates, teaches us this. At the same time, however, it seems for Girard to be that the Gospels do not teach so much as reveal to us something. Girard writes, "The gospels are the first texts in which this mechanism is fully revealed as a human and purely mimetic phenomenon." [12] This revelation is more than a teaching. It is for Girard the disclosive event that constitutes the truth of the Gospels.

Jesus, therefore, is a very special victim who refuses not only the vicious circle of mimetic violence but also the breaking of that circle through the mimetic violence of unanimous scapegoating. Regarding the relationship of sacrifice and victimization, social unity and victimization, the gospels spell out a truth that is nowhere else to be found. [13]

Here Scripture "spells out a truth," in an apparently unique fashion. Unlike the novels he analyzes in *Deceit, Desire, and the Novel*, which seem each to reveal the same phenomenon of mimetic desire, Girard claims that Scripture is the only place for this revelation. Literature has receded entirely from the scene despite the continued deployment of the notion of realism that Girard himself derived from his work on the French novel.

Even the terms "teaching" and "revealing," however, do not as terms evoke the kind of performative intervention that Girard ultimately wants to ascribe to Scripture. For Girard Scripture does not simply show and does not simply instruct; it is the possibility, in itself, of a world beyond violence. Indeed Girard describes in *Things Hidden Since the Foundation of the World* the peculiar kind of reading that he believes is happening with the Gospels. Girard in effect displaces agency from the reader to the text itself, such that it is not a matter of our reading of the Gospels, but of the happening of the Gospels themselves. He writes,

We can no longer believe that it is we who are reading the Gospels in the light of an ethnological, modern revelation. . . . We have to reverse this order. It is still the great Judaeo-Christian spirit that is doing the reading.[14]

Girard's displaces readerly subjectivity from human readers onto a "Judeo-Christian spirit" itself. In a philosophical vein we might ask whether the great Judeo-Christian spirit to which Girard refers acts in the same fashion as Hegel's absolute spirit, which the *Phenomenology of Spirit* suggests is not only described in its pages, but actually is supposed to be unfolding in the world by way of the *Phenomenology*. But this same comparison evokes the problem with claims of absolute textual effectivity: the mixed reception of Hegel has shown that there is no guarantee that absolute spirit will be recognized. Where Girard seems to evoke the absolute effectivity of Scripture, as the extreme of the realism he has described with respect to an unmasking that breaks into truth, then as with Hegel's *Phenomenology* we might ask about the guarantee that the event of scriptural revelation will succeed. If we were to take up Walter Benjamin's evocation of a Jewish notion that "every second was the small gateway in time through which the Messiah might enter," we could suggest that for Girard every page of Scripture is a place where the exodus from scapegoating is already happening.[15] And yet given the uncertainty of this effectivity, the messiah to whom Benjamin refers, who might enter our history in any moment, and for Girard who emerges out of every scriptural page, could in this respect turn into the messiah in Kafka, who comes and goes and makes no difference.[16]

Let me say more about the uncertainty of textual effectivity. With the notion of a Scripture that not only represents, but itself is the entrance into the world of the Judeo-Christian spirit and the messianic possibility of redemption, Girard thereby evokes the questions of the bounds of literary study for literary critics and scholars of texts: The text announces, reveals, or even performs or dramatizes; but what is the axis of intervention in the world? How does this intervention gain its proper audience? Where does it get its effectivity? Has the "exodus" from sacrifice already happened? What is the temporality of this exodus, since we can always put aside this object that is a book, or reread and open it again, or close it again? If Scripture must be read for the world-intervention to take place, what guarantees that it is read properly and thus that the intervention in the world is the one that the literary critic says it is? And what is the guarantee of its being understood, and not, for instance, misused?

Robert Alter and the Literary Girard

Despite the hope that Girard places in Scripture, the agency of the Bible in the world cannot, it seems, be guaranteed; its proper reception also not; and its effectivity is—and has been—wayward, violent, and persecutory. These might be effects of misreadings, misappropriations, and perversions of the revelation of Scripture, but they nonetheless belong to the history of the Scripture. The bare presence of the Scripture in our midst seems to provide no guarantee to its effectivity: in other words, there looks to be no risk on this earth of coming to a peaceful end with scapegoating, violence, and rivalry.

The present objection to Girard's considerations might be couched as a criticism that Girard's practice when it comes to Scripture is not literary enough, where literariness involves not the revelation of one single meaning but the possibility of multiple, perhaps even infinite, meanings. For Scripture is above all narrative, and thus it partakes of all the complications of narrative—as Robert Alter argues at length in his book *The Art of Biblical Narrative*. The art of the Bible is such that, like any art, it may offer certain interpretive possibilities or even messages, teachings, and demystifications, but without guarantee. The central reality of mimetic desire is, as Girard shows, indeed portrayed in Scripture, and thus I would agree that it is a "truth" in Girard's sense that is unmasked in Scripture. But the literary complexity of Scripture also exceeds this revelation of mimetic desire, victimage, and scapegoating, and reveals more about human relations than this.

We could compare, for instance, Alter's reading of the Joseph chapters of Genesis with Girard's.[17] While Girard's account is a stunning reading of the story as a turning point in human history with regard to the recognition of scapegoating, and Judah is properly rendered the real hero for his offer of self-sacrifice in the place of Benjamin—in which context Joseph exhibits an unprecedented capacity for forgiveness and reconciliation—nonetheless Girard's reading in my view does not give us the full literary scope of the Joseph story. For instance, where is a literary analysis of the narrator in Girard's scriptural exposition? Alter points out that the position of the narrator is crucial, even the omniscience of the biblical narrator. With regard to the Joseph chapters, Alter writes of the "purposeful reticence of this kind of narration."[18] In fact, Alter's study of the manifold narrative techniques in the story of Joseph uncovers the literary strategies that go in many directions, and to many ends. He investigates the range of narrative and writerly choices: for instance, withholding comment, flaunting an omniscient overview, montage of sources, repetition of thematic key words, reiteration of motifs, subtleties of dialogue. The change in Judah is in Alter's reading a revelation that "shake[s] Joseph" and provokes Joseph's revelation of himself to his brothers.[19]

In the literary reading, the stakes are not monolithic as they are for Girard. Hence for Alter the question is multifarious. He writes:

> What is it like, the biblical writers seek to know through their art, to be a human being with a divided consciousness, intermittently loving your brother but hating him even more, resentful or perhaps contemptuous of your father but also capable of the deepest filial regard, stumbling between disastrous ignorance and imperfect knowledge, fiercely asserting your own independence but caught in a tissue of events divinely contrived, outwardly a definite character and inwardly an unstable vortex of greed, ambition, jealousy, lust, piety, courage, compassion, and much more?[20]

Alter's reading of the story of Joseph and his brothers excludes none of the passions, desires, and literary moments that make up this part of the Hebrew Scripture. His literary reading examines each pause, each turn of phrase, each writerly choice, for its own contribution to the power of the narrative. His reading is thus more complete, in acknowledging the open-endedness and instability that Scripture reveals, along with the mechanisms of victimage. Girard must overlook or underplay the moments that do not conform to the reading of the story of Joseph that he proposes; this is theologically or anthropologically useful but literarily unsatisfying.[21] Hence Françoise Meltzer has argued that Girard evokes an ideological "communal inevitability" in which a basic character of human nature is asserted, whereas in fact he has produced the story of the human nature that he then believes to have found in his biblical investigations. Meltzer adds, "With Girard, any text will do—since it always 'means' the same thing," and "Girard's obsession with resolving differences and rivalry can only be accomplished by omissions and doublings." Of course not only within the literary unfolding of Scripture, but also in its reception, there are waywardness, ungovernability, and historicity that affect how it breaks through representation into truth in any particular time, place, and context. There is a wayward, ungovernable literary and worldly range of readings and historical effects that appear around Scripture. The scriptural texts in their very materiality stand for a foregone dispersion, diaspora, heterogeneity, miscommunication, and conflict. For Scripture is not ever there for us pure of reception, but is always placed and received. The Girardian claims for a biblical epistemology in this respect reduce the wild ungovernability of scriptural potential into one dimension only— namely the dimension of the exodus from scapegoating and the revelation of the mechanisms of victimage. The yield for a monolithic anthropology of scapegoating is thereby high, but the literary and historical possibilities are thereby dramatically reduced.

Girard and the Hebrew Scripture

In closing we return to the broader questions about the ungovernability of literary effects and the implications of this ungovernability for Girardian biblical epistemology and auto-critique. Girard draws out neglected or underread moments of mimeticism in the Scripture in order to argue for its revelatory and transformative character with respect to scapegoating. But in literary terms, I suggest that Girard underreads other biblical elements in order to strengthen a monolithic focus on mimeticism—which as a humanitarian project is understandable, but as a literary project is untenable. For in Girard's anthropological impulse, he in my view actually loses much of the literary or aesthetic yield of Scripture, not least because the Bible contains more than what Girard states—more words, more stories, more figures, more possibilities. If Scripture is also a literary work, then there is a logic to it—to every line, to every word even, and to its flow and sequencing. For instance, Girard's reading of Joseph and his brothers focuses on brotherly rivalry, sacrificial attempts, and ultimately on change on Judah's part and forgiveness on Joseph's; it is an illuminating reading. But Alter's reading of Joseph and his brothers, for instance, includes the apparent scriptural detour through the stories of Judah and Tamar, and Joseph and Potiphar's wife—which in the Girardian analysis (and the analysis of many biblical scholars) do not seem to fit well into Genesis. The story of Judah and Tamar is a particularly glaring interruption in the Joseph sequence.

Unlike Girard, however, Alter's literary focus on words, phrases, and scenes multiplies the themes of the story. Alter takes his cues from midrashic exegetes and assumes that the biblical text is "an intricately interconnected unity."[22] But beyond that midrashic assumption Alter argues for a narrative unity, a literary integrity, and renders the story of Judah and Tamar utterly comprehensible within the narrative's own terms. Alter—also indebted in his own ways to Auerbach—suggests that the Scripture contains an "indeterminacy of meaning, especially in regard to motive, moral character, and psychology."[23] Girard, on the other hand, eliminates that indeterminacy. The literary elements of the Bible—the necessity of every line, every word choice, the flow and sequencing of elements—are not for Girard part of its import. He reduces the Scripture to one effect: the unmasking of scapegoat logic. He thereby surrenders its literary and even theological complexity. Alter's detailed analyses of biblical narrative, in contrast, argue precisely for the authorial brilliance of the Hebrew Bible, whereas Girard's analyses argue for the bare, disruptive truth of exodus from Sacrifice contained in the Scripture. Just as the characters in a novel are not simply there, but are authorially presented in a crafted fashion, and just as the narratives of the novels involve demystifications in precisely how they are written, likewise the scriptural personages are literarily presented, and the demystifications that operate in Scripture are narratively constructed.

This takes us to a question of any literary critical practice that concerns itself with politics, society, and "making a difference." How can books make the world better? How can they be read to "proper effect"? Girard's single focus on scriptural moments of forgiveness and renunciation of violence renders the Bible less literary, which is to say reduces the overdetermination that makes it relevant in more than one way. What is more, with regard to worldly effectivity, the monolithic focus on the revelation of mimetic and scapegoating mechanisms also underestimates the ungovernable, wild possibilities of worldly reconciliations. Does the setting aside of violence take only one form, and is it necessarily by way of the revelation of the logics of victimage and scapegoating? Or are there many different possibilities here?

There is, for instance, forgiveness, which as Hannah Arendt describes it disconnects the past from the present, thereby allowing for a different future.[24] There are, also other, less emphatic, ways that people set aside violence—for instance, in the face of distractions, better things to do, or even instead just in settling instead for holding a deep but quiet grudge. It is obviously difficult to consider these as programmatic possibilities for a way past victimage, and they are not as perfectly satisfactory as forgiveness as a solution. But then again the world could do worse than holding a few more quiet grudges, or getting distracted with better things to do. Scripture even presents some of these other solutions, in all their finitude and fragility. A less anthropological and more literary approach to the biblical reading multiplies the possibilities for finding in Scripture a realism that breaks through toward truth; but this requires precisely a literary dedication to the multiplicity of scriptural potential—precisely not the reproduction through mimesis of one dynamic throughout, but instead a densely layered, multidirectional possibility of literary epistemology.

Notes

1. Chris Fleming, *René Girard: Violence and Mimesis* (Cambridge: Polity, 2004), 114.

2. Thomas Bertonneau, "The Logic of the Undecidable: An Interview with René Girard," *Paróles Gelées* 5.1 (1987): 9.

3. Markus Müller, "Interview with René Girard," *Anthropoetics* 2.1 (1996), http://www.anthropoetics.ucla.edu/AP0201/interv.htm.

4. See, for instance, Françoise Meltzer, "A Response to René Girard's Reading of Salomé," *New Literary History* 15.2 (1984): 325–32.

5. Fleming, *René Girard*, 123; Robert Alter and Frank Kermode, *The Literary Guide to the Bible* (Cambridge: Harvard University Press, 1990), 24.

6. René Girard, "Peter's Denial and the Question of Mimesis," *Notre Dame English Journal* 14.3 (1982): 187–88, emphasis added.

7. Hayden White, "Ethnological 'Lie' and Mythical 'Truth,'" *Diacritics* 8.1 (1978): 5.

8. White, "Ethnological Lie," 5.

9. Girard, "Peter's Denial," 186.

10. See Erich Auerbach, "Figura," in *Scenes from the Drama of European Literature* (Minneapolis: University of Minnesota Press, 1959), 11–78.

11. Girard, "Peter's Denial," 187.

12. Girard, "Peter's Denial," 187.

13. Girard, "Peter's Denial," 186.

14. René Girard, *Things Hidden Since the Foundation of the World*, research undertaken in collaboration with Jean-Michel Oughourlian and Guy Lefort, trans. Stephen Nann and Michael Metteer (Stanford: Stanford University Press, 1987), 177.

15. Walter Benjamin, "On the Concept of History," in *Selected Writings*, vol. 4, ed. Howard Eiland and Michael W. Jennings (Cambridge: Belknap Press of Harvard University Press, 2003), 397.

16. James Martel, "The Messiah Who Comes and Goes: Franz Kafka on Redemption, Conspiracy and Continuity," *Theory and Event* 12.3 (2009), n.p.

17. There are two main sources for this: Robert Alter, "Joseph and His Brothers," *Commentary* 70.5 (1980): 59–69; and Alter, *The Art of Biblical Narrative* (New York: Basic Books, 1981), 155–77.

18. Alter, *Biblical Narrative*, 158.

19. Alter, *Biblical Narrative*, 175.

20. Alter, *Biblical Narrative*, 176.

21. Meltzer, "Response to Girard's Salomé," 328–29.

22. See Alter, *Biblical Narrative*, 11.

23. See Alter, *Biblical Narrative*, 12.

24. Hannah Arendt, *The Human Condition* (Chicago: University of Chicago Press, 1958), 243–47.

Creative Renunciation

The Spiritual Heart of *Deceit, Desire, and the Novel*

eceit, Desire, and the Novel is a masterpiece of Christian spirituality. This thesis might surprise if we just look at the reception that this book found immediately after its publication. It was not theologians or church people who praised this book but Lucien Goldmann, a Marxist philosopher and sociologist. When Goldmann founded in 1961 the Centre de sociologie de la littérature in Brussels he referred to Karl Marx, George Lukács, and the young René Girard—who had just published his first book—as the theoretical pillars on which he based his new-founded sociology of literature research group.[1] Goldmann summarized the religious thesis that concludes Girard's book in the following way: "For Girard, the novelist has left the world of degradation and rediscovered authenticity, vertical transcendence, at the moment he writes his work. This is why he thinks that most great novels end with a conversion of the hero to his vertical transcendence."[2] Goldmann, however, does not share Girard's view and sides with Lukács in this regard, who rejects any possibility of returning to vertical transcendence: "The ultimate conversion of Don Quixote or Julien Sorel is not, as Girard believes, a discovery of authenticity, vertical transcendence, but simply an awareness of the vanity, the degraded character not only of the earlier search, but also of any hope, of any possible search. That is why it is an end and not a beginning."[3]

The last sentence of this quotation marks most strongly Goldmann's opposition to Girard, who claimed that "every novelistic conclusion is a beginning."[4] Goldmann also understood Girard's insight that mimetic rivalries govern human beings only as the expression of the capitalist period in human history. He was not willing to accept these insights as the expression of a much more general anthropology.[5] Girard responded with his essay "The Mimetic Desire of Paolo and Francesca" (1963), showing how Augustine and Dante reveal the same structures of desire as the great novelists of the modern era and how the fathers of the church criticized idolatrous forms of monetary fetishism.[6]

Girard's first book highlights conversion as the precondition of the masterpieces of the great novelists. Cervantes, Stendhal, Flaubert, Proust, and Dostoyevsky overcame their own entanglements in mimetic rivalries and their seeking of death as the meaning of life, all of which follow from metaphysical desire, by letting their own prideful egos die. Metaphysical desire is the result of an extreme escalation of rivalry that turns objects and rivals into idols and that seeks death as the ultimate and insurmountable obstacle.[7] Metaphysical desire takes root in a paradoxical entanglement of mimetic desire and religious longing. Every human attempt at self-divinization results ultimately in the divinization of the other because only the approval of the other can really assure us of our own divine status. This "double idolatry of self and other," however, leads necessarily to rivalry and hatred: "The more desperately we seek to worship ourselves and to be good 'individualists,' the more compelled we are to worship our rivals in a cult that turns to hatred."[8] All our attempts to reach divine status by ourselves end in seeking death as the most inaccessible obstacle. What starts as self-divinization ends as enslavement by death.

The great novelists, however, not only narrate this mimetically generated seeking of death. They also deal with death in those chapters where they focus on the death of their heroes. And here we discover suddenly a type of death that is not a nihilistic death as the result of metaphysical desire but a death that results in resurrection, enabling these authors to write their masterpieces: "The unity of novelistic conclusions consists in the renunciation of metaphysical desire. The dying hero repudiates his mediator. . . . Repudiation of the mediator implies renunciation of divinity, and this means renouncing pride. . . . In renouncing divinity the hero renounces slavery."[9]

Girard claims in this book that the conversion he discovered in the great novels is not only an "aesthetic experience" but also a "religious" one.[10] He goes so far as to claim that he does not see a real difference in this regard between Dostoyevsky, a Christian thinker, and the agnostic writer Proust. A verse in the Gospel of John illustrates this thesis perfectly well: "Unless a grain of wheat falls into the earth and dies, it remains just a single grain; but if it dies, it bears much fruit" (John 12:24). Dostoyevsky uses this verse as an epigraph for his book *The Brothers Karamazov* and turns to it in several of its episodes. But Proust, too, alludes to this verse when he reflects on how sickness brought forward his creative work. Girard quotes the following passage: "When sickness, like a harsh spiritual director, caused me to die to the social world, it did me a good service for if the seed does not die after it is sown it will remain alone and will not bear much fruit."[11] Girard concludes that this verse "could serve as an epigraph for all novelistic conclusions."[12] This is one of the clearest expressions of Girard's religious point of view.

But we can find some more hidden traces of Girard's spiritual attitude, too. In a very interesting passage Girard summarizes his view of the novelistic conversion visible in all the great conclusions: "When he renounces the deceptive divinity of pride, the hero frees himself from slavery and finally grasps the truth about his unhappiness. There is no distinction between this renunciation and the creative renunciation. It is a victory over metaphysical desire that transforms a romantic writer into a true novelist."[13] The expression that deserves our special attention is as paradoxical as the verse from the Gospel of John: "creative renunciation." It was coined by the French philosopher and mystic Simone Weil. Girard does not mention Weil in his first book, but an interview with Christian de Maussion from 1987 tells us that he read Weil during the time he was working on this book.[14] If we read Weil's *Waiting for God*—the book in which we find the expression "creative renunciation"—we discover important parallels between Weil and Girard.

One indication may be seen in their shared appreciation of Proust, an author who played a key role in Girard's reflections on conversion and whom Weil praised for his "subtle analyses" of love.[15] But there are more striking parallels. Both Girard and Weil differentiate in a very similar way between first-rate authors and second-rate authors.[16] Girard distinguishes between novelists whose pride has died and romantic writers who idolize their apparent autonomous selfhood. Weil makes a similar distinction, claiming that only renunciation leads to first-rate art: "Even in art and science, though second-class work, brilliant or mediocre, there is an extension of the self; work of the very highest order, true creation, means self-loss."[17] In his introduction to a 1962 collection of essays on Proust, Girard uses Weil's distinction to express his insight into novelistic conversion: "*Jean Santeuil* and *Remembrance of Things Past* illustrate Simone Weil's distinction between those works of art which remain second rate, however brilliant they may be, because they do nothing but 'enrich' their author's personality, and true masterpieces, which originate from an impoverishment, a mutilation of the unauthentic self."[18]

Weil's emphasis on renunciation has a deeply religious meaning, too. Like Girard she insists on the religious nature of great art: "All art of the highest order is religious in essence."[19] According to Weil, it is God himself who has inspired great art: "God has inspired every first-rate work of art, though its subject may be utterly and entirely secular; he has not inspired any of the others."[20] If we examine how Weil relates great art to God, we realize the deeper meaning of her term "creative renunciation." Great art that stems from renunciation and self-loss imitates God's way of creation that consists primarily in renunciation: "On God's part creation is not an act of self-expansion but of restraint and renunciation. . . . God permitted the existence of things distinct from himself and worth infinitely less than himself. But through this creative act he denied himself, as Christ has told us to deny ourselves. God denied himself for our sakes in order to give us the possibility of denying ourselves for him."[21]

God's "creative renunciation" enables us to love our neighbor and also the order and the beauty of the world. This renunciation inspires great art, too. Only when we give up our self-centeredness are we able to open up to others in a loving way and to what is real and eternal.[22] Like Girard, Weil knows that we cannot love ourselves in an egoistical and self-divinizing way. Whenever we try to do that we end up as the slaves of idolatry, as the worshippers of the "collective."[23] The only way out of this dangerous path is, according to Weil, the imitation of God's creative renunciation. Only through "decreation"— the imitation of God's creative renunciation—can we overcome idolatry.[24] This imitation comes again close to Girard's positive mimesis, the imitation of Jesus Christ that does not lead us into the "trap of rivalries in which we are ensnarled more and more."[25]

By comparing Girard with Weil we also realize some differences between these two eminent spiritual thinkers. Whereas Weil reached out broadly to other religions, even beginning to build a bridge to the East, Girard has tended to confine himself until recently to the Judeo-Christian tradition, or even to Christianity alone.[26] This tendency is already visible in his first book, where he says that "the Christian symbolism is universal for it *alone* is able to give form to the experience of the novel."[27] In a later article he very openly talks about the novelistic conversion that we can find at the spiritual center of his first book, connecting it to Dante, Augustine, and the disciples in the Gospels. This very explicit unfolding of his Christian conviction reveals what Girard addressed more indirectly in "The Conclusion" of his first book. In his most recent book, *Battling to the End*, Girard expresses most openly his true agenda that started with "The Conclusion": "Since the beginning of the 'novelistic conversion' in *Deceit, Desire, and the Novel*, all of my books have been more or less explicit apologies of Christianity" (xv).

Girard justly distanced himself from Weil's harsh criticism of Judaism. This was surely one of the reasons why he did not want to be identified with her too much. But I think Weil's work can help to broaden Girard's perspective beyond Judaism and Christianity because it is truly "a great Revelation" that shares with the Bible the emphasis on renunciation and on decreation.[28] Weil built a bridge between West and East by turning toward Asian religions. There is a possible opening in this direction also in Girard's first book. After his description of genuine conversion as the death to pride, he refers to a traditional Asian tale: "The conclusions of all the novels are reminiscent of an oriental tale in which the hero is clinging by his finger-tips to the edge of a cliff; exhausted, the hero finally lets himself fall into the abyss. He expects to smash against the rocks below but instead he is supported by the air: the law of gravity is annulled."[29]

Leo Lefebure, a theologian familiar with Girard's mimetic theory as well as with Asian religions, refers to this passage to show how this type of renunciation or letting go comes close to practices of Buddhist meditation.[30] Girard himself points to certain parallels between the biblical revelation and Asian traditions in one of his more recent books, *Sacrifice* (2011). Creative renunciation as discussed by Weil and Girard is also part of the Muslim tradition. Reza Shah-Kazemi, a Muslim scholar, understands the need to renounce self-deification and pride in a way that is very close to Weil and Girard. Shah-Kazemi shows how true compassion flows from a "proper awareness of reality," by a reaching out to God that becomes only possible by giving up our self-centeredness: "Self-effacement is the *conditio sine qua non* of Self-realization."[31] Ultimately the realization of God's true Selfhood enables us to overcome our pride and to become humble: "Self-effacement is the consequence of true Self-realization. When the subjective core of individuality is effaced, there can be nothing to which pride can attach itself: with the effacement of individuality, there is the uprooting of pride, and the consummation of a humility that is as ineradicable as the knowledge upon which it is based is indubitable."[32]

Let me come to a final point. In Girard's later article on the "novelistic conversion," he makes the claim that his first book challenged fundamentally the thesis that the work of an author has nothing to do with his or her life: "When I was writing about Proust, it was already fashionable to say that Marcel the narrator is a pure invention of the novelist, that the art of a writer has nothing to do with his life. This is not true, of course."[33] After publishing his first book, Girard again and again emphasized the "existential" or "spiritual" form of autobiography that reveals a deeper connection between author and literary work.[34]

What Girard observes systematically in the great works of literature also takes on meaning for his own work. Just as the great novelists based their works on insights—obtained in a kind of conversion—into their own mimetic desire, Girard's mimetic theory, too, results from such an experience of conversion. The discovery of conversion among the great novelists of European literature coincided with Girard's own experience of conversion. He began to turn away from his own pride and to see himself as a puppet of his own mimetic desire. Just as with Dostoyevsky, this reversal was accompanied by a turning toward Christianity, as his intellectual work led him to a new understanding of the Gospels. From the age of ten to thirty-eight years, Girard was an agnostic, even siding with left-leaning atheists. He sympathized with the intellectual, revolutionary avant-garde. Girard's intense study of major novelistic authors eventually led him back, after decades of indifference, to the Christian faith and the Catholic Church.

At first, this conversion applied merely to his intellectual stance, but Girard eventually returned to the Catholic Church and began once again to practice his faith. He described the decisive moments of his conversion and how it led to "The Conclusion" of his first book in an interview in the mid-1990s.[35] Shortly after his intellectual conversion, which coincided with the writing of *Deceit, Desire, and the Novel*, Girard underwent treatment during Lent for an ultimately harmless, but worrisome, form of skin cancer on his forehead. The period of treatment and the resultant cure triggered his final conversion, which was sealed during the liturgies of the Easter Triduum. "I realized," Girard recalls, "that I had just . . . had an experience similar to that which I had just wanted to describe [in the case of the novelists]. The religious symbolism, which in the novelists is there in embryo, began to work in my own case, spontaneously bursting into flame."[36] Like the great novelists he studied, Girard finally renounced his pride, a conclusion that was also the beginning of his unfolding of mimetic theory, an anthropological apology for Christianity.

Notes

1. Lucien Goldmann, *Towards a Sociology of the Novel*, trans. Alan Sheridan (London: Tavistock Publications, 1975), 1–17. Cf. René Girard, *Evolution and Conversion: Dialogues on the Origin of Culture*, with Pierpaolo Antonello and João Cezar de Castro Rocha (New York: Continuum, 2007), 22. The original article "Marx, Lukacs, Girard et la sociologie du roman" was published in 1961 in the journal *Médiations*.

2. Goldmann, *Sociology of the Novel*, 4.

3. Goldmann, *Sociology of the Novel*, 5.

4. René Girard, *Deceit, Desire, and the Novel: Self and Other in Literary Structure*, trans. Yvonne Freccero (Baltimore: Johns Hopkins University Press, 1965), 297.

5. René Girard, *"To Double Business Bound": Essays on Literature, Mimesis, and Anthropology* (Baltimore: Johns Hopkins University Press, 1978), viii, 200; Girard, *Evolution and Conversion*, 33.

6. Girard, *"To Double Business Bound,"* 1–8; cf. René Girard, *Battling to the End: Conversations with Benoît Chantre*, trans. Mary Baker (East Lansing: Michigan State University Press, 2010), 59–60.

7. Girard, *Deceit, Desire, and the Novel*, 286.

8. René Girard, *I See Satan Fall Like Lightning*, trans. James G. Williams (Maryknoll, NY: Orbis Books, 2001), 11.

9. Girard, *Deceit, Desire, and the Novel*, 293–94.

10. Girard, *Deceit, Desire, and the Novel*, 310; cf. Girard, *Evolution and Conversion*, 181.

11. Girard, *Deceit, Desire, and the Novel*, 311.

12. Girard, *Deceit, Desire, and the Novel*, 312.

13. Girard, *Deceit, Desire, and the Novel*, 307; cf. Wolfgang Palaver, *René Girard's Mimetic Theory*, trans. Gabriel Borrud (East Lansing: Michigan State University Press, 2013), 220–21.

14. René Girard and Christian de Maussion, "Simone Weil vue par René Girard," *Cahiers Simone Weil* 11.3 (1988): 201–2; Girard, *Evolution and Conversion*, 150–51. Michel Serres has emphasized again and again how important Weil was for both of them at the beginning of their work: Michel Serres and Bruno Latour, *Conversations on Science, Culture, and Time*, trans. Roxanne Lapidus (Ann Arbor: University of Michigan Press, 1995), 35; Michel Serres, "Receiving René Girard into the Académie Française," in *For René Girard: Essays in Friendship and in Truth*, ed. Sandor Goodhart, Jørgen Jørgensen, Tom Ryba, and James G. Williams (East Lansing: Michigan State University Press, 2009), 14.

15. Simone Weil, *Waiting for God*, trans. Emma Craufurd (New York: Perennial Classics, 2001), 109.

16. Weil, *Waiting for God*, 92; Girard, *Deceit, Desire, and the Novel*, 5, 38, 309.

17. Weil, *Waiting for God*, 92.

18. René Girard, *Mimesis and Theory: Essays on Literature and Criticism, 1953–2005*, ed. R. Doran (Stanford: Stanford University Press, 2008), 67.

19. Simone Weil, *Gravity and Grace*, trans. Emma Crawford and Mario von der Ruhr (London: Routledge, 2002), 150–51.

20. Weil, *Gravity and Grace*, 107.

21. Weil, *Waiting for God*, 89.

22. Weil, *Waiting for God*, 100; see Ann W. Astell, "Saintly Mimesis, Contagion, and Empathy in the Thought of René Girard, Edith Stein, and Simone Weil," *Shofar* 22.2 (2004): 126–27.

23. Weil, *Gravity and Grace*, 144.

24. Weil, *Gravity and Grace*, 28–34; see Marie Cabaud Meaney, "Simone Weil and René Girard: Violence and the Sacred," *American Catholic Philosophical Quarterly* 84.3 (2010): 584.

25. Girard, *I See Satan Fall*, 15.

26. In 2002 Girard gave a series of lectures at the Bibliothèque nationale de France in Paris in which he undertook a mimetic reading of Hindu mythology. These lectures have since been published in English translation: René Girard, *Sacrifice*, trans. Matthew Pattillo and David Dawson (East Lansing: Michigan State University Press, 2011).

27. Girard, *Deceit, Desire, and the Novel*, 310, my emphasis.

28. Weil, *Waiting for God*, 89.

29. Girard, *Deceit, Desire, and the Novel*, 294.

30. Leo D. Lefebure, "Mimesis, Violence, and Socially Engaged Buddhism: Overture to a Dialogue," *Contagion* 3 (1996): 136.

31. Reza Shah-Kazemi, "Jesus in the Qur'an: Selfhood and Compassion—an Akbari Perspective," in *Sufism: Love and Wisdom*, ed. Jean-Louis Michon and Roger Gaetani (Bloomington, IN: World Wisdom, 2006), 226.

32. Shah-Kazemi, "Jesus in the Qur'an," 232.

33. René Girard, "Literature and Christianity: A Personal View," in this volume.

34. Cf. Girard, *Mimesis and Theory*, 56, 67; Girard, *"To Double Business Bound,"* 11–12; René Girard, *A Theater of Envy: William Shakespeare* (Oxford: Oxford University Press, 1991), 298, 339; and Palaver, *René Girard's Mimetic Theory*, 1–3.

35. René Girard, *Quand ces choses commenceront . . . Entretiens avec Michel Treguer* (Paris: Arléa, 1994), 190–94; *The Girard Reader* (New York: Crossroad, 1996), 283–88.

36. Girard, *Quand ces choses*, 180.

PART TWO

Mimetic Hermeneutics in History

The Desire to Be You

The Discourse of Praise for the Roman Emperor

Marco Formisano

Because Girard's approach is not simply a hermeneutical tool to be applied to certain texts, but has the nature of an anthropological insight with a claim of universal validity, it invites application to textual cultures, such as those of ancient Greece and Rome, which are beyond those that are Girard's own primary focus.[1] For its part, the discipline of classics is based on textual analysis and close reading, but is often rather impermeable to modern literary theories. Conversely, theorists frequently avoid discussing Greek and Latin texts, even though they offer an unexpected interpretive wealth, perhaps especially because of the gap in time that makes these texts appear both exemplary and at the same time surprisingly familiar. This chapter is thus intended to bridge a certain gap by representing the field of ancient literature within a volume devoted to the reception of René Girard's mimetic theory in contemporary literary studies.

A theory of mimetic desire turns out to be a fundamental perspective from which to read and analyze ancient texts for one reason in particular: within the Greek and Latin textual tradition, as is well known, the concept of imitation is absolutely central not only as aesthetic but also as ethical criterion. If it is true that the modern theorists (such as Girard, Adorno, or Ginzburg) who have discussed the concept of imitation cannot be seen as continuing ancient discussion on mimesis or *imitatio* as "imitation of nature,"[2] it should nonetheless not be forgotten that even in antiquity those terms were flexible and received different treatments. It will be not possible here to sketch the long history of the Greek term "mimesis," as discussed among others by Plato in the *Republic*, Aristotle in his *Poetics*, and the anonymous author of *On the Sublime*,[3] or the Latin terms "*imitatio*" and "*aemulatio*," very much present in texts from early rhetorical treatises such as *Rhetorica ad Herennium* (circa 80 B.C.), through Horace's famous *Ars poetica* (18 B.C.) until late antiquity, when Christian theorists such as Lactantius and Augustine further developed the classical concept of *imitatio* by combining it with the necessities of integrating allegory and biblical hermeneutics.[4] One aspect in particular deserves our attention in this context: mimesis on the one hand was originally meant as *Naturnachahmung*, "imitation of nature" (as it has generally been received within Western culture) and hence the creation of fictional worlds. On the other hand it also meant—especially if we consider the Latin terms "*imitatio*" and "*aemulatio*"—imitation and emulation of other authors. Virgil, for instance, aimed in the *Aeneid* at imitating and emulating, that is, challenging, Homer. The very core of ancient literary aesthetics is based on competition with exemplary models; behind an apparently slavish admiration is concealed a sense of rivalry and a drive to overcome the model.

This sense of imitation as emulation brings us very close to some aspects of Girard's mimetic theory. Although strictly speaking there is no exact ancient equivalent to the (early) modern novel to which Girard mainly directs his attention in *Deceit, Desire, and the Novel*, Greek and Roman literature offers a textual type that is often called "the ancient novel" (Petronius, Apuleius, Longus, Achilles Tatius, and others) and in addition to these a broad spectrum of fictional narrative texts. In particular, epic poetry and drama (both tragedy and comedy) are obvious candidates. But there are a number of other genres that also could be explored from a Girardian perspective, among others the Latin love elegy, practiced by authors such as Propertius, Tibullus, and, of course, Ovid, a master in disguising human desire, or epistolography (Cicero, Pliny, Symmachus). Although these last genres are not narrative in their own terms, they manifest many of the aspects emphasized by Girard, namely a constant doubleness of the constellation of the involved personae in the communication (for instance, the lover and the beloved in elegiac poetry, the addresser and addressee within epistolography). Precisely this constellation turns out to be regulated by the kind of triangulation theorized by Girard, in which desire and competition are tightly connected and inter-dependent.

The methodological implications that Greek and Roman texts bring with them are especially interesting: they belong to a different literary system, one that from certain perspectives was little affected by the kind of romantic criticism so clearly attacked by Girard. The ubiquitousness of *imitatio* and *aemulatio* in ancient literary discourses allows the use of Girard's theory at its best by systematically applying imitation as the key criterion to analyse these texts. However, precisely because imitation is so ubiquitous, the distinction between "*mensonge romantique*" and "*vérité romanesque*"—that is, the tension between the romantic pretence of originality and genuinity, which Girard marks as "*mensonge*," and the resort to imitation typical of the "*vérité romanesque*"—is weakened if not seriously undermined.

Given these premises, in this essay I will concentrate on one of the central literary genres of Roman imperial literature, panegyric, that is, speech in praise of Roman emperors. Discussing this genre as the archaeology of the discourse of praise leads us to a fundamental aspect: admiration as the fundamental mode of mimetic theory, since it is the vehicle of the discourse of the mediator. In other words, I wish to present this textual genre as the one in which more than in others, "metaphysical desire," as it has described by Girard, manifests itself in all its evidence and power. Much more than other literary genres, panegyric presents the tension between the self and the other in an exemplary way, one that arguably does not even need to be detected with the use of particularly sophisticated interpretive tools: it is the essence of this kind of text, and clearly manifests itself at every step.

The Corpus of the *Panegyrici Latini*

As happened to so many Greek terms imported to Rome, the word *panegyricus* was transformed. In Greek, *panegyrikos logos* means literally "speech in front of an assembly," and this was the title of a famous speech delivered by Isocrates in 380 B.C. In Rome, although it still remains within the field of the epideictic genre (i.e., display texts), panegyric specifically focuses on the public praise of the emperor, and the term *panegyricus* was formalized during late antiquity. In particular a corpus has been handed down to us with the title *Panegyrici Latini*, which was very probably put together at the end of the fourth century A.D. It contains twelve speeches held in honor of different emperors for various occasions such as birthdays, celebrations of the foundation of Rome, or a victory. The first text included is the famous *gratiarum actio* (speech of thanksgiving) for the emperor Trajan held in Rome by Pliny the Younger in A.D. 100, while the last is a speech for Theodosius the Great written in A.D. 389 by a certain Latinus Pacatus Drepanius, who might be also the one who compiled the corpus,[5] although in fact we know very little about the authors of the various speeches or the circumstances of the composition of the collection itself; in any case the arrangement does not follow a chronological criterion.[6]

This corpus also contains a unique aspect that makes it a paradigm of a genre: it shows both the text believed to be the model of the panegyric genre (i.e., Pliny's speech) and a sample of the textual tradition that derives from it (i.e., the eleven other speeches). Yet the majority of classical scholars, driven by the necessity of reconstructing the historical context, tend to read the individual speeches in isolation and in doing so they undermine the sense of interconnections that are implicitly emphasized by the corpus. Not only do the twelve speeches need to be read as a textual cluster so that the recurrence of certain themes can be appreciated, but also, and more importantly, the collection itself, having its own textual voice, manifests certain characteristics that are so different from those presented in the single speeches taken singularly that they actually seem to contradict panegyric in its generic expectations. In other words, the corpus of the *Panegyrici*, if read as a macrotext,[7] arguably contains a potential of rivalry and subversion instead of the eulogy and admiration that, as required by the rules of the genre, is programmatically displayed within the individual textual units, that is, in each of the twelve discourses of praise.

Competition, Reflexivity, and Desire

Since the rise and diffusion of political and ethical values inherited from the French Revolution, modern Western readers are accustomed to conceiving a speech written in order to celebrate established power as an act of submission, flattery, and adulation and to seeing such a speech as self-serving, lying, hypocritical.[8] New perspectives over the past decades have suggested that such a text can be treated differently, by trying to make this almost inevitable prejudice milder, if not to attempt to eliminate it entirely. Indeed, ancient panegyric is now mainly treated as a source for historical reconstructions of the political and social context on the one hand,[9] and of ancient rhetoric and ethics on the other.[10] More recently, by combining literary analysis and historical expertise, many scholars have also tried to reestablish some positive political values the panegyrical texts may have had, almost as if their supposed engagement could somehow make up for aesthetical defects.[11] Thus the intrinsic protreptic function of encouraging and instructing has received attention: the panegyrist not only praises the emperor but also offers him a concrete "programme of behaviour."[12] Also, it has been argued that "flattery is a kind of aggression," since he who believes in the truth of flattery easily succumbs to mockery.[13] In an important study, which surprisingly does not consider panegyric, Frederick Ahl thoroughly discusses ancient literary manifestations of "safe criticism," recurring in particular to the analysis of the rhetorical concept of figured speech, which allows the speakers to implicitly express a criticism instead of presenting it as such.[14]

This essay focuses on another type of question, more precisely having to do with the kind of communication established between the two actors of what we might call the "panegyric constellation," namely the orator and the *princeps*, that is, the one who praises and the one who is praised. Latin panegyric, when observed from a Girardian perspective, becomes a very engaging genre indeed: the reader can fully appreciate the kind of obsession with the admired model that is so relevant for the mimetic desire. The panegyrist is "obsessed" with the figure of the emperor, who thus becomes his model-obstacle. Panegyric, moreover, contains an exemplary kind of mimetic desire in which the Girardian triangulation involves the orator, the emperor, and the textual dimension itself. The desire of the panegyrist is directed to the emperor but also to the text itself, which produces competition with the preceding textual tradition.

This aspect emerges when considering two themes in particular: the perception of truth and falsity, and the nature of the relationship between the two parties in panegyric. In the most general terms, my aim is to show that the panegyric mode contains its opposite in itself, that is, it contains a potential of destabilization of power by establishing a type of communication inspired by competition, reflexivity, and desire. Given these premises, the category of metaphysical desire as theorized by Girard represents the most apt perspective from which to shed light on these particular textual features.

The discourses of truth and the eulogy have been tightly connected since the beginning of Western civilization. In his illuminating book *Les maîtres de vérité dans la Grèce archaïque* (1967),[15] Marcel Detienne rightly places emphasis on this connection, but he also sheds light on another connection, which in the eyes of modern readers seems more dangerous, namely that established between *aletheia* and *pseudes*, truth and lie. Detienne points out the inner duplicity and ambiguity that constantly characterize the discourse of truth in religious and poetic discourse in archaic Greece. This productive ambiguity was eventually dissolved with the rise of philosophy, which provided a new set of concepts suited to distinguishing *aletheia* from *doxa*, truth from appearance. Turning to imperial Rome: since panegyric notoriously tends to mix historical reality with mythology and fictional events, the genre has been traditionally seen as the place for historical distortion in order to please the emperor, the representative figure of established power.[16] Praising his addressee, the panegyrical speaker does not care about historical accuracy in referring to deeds and events, and does not hesitate to confound the level of reality with that of myth. Yet perhaps the most curious thing for the modern reader is that the panegyrists deliberately insist on the truth of what they are telling: they do not want to make fiction but to tell the truth, although this truth is seemingly impossible. This motif clearly emerges in a number of passages from the corpus.

> For neither is it a fable stemming from poetic license nor mere belief based on the assertions of bygone eras, but a manifest and confirmed fact.[17]
>
> Do not fear, most eminent authors, for the veneration of your writings; we who have now seen greater things believe in those deeds. Our leader's greatness wins credence for the ancients' accomplishments, but removes the miraculous element.[18]
>
> To this, to this, you pious bards, devote all the labors of your learned nights; celebrate this in all your writings and in every tongue, nor be anxious as to whether your works shall last. That eternity which you are accustomed to confer on histories shall come from history.[19]

But let us set aside the fables of the ignorant and speak the truth: your piety, most sacred Emperor, gave you winged course. And since nothing is swifter than the spirit, you, whose fiery and immortal minds scarcely perceive the body's delays, rode to each other on the swiftness of mutual longing.[20]

The texts do not want to escape the problem of historical verisimilitude; instead they aggressively use the comparison between reality and myth as a rhetorical strategy. Thus they do not refer to historical events as the readers might expect in historiography or other genres. They prefer to allude to them, recurring to their symbolical and mythical significance for the audience they wish to reach. Since the emperor is represented as the interpreter of divine will, the panegyrist constructs history using the mythological frame. History remains in the background as something that everybody knows, but which it is not important to cite accurately in the moment; it is, one could say, something not to be taken very seriously. As we will see, it is by challenging history in its truthfulness that the orator also implicitly challenges the figure of the *princeps*, who is constantly presented and depicted precisely as an emanation of Roman history.

More particularly, the emperor is confronted with history, and he competes with the past as celebrated by the poets. The panegyrist is able to stage a rather paradoxical contest between the past, which ends up becoming a lie, and present reality, which is the only possible truth. History competes with myth, or—better put—myth is replaced by contemporary events. Myth is made present, while history dissolves into the domain of fiction. The *princeps* floats between fiction and reality, between ideal exemplum and real person: "I shall omit the rest and seize above all upon what perhaps will seem astonishing to many, yet which is absolutely true."[21] Here the text again puts emphasis on the contraposition of *mirum* and *verissimum*, practically compelling the audience to mix them up. Another passage from Pacatus's Panegyric for Theodosius shows with exemplarity the vertiginous mixture of reality and fictionality:

If the favor of the gods is to be measured by the worthiness of the cause, I for one would contend with good reason that your cavalry were carried along, born aloft, by Pegasuses, your infantry on winged feet. Simply

because divine things disdain to show themselves to mortals, we shall not
on that account doubt that things that were not seen were done, since we
see things done which we would have doubted could have been done.[22]

As this passage well illustrates, the panegyric genre requires excess, exag-
geration, and hyperbole as marks of its own discourse.[23] But the most
interesting point for us is that the imitation of literary past and imaginary is
deeply marked by a sense of competition. Within this peculiar constellation
we find a particular kind of triangulation of desire, which, I would argue,
is specifically typical of Latin textuality, which is in its own nature greatly
allusive and intertextual (and thus the opposite of the romantic "truth"). The
triangulation is constituted by the one who praises, the one who is praised,
and the literary tradition—in particular the epic and historiographic genres
with which the panegyrist establishes a sort of competition. Precisely this
textuality assumes the role of the mediator, as Girard argues in the case of
Don Quixote and chivalric romance.[24]

     Another key point is that behind the one who is praised is the one who
praises, that is, the figure of the author, who by means of his art competes
with other authors and other genres. The corpus in its very structure is, after
all, a product of competition and subversion. There is competition first with
the primary panegyrical model, Pliny's speech, which is presented as the first
and to which every other text in the series invites being compared. Second
and more subtly, there is competition with the figure of the emperor itself.
Every speech is meant, at least theoretically, to be delivered in front of the
emperor, but by putting those speeches in writing and making them parts
of a series, the corpus produces a very different effect from that of the individual speeches. If praise of the emperor and admiration for the model are
the marks of the individual speeches taken in isolation, the series itself, by
dissolving the uniqueness of that single moment of delivery—whether real or
ideal—dangerously undermines the representation of the emperor precisely
by launching him into a web of references that annuls his individual personality. In the end, I would suggest, this is the result of a compulsive mechanism
of comparisons with the past and with other emperors that implicitly transforms eulogy into its opposite.

     An important set of themes more directly involves the relationship
between the panegyric speaker and the person being praised. The figure of

the *princeps*, as we have already seen, is forged by the panegyrist: the latter gives life to the former by representing him through traditional qualities. In praising the emperor, the panegyrist ascribes to his creation the highest level of veracity. And yet his creation, the *laudandus*, is unavoidably represented as a fictional figure. In order to clarify the kind of mechanism working within this particular constellation, I would suggest that the author ascribes to the *princeps* a function similar to that of a mannequin in an artist's studio, which is a model of and model for someone, since it reproduces a previous human figure but its aim is to help the artist in representing another human figure.[25] The comparison between the mannequin and the figure of the emperor as it emerges within panegyric brings us to several points of interest. First, by modeling the qualities of the *princeps* the author deprives his creature of individuality. Second, as has been argued for the mannequin by Claudia Peppel, precisely the act of modelization has the effect of projecting the praised person into a fictional universe.[26] Finally, another point that is the most interesting from a Girardian perspective is this: mannequins within art history have been created not only as a tool for the work of artists in their studios but also in order to represent sacred figures such as Christ or kings, which were then carried in religious and political processions. Transferred from the materiality of the mannequins to the textual dimension of panegyric, this point brings us to the inner connection between royalty and victim that is one of the most famous concepts explored by Girard.[27]

Consider, for example, this passage:

> Whether you knew and followed this example, or did it on your own initiative, in either case it was a very fine accomplishment. For those emulating great deeds deserve no less praise than the authors themselves. Nay more, the enterprise of something untried, however well conceived, is entrusted to Fortune, but the reiteration and repetition of the same stratagem surely redounds to the fame of one's judgement. And for this reason, most sacred Emperor, both of you are now greater than Scipio, for you imitated Africanus, and Diocletian imitated you.[28]

These lines well illustrate the panegyrical constellation in the terms I have suggested. The exemplum and its imitators (*aemuli*) are paramount; only in comparision with a model can the existence of the emperor be assured, only by reiterating and repeating (*iteratum atque repetitum*) can he achieve glory. In this case, though, the procedure is rendered more complex by the fact that the panegyrist addresses not only one but two emperors, Maximian and Diocletian, so that the reader is vertiginously confronted with a doubled effect of mirroring between exemplary model and imitator.

Related to this is another aspect of panegyric communication that needs emphasis and further exploration: the constant duality that underlies the language of these texts and their situation. The readers are confronted with binary oppositions at every level. Reciprocities between the praising and the praised are virtually infinite and represent the very rules of the genre: history versus myth, reality versus fiction, sincerity versus lie, current emperor versus past emperors, *princeps* versus tyrant, praise versus blame, exemplum versus reality, being a model for someone versus being a model of someone, and so on. The whole communication is based on the axis of a double parler and double entendre, as Shadi Bartsch has put it in connection with the Plinian panegyric.[29] But this also implies that every element is at one and the same time its opposite: history becomes myth, exemplum becomes imitation, praise becomes blame, and so on. Furthermore, an extreme kind of communication takes place within panegyric. The *princeps* appears simultaneously as the one who commissions the speech, as dedicatee, and as the praised one; his deeds shall be the only content of the text. But the other protagonist is the orator himself. In fact, one might argue that he actually is the true protagonist, and that in addressing his speech to the *princeps* he praises himself.[30] In countless passages of the corpus this liaison is more or less explicitly present. I cite only a few examples:

> The Emperor who has given me his approbation will provide a supply of material for my speech that is inexhaustible.[31]
>
>   I propose for myself a new mode of speaking to show that, although I seem not to speak of all the greatest things, there are nonetheless among your praises other things which are greater.[32]

Another intriguing element in the relationship between orator and *princeps* requires attention. Some scholars have argued that the majority of the speeches contained in the collection were actually never delivered in front of the emperor, and that they remained unspoken words, on paper alone. In this connection I would point out that the theme of absence and the interrelated theme of presence are figures of desire: writing in general is a medium aimed at catching and representing the absence of the desired object. Interestingly, the concept of the portrait (both in visual arts and in literature) has been also put into relationship with absence and desire. According to Maurizio Bettini, for example, the impulse behind a portrait is *pothos* or *desiderium* for the absent.[33] The affinity between panegyric and portrait is obvious, since the art of verbal eulogy can be easily be compared to the art of a painter or a sculptor while rendering a human figure. Within the corpus, in fact, there are a number of passages that combine the themes of desire, absence, and portraiture.

> But now your injury will make his patience the more commendable: they will long more keenly for him if no picture represents him. The desires of the spirit are more passionate when they have lost the consolation which eyes provide.[34]

Here absence, a portrait, and desire are tightly interrelated. In many other cases a great attention is directed to seeing (*videre*) as the mark of veracity, but this aspect is continuously negotiated with the actual absence of the emperor. In one passage we read of the desire of the emperor Constantine to be seen:

> No one may pass judgment upon rulers, for confrontation with an object of veneration repulses the seeker in the entranceway, and any who have approached closer have been blinded and lost faculty of sight, which is what happens to the eyes when they are directed to the sun. But you bring it to pass, greatest of rulers, that things which had previously been shut away are seen to lie open, you who desire as much to be seen in your entirety as the rest were reluctant.[35]

And later in the same speech we read the following:

> There is but one thing by which Rome could be made happier, a very great thing but yet the only one, that it see Constantine its preserver, that it see the blessed Caesars, that it obtain the means of enjoyment in proportion to the measure of its longing, that it receive you joyously and, when reasons

of state have made you depart, that it send you away with a promise of your return.[36]

In fact, the corpus of the *Panegyrici* is full of passages referring to the *praesentia* of the princeps, and *praesentia* is, after all, a mark of absence and desire.

> We saw you, Caesar, on the very same day taking up vows on behalf of the state and incurring the debt of them being answered. . . . We saw you, Caesar, on the same day both in the most splendid garb of peace and in the magnificent accoutrements of war.[37]

And at the end of the same speech:

> You perceive, O Emperor, how much power there is in the heavenly benefits you have conferred upon us: we still enjoy your presence; we already long for your return.[38]

In the following passage a sort of echoing of the vision of the emperor is put on the stage: first he is seen, then people talk about the fact that they have indeed seen him. The effect is that the direct vision is overcome by hearsay.

> But when you came closer and closer and people began to recognize you, all the fields were filled not only with men running forth to see but even with flocks of beasts leaving their distant pastures and woods, farmers rushed about among each other, told everyone what they had seen.[39]

Elsewhere, barbarians are defined as "blind" precisely because they could not see the emperor's face: "O truly blind barbarians, who did not see the marks of a ruler on that face!"[40]

Within the same series, particularly revealing is a passage from Pacatus's Panegyric for Theodosius:

> What crowds of admiring people, how great an audience, shall surround me when I say: "I have seen Rome; I have seen Theodosius; and I have seen both together; I have seen the father of the ruler himself, I have seen the avenger of the ruler; I have seen the restorer of the ruler."[41]

Here the fact that the orator has seen the emperor is connected with the admiration of the crowd for the orator himself, and for his part, Theodosius is represented not alone but in the company of his fellows Honorius, Gratian, and Valentinian II.

The Panegyric Pact

In *A Theater of Envy*, Girard discusses Shakespearean dramas as texts where the mimetic dimension emerges with particular clarity. In particular he analyzes the "deeper play" of *Julius Caesar*, in which he detects a mimetic rivalry that leads to the sacrificial quality of the murder of Caesar as representant of supreme power. In a comparable way, I would here like to shed light on the deeper play of Roman panegyric by focusing on the relationship between the two parties in the panegyric "pact" in order to show how panegyric, by contradicting its own generic essence, bears a potential of subversion and destabilization of power. This potential is not necessarily or exclusively to be detected in more or less open mechanisms of critique—consider the rhetorical device of *synkrisis* or *comparatio*, which allows the orator to admonish his *princeps* by recalling the bad deeds of his predecessors, presented to him as tyrants—or in the so-called double speak, that is, hidden allusions to behaviors to avoid. More than this, I would argue, praise itself contains a highly subversive potential, since it deliberately contains a perfect and ideal model, almost unreachable for a human *princeps*. Consider what the Romanian philosopher Emil Cioran affirms regarding the ideal pope described by Joseph De Maistre in *On the Pope* (1819):

> There is only one way to praise: to inspire fear in him whom we extol, to shake him, to force him to hide away from the statue that was erected to him, to compel him, by generous hyperbole, to measure his mediocrity and to suffer from it. What is a plea that neither torments nor disturbs, what is praise which does not kill? Any apology should be a murder by enthusiasm.[42]

This quotation from Cioran brings us very near to the main thesis of Girard himself, who discusses the figure of the king or of the emperor in their sacrificial dimension: any royal figure is destined to become a victim, a scapegoat sacrificed by the crowd reproducing the original identification of divinity and political power.[43] Thus, for Girard, Shakespeare's *Julius Caesar* "is not about Roman history but about collective violence itself,"[44] and, more significantly for our treatment of ancient panegyric, Girard establishes an ontological equivalence between Brutus the murderer and Caesar the victim. The latter turns out to be "the hated rival and the beloved model, the incomparable guide, the unsurpassable teacher." Brutus fully identifies with his victim, and "the more he reveres Caesar, the more he hates him as well."[45] Admiration and the speech genre that most represents it, panegyric, are inevitably and fatally linked with murder.

◆ ◆ ◆

The suspicion that under eulogy is concealed a sharp criticism is found in many other authors, in particular those who wrote aphorisms such as François de La Rochefoucauld and Friedrich Nietzsche. The latter points out in *Human, All Too Human II*:

> Sharpest criticisms: We criticize a man or a book most sharply when we sketch out their ideal. (157)
>
> The one who is praised: So long as you are praised think only that you are not yet on your own path but on that of another. (340)
>
> Danger in admiration: Through too great admiration for the virtues of others it is possible to lose interest in one's own and from lack of practice finally lose them altogether without acquiring those of others in return. (355)

Apart from these considerations, the potential I wish to illustrate is structural, I would argue, to the very discourse of the genre. Roland Barthes suggests that every literary genre and text contain an inner conflict of opposites; he illustrates this conflict in authors considered rather marginal to the literary system—Sade, Fourier, and Loyola—precisely in order to reveal their high literariness.[46] To illustrate my point about panegyric, I recall the concept of masochism, which overlaps in some ways with the panegyric constellation. Girard devotes an entire chapter of *Deceit, Desire, and the Novel* to the figure of the masochist, making of him a specific actor of metaphysical desire (176ff). Girard suggests that the masochist will always tend to avoid the people who manifest love and affection for him or her, and will direct his or her attention to those who overtly show their contempt. He writes: "we are masochists when we no longer choose our mediator because of the admiration which he inspires in us but because of the disgust we seem to inspire in him" (178).

More importantly for my purposes in this essay, Girard focuses on the fact that a masochist, precisely like any other victim of metaphysical desire, beyond the facade of suffering seeks actually to reach the power and divinity of the mediator. Thus the panegyrist, while praising the emperor and humiliating himself in front of him, actually renders the object of his eulogy an instrument of a strategy devoted to reach the level of his addressee, and possibly to overcome him by means of words. A masochist, as Girard points out, desires "autonomy and a god-like self-control, his own self-esteem and the esteem of others; but by an intuition of metaphysical desire . . . he no longer hopes to find these inestimable treasures except at the side of a master whose humble slave he will be."[47]

In a famous essay on masochism, Gilles Deleuze provides another useful consideration in order to better understand the phenomenon of masochism He first introduces important conceptual divergences between masochism and sadism: while sadism practices an "institutionalized possession," masochism thinks in terms of a "contracted alliance."[48] While the obession of the sadist is possession, that of the masochist is the pact. The masochist, after all, enters into an agreement with his or her partner: "You will cause me pain—but only up to a certain point." The sadist, on the other hand, ideally is not interested in what his or her partner wants (hence Deleuze keeps quite distinct the two categories, and thus does not speak of "sadomasochism"). In particular, in the novels of Sacher-Masoch a "dialectical reversal" takes place: while the masochist seems to be educated by his dominatrix, he is in fact the one who forms and educates her. It is he who gives her the words to use with him. As Deleuze points out:

> It is the victim who speaks through the mouth of his torturer, without sparing himself. Dialectic does not simply mean the free interchange of discourse, but implies transpositions or displacements of this kind, resulting in a scene being enacted simultaneously on several levels with reversals and reduplications in the allocation of roles and discourse.[49]

Furthermore, the masochist needs to create an impossible model for his or her fantasies, and it is necessary that this ideal model be more valid than reality, in order to avoid any possible disappointments deriving from an imperfect reality.

◆ ◆ ◆

Girard and Deleuze provide both a profound insight and a useful tool, one well suited for illustrating the panegyrical constellation in the terms we have seen. On the one hand, the panegyrist renders the historical emperor a literary figure, placing his subject within the realm of fiction and myth, which turns out being a kind of "novelistic truth." Thereby his relationship to the model is made present at every step; to use Girardian terminology, the mediator is in this case the Latin literary tradition itself. By means of this mediator, the panegyrist establishes a relation of competition, and at the same time he tends to destabilize historical truth, which turns out to be nothing but "romantic lie." The one who desires—says Girard—wants to transform himself into the mediator. Within the panegyric constellation, the Roman emperor becomes a fictional figure like Emma Bovary. His principal trait is an absolute lack of originality, since all his deeds, all his battles, all his gestures have been already told and retold a myriad of times within previous texts.

On the other hand, the panegyrist reveals himself as a masochistic stage director of his own desire. The masochist and the panegyrist set up a direct confrontation with power. Both create their own image of power; both are marked by desire for the other and for the self; and both enter into a pact or agreement between the parties involved. In both discourses, a eulogy of the desired object—whether the beloved or the *princeps*—turns out to be a eulogy of the self.

Notes

1. Although Girard extensively treated some figures and narratives from classical myth (e.g. Oedipus and Dionysos in *Violence and the Sacred*, and in *Oedipus Unbound*), ancient texts per se are not at the center of his system. Conversely, Girard's theory has only very rarely had an impact within the study of ancient literatures; one exception is Cesareo Bandera's *The Sacred Game: The Role of the Sacred in the Genesis of Modern Literary Fiction* (University Park: Penn State University Press, 1994) approaching Virgil among other premodern authors from a Girardian perspective.

2. See L. Costa Lima, "Mimesis," in *Ästhetische Grundbegriffe*, ed. K. Barck et al., vol. 4 (Stuttgart: Metzler, 2002): 84–120.

3. For a treatment of mimesis in ancient Greek thought and its reception see S. Halliwell, *The Aesthetics of Mimesis: Ancient Texts and Modern Problems* (Princeton: Princeton University Press, 2002).

4. For an overview of mimesis and imitatio see the entry "Mimesis" in *Historisches Wörterbuch der Rhetorik*, ed. G. Ueding (Berlin: De Gruyter, 2001).

5. For an edition of the corpus with introduction, English translation, and commentary see C. E. Nixon and B. Rodgers, *In Praise of Later Roman Emperors: The Panegyrici Latini* (Berkeley: University of California Press, 1994).

6. For a discussion of the particular contexts of the various speeches contained in the corpus see M. Mause, *Die Darstellung des Kaisers in der lateinischen Panegyrik* (Stuttgart: Franz Steiner, 1994); and R. Rees, *Layers of Loyalty in Latin Panegyric* (Oxford: Oxford University Press, 2002).

7. For a definition of "macrotext" see M. Corti, *Introduction to Literary Semiotics* (Bloomington: Indiana University Press, 1978); and C. Segre, *Introduction to the Analysis of the Literary Text* (Bloomington: Indiana University Press, 1988).

8. See I. Cogitore and F. Goyet, eds., *Devenir roi: Essais sur la littérature adressée au Prince* (Grenoble: Ellug, 2001); *Eloge du Prince: De l'antiquité au temps de Lumières* (Grenoble: Ellug, 2003).

9. Exponents of this tendency are, among others: A. Giardina and M. Silvestrini, "Il principe e il testo," in *Lo spazio letterario di Roma antica*, ed. G. Cavallo et al., vol. 2 (Rome: Salerno, 1989): 579–613; M.-C. L'Hullier, *L'empire des mots: Orateurs gaulois et empereurs romains* (Paris: Diffusé par Les Belles Lettres, 1992); Nixon and Rodgers, *In Praise of Later*; M. Whitby, ed., *The Propaganda of Power: The Role of Panegyric in Late Antiquity* (Leiden: Brill, 1998).

10. See in particular L. Pernot, *La rhétorique de l'éloge dans le monde gréco-romain* (Paris: Institut d'études augustiniennes, 1993; D. A. Russell, *Menander Rhetor* (Oxford: Clarendon, 2004); Russell, "The Panegyrists and Their Teachers," in Whitby, *The Propaganda of Power*, 17–50.

11. In an important article, Sabbah sought to find positive value in the activity of a panegyrist by affirming that those were "true orators, whose word, active in the real and the present, was also action" (363); G. Sabbah, "De la rhétorique à la communication politique: Les Panegyriques latins," *Bulletin de l'association Guillaume Budé* 4 (1984): 362–85.

12. S. Morton Braund, "Praise and Protreptic in Early Roman Imperial Panegyric: Cicero, Seneca, Pliny," in Whitby, *The Propaganda of Power*, 66.

13. F. Ahl, "The Art of Safe Criticism in Greece and Rome," *American Journal of Philology* 105 (1984): 199.

14. The article by Ahl is relevant and would require a longer discussion, especially because many of his assumptions, being characteristic of the way in which classical scholars read ancient texts, would need to be revised. I mention here only one point in particular: Ahl analyzes only the kind of criticism that ascribes intention to the authors, firmly believing that we must read the text according to it. This chapter takes a different approach by showing how the text itself, independently of any intentionality, produces a discourse of rebellion and subversion.

15. Marcel Detienne, *Les maîtres de vérité dans la Grèce archaïque* (Paris: Maspero, 1967).

16. See, for instance, Mause, *Die Darstellung des Kaisers*.

17. Nixon and Rodgers, *In Praise of Later*, 10.1.3, p. 53. All English translations of the *Panegyrici Latini* are from Nixon and Rodgers, *In Praise of Later*.

18. Nixon and Rodgers, *In Praise of Later*, 4.15.6, p. 360.

19. Nixon and Rodgers, *In Praise of Later*, 2.44.4–5, p. 511.

20. Nixon and Rodgers, *In Praise of Later*, 11.8.4–5, p. 94.

21. Nixon and Rodgers, *In Praise of Later*, 10.3.1, p. 57.

22. Nixon and Rodgers, *In Praise of Later*, 2.39.5, p. 507.

23. See Rees, *Layers of Loyalty*.

24. René Girard, *Deceit, Desire, and the Novel: Self and Other in Literary Structure*, trans. Yvonne Freccero (Baltimore: Johns Hopkins University Press, 1965), 1ff.

25. See B. Mahr, "Modellieren. Beobachtungen und Gedanken zur Geschichte des Modellbegriffs," in *Bild—Schrift—Zahl*, ed. S. Krämer and H. Bredekamp (Munich: Wilhelm Fink, 2003), 59–86.

26. C. Peppel, *Der Manichino. Von der Gliederpuppe zum technisierten Kultobjekt. Körperimaginationen im Werk Giorgio de Chiricos* (Bonn: VG Bild-Kunst, 2008), 123.

27. René Girard, *Things Hidden Since the Foundation of the World*, research undertaken in collaboration with Jean-Michel Oughourlian and Guy Lefort, trans. Stephen Nann and Michael Metteer (Stanford: Stanford University Press, 1987), 59–66.

28. Nixon and Rodgers, *In Praise of Later*, 10.8.3–6, p. 65–66.

29. S. Bartsch, *Actors in the Audience: Theatricality and Doublespeak from Nero to Hadrian* (Cambridge: Harvard University Press, 1994), 174.

30. Though from a completely different perspective a recent article reads the panegyric of Pliny as an act of "self-fashioning"; C. Noreña, "Self-fashioning in the Panegyricus," in *Pliny's Praise: The "Panegyricus" in the Roman World*, ed. P. Roche (Cambridge: Cambridge University Press, 2011), 29–44.

31. Nixon and Rodgers, *In Praise of Later*, 6.23.3, p. 253.

32. Nixon and Rodgers, *In Praise of Later*, 11.5.5, p. 89–90.

33. M. Bettini, *The Portrait of the Lover* (Berkeley: University of California Press, 1999).

34. Nixon and Rodgers, *In Praise of Later*, 10.12.5, p. 73.

35. Nixon and Rodgers, *In Praise of Later*, 4.5.1–2, p. 348.

36. Nixon and Rodgers, *In Praise of Later*, 4.38.6, p. 385.

37. Nixon and Rodgers, *In Praise of Later*, 10.6.3, p. 63.

38. Nixon and Rodgers, *In Praise of Later*, 10.14.5, p. 75.

39. Nixon and Rodgers, *In Praise of Later*, 11.10.5, p. 96.

40. Nixon and Rodgers, *In Praise of Later*, 4.18.4, p. 364.

41. Nixon and Rodgers, *In Praise of Later*, 2.47.5, p. 515.

42. E. Cioran, *Excercises d'admiration* (Paris: Gallimard, 1986): 17.

43. Girard, *Things Hidden*, 51ff.

44. René Girard, *A Theater of Envy: William Shakespeare* (Oxford: Oxford University Press, 1991), 223.

45. Girard, *A Theater of Envy*, 189.

46. Roland Barthes, *Sade, Fourier, Loyola* (Paris: Editions du Seuil, 1980).

47. Girard, *Deceit, Desire, and the Novel* 184.

48. Gilles Deleuze, *Coldness and Cruelty*, trans. Jean McNeil, published with Leopold von Sacher-Masoch, *Venus in Furs* (New York: Zone Books, 1991), 20–21.

49. Deleuze, *Coldness and Cruelty*, 22.

René Girard
and (Medieval) Sanctity

A Reappraisal

Bill Burgwinkle

For someone who has spent a good deal of his scholarly career charting the sacred—what it is, how it is created, sustained, and memorialized—René Girard has done remarkably little work on sanctity in the ecclesiastical sense or on saints as figures of devotion, sacrifice, and transcendence. This is slightly puzzling since so many of the Christian martyrs lend themselves so well to the categories he has by now practically institutionalized, especially that of the sacrificial victim.[1] In giving up their lives under mostly false accusations (e.g., of being magicians and political saboteurs) and condemned under extrajuridical conditions, these saints occupy a position very close to what Girard has identified as a sacrificial status and what Giorgio Agamben has called "bare life," beings unable to be sacrificed (presumably to God or the sovereign) because of their nonstatus (or their guilt), and whose death entails therefore no accusation of murder.[2] One of the complications that arise from the Girardian point of view is, of course, these saints' status as mimetic followers of Christ: they are victims who call out for their killing, whose desire operates with God alone as their mediator, who reject the baseness of human society as well as its treasures, and who move, at death, to a status lesser than that of a God but more than that of the venerated dead. Saints thus become eternal (usually external) mediators, without the benefits of absolute sovereignty: locally revered, their power often limited to specific ailments and complaints, they benefit from some of the power of the sacrificed victim but without being able to claim the status of saviour.

One of the striking features of *Deceit, Desire, and the Novel* is the unique power that Girard attributes to the literary text to bear witness to the sort of institutionalized scapegoating that underlies mythmaking, and, in bearing such witness, to demystify it. Historical accounts might be able to map the process, but, in Girard's account, only a gifted author can unveil the unconscious processes of mimeticism and collective violence that lie at the base of our myths of victimization and which found, in their wake, our notion of the sacred. In his words, "Great writers apprehend intuitively and concretely, through the medium of their art . . . the system in which they were first imprisoned. . . . Literary interpretation must be systematic because it is the continuation of literature."[3]

This citation is interesting on many levels: first of all, because it betrays Girard's early interest in structuralist thinking and, second, in the modern as the privileged era in which this unveiling of victimization takes place. There are, no doubt, very good reasons why he chose to focus on texts from the postrevolutionary nineteenth century and the fallout from the industrial revolution to make his case, but I want to suggest here that some of that demystifying energy was already at work—admittedly in a problematic sense—in the supposedly traditional Middle Ages, and especially in works produced in the southern French lands that might be called Occitania.

To that end, I will be focusing on a single Occitan saint's life that undertakes this demystification while also questioning whether that unveiling, from within a vernacular (and therefore secular) saint's life, can ever really effect significant change in cultural practice. The text I have chosen is the oldest known saint's life in Occitania, the *Cancó de Santa Fe*, dated to the second half of the eleventh century.[4] In its famous opening stanzas, the author first claims that he heard the Latin life of Saint Faith recited as he sat under a pine tree, before announcing that he will now sing the tale as a dance song, "*a lei francesca*," to inspire his readers.[5] This odd solicitation to pleasure, the first of several pre-Occitan-lyric references, is followed by a mini-history of the pagan city of Agen and a first metaphorical allusion to the young saint in terms borrowed from the *Song of Solomon* (2:3). The biblical apple tree, which is choked by forest growth but gives birth nonetheless on its upper branches to lovely flowers, is assimilated here to the new religion, with the flowers playing the role of the young girl's faith and the encroaching growth the repressive power of the pagan state:

> The pagan Gascons were such an evil presence
> for they refused to recognize God in his heavens.
> Their pressing shade similarly strangled the young plant
> about whom we are singing this song;
> and God took from that tree the sweet and good fruit.[6]

The figure of this menaced young plant, reaching toward heaven, introduces a note of violence and self-sacrifice from the very beginning. God himself, who "took the sweet and good fruit," is implicated in the sacrifice through the active role he plays in allowing for the murder of the girl and the taking of her body for himself. God does not wait passively for the offering of the saint's body but actively takes the fruits that he sees as legitimately his. Furthermore, his role as external mediator in the mimetic scenario is established when the young saint's imitation of Christ's martyrdom leads not to a cessation of violence through her sacrifice but to another more deadly cycle of violence that will soon thereafter spin out of control. Let us then look at this text more closely.

Faith's martyrdom is described as a rhetorical and ritualistic piece of theater. Instead of having martyrdom inflicted upon her, as one might have expected, the author of this life opts for the active voice, saying that Faith, like God, took martyrdom upon herself ("*Martiri pres, e fort assaz*" [82]). We learn furthermore that the world is very much honoured/bettered by her death ("*O Deus! tant n'es est monz honraz*" [84]) because it has an immediate bearing on all that surrounds her, including the political institutions of the state and church. Her sacrifice seems to be required in order to ensure the integrity and stability of God's creation. In the final line of the stanza ("*O Deus! tant n'es est monz honraz*" [84]), God is even addressed directly as an ally and witness to her action.

It turns out that young Faith has been divesting herself of her luxurious gold, silks, and furs, the trappings of her noble birthright, for some time, in order to give them to the poor and the lepers. We learn shortly thereafter, however, that the pagans, not at all the opposite of the Christian saint, do very much the same, giving up in turn their own golden rings ("*l'anel del man*" [49]) or even just a tiny bit of bread if that is all they can afford ("*pecza de pan*" [50]). The two religions emerge in this example as "*frères ennemis*," insufficiently differentiated and bound in a pact of ritual sacrifice and murder. All that Faith can do to distinguish herself from these self-denying pagans is to perform her ascetic practices in an even more single-minded and obsessive way, and cleave to the model of Christ. This behavior, in turn, further sharpens her enemies' enmity, especially in the case of the devil, and the passages in which this dynamic is described bristle with mimetic energy.[7] God needs the sacrifice of his people to be God, that much is clear, but though both pagans and Christians oblige him, one does so in vain (the pagans) and the other in exchange for favor (i.e., her salvation, in the case of Faith). The devil essentially imitates this primordial desire to be desired—a taste acquired from God—as he works endlessly to circumvent this flow of desire and adoration and redirect it toward himself.

Faith emerges as the ultimate Christian, a sacrificer who is also willing to make of herself the object to be sacrificed. Her first renunciation is of her people and possessions, in keeping with God's plan:

> For God's sake she lowered herself to great poverty;
> she left behind the others of her land
> and became single-minded in her devotion, as God wishes (or: in searching
> for God).[8]

This behavior is, of course, doubly offensive to the pagan rulers because it goes against all of their interests, material and ideological. If they cannot be the model that inspires her imitation, or if she insists on being so much like them that she weakens their claims to singularity, then she and others like her must die so as to eliminate all models of worship and governance that would rival their own. The pagan's religion emerges thereby as a sham: their idols simply images of themselves, totems of political worship. These men kill saints with their bare hands, we are told ("*aucis lil[s] saintz ab ambas mans*" [line 129]) and delight in it ("*els Cristians prend'et eschar / els destrenga fort & amar*" [lines 130–31]); and for this crime they will suffer eternally, "under a thousand devils" (line 121).[9] The world that we live in appears always as larger and more menacing than we could possibly imagine—one religion up against another, unable to establish its own brand of sovereignty—and marked by unavoidable conflict. Even eternal punishment takes place within a social setting, the dead piled up upon the dead. And this life is but a foretaste of what is to come.[10]

Faith's defiant stance is hardly welcomed by her people either, at least not at first. The Agenais are easily impressed by political power and urge the pagan rulers to discipline the young girl, warning their rulers that what they covet will soon be hers through inheritance and that she will in turn use that inheritance to defeat them. Her noble family has however always supported the people and the community, as befitting such a family in a gift economy, but Faith's abandonment of their pagan beliefs involves as well a relinquishing of her family destiny and its responsibility (*"Sos linz nos a totz temps nuiriz, / elle per mal anz relinquiz"* [lines 163–64]). The Agenais pagans agree that they cannot tolerate individuals who relinquish hereditary duties and they urge Dacien to slice the girl's throat or risk losing their hold on legitimacy, power, and the right to life:

> And you will all end up dead and humiliated
> if you do not bleed her brain
> as you did with Saint Felix.[11]

This public call to murder is, of course, the cry of the mob, the incitement to sacrificial violence, but it is also a knowing warning that sovereignty is nothing more than a theatrical pantomime. Should Dacien fail to follow their wishes, his power will crumble and his bogus gods will go down with him. So far all agree that Faith must die, each from his or her own perspective, but no one is as keen on that prospect as Faith herself.

After her arrest, she raises her voice against her persecutors, calls openly for death and begs God to send relief and take her soul (*"Mais voil morir o pendr'al vent"* ["I would prefer to die and hang, swaying in the wind," lines 260]). Decapitation follows an unsuccessful grilling (she is saved by angels), upon which the attitude of the people reverts suddenly to mourning, all calls for violence forgotten. They sigh (*"gentz suspira"*) as they watch her burn, then turn on the rulers once they have witnessed her death.[12] The mob acts here, at one and the same time, as the voice of the prosecution and the voice of the defence. They make and support the initial accusation that Faith is undermining social structure and that her defiance will lead to social disruption, then they sanctify her death by reinstantiating the sacred in the form of her body and proceed to turn on their sovereign. In other words, they call for her sacrifice, then close ranks around her dead body to sanctify it through collective hysteria. From this point on, there is no further question of the saint's murder being an isolated phenomenon. The slaughter that follows actualizes the mob's worst suppositions, with rivers of blood and unburied bodies ("*Ar audirez un mot eschiu: lo sangs en terra fez gran riu*" [lines 402–3]). All that they had predicted had Faith lived comes true with Faith's death. As long as her body lies unburied and unprotected, the people await with fear a renewed outbreak of the violence ("*paor an gran qel mals reziu*" [line 411]).

The role that God plays in this cycle of violence is muted but not inconsequential. Though Girard's later work, like *Violence and the Sacred* and *Things Hidden*, focuses more on the sacrificial figure of Jesus Christ as the victim who proclaims his innocence and thereby undoes the myth of the solitary victim at whose feet the social crisis is laid, the pattern does not exactly fit this particular tale of sacrifice. It is God, after all, who sent his son to earth to experience that sacrificial death; and God, however you spin it, who is complicit with the mechanism unleashed in this tale through mimetic rivalry. Though the death of the victim initially calms the violence, dependent of course upon the safe burial of the sacred body, the threat of more of the same is palpable. The God of this tale is a passive yet curiously engaged spectator rather than a clear arbiter of justice and this emerges even in the manner in which he is addressed. Like the courtly lady, several decades before her first official appearance in the *cansos* of the early troubadours, he is addressed as a *domna*, a superior presence, a sovereign, whose every whim becomes law and whose desires are never expressly enunciated. In lines 230–35, for example, Faith has just spent her first night in prison after having been beaten very badly earlier that evening. When called upon now to renounce her false beliefs, having learned her lesson, she instead recites the following incantation:

> I want to get closer to my lord . . .
> There is nothing I admire so much as him.
> If I do not have him with me, I cannot be cured (saved).
> I love nothing so much as him and I cannot lie about it:
>   it is with him that I want to laugh and take my pleasure.[13]

With little or no manipulation, this passage could have been inserted into the middle of almost any standard twelfth-century love song (*canso*) and the same could be said for Faith's second declaration of love, a hundred or so lines later:

> He is the one I would want to take as my spouse,
> no matter what you put me through today,
> for to me he is beautiful and loving.[14]

Faith will also be placed into this *domna* position after her death as she becomes for her followers the intermediary between their needs and the God to whom they pray. Calling her explicitly their "*domna*," they laud her power of intercession, claiming that she can cure whatever ails them. One piquant example that they cite is worth repeating:

> Giraud, a badly tonsured monk,
> took out the eyes of his closest companion, Guibert.
> Then, a year later,
> God returned his sight to him through the intercession of Faith.
> If a man comes to her, blind or dumb,
> or with an ailment that greatly afflicts him,
> or if he is held in prison
> or in ruins after a war,
> provided that he stretches himself out before her,
> regardless of whether he is young or old,
> joy and blessings will always thereafter rain upon him.
> So now let us pray, my lady, that you come to our aid.[15]

The association here between acts of violence, warfare, and the devotion to the saint is not coincidental. Faith is clearly one who was always associated with rivalry and its consequences and this could not be any clearer than in the fate of her corpse. According to a ninth-century legend, her body was stolen from its grave in Agen in order to be incorporated into the sacred space of the new abbey at Conques. This theft, which resulted in the building of one of the jewels of pilgrimage architecture, involved monks stealing from monks in the interests of commerce.[16] Once again, the mimetic energies produced by a state of sanctity overflow any text that tries to contain them and it is with such a state of crisis that the author ends his *Vida*. Abandoning the holy saint altogether and defying generic expectations, he turns his attention back to the bloodshed that the city of Agen experienced after the murder of the saint. Such a dispiriting ending frankly mystifies: why focus on destruction and disgust rather than exult over the final victory of the saint? Here is a sampling of the text's closing stanza:

> Only a madman would take the trouble
> to seek to better his family's fortunes by doing evil.
> God saw to it that hardly a day goes by
> that the sons of one of those men don't attack the sons of the other
> . . . .
> Blood flows from their necks
> and there they are, dead on the straw, the two kings,
> each wrapped in a sheet.
> God burned that family like a fire burns a torch;
> never will their remains be seen.
> If they ended up slaughtering each other,
> that shouldn't upset you for it doesn't bother me a bit.
> Just the thought of singing any more about them disgusts me.[17]

This author, who began his song with a call to pleasure, followed by a meditation on violence in the pagan world, switches, after recounting the life of martyred victim, to a dispiriting reminder that violence can only ever beget more of the same; and that violence always afflicts one side and the other. His saint is one who imitates her lord, thinking him unique, but she is matched by the pagans who do much the same, all craving as well the blessing of their sovereign. The sovereigns, meanwhile, and in both cases, are so anxious about their status that they rely on violence to put an end to violence, as we see in the parable cited above that appears in the final stanza of the saint's life. Faith's sacrifice is supposed to ensure the well-being of her land and its people but it is ultimately unable to undo the links between mimetic desire and violence. Her story is instead a reminder of its ravages. So why is it that this early Occitan text takes the trouble to reveal the mechanism of victimization only to deny its power to undo that violence?

Part of that explanation might involve the status of the saint's life itself as a genre. Neither a text of revelation or of liturgy, the early vernacular saint's life walks the line between entertainment and didacticism. The authors veer from celebration of the saints' courage and forthrightness, and veneration of their beauty and singularity, to outright delight in their torture and ability to withstand repeated attempts at murder. Diegetically, the texts are equally ambivalent. The saint, too, is subject to the mimetic machine and imitates her desire from the example of the Christ figure; but that figure operates as both an internal and external mediator, thus destroying any attempt at classification. Christ is both a figure from outside the mimetic circle and a figure internal to the subject. In Faith's case, Christ is a projection of her "faith," in an abstract sense, and a body with which she craves union, in an arguably material and internal sense. Religion, too, finds itself embedded in processes of mimetic return, and as the structural differences between one religion and the other dissolve, the listener is left with divided sympathies: Faith is a young girl victimized by political forces and a young lover separated from her desired mate. The personal and political merge in this tale and one is unsure of where to read it finally: as a religious parable on faith? A didactic parable inciting imitation? A political parable on the curse of power's abuses? In an interesting discussion of Girard and Giorgio Agamben, Rey Chow makes the following statement that strikes at the heart of my unease in analyzing the *Life of Saint Faith*:

> this is also the point at which Girard's seemingly amoral, religion-oriented argument of mimetic violence comes closest to Agamben's nihilistic, atheist understanding of law and power. As the fundamental vacuity of the sovereign relation is exposed by the increasingly arbitrary abuses by those in power, what is so-called law is revealing itself—and here is the logical transition from Agamben into Girard—to be nothing more than a collectively ordained exercise of violence, intended once upon a time to preserve the social equilibrium, perhaps, but now functioning as nothing more than a killing machine.[18]

To return to the citation cited at the beginning of this essay, Girard claimed that "great writers apprehend intuitively and concretely, through the medium of their art . . . the system in which they were first imprisoned."[19] This system, we might say, is one that our Occitan author understands only too well, and it consists in the workings of mimetic desire and the prison in which it holds us. In the *Cancó de Santa Fe* mimetic desire is voracious, mutating when disempowered so as to resurrect itself in another form, afflicting both sides in the conflict. Even the impulse to imitate and worship the sovereign is embedded in tangled economic hierarchies that subordinate one mimetic practice—victimization—to another—the economic well-being that is born of the possession of a holy relic. *Cancó de Santa Fe* may provide us with a rare eleventh-century reading of this operation, but its author never claims that revelation alone, Christian revelation, can lead to reformation. On the contrary, he suggests that the violence that gives rise to and defends the inviolability of the sacred is no different from the violence that gives rise to the political. Rather than try to separate out those two domains as incommensurable, as we are often wont to do, we should instead listen more closely to the text itself: a text that reveals not that violence can be overcome by sacrifice, as in a myth, but that violence can never be overcome so long as both discourses—the religious and political—feed on the blood that gives rise to their institution and on which they lay their sovereign claims. A dance "à lei francesca," our author called his text at the beginning of the life he was to recount: a dance indeed, a dance of death, and one whose genre would benefit from the riches of Girardian analysis.

Notes

1. These are some of the criteria for determining sacrificial status according to Girard's model: (1) The victims are charged with being guilty of a crime that they did not commit. (2) The crime is so heinous that it could undermine safety and order. (3) They are not given a trial at which their innocence could be established. (4) Their death instantiates a period of calm following one of high political tension. (5) They become more powerful and more threatening after their deaths. (6) Their once vilified bodies become conduits of some sort of blessing (often healing oils and grace). (7) Their afterlives as protectors of the community and mediators between the individual and the divinity make them much more useful after death than ever they were while living.

2. Giorgio Agamben, *Homo Sacer: Sovereign Power and Bare Life*, trans. D. Heller-Roazen (Stanford: Stanford University Press, 1998), 14.

3. René Girard, *Deceit, Desire, and the Novel: Self and Other in Literary Structure*, trans. Yvonne Freccero. (Baltimore: Johns Hopkins University Press, 1965), 14.

4. *La Chanson de Sainte Foi d'Agen, poème provençal du XIe siècle*, ed. Antoine Thomas (Paris: Champion, 1974).

5. *Chanson*, 3, line 20.

6. *Chanson*, lines 60–64. "King Solomon once told a parable about an apple tree that grew in the woods, surrounded on all sides by thorns and thistles and hawthorne. The tree grew straight upward nonetheless and produced flowers at its summit and the fruits that follow in their season. The pagan Gascons were such an evil presence for they refused to recognize God in his heavens. Their pressing shade similarly strangled the young plant about whom we are singing this song; and God took of that tree the sweet fruit and the good" (*Chanson*, lines 53–63, p. 5).

7. Her heart is said to lie with God's heart [line 87] and she cannot wait to join him in death [lines 89–90], actions that heighten the devil's taste for revenge [line 91].

8. *Chanson*, lines 102–4.

9. *Chanson*, 9.

10. See Rey Chow's meditation on the differences between Girard, Agamben, and Foucault on the question of mimetism, sacrifice, and the law in "Sacrifice, Mimesis, Victimhood," in *Entanglements, or Transmedial Thinking about Capture* (Durham, NC: Duke University Press, 2012), 81–105. See also Girard on war at http://www.rene-girard.com/rene-girard-war-is-everywhere.

11. *Chanson*, lines 169–71. "May she find no source of support in you until she gives up her offensive belief in that God she worships. She really has treated us like a bunch of fools. Her hostility has weakened us and you are dead and dishonored if you don't see to it that blood is soon flowing from her neck as it did with Saint Felix" (lines 165–71).

12. *Chanson*, lines 380–83.

13. *Chanson*, lines 231–36.

14. *Chanson*, lines 311–13.

15. *Chanson*, lines 441–53. The miracle tradition that surrounded Saint Faith was chronicled throughout the eleventh century by Bernard of Angers and his followers in a collection now known as the *Liber miraculorum sancta Fidis*. A recent publication on this account of miracles brings out the ways in which the saint's deeds were seen either as miracles or as tricks. See Kathleen Ashley and Pamela Sheingorn's *Writing Faith: Text, Sign and History in the Miracle of Saint Faith* (Chicago: University of Chicago Press, 1999).

16. *Chanson*, lines 433–36.

17. *Chanson*, lines 586–93.

18. Chow, *Entanglements*, 104.

19. Girard, *Deceit, Desire, and the Novel*, 3.

Dubbiosi Disiri

Mimetic Processes in Dante's *Comedy*

Manuele Gragnolati and Heather Webb

This essay explores the potential uses of René Girard's theory of mimetic desire to shed new light on the ways in which desire is articulated and structured in the *Commedia*. Girard's mimetic theory is based on human interaction and it branches outside the limits of the literary text per se to propose a veritable social theory; in a similar fashion, Dante's poetic journey into the redemptive potentiality of the human seeks to illustrate how the individual, in its historical uniqueness, could progressively and painfully move from a state of self-enclosure and sterility to the openness of constructive desire, communication, and communal sharing.

Girard's mimetic theory teases out what texts can tell us about human relationships. According to Girard, the great writers are the best "theoreticians," because they "apprehend intuitively and concretely, through the medium of their art, if not formally, the system in which they were first imprisoned together with their contemporary."[1] Because of the wide variety of characters and human case studies that Dante proposes in the *Commedia*, alongside the overall structural, philosophical, and theological coherence of his work, Dante illustrates a theory of desire that not only prefigures some of Girard's points about the novelistic revelation of the mechanisms of imitative desire, but also considers a greater variety of aspects of these mechanisms than does Girard. Most importantly, perhaps, Dante illustrates a range of modes of mimetic desire that include positive and even salvific modes, while Girard's articulation of mimetic desire sees the mechanism as fundamentally negative.

In his discussion of the mimetic nature of desire, Girard has put almost exclusive emphasis on its conflictual and antagonistic aspects (envy, jealousy, rivalry, resentment, blaming, scapegoating, violence, sacrifice), leaving aside the positive and constructive ones (empathy, the pedagogical modeling of desire, reciprocal positive mirroring, nonconflictual love, and the emancipatory role of art).[2] What is striking in Dante is the fact that the *Commedia*, and in particular the *Purgatorio*, provides what we could call a medieval version of therapy, an approach that intends to heal the individual of the dangerous aspects and involutional dynamics of desire, and that intends to direct her from the mechanisms of rivalry and self-referential compulsions typical of the *Inferno*, through a difficult and painful redirection and remodeling of desire in Purgatory, to the complete openness of desire in Paradise.

This essay focuses on the episode of Paolo and Francesca in *Inferno* 5, to which Girard has dedicated his only essay on the *Commedia*: "The Mimetic Desire of Paolo and Francesca."[3] Girard parallels Dante's episode with Don Quixote. In Cervantes's novel, the protagonist constructs his identity and lives his life through the mediation of the chivalric epic tales of Amadis of Gaul; his desire is mediated by an external model—somebody who does not belong to the same realm of social interaction as Quixote; Girard calls this triangular structuring of desire "external mediation."[4] In a similar way, Francesca's desire for Paolo is triggered by reading a courtly tale, the romance of Lancelot and Guinevere. Just as Madame Bovary becomes victim of her reading of feuilletons, or Quixote is enslaved by the epic mythical frame of mind, Paolo and Francesca become victims of a desire that is not the spontaneous outburst of an authentic passion, as the Romantic critics held, but the production of a mediation—the mediation of literature.

The episode of Francesca and Paolo is obviously a very complex one, precisely because Francesca is constructed in such a way that she continues to elicit fascination and sympathy from the reader.[5] It may be that in Dante's mapping of the constituents of an ideal subjectivity there are some elements of Francesca having to do with both intersubjectivity and language that do not need to be relinquished but transformed. The angle that we are taking at this point, however, is to pursue Girard's emphasis on the fact that Francesca's and Paolo's desire is mediated by a literary model, and to see whether we can engage Girard's concept of mimesis to look at *Inferno* 5 and Dante's poem more generally.

Francesca belongs to the category of the carnal sinners, who are defined as those who subjugate reason to their desire: "the carnal sinners, who subject their reason to their lust" (*Inf.*, 5:38–39).[6] Unlike most popular representations of Hell, which depict the punishment of the lustful in very physical terms—such as having their genitalia devoured by snakes or being forced to enact monstrous and parodic copulations—Dante is more interested in the psychology of love and insists on the lack of control that lust entails:[7] as Dante indicates in several passages of his works and throughout the *Commedia*, reason is the quintessentially human faculty created directly by God that empowers humans with free agency, and the carnal sinners are defined precisely by their inability to use their rational faculty to master their own desires.

The sinners' lack of control over their own desires is reflected in their punishment, which consists of being carried away by a violent hurricane without having control over their bodies: "The infernal whirlwind, which never rests, drives the spirits before its violence; turning and striking, it tortures them" (*Inf.*, 5:31–33);[8] and "so does that breath carry the evil spirits here, there, down, up; no hope ever comforts them, not of lessened suffering, much less of rest" (*Inf.*, 5:42–45).[9] The punishment of the carnal sinners in Hell can be understood as the eschatological dramatization of their earthly experience of sin. Indeed, the verb *menare*, "to drive," which refers twice to the hurricane tormenting the damned, is also used by Virgil to refer to the love that still controls them: "You will see when they are closer to us; and then beg them by the love that drives them, and they will come" (*Inf.*, 5:76–78).[10] As Elena Lombardi also indicates, "The love that drives them" (*l'amor che i mena*) is at the same time the lovers' desire, their sin and their punishment for it.[11] As often in Hell, it is therefore a case of *contrapasso* by analogy inasmuch as punishment consists in being stuck in the same condition of sin that condemned the spirits to Hell in the first place: infernal punishment can be understood as the condition of experiencing one's own sin, that is, as both a manifestation of sin and a fitting punishment for it.[12]

In the case of the carnal sinners, the passivity with which they followed the model imposed on them by literature is reflected not only in their lack of control over their own bodies within the infernal hurricane, but also in the way in which Francesca gives an account of her adultery: "Love, which is swiftly kindled in the noble heart seized this one for the lovely person that was taken from me; and the manner still injures me. Love, which pardons no one loved from loving in return, seized me for his beauty so strongly that, as you see, it still does not abandon me. Love led us on to one death. Caina awaits him who extinguished our life" (*Inf.*, 5:100–108).[13] Francesca credits love for her passion for Paolo and, as has been noted by several critics, always presents herself—also grammatically—as a passive object, claiming that she had no power over the irresistible force of love. It is also interesting to note that "swiftly" (*ratto*) indicates the automatic, unreflective way of falling in love.

As is well known, Francesca's words are a collage of new phrases and passages from texts by courtly poets and theoreticians, from Andrea Cappellanus to Guido Guinizzelli to Dante himself:[14] the impossibility of resisting love was quite a dominant motif of courtly literature, and what we would like to point out is that Francesca has so much interiorized the models for her desire that her words, which do not accurately represent her earthly reality, have indeed become her eternal reality in Hell: according to Dante, Francesca was not—as she claims in her mechanical repetition of a topos of courtly literature—a passive object conquered by love, but a free agent who decided not to control her misplaced desires, and in Hell she has become precisely what she performed on earth and is now deficient of all control. This is a performative concept of identity and it is precisely this that we find particularly compelling about looking at Dante's *Commedia* with the lens of mimetic desire: performance of or acting upon mimetic desire in life becomes real, unchangeable, substantial identity in Hell.

Francesca's infernal condition consists of eternally repeating the models that she accepted passively without ever seeing their false premises. In other words, one could say that Hell for Francesca means being trapped within the consequences of her mimetic desires: she does not read or imitate anymore but has become what she read. This condition refers to not only Francesca's specific eschatological destination, but also to a human experience, in the form of a pathological narcissism that corresponds to the radical closure of the self: Francesca echolalically repeats the words of the poets, while she also seems to lack any form of communication with Paolo, the person who, supposedly, she should be in love with.

There is more to be explored in term of mimetic processes in canto 5 of *Inferno*, and something that interests us is what it means that Dante-the-character and Francesca engage with each other in a way that assimilates them, through a process of mimetic mirroring of each other: as we mentioned before, Francesca speaks by referring to a line from Dante's lyric poetry and Dante-the-character also mirrors her words and falls into her rhetorical patterns when he says: "by what and how did Love grant you to know your dangerous desires [*dubbiosi desiri*]," (*Inf.*, 5:119–20)[15] attributing agency to love, just as she does.[16] Moreover he also faints like a dead body in the same way as Francesca was led to death by love: Francesca's "Love led us on to one death" is mirrored in Dante's "and I fell as a dead body falls" (*Inf.*, 5:106).[17]

These considerations bring to light a comparison between Francesca in *Inferno* 5 and the lustful in Purgatory, for whom the experience of pain is not only punishment, as in Hell, but also an opportunity for growth and transformation. The only eschatological realm set in time, Purgatory is also the only realm where the soul changes, entering contaminated by sin and leaving after having recuperated and reactivated its original goodness. This process of change consists of transforming one's desires and occurs through a complicated process centered on the model of Christ and involving several actions, such as praying and meditating upon positive and negative examples taken from the Bible and classical mythology.[18]

In the terrace of lust, which is the last terrace of purgatory proper and is situated just below the garden of Eden, souls are burned in fire and divided into two groups that seem to fit and not to fit modern categories of homosexuality and heterosexuality. As in all other terraces, the purging souls are confronted with positive examples to imitate (the first of which is always Mary, Christ's mother) and with negative examples to reject. As a negative example of lust the first group of souls (usually referred to as "homosexuals" by twentieth-century commentators) recalls Sodom and Gomorrah. Guido Guinizelli, one soul belonging to the other group of lustful (usually referred to as "heterosexuals" by twentieth-century commentators), further characterizes the first group by referring to Julius Caesar when he was called "queen" (*regina*) by his army for his relationship with King Nicomedes,[19] while his own group recalls Pasiphaë, the queen of Crete who was forced to fall in love with a bull and had a wooden cow built so that she could enter it and be mounted by the bull: "Into the cow goes Pasiphaë, so that the young bull will run to her lust" (*Pur.*, 26:41–42).[20] Unlike Francesca, who continues to mechanically repeat the formulas of lyric poetry without understanding that they do not fully represent the truth of her situation, the lustful in Purgatory gain awareness of their sin and unveil what they believe is the true nature of their wrong desires—or what is presented as such by the examples of purgatory. It is the soul of Guido Guinizzelli, one of the poets whose words Francesca was ventriloquizing in her celebration of the power of love, who confesses his sin to Dante and acknowledges having been a carnal sinner: "because we did not keep human law, following our appetite like beasts, in our own reproach we read out when we part, the name of her who made herself a beast within the beast-shaped planks" (*Pur.*, 26:41–42).[21] To subjugate reason to desire ("who make reason subject to desire" in the words of *Inferno* 5.39) is here described as following one's appetite as beasts, "following our appetite like beasts"—which amounts to transgressing humanity ("we did not keep human law"). On this score, one may need to recall the distinction made by Girard between appetite and desire (appetites are biological and instinctual and proper also to animals; desires are social and therefore radically human).[22] Here, the souls' self-accusation suggests that their pursuit of their desires manifested itself in a bestial way, leading them to translate human desire into animalistic appetite. As we will see later, Dante makes crucial distinctions between forms of love and desire, as well as the pursuit of those desires. The souls in Purgatory see the difference between human desire and its potential outcomes; Francesca's speech conflates love, desire, seduction, and adultery in simplistic, if incantatory, formulas.

Among the passages in Latin authors that mention Pasiphaë it is to our knowledge Ovid's *Ars Amatoria* that gives the most thorough account of her story.[23] Reading it, we were struck by the extent to which it is structured according to the paradigm of antagonistic mimetic desire and its monstrous transformations. While in the case of Francesca and Paolo, mediation was "external," in the case of Pasiphaë in Ovid's account in the *Ars Amatoria* it is "internal" and leads to a negative loop of identification and rivalry: it is by looking at cows desiring to be mounted by the bull that Pasiphaë's desire and jealousy are aroused. On the one hand, Pasiphaë feels more and more jealous of the cows ("she hated the handsome heifers with jealousy") and considers them her rivals, while, on the other hand, she wishes to be like them ("How you wish that brow of yours could bear horns") and behaves like a cow so that she can approach the bull. Devoured by jealousy and mad like a Maenad, Ovid's Pasiphaë punishes her rivals by having them either work under a yoke or be "felled before the altar, forced to be a false sacrifice," rejoicing to hold "her rival's entrails in her hands." Pasiphaë's delirious mimetic frenzy culminates in taking the same shape as her rivals: she has a wooden cow built with which she can "deceive" the bull and be impregnated by him (and the offspring will be the Minotaur). Pasiphaë has literally turned into a monstrous double of the rivals upon which she has modeled her own desires; mimesis has turned her into a beast. In Girardian terms, this would correspond to the mythical transfiguration that the mimetic frenzy would eventually produce, the scapegoating of rivals, and the sacrificial gesture as the ultimate end point of the mimetic paroxysm.[24] From our perspective, it seems to confirm the performative nature of desire that we had already proposed with Francesca: it is by desiring what cows desire that the human Pasiphaë literally takes on the shape of a cow.

The cases of Francesca and Pasiphaë indicate not only that their desire is not spontaneous but mimetic, but also that mimesis is performative and can enchain the subject into an identity of (self-)obsession and closure. Yet considering Francesca and Pasiphaë from a Girardian perspective also highlights differences between the two figures: Pasiphaë's desire is a case of internal mediation that leads to rivalry and to the paroxysm of monstrous doubling, while Francesca's case, which shares with Pasiphaë a monomaniac closure, is more complicated and ambivalent, as the long history of its reception shows. Indeed, while mimesis turns Pasiphaë into an animal controlled by its sexual appetite, Francesca becomes a sort of literalization of the refined and elegant courtly literature that she reads and follows. The figure of the fully bestial and almost schematic case of Pasiphaë can work well in Purgatory, where the souls are confronted with fully negative examples that must help them to change. The figure of Francesca would be less suitable, as it expresses some ambivalent elements that have the potential for seduction (and indeed continue to seduce the reader of the episode).

Something that interests us and that we would like to investigate further is precisely how the difference between Francesca and Pasiphaë relates to the fact that in spite of Pasiphaë's fully negative example, the terrace of lust in Purgatory does not lead to the cessation of desire (as one may have expected) but to Dante's reunion with Beatrice in the garden of Eden. That is, the process of purgatory does not seem to aim at eradicating interpersonal desire from the subject, but at correcting and transforming it.[25]

We are also very interested in exploring how Purgatory's positive mimetic process functions and how it breaks the negative loop typical of Hell. A hypothesis could be that awareness, voluntariness, and Christ's mediation play an all-important role in this process, which helps the souls overcome the closure and self-obsession typical of Hell, and open up to others.

The central cantos of *Purgatorio*, and of the *Comedy* as a whole, unfold a comprehensive "theory" of the causes of sin and the problem of desire that provides some key tools for such an investigation of the mechanisms of the recuperation and reshaping of desire. It is a discourse that relates to desire in general and not solely to lust; therefore, for the purposes of the present investigation, we will briefly treat the comprehensive theory with an eye to arriving at what we are reading as a response to Francesca's misguided explanation or rather justification of her own actions.

The discussion takes place as the pilgrim has just passed through the terraces of pride and envy, and is now among the wrathful. These three sins in particular may be understood to be at the center of the problem of mimetic rivalry in a way that resonates with Girard's meditation. Girard speaks of the *vaniteux*, of envy, and of hatred (which we may relate to wrath) in the very first pages of *Deceit, Desire, and the Novel* as key concepts in his theory of triangular desire.[26] Envy is of particular importance here; for Girard, envy does not begin around the object of rivalry, but rather with the subject's relation to the rival himself. In a similar vein, for Dante, envy is not coveting something that belongs to another, but rather desiring that the other be deprived of that thing. Dante's sense of mimetic rivalry in envy has much in common with Girard's; he actually removes the object of rivalry from the equation. This is shown, for instance, by the sinner Sapia, who explains that her envy consisted in rejoicing more for other people's ill fate than for her own good fortune: "I rejoiced at other's harms much more that at my own good luck" (*Pur.*, 13:110–11).[27]

Envy is important for our discussion for two reasons. First, in the context of lust: if we consider Ovid's description, envy is a strong component of Pasiphaë's madness. She delights in destroying her rivals by either having them put under a yoke or even sacrificed on the altar in what Ovid names a "false sacrifice." As she holds the entrails in her hand, saying "go, please him for me," we get the sense that she joys above all in the knowledge that her slaughtered rivals can no longer enjoy the attentions of the bull. Second, and more generally, the discussion in the central cantos of *Purgatorio* focuses on the invidious nature of desire and its individual and social causes. Desire, when it leads to the unleashed pursuit of limited, earthly goods, swiftly and inevitably gives rise to envy and resulting conflict.

It is one of the envious, Guido del Duca, who raises the issue that begins this larger consideration of the problems of desire: "O human race, why do you set your heart where sharing must be forbidden?" (*Pur.*, 14:85–87)[28]—a rhetorical question indicating that humankind makes the mistake of directing its affection and desires toward those goods that are diminished by sharing. Later, Dante is still pondering this problem, an issue that we have come to see as a central one in the *Commedia*: Why do we tend to desire things that cannot be properly shared? Is it possible to desire noncompetitively? And if so, how?

When Dante asks for clarification, Virgil explains: "Because your desires point to where sharing lessens each one's portion, envy moves the bellows to sighing. But if the love of the highest sphere bent your desire upward, you would not have that fear in your breasts: for the more say 'our' up there, the more good each one possesses, and the more charity burns in that cloister" (*Pur.*, 15:49–57).[29] Human desires, when they are focused on the wrong things, enter into competition with the desires of others, a notion that resonates with Girard's concept that desire, being mimetic, must often impel competition in a similar way. According to Virgil, many objects of desire cannot be shared without being diminished, if they can be shared at all. It is only through the love of God, which redirects desire upward, to heavenly goods that are infinitely shareable, and in fact, increased by sharing, that this infernal pattern of rivalry and envy may be avoided.

While each individual is held responsible for his or her own misdirected desires, mimetic patterns are invoked to explain why it is that things have come to be so very troubled in Dante's world. When the pilgrim asks the penitent Marco Lombardo to explain the reasons for which the world is barren of virtue, Marco begins by a description of the individual soul and the ways it may fall into sin but transitions quickly to a discussion of earthly political leaders that is famous for the image of the two suns as representing the ideal independence of Papacy and Empire from each other. But this discussion can also offer a meditation on the function of models in the mechanisms of desire. Marco Lombardo explains that it is wrong to look to heavenly causality for the evils of the world, but that one must, instead, look to humans and to their human leaders. He first explains God's creation of the individual soul, and almost simultaneously, the creation of its desires: "From the hand of him who desires it before it exists, like a little girl who weeps and laughs childishly, the simple little soul come forth, knowing nothing except that, set in motion by a happy Maker, it gladly turns to what amuses it" (*Pur.*, 16:85–90).[30] The human soul's first model is God. Just as God looks with love upon the soul and is described as a joyful maker, so the human soul happily turns toward those things that bring delight. But the soul has issued forth from the hand of God ("From the hand of him who desires it") and so enters the body and world, leaving behind an innocent and direct mode of relating to God. At this point, the turning soul and its accompanying body can go astray if, for example, the soul follows a lesser good with excessive enthusiasm.

Here, according to Marco, is where human models and structures are needed. The problem is that the current leaders of the spiritual realm act in a way that is invidious of the temporal realm and of imperial power. They pursue earthly and diminishable goods, thus guiding the people into cupidity by example: "therefore the people, who see their guide striking at the thing that they themselves are greedy for, feed there and seek no further" (*Pur.*, 16:100–102).[31] This introduces a similarity, a vicinity of desires between the people and the pope that should not exist, and this vicinity of desire makes the pope's greed for temporal power work as a perverse model for humans, focusing not on the higher, spiritual goods that can be shared but on earthly things that cannot. The terminology introduced here, of greediness, feeding, and satiation, likens the pursuit of these mimetic desires to the trajectories of baser appetites. The people do not seek beyond the satisfaction of this hunger; appropriate desire, in Dante, is not so easily sated.

Girard in *Deceit, Desire, and the Novel* also speaks at length of the importance of distance between the subject and the mediator.[32] The distance is above all a spiritual one, not physical or even necessarily structural. When the people see the pope grabbing for the same goods that they themselves desire, the distance between people and pontiff is reduced to a relationship of similarity. The structuring hierarchy is flattened. Further, the power of the model is such that the people do not seek to desire anything other than that which the model desires. Cupidity is thus reinforced in a cycle of blockage from which there is no outlet without the introduction of a different kind of model. Marco even describes a kind of monstrous doubling between the church and the empire: "Rome, which made the good world, used to have two suns that made visible the two paths of the world and of God. One sun has extinguished the other, and the sword is joined to the shepherd's staff, and it is ill for those two to be violently forced together" (*Pur.*, 16:106–11).[33] The church, placing itself in rivalry with the empire, has become fixated upon subsuming that power into itself, as if it were an institutional Ugolino, devouring his rival.

An effective emperor would rein in the chaotic forces of cupidity and maintain dominion over the earthly realm as separate from the spiritual. Once secure under the emperor, humankind would be free to desire those goods that unify society, rather than those goods that lead to conflict. Again, a distinction between desire and appetite might be crucial here. In chapter 12 of book 1 of the *Monarchia*, Dante explains that judgment can be swayed when it is in some way hindered by appetites. In that case, judgment cannot be free because it cannot act with authority, but is "dragged away" as if captive to another force: "Now if judgment controls desire completely and is in no way pre-empted by it, it is free; but if judgment is in any way at all pre-empted and thus controlled by desire, it cannot be free, because it does not act under its own power, but is dragged along in the power of something else."[34] In other words, unrestrained appetites impede the ultimate freedom of desire, the freedom to desire goods beyond those that engender conflict even as they promise quick and satisfying rewards. This suggests that desire can be liberated when judgment is also free.

When there is no rein on the fractious forces of cupidity in society, and those who should be providing that rein are instead modeling unrestrained acquisitive responses to desire, humans are not entirely free to choose the greater good.[35] Dante is acutely aware of the power of models, seeing both pope and emperor as supreme models of behavior. The ideal emperor, in fact, is, by Dante's definition in the *Monarchia*, someone who sounds almost other than human, in that he is free of desire for earthly possessions—the *cupiditas* that all of humankind suffers as a consequence of Original Sin—by virtue of the fact that he already possesses everything. There is, therefore, a great distance between the people and such a model or mediator. He becomes a "safe" model for two reasons: first, he is himself free of dangerous, competitive desires, and second, this difference of desire locates him at a safe spiritual distance from the people he governs. Since humans imitate the desires of others, people cannot competitively desire what the emperor has (even if he has everything) simply because the emperor himself does not desire any earthly goods. Likewise, the pope should be free of desire for earthly possessions, not actively envying and pursing that which ought to belong to the emperor. The pope's mediator should not be the emperor, but Christ alone, who did not desire any material good and whose best representative in this respect, St. Francis—as St. Dominic tells us in Heaven of the Sun—united with Lady Poverty in a mystical marriage and whose conformity with Christ was signaled by his stigmata ("the final seal"; *Par.*, 11:107).

After canto 17, which explains the structure of Purgatory according to three different ways of desiring badly ("with an evil object or with too much or too little vigor"; *Pur.*, 16:95–96) canto 18 continues the discussion on desire with an analysis of the nature of love. It seems to us that Virgil's words suggest an important distinction between love, desire, and the modes of pursuit of objects of desire that could be developed further:

> The mind, created quick to love, can move toward everything that is pleasing, as soon as it is wakened into act by pleasure. Your power of apprehension takes from some real thing an intention and unfolds it within you, so that it causes the mind to turn toward it; and if, having turned, the mind bends toward it, that bending is love, that is nature which by pleasure is first bound in you (*Pur.* 18:19–25).[36]

Love thus occurs when an image is taken from a real thing and unfolded within. The soul bends toward that image and that bending is love.

Desire occurs in a second phase: "Then, as fire moves upwards because of its form, which is born to rise to where it may last longer in its matter, so the captured mind enters into desire, which is a spiritual motion, and it never rests until the beloved thing causes it to rejoice" (*Pur.*, 18:28–33).[37] Desire here is cast as the state of the soul that does not rest until the beloved object makes it rejoice.[38] Note that "seized" (*preso*) is used here to describe the soul that has come to love and thus enters into desire, recalling Francesca's "Love, which is swiftly kindled in the noble heart, *seized* this one for the lovely person that was taken from me" (*Inf.*, 5:100–101; emphasis added).[39] Thus far, Virgil's explanation and Francesca's formulation are consistent. Love takes hold of a person, causing him or her to enter into a state of desire.

But Virgil's discussion does not conclude here. He continues a bit later to say: "Therefore, supposing that *every love kindled in you* arises by necessity, in you is the power to restrain it. This noble power Beatrice understands as free choice, and therefore see that you remember it, if she speaks to you about it" (*Pur.*, 18:70–72; emphasis added).[40] Within these lines, the "every love kindled in you" (*amor che dentro a voi s'accende*) seems to be another clear recall of those same lines of Francesca's "love, which is swiftly kindled in the noble heart" (*amor, ch'al cor gentil ratto s'apprende*; *Inf.*, 5:100). Such a systematic reworking of those lines shows that what Virgil offers here can also be understood as a response to Francesca's speech. Love is not adequate justification for pursuing the object of one's desire: "in you is the power to restrain it"; love can be controlled. Even if one must love by necessity (or, in Girardian terms, even if desire is always mimetic and "mechanically" induced through mediation), there is always freedom, "free choice" (*libero arbitrio*), that allows humans to govern their subsequent actions in response to their desires. Love may be restrained when necessary; it is not impossible to resist. This is a crucial revision to the doctrine of courtly love on display in Francesca's speech. As she claimed passivity, Dante here counters with the notion that agency and the exercise of free will can and must prevail. While Francesca is eternally stuck in her false notion of helplessness in the face of the power of love, the pilgrim and the reader who have made it thus far have learned that the truth is far more complicated indeed.

The preceding discourse has shown that, according to Dante, Francesca's sin lies in taking for granted that love cannot be controlled and therefore necessitates lustful action (which is precisely defined as the act of subjugating reason to desire). She conflates love, desire, and the pursuit of the object of desire, understanding love as setting into motion an unstoppable chain of events. Instead, propensity to love, which is not denied as a powerful force, is but a first phase. From that love comes desire, or the spiritual motion toward some kind of union with the beloved, a "rejoice" (*gioire*) that only the beloved can provide. It is this striving that can take numerous forms, from the eternal ardent desire for God visible throughout the *Paradiso* to the acquisitive, appetitive scramble for earthly goods and individual bodies. This is a lesson in part learned in the *Vita nuova*, when Dante transitions from desiring something from Beatrice to shifting his emphasis to that beatitude that may be derived from praising his lady alone, without any expectation of that which the troubadours called *mercé* (the conferral of favors upon the poet-lover, for example, or the greeting in the case of Beatrice). When love moves into the realm of acquisitive desire it may be compared to the desire for earthly goods and understood in that context. In those cases, it enters into the world of envy and rivalry.

Love, in Virgil's and Marco's definition, is natural, modeled on God's love, and as such escapes negative mimetic patterns. But desire takes place in the social realm and is therefore acutely vulnerable to negative mimetic mechanisms. As soon as one passes from the initial bending of the soul toward a pleasing image and steps into the bodily world of acquisition, whether of goods or of favors, amorous desire can take the same form as the pope's desire for the emperor's wealth, or Ugolino's desire for Ruggieri's power, or that of any person who competitively seeks to acquire.[41] The transition from love to desire is a transition from the individual workings of the soul, taking the divine model of its source, to the "interdividual" workings of multiple people, to use Girard's terminology,[42] and as such has the power to effect total redemption or to release the mechanisms of rivalry.

When Francesca says that love is "swiftly kindled in the noble heart" she is not wrong: that happens and has happened with Francesca. The problem enters with the mediator, later. It is the mediator that shapes the form that desire will take, but above all, it is the mediator that models the ways in which that desire will lead to action and to pursuit of the object. Consider the way in which Dante probes further, having heard Francesca's first statements about love's inescapable power: "by what and how did Love grant you to know your dangerous [*dubbiosi*] desires" (*Inf.*, 5:119–20).[43] He wants to know the way in which love allowed Francesca and Paolo to know their desires. We may think, here, of original sin. Eve does not know that she desires the apple until the serpent tells her so.[44] The object of desire is suggested by another. As we have seen in Virgil's explanation in *Purgatorio*, love precedes desire. It is desire, not love, that can take on "dubious" forms. It is hard for us now to recapture what a first glance at that sentence might feel like, since these lines are so extremely well known, but if we think about it, Dante's question could seem a bit odd. What we are proposing here is a different sort of reading of

Francesca's speech that can come into being only when we read backward from *Purgatorio* 18. Francesca has already explained that love led to their deaths. So what is it that Dante wants to know? For him, the consequences of love are not self-evident. It's not clear what desires would arise from this love. Francesca's speech is thus divided into two parts: the first explains the all-powerful qualities of love, something that the discourses of *Purgatorio* do not feel the need to deny; and the second explains how that love granted them to know specific forms of their desires.

It is in this second part of the speech that the mimetic mechanism comes into play. Love transitions to specific desires for specific things when a model is presented: "When we read that the yearned-for smile was kissed by so great a lover, he, who will never be separated from me, kissed my mouth all trembling" (*Inf.*, 5:133–36).[45] This is no longer the bending of a single soul toward an image taken from an object. Here, the interpersonal dimension in the form of the model or mediator suggests the desire to obtain something from the object. "He . . . kissed my mouth," in this context, is a strong statement of this transfer, via the mediator of the romance of Lancelot and Guinevere, from the spiritual to the physical realm, and indeed the act of kissing is striking within the lyric context evoked in the episode. Love is thus the soul's natural and sin-free bending toward beauty and that which gives pleasure, as described in the speech in *Purgatorio* 18 cited above. Desire can instead take the form of projecting an individual toward a specific thing. But we cannot know without a model what specific thing it is that we want. Reading of a kiss, Francesca and Paolo kiss. In so doing, Paolo and Francesca act as "the carnal sinners, who subject their reason to their lust" (*Inf.*, 5:38–39).[46] They do not control their desire through reason or the exercise of free will. Paolo takes something that cannot and should not properly be shared with his brother. It is precisely in these desires for specific things, desires that must be modeled upon someone else's desires, that earthly loves are transformed into infernal obsessions that set humans against one another. *Purgatorio* and *Paradiso* will teach the pilgrim to understand the boundaries between love, praiseworthy in itself, and those desires that derive from improper models and thus tell us that we want those things "where sharing lessens each other's portion" (*dove per compagnia parte si scema*; *Pur.*, 15:50).

After therapy in Purgatory, Heaven is the place that will show the correct way of desiring. We would like to conclude by mentioning a tercet from

Piccarda Donati's speech on heavenly bliss as an example of this correct modality of desire. On Earth Piccarda did not fulfill her vows and thereby in Heaven enjoys a lesser degree of beatitude than other souls, and when she is explicitly asked whether she desires to have the same beatitude as souls higher up in Paradise, she indicates that desire in Heaven works in a different way than on Earth: "Brother, our will is quieted by the power of charity, which causes us to desire only what we have and does not make us thirsty for anything else" (*Par.*, 3:70–72).[47] Dante's Heaven shows that once freed from a self-centered and myopic loop of competition and rivalry, human desire can be noncompetitive, but open to others and a source in itself of joy and happiness.

While *Inferno* 5 develops a model of mimetic desire that is particularly useful for Girard's consideration of envy, rivalry, and violence, the *Purgatorio* offers theorizations of desire that account for a spectrum of possibilities, and the *Paradiso* provides models of joyful, noncompetitive desire. Precisely how does this paradisiacal desire work? Is it possible in earthly existence? How does a performative concept of identity allow us to explore such various modes of being? These preliminary experiments in thinking mimetic desire in the *Comedy* would suggest that this is a rich field for further inquiry.

Notes

1. René Girard, *Deceit, Desire, and the Novel: Self and Other in Literary Structure*, trans. Yvonne Freccero (Baltimore: Johns Hopkins University Press, 1965), 3.

2. For a preliminary discussion on the positive aspects of mimetic dynamics see, for instance, René Girard's *Evolution and Conversion: Dialogues on the Origin of Culture*, with Pierpaolo Antonello and João Cezar de Castro Rocha (New York: Continuum, 2007), 74ff and *Battling to the End: Conversations with Benoît Chantre*, trans. Mary Baker (East Lansing: Michigan State University Press, 2010), 130–35; but also G. Fornari, *La bellezza e il nulla: L'antropologia cristiana di Leonardo da Vinci* (Milan: Marietti, 2005), 139; Petra Steinmair-Pösel, "Original Sin, Grace, and Positive Mimesis," *Contagion* 14 (2007): 1–12; Martha Reineke, "After the Scapegoat: René Girard's Apocalyptic Vision and the Legacy of Mimetic Theory," *Philosophy Today* 56.2 (2012): 141–53.

3. René Girard, *"To Double Business Bound": Essays on Literature, Mimesis, and Anthropology* (Baltimore: Johns Hopkins University Press, 1978), 1–8.

4. Girard, *Deceit, Desire, and the Novel*, 5.

5. A key text for the construction of this episode as an archetype of Romantic love is Denis de Rougemont, *Love in the Western World* (New York: Doubleday Anchor, 1958); a similar interpretation is presented, for instance, by Francis Fergusson, *Trope and Allegory: Themes Common to Dante and Shakespeare* (Athens: University of Georgia Press, 1977), 17ff.

6. "i peccator carnali / che la ragion sommettono al talento"; all citations from the *Comedy* are from Dante Alighieri, *Commedia*, ed. Anna Maria Chiavacci Leonardi (Milan: Mondadori, 2008). Translations are from *The Divine Comedy of Dante Alighieri*, ed. and trans. Robert M. Durling (Oxford: Oxford University Press, 1996–2011).

7. Cf. Teodolinda Barolini, "Dante and Cavalcanti (On Making Distinctions in Matters of Love): *Inferno* 5 in its Lyric Context," *Dante Studies* 116 (1998): 31–63. Scholarship on Dante and in particular on the fifth canto of the *Inferno* is limitless, and here we mention only the studies directly relevant to our argument. Two books on *Inferno* 5 provide an extensive bibliography on it: Lorenzo Renzi, *Le conseguenze di un bacio: L'episodio di Francesca nella "Commedia" di Dante* (Bologna: Il Mulino, 2007); and Elena Lombardi, *The Wings of the Doves: Love and Desire in Dante and Medieval Culture* (Montreal: McGill Queens University Press, 2012). See also Manuele Gragnolati's recent *lectura* of the canto in *Lectura Dantis Bononiensis*, vol. 2, ed. Emilio Pasquini and Carlo Galli (Bologna: Bononia University Press, 2012), 7–22.

8. "La bufera infernal, che mai non resta, / mena li spiriti con la sua rapina; / voltando e percotendo li molesta."

9. "così quel fiato li spiriti mali / di qua, di là, di giù, di sù li mena; / nulla speranza li conforta mai / non che di posa, ma di minor pena."

10. "Vedrai quando saranno / più presso a noi; e tu allor li priega / per quello amor che i mena."

11. Lombardi, *Wings of the Doves*, 88.

12. See Manuele Gragnolati, "Gluttony and the Anthropology of Pain in Dante's *Inferno* and *Purgatorio*," in *History in the Comic Mode: Medieval Communities and the Matter of Person*, ed. Rachel Fulton and Bruce Holsinger (New York: Columbia University Press, 2007), 238–50.

13. "Amor, ch'al cor gentil ratto s'apprende, / prese costui de la bella persona / che mi fu tolta; e 'l modo ancor m'offende. / Amor, ch'a nullo amato amar perdona, / mi prese del costui piacer sì forte, / che, come vedi, ancor non m'abbandona./ Amor condusse noi ad una morte. / Caina attende chi a vita ci spense."

14. See, among many others, Gianfranco Contini, "Dante come personaggio-poeta della *Commedia*," in *Un'idea di Dante* (Turin: Einaudi, 1976), 33–62; and Teodolinda Barolini, *Dante's Poets: Textuality and Truth in the "Comedy"* (Princeton: Princeton University Press, 1992).

15. "a che e come concedette amore/che conosceste i dubbiosi disiri?"

16. For further discussion on this see Heather Webb, "Deceit, Desire, and Conversion in Girard and Dante," *Religion and Literature*, special issue: "*Deceit, Desire and the Novel* 50 Years Later: The Religious Dimension," ed. Ann W. Astell and Justin Jackson, 43.3 (2011): 200–207.

17. "Amor condusse noi ad una morte," (*Inf.*, 5:106); "E caddi come corpo morto cade." *Inf.*, 5:142.

18. See the chapter "Productive Pain" (and especially the section "The Pattern of Purgatory as a Journey to/as Christ") in Manuele Gragnolati, *Experiencing the Afterlife: Soul and Body in Dante and Medieval Culture* (Notre Dame: University of Notre Dame Press, 2005), 89–137.

19. See Heather Webb, "Power Differentials, Unreliable Models, and Homoerotic Desire in the Commedia," *Italian Studies* 68.1 (2013): 17–35.

20. "Ne la vacca entra Pasife, / perché 'l torello a sua lussuria corra."

21. "perché non servammo umana legge, / seguendo come bestie l'appetito, / in obbrobrio di noi, per noi si legge, / quando partinci, il nome di colei / che s'imbestiò ne le 'mbestiate schegge."

22. Girard, *Evolution and Conversion*, 58.

23. Ovid, *Ars Amatoria*, I, 289–326. Ovid's text is quoted in the English translation by A. S. Kline (2001), available online at http://www.poetryintranslation.com/PITBR/Latin/ArtofLoveBkI. htm.

24. René Girard, *Things Hidden Since the Foundation of the World*, research undertaken in collaboration with Jean-Michel Oughourlian and Guy Lefort, trans. Stephen Nann and Michael Metteer (Stanford: Stanford University Press, 1987), 23ff.

25. See Manuele Gragnolati, "Nostalgia in Heaven: Embraces, Affection and Identity in Dante's *Comedy*," in *Dante and the Human Body*, ed. John Barnes and Jennifer Petrie (Dublin: Four Courts Press, 2007), 91–111; and Gragnolati's recent book *"Amor che move": Linguaggio del corpo e forma del desiderio in Dante, Pasolini e Morante* (Milan: il Saggiatore, 2013). On Dante's fidelity to lyric poetry and to the relationship with the beloved, see Regina Psaki, "Dante's Redeemed Eroticism," *Lectura Dantis* 18–19 (Spring–Fall 1996): 12–19; "Love for Beatrice: Transcending Contradiction in the *Paradiso*," in *Dante for the New Millennium*, ed. Teodolinda Barolini and Wayne Storey (New York: Fordham University Press, 2003), 115–30. Crucial also, albeit with a different perspective, are Lino Pertile's following studies: "Dante's *Comedy* Beyond the Stilnovo," *Lectura Dantis* 13 (1993): 47–77; "Does the *Stilnovo* Go to Heaven?" in Barolini and Storey, *Dante for the New Millennium*, 104–14; *"La punta del disio": Semantica del desiderio nella "Commedia"* (Fiesole: Cadmo, 2005).

26. Girard, *Deceit, Desire, and the Novel*, 6.

27. "fui de li altrui danni / più lieta assai che di ventura mia."

28. "o gente umana, perché poni il core / la 'v' è mestier di consorte divieto?"

29. "Perché s'appuntano i vostri disiri / dove per compagnia parte si scema, / invidia move il mantaco a' sospiri. Ma se l'amor de la spera supprema / torcesse in suso il disiderio vostro, / non vi sarebbe al petto quella tema; / ché, per quanti si dice più lì 'nostro,' / tanto possiede più di ben ciascuno, / e più di caritate arde in quel chiostro."

30. "esce di mano a lui che la vagheggia / prima che sia, a guisa di fanciulla / che piangendo e ridendo pargoleggia, / l'anima semplicetta che sa nulla, / salvo che, mossa da lieto fattore, / volontier torna a ciò che la trastulla."

31. "per che la gente, che sua guida vede / pur a quel ben fedire ond' ella è ghiotta, / di quel si pasce, e più oltre non chiede."

32. Girard, *Deceit, Desire, and the Novel*, 9.

33. "Soleva Roma, che 'l buon mondo feo, / due soli aver . . . L'un l'altro ha spento; ed è giunta la spada / col pasturale, e l'un con l'altro insieme / per viva forza mal convien che vada."

34. "Si ergo iudicium moveat omnino appetitum et nullu modo preveniatur ab eo, liberum est; si vero ab appetitu quocunque modo preveniente iudicium moveatur, liberum esse non potest, quia non a se, sed ab alio captivum trahitur." Dante Alighieri, *Monarchia* I, 12, 4, ed. and trans. Prue Shaw (Cambridge: Cambridge University Press, 1995).

35. On the notion of the "bridle" in this canto, see John Scott, "Canto XVI: A World of Darkness and Disorder," in *Lectura Dantis: Purgatorio*, ed. Allen Mandelbaum, Anthony Oldcorn, and Charles Ross (Berkeley: University of California Press, 2008), 167–77.

36. "L'animo, ch'è creato ad amar presto, / ad ogne cosa è mobile che piace, / tosto che dal piacere in atto è desto. / Vostra apprensiva da esser verace / tragge intenzione, e dentro a voi la spiega, / sì che

l'animo ad essa volger face; / e se, rivolto, inver' di lei si piega, / quel piegare è amor, quell'è natura/ che per piacer di novo in voi si lega."

37. "Poi, come 'l foco movesi in altura / per la sua forma ch'è nata a salire / là dove più in sua matera dura, / così l'animo preso entra in disire, / ch'è moto spiritale, e mai non posa / fin che la cosa amata il fa gioire."

38. According to another interpretation of lines 31–33, which offers a more positive understanding of desire as a joy in itself rather than a lack that needs to be satiated, this passage could also mean that the spiritual motion of desire continues to be active as long as the beloved object makes the enamored soul rejoice. See Pertile, "*La punta del disio*," 268–69: "Desire continues as long as the loved thing gives joy."

39. "Amor, ch'al cor gentil ratto s'apprende, / *prese* costui della bella persona / che mi fu tolta."

40. "Onde, poniam che di necessitate / surga ogne *amor che dentro a voi s'accende*, / di ritenerlo è in voi la potestate. / La nobile virtù Beatrice intende / per lo libero arbitrio, e però guarda che l'abbi a mente, s'a parlar ten prende."

41. On the relation between amorous desire and other sorts of earthly desires, see Teodolinda Barolini's chapter "Guittone's *Ora Parrà*, Dante's *Doglia mi reca*, and the *Commedia*'s Anatomy of Desire" in *Dante and the Origins of Italian Literary Culture* (New York: Fordham University Press, 2006), 47–69.

42. Girard, *Things Hidden*, 283ff.

43. "Ma dimmi: al tempo de' dolci sospiri, / a che e come concedette Amore / che conosceste i dubbiosi disiri?"

44. For a reading of this biblical passage through a Girardian lens see Jean-Michel Oughourlian, *The Genesis of Desire*, trans Eugene Webb (East Lansing: Michigan State University Press, 2010), 53–55.

45. "Quando leggemmo il disiato riso / esser baciato da cotanto amante, / questi, che mai da me non fia diviso, / la bocca mi baciò tutto tremante."

46. "i peccator carnali / che la ragione sommettono al talento."

47. "Frate, la nostra volontà quïeta / virtù di carità, che a volerne / sol quel ch'avemo, e d'altro non ci asseta."

For a Comparative Topography of Desire

Mimetic Theory and the World Map

Rosa Mucignat

When Girard opposes "Romantic lies" to "novelistic truth," in *Deceit, Desire, and the Novel*, he is not thinking of Keats or Shelley but of the secondhand romanticism of some literary critics whom he never names. "Romantic critics" extol Don Quixote for living his dream and admire Julien Sorel's ambition, seeing in them the embodiment of the bogus ideals of originality and spontaneity that they cherish. Literary criticism of this kind, Girard observes, is the victim of the same form of mediated desire that controls the characters of novels. If we want literary criticism to be "real knowledge," Girard argues, we have to think comparatively and systematically.[1] There are two points I would like to make about Girard's idea of systematic comparative criticism and about the particular hermeneutic system he constructs in *Deceit, Desire, and the Novel*. In the first part of my essay I will look at what mimetic theory can tell us about the organization and functioning of space in realist novels. In particular, I am interested in seeing how far Girard's structural model can be inscribed in a physical geography of the novelistic world. In order to investigate this, I will look at two of the novels Girard discusses in his book, namely Stendhal's *The Red and the Black* (1830) and Flaubert's *Sentimental Education* (1869). Second, I will discuss ways in which triangular desire is active in novels outside of the cultural area of Western realism, again with a focus on space and geography and using the example of Orhan Pamuk's novel *Snow* (2002).

"Literary interpretation must be systematic because it is the continuation of literature," says Girard.[2] As Robert Doran has explained, Girard does not offer us a theory of literature but rather a reading of "literature *as* theory."[3] In an essay of 1963 entitled "Formalism and Structuralism in Literature and the Human Sciences" Girard has a bit of fun finding passages that look like Lévi-Strauss in Proust and vice versa.[4] This is where, I think, Girard differs from the typical structuralist position: he is always eager to show that he has not invented or designed structural models such as the triangle of metaphysical desire. He has found them in the texts. In Girard's view, the professional reader (i.e., the critic) sees structures emerge from the "unsystematic, irrational, and chaotic" conglomerate that is a literary text.[5] Systems are not the product of systematic thinking; systematic thinking only brings to the surface and makes evident what is hidden in the texts and in human civilization itself. I will come back to this point later.

In the first pages of *Deceit, Desire, and the Novel*, Girard explains the functioning of mediated desire: we imagine that desire connects the desiring subject and the object of his or her desire with a straight line. But this is just a Romantic lie. Novels show us characters who desire by imitation, copying someone else's ambitions and desires. The straight line is deviated and forms a triangle whose three corners are occupied by the desiring subject, the mediator, and the object of desire. The relative distance between the points can vary, but the mechanism remains the same: desires do not come spontaneously but via the influence of a mediator (who can be a model, a rival, or himself the object of desire). Early on in the book Girard makes clear that "the triangle is no *Gestalt*. The real structures are intersubjective. They cannot be localized anywhere; the triangle has no reality whatsoever; it is a systematic metaphor, systematically pursued" (2). This means that the triangle is a topology and not a topography, which does not exist in actual space but only as an abstract representation of the relationship described above. It is a spatial metaphor, not the actual shape that space takes. Even if Girard never addresses the issue of space directly, the constant references he makes to places and settings end up calling his reader's attention to where the three poles of mediated desire are actually located and why. What I am asking here is whether the triangle as a structural model finds any correspondence in the actual geography of novels where triangular desire is active. Girard claims to have "found" the model in the texts. Might he have found it in the landscape of the text? In other words, does the structure of triangular desire also play a role in the way space is organized?

A good example of the spatial embeddedness of desire is the switch Girard describes from external to internal mediation, which presupposes a closer proximity between the desiring subject and his or her mediator. Girard makes it clear that "obviously is not physical space that measures the gap between mediator and the desiring subject."[6] Even if they ride side by side, Don Quixote always remains an external mediator for Sancho Panza, whose vicarious dreams of owning an island are never in competition with his master's plans. Later on, however, Girard makes some considerations on the reciprocal position of subject and mediator: "At the beginning of *The Red and the Black* the distance between the hero and his mediator is as great as in *Madame Bovary*. But Julien spans this distance; he leaves his province and becomes the lover of the proud Mathilde; he rises rapidly to a brilliant position."[7] In Stendhal's novel the move from external to internal mediation happens by means of a transfer in space, from the small town of Verrières to Parisian high society, the setting of so many of his dreams of glory and success.

Girard argues that internal mediation is facilitated by the structure of modern society, where differences between men have become less marked and there is increased social mobility. Julien Sorel, the protagonist of *The Red and the Black*, lives in a world governed by the laws of "vanity" (*vanité*), where actions and even feelings are motivated by envy, mutual suspicion, and an exaggerated pride. It seems that at every stage of his advancement Stendhal's plebeian hero is helped along by the fortuitous combination of multiple currents of mimetic desire. First, M. de Rênal takes him on as tutor for his children only to outdo his rival Valenod. The brainy, self-absorbed Mathilde, daughter of the Marquis de la Mole, falls in love with him because he fits the Romantic picture of fervent passion and courage she has derived from her own family history (she wants to emulate Queen Marguerite and her lover Boniface de la Mole, who was beheaded on Place de Grève in 1574) and from novels (she measures her own feelings against "the descriptions of passions she had read in *Manon Lescaut*, *La Nouvelle Héloïse*, the *Letters from a Portuguese Nun* etc.").[8]

Stendhal sees postrevolutionary France as a permeable, traversable space, but one where linear movement is impossible: the force of internal mediation has caused a curvature in space. Julien crosses and gets caught in a multitude of triangular force fields that divert, accelerate, or reverse his trajectory, while all of the time thinking he is moving in a straight line. Julien flatters himself that he can use other people's "vanity" to his own advantage. Upon learning that the Marquis has given him a bogus aristocratic title and made him a lieutenant, he declares: "My story is ended, and all the credit goes to me alone. I've succeeded in making this monster of pride [Mathilde] fall in love with me; her father can't live without her, nor she without me."[9] But this is a mere romantic illusion: as Girard explains, the world is now better described by means of a more complex, nonuniform "Einsteinian" geometry, where "the straight line is in reality a circle which inevitably turns us back on ourselves."[10] At the height of his success Julien is so close to the mediator he almost *becomes* him, and starts believing that he might actually be "the natural son of some great lord."[11] But proximity fosters understanding, which inevitably leads to disappointment and then hatred, both of the Other and of oneself. This psychological circle is expressed spatially in the novel, and is one of the possible explanations of Julien's sudden decision to travel back to Verrières and revenge himself on Madame de Rênal, who had sent a letter to the Marquis denouncing Julien as a fortune seeker. The letter, besides wrecking his plans, also reveals to Julien how similar he has become to the scheming courtiers he despised so much. Wounded pride and deep self-loathing then, more than rancor, fuel the blind fury that takes possession of Julien as he fires his pistols at Madame de Rênal.

The space of *The Red and the Black* is apparently docile and traversable but it hides a secret resistance. Julien crosses and gets caught in a multitude of triangular force fields that divert, accelerate, or reverse his trajectory, and the physical topography of the novel maps this intricate web of competing desires. It should be noted that the city of Paris is almost nonexistent in the novel. Whenever the action moves to the city, the focus remains on the residence of the Marquis de la Mole, who entertains close relations with Julien's native Jura district as the major landowner and main political influence. Stendhal's map is not centered on the capital but embraces a number of small and middle-sized cities: the fictional towns of Verrières and Vergy in the Jura, as well as Besançon, Strasbourg, and Metz.

The modern metropolis is central to the type of experiences Girard associates with a further stage of mimetic desire: extreme metaphysical desire, which is entirely concentrated on the mediator and completely disregards the nature of its object. This development becomes evident when comparing the map of Flaubert's *Sentimental Education* with that of Stendhal. "The environment of *Sentimental Education* is the same as that of *The Red and the Black*," says Girard: "again the provinces and Paris are opposed to one another, but it is clear that the center of gravity has moved toward Paris, the capital of desire, which increasingly polarizes the forces of the nation."[12] Stendhal's map is a network of small towns, medium-sized cities, and the capital—the sides of the triangle are long, and movement, although it ends up being circular, nevertheless spans some distance. Flaubert's map instead reflects the obsessive nature of metaphysical desire. The circle narrows, Paris dominates the scene, and Frédéric Moreau, the protagonist, is clearly going nowhere.

Frédéric is a much less purposeful character than Julien Sorel. He actually moves around a lot more: he is always walking around Paris, meeting people, starting some new initiative, spending money, traveling. And he does not lack desire either, most of which is directed toward Madame Arnoux. But for all his hectic movement he achieves very little, and his desire too is stunted and ineffectual. The concept of metaphysical desire offers an elegant explanation of Frédéric's irritating inconclusiveness. But does space have something to do with it, too? Girard talks about the multiplication of mediators that takes place in modern "democratic" societies. "Beginning with Proust," he explains, "the mediator may be literally *anyone at all* and he may pop up *anywhere*. Mystical revelation presents a constant danger. A chance encounter along the promenade at Balbec decides Marcel's fate."[13] In the populous anonymity of bourgeois society, individuals become vulnerable to the magnets of countless mediators. This is also a prevailing mode in *Sentimental Education*. The "apparition" of Madame Arnoux at the beginning of the novel tends to eclipse the rest of what happens on the ferryboat that takes Frédéric back home from Paris. But actually Madame Arnoux is not the first to capture his attention. He notices her husband first, and recognizes him as the proprietor of a well-known art-journal and gallery, *L'Art Industriel*. Frédéric is struck by Arnoux's genial and worldly manners: he offers advice on women, talks confidently about politics and business, knows famous people, and has traveled widely.

To some extent Arnoux becomes Frédéric's mediator: he desires Arnoux's wife and later his lover, and acquires a taste for the same objects d'art and orientalist furniture that fill Arnoux's apartment. In Flaubert's novel, internal mediation spreads and grows stronger thanks to the way people interact in the city. The whole Arnoux affair would be all but forgotten, if one day Frédéric did not chance upon the L'Art Industriel shop on the boulevard. A few days later, in the midst of a clash between rioting students and the police, he makes friends with one Hussonnet, who, it turns out, works for Arnoux and introduces Frédéric to his circle. The "ontological sickness" induced by mediated desire spreads via chance encounters on the street, on public transport, at the theater, in shops, cafés, and other characteristic sites of modern city life.

"In the world of internal mediation, the contagion is so widespread that everyone can become his neighbor's mediator without ever understanding the role he is playing."[14] Paris in *Sentimental Education* is a space of promiscuity and convergence, where accidental multiple mediations solidify around Frédéric into a hard and inescapable reality, and other people's desires become introjected and part of his own life. Isabelle Daunais makes this point clear when she argues that Frédéric, "subjected to the geographic and architectural contingencies of his environment, adopts its curves and accidents, which instantaneously replicate themselves in the itinerary of his life course."[15] Just like in *The Red and the Black*, the configuration of space determines movement and shapes the course of the events in the character's life, but Flaubert has replaced the map of France with Paris's city plan. Paris has become the center of the magnetic field, attracting a crowd of young men from the provinces, whose paths constantly cross and hinder one another in a narrow space that condemns them to a limited horizon made of "bitterness, malice, and petty rivalries."[16]

What I have tried to show with these examples is that the presence of mediated desire causes major shifts in the representation of space and the choice of setting. The measures of Girard's metaphorical triangle, which grows smaller and smaller as the mediator gets closer, are translated into physical distances in the novel's geography. What is still a relatively wide scenario in *The Red and the Black* becomes a claustrophobic urban world where the eyes of the mediator are always upon you. Girard continues his analysis with Proust and Dostoyevsky, charting a process by which metaphysical desire intensifies as the mediator moves nearer, from the same city to the peer group to the family (as among brothers or between father and son), until it brings its disaggregating force inside the psyche of the character. The extremity of the "ontological sickness" ultimately causes "the complete disintegration of the subject," which Dostoyevsky represents in the physical and spiritual self-destruction of his characters.[17] Girard develops his topography of desire on two dimensions: one the one hand, as we have seen, space tends to shrink following the progressive contraction of the distance between subject and mediator; on the other hand it expands as society becomes more and more "democratic." The increased political and economical equality paradoxically aggravates the malady of desire, because it multiplies the potential mediators and rivals ad infinitum. And if everything is up for grabs and competition is open to everyone, the intensity of desire, envy, and impotent hatred becomes intolerable. Stendhal, Proust, and Dostoyevsky have described the effects of vanity in a society where differences among classes and individuals gradually disappear. But what happens when Western modernity is "exported" elsewhere, and the logic of mediation invests other nations and cultures?

At the end of the chapter on *The Red and the Black*, Girard looks ahead to the consequences of imitative desire in the twentieth century. In an ominous-sounding passage he describes the double impact of mediation on the individual and the global sphere: "Double [i.e., reciprocal] mediation has invaded the growing domain of collective existence and wormed its way into the more intimate depths of the individual soul, until finally it stretches beyond national boundaries and annexes countries, races, and continents, in the heart of a universe where technical progress is wiping away one by one the differences between men."[18] Girard gives no further explanation and never returns to discuss the present time in the rest of the book. So it is hard to say what this apocalyptic vision exactly refers to. Totalitarianism? Globalization? Or perhaps materialism and the erosion of traditional values? Yet, if we remain within the domain of cultural politics, it might be possible to read this statement by Girard in the light of more recent theories of world literature, as developed among others by Franco Moretti, which construct world literature as a system of power relations connecting literary cultures across the globe. Can mimetic theory also describe relations of admiration, imitation, and antagonism that exist between cultures?

In his essay "Conjectures on World Literature" (2000), Moretti talks about the system of world literature as being "one and unequal: with a core and a periphery . . . that are bound together in a relationship of growing inequality."[19] Peripheral literatures "borrow" and "imitate" the more prestigious and fashionable forms from the core (which still corresponds to Europe and North America), while the core completely ignores the culture of the periphery. The realist novel, for example, has been "imported" into various literary cultures outside of Europe, which by doing so have entered into a form of debt with the West. Moretti's conjectures are sketched in broad and rapid strokes, and are heavily dependent on economic and political theories. Perhaps Girard's psychology of the triangular desire can be used to complicate the picture, and shed light on the workings of global mediation as represented in world novels. It is Girard himself who claims that mimetic theory can help us understand relationships between texts: "the idea of mediation encourages literary comparisons at a level which is no longer that of *genre* criticism or thematic criticism. It may illuminate the works through each other; it may unite them without destroying their irreducible singularity."[20] In other words, it can provide the tools for a new kind of comparative analysis that considers how different texts represent the workings of mediated desire, comparing, for instance, Stendhal's vanity and Flaubertian bovarism. In what follows I will try to apply the same method to literature outside the European "center," to see whether the triangle of resentful, imitated desire is still present and what shape it takes.

Ka, the hero of Pamuk's novel *Snow*, returns to Istanbul after a twelve-year stay in Germany. Once there, and for no clear reason, he decides to travel to the remote city of Kars, in northeast Turkey. According to Moretti, the system of world literature is dominated by the tension between center and periphery. The geography of Pamuk's novel seems to mirror that tension. Places are defined by their respective positions in the East-West, center-periphery polarity: Frankfurt is West compared to Istanbul; Istanbul is a Westernized city and the center of cultural innovation compared to the poor, isolated city of Kars. Tucked away in a corner of Eastern Anatolia, Kars's function in the novel has been interpreted as emblematic of the peripheral position of Turkey in relation to the Western world, as well as "the repressed 'East' within Westernized Turkey."[21] In Girard's topology mediator and desiring subject are relative functions, and depending on what triangle you are looking at, each player can be playing different roles at the same time. On a bus to Kars, Ka strikes up a conversation with fellow passenger from a local village. The narrator comments: "It had been a long time since [Ka] had enjoyed the fleeting pleasure of empathizing with someone weaker than himself."[22] Ka feels inferior and provincial in Frankfurt, but in Kars he is an upper-class intellectual and people treat him as a sophisticated representative of the center. Positions of inferiority and superiority, center and periphery, and the role of desiring subject and of mediator are shown to be mobile, relative.

Girard argues that "imitative desire is always a desire to be Another."[23] Ka is the son of a bourgeois Istanbul family who have long adopted Western ways. In Istanbul, Ka has never been to a mosque to pray. In Kars, he has long conversations about faith and attends religious gatherings. At the sheikh's house he makes a public confession: "I grew up in Istanbul, in Nişantaşı, among society people. I wanted to be like the Europeans. Because I couldn't see how I could reconcile my becoming an European with a God that required women to wrap themselves up in scarves, I kept religion out of my life." But after twelve years in Germany, he now wishes to end his isolation and become just like all other "common" Turks who believe in God, talk politics all of the time, and are never tired of watching television. "I'm provincial, too," he says, "and I want to become even more provincial. I want to be forgotten in the most unknown corner of the world under a blanket of snow."[24] Ka hopes that Kars's Eastern authenticity and remoteness will help him shake off the European mediator, but that is a mere illusion. Kars is no safer than Istanbul from the large-scale metaphysical desire that makes secularized Turkey the "slave" to "ruthless Europeans."[25] On the contrary, in the microcosm of the provincial town these tensions become magnified, and a cascade of double and multiple mediations flows down from the global to the national and then the personal sphere.

The most serious case of ontological disease is Ka's relationship to Blue, the charismatic leader of the "Pilgrims," an underground Islamist group. In a brilliant reversal of the stereotype of the long-bearded fanatic, Pamuk makes Blue an exceptionally handsome man and a high-minded freedom fighter who has read Franz Fanon and is adored by women.[26] After his last meeting with Blue, Ka writes a poem entitled "Jealousy" whose subject is "the link between love and hate," a very Girardian feeling that unites "an unveiled contempt and a secret adoration."[27] Ka suffers the emotional agony of a subject who has lost his autonomous identity and agency to an overpowering mediator, or, in his case, two mediators that pull in opposite directions: first, the European culture that he cherishes, but has alienated him from his Eastern roots; and second, his rival Blue, who has emancipated himself from Western influence (and has been Ipek's lover before Ka). Pamuk reaches new heights of "vérité romanesque" when he constructs a further triangle around his narrator, who, as it is often the case in Pamuk's novels, is a novelist called Orhan Pamuk. Orhan the narrator has taken up the task of collecting Ka's lost notebooks and reconstructing the events of his life. Soon Orhan's admiration for his dead friend transfigures into jealousy and a desire to replace him, particularly in Ipek's affection. Showing off his writerly skills in self-mastery and analysis, and perhaps his knowledge of literary theory, he comments: "A man can shut out love if he so desires. However, to do so, he must free himself not only from the woman who has bewitched him but from the third person in the story: the ghost who has put temptation in his way."[28] Here, Pamuk makes explicit how the feelings of a writer toward his character might take the shape of mimetic desire.

Depending on where he stands, Ka is in turns Turkish or Westernized, the subject of imitative desire (via Blue) or the mediator (for Orhan). One of Ka's defining features is the complete, despairing solitude he lives in, unable and unwilling to learn German, living like a recluse in a city where he knows nobody. As mentioned above, it is not clear what causes Ka's sudden decision to travel to Kars. At one point the trip is presented as "an attempt to step outside the boundaries of his middle-class upbringing" and "the desire to look further afield for childhood and purity" in what is now the "poorest, most overlooked corner of Turkey."[29] As Irzık has noted, Pamuk deliberately accentuates the "Orientalist ring" of Ka's nostalgia. Imitating Western fantasies about the East, he sees the poverty and backwardness of the Eastern town as an opportunity for spiritual regeneration and personal fulfillment.[30] So even Ka's search for autonomy and authenticity ends up being guided by precisely the Western models he is trying to escape.

But no matter how far it is from the European core, Kars is not safe from the destructive influence of its mediation. The city is ripped apart by political strife. Pamuk enacts long debates about the most controversial issues of the moment: the headscarf ban, the status of Turkey in Europe (Turkey is currently in the process of applying for membership of the EU), the cultural and religious identity of Turkey and the influence of the West. All areas of the political spectrum are represented: the old communists (Ipek's father), the political Islamists (Blue), the more moderate God's party (Muthar and the group that meets at the sheikh's house), the army and the Kemalists (Colonel Colak, Sunay Zaim, the director of the Institute of Education), ethnic minorities (Kurds, Georgian immigrants) and the liberal intellectuals (Ka himself). As explained by Girard's theory, the differences between factions are only superficial. What they are really competing for is a place under the sun of the mediator. In fact there is one thing on which they all agree: they are unhappy about their image as Turks in Europe, and they want to send a message to the West. Ka gathers them all together with the pretext of composing a statement for a German newspaper where he claims he can get it published. One voice rises above the others in the confusion of the assembly. It is a young Kurd who cries out: "In Germany, they can spot people from Turkey just by the way they look. There's no avoiding humiliation except by proving at the first opportunity that you think exactly as they do. But this is impossible, and it can break a man's pride to try."[31] Girard wrote that Stendhal's novels ask the question "Why are men not happy in the modern world?"[32] Pamuk asks the same question about the inhabitants of the global periphery. Stendhal's answer was that men are *vaniteux* and they let themselves by ruled by metaphysical desire. Characters in Pamuk's novel have become victims of the same "ontological sickness": they feel painfully conscious of their provinciality because they have become aware of the presence of a center, elsewhere. The interference of the culture of the center has the effect of replacing the old "innocence and purity" with a subordinate peripheral identity.

The flow of mediated desire in this global system forms a new type of triangle. The asymmetry Moretti sees between a marginal culture intersected and altered by a source culture that completely ignores it is reproduced in the world of the novel. Ka and the people of Kars constantly talk about how Turkey could make itself visible and acceptable to European eyes without losing its pride, while the West seems to take no notice of their agonizing preoccupation. Europe would then be in the position of an absent, external mediator. But other elements suggest that we are dealing with a form of metaphysical desire: the mixture of reverence and hatred Ka feels for Europe and its culture, the fits of self-loathing in which he falls and the dilemma he faces between the impossibility of being on an equal footing with Westerners and his inability to be a real Turk. These are all symptoms of extreme internal mediation. Girard claimed that triangular desire had invaded all areas of contemporary society, stretching from "the more intimate depths of the individual soul" to "countries, races, and continents."[33] The new triangle resembles the shapes of fractal geometry, where the same pattern is reproduced in an infinitely small and infinitely large scale. The space in which it is inscribed is no longer the nation-state or the metropolis. The entire planet is divided into a center and an extended periphery, which in turn are fragmented into smaller, relative centers and peripheries, until we reach the inner world of the individual's consciousness, also composed of multiple, constantly shifting centripetal and centrifugal tensions.

Snow offers no possibility of reconciliation between the hero and the world comparable to the Julien's "reawakening" at the end of The Red and the Black and his renunciation of sick metaphysical desire, which allows him to go to his death with a mindful and serene attitude. Ka too is executed, shot down on the street in Frankfurt, apparently in retaliation for informing on Blue, and his notebook of poems is never found. The poems, we are told, were made of apparently meaningless fragments ordered in a perfect geometrical structure, so as to reveal "the world's hidden symmetry."[34] The form the collection should take is revealed prodigiously to Ka in "a vision of extraordinary power" that shows him how "everything is interconnected," and he, too, is "inextricably linked to this deep and beautiful world."[35] Knowledge of, and liberation from, the twisted schemes of triangular desire are achieved only in the poems—which are lost forever.

A space-oriented analysis of The Red and the Black and Sentimental Education suggests that the triangle of imitative desire might have a much stronger physical presence in the space of the texts than Girard himself had imagined. Following Girard's method of using literature as theory, the example of Pamuk's Snow has served to illuminate the mechanism of triangular desire in the context of world literature. Pamuk's oeuvre is an interesting case because it is self-consciously the locus of triangular desire, where the mediator is the European novel. At the same time, it is also an attempt to resolve this tension productively and reach a new synthesis through literary appropriation and innovation. In his Nobel lecture Pamuk talked about his struggle as a young writer caught between his own literary heritage and the attraction of Western models: "At one end, there were Istanbul's books—our literature, our local world, in all its beloved detail—and at the other end were the books from this other, Western, world, to which our own bore no resemblance, to which our lack of resemblance gave us both pain and hope"[36]—the same pain and hope that Ka has inherited from his European ancestors (and perhaps mediators) Julien Sorel and Frédéric Moreau.

Notes

1. René Girard, *Deceit, Desire, and the Novel: Self and Other in Literary Structure*, trans. Yvonne Freccero (Baltimore: Johns Hopkins University Press, 1965), 3.

2. Girard, *Deceit, Desire, and the Novel*, 3.

3. Robert Doran, introduction to René Girard, *Mimesis and Theory: Essays on Literature and Criticism, 1953–2005* (Stanford, CA: Stanford University Press, 2008), xiv.

4. Girard, *Mimesis and Theory*, 80–95.

5. Girard, *Deceit, Desire, and the Novel*, 3.

6. Girard, *Deceit, Desire, and the Novel*, 9.

7. Girard, *Deceit, Desire, and the Novel*, 8.

8. Stendhal, *The Red and the Black: A Chronicle of the Nineteenth Century*, trans. Catherine Slater (Oxford: Oxford University Press, 1998), 322.

9. Stendhal, *The Red and the Black*, 463.

10. Girard, *Deceit, Desire, and the Novel*, 74.

11. Stendhal, *The Red and the Black*, 465.

12. Girard, *Deceit, Desire, and the Novel*, 135.

13. Girard, *Deceit, Desire, and the Novel*, 92.

14. Girard, *Deceit, Desire, and the Novel*, 99.

15. Isabelle Daunais, *Flaubert et la scénographie romanesque* (Paris: Nizet, 1993), 112.

16. Girard, *Deceit, Desire, and the Novel*, 136.

17. Girard, *Deceit, Desire, and the Novel*, 279.

18. Girard, *Deceit, Desire, and the Novel*, 138.

19. Franco Moretti, "Conjectures on World Literature," *New Left Review* 1 (2000): 56.

20. Girard, *Deceit, Desire, and the Novel*, 23.

21. Sibel Irzık, "Orhan Pamuk's *Snow*: Reimagining the Boundaries between East and West, Art and Politics," in *Europe and Its Boundaries: Words and Worlds, Within and Beyond*, ed. Andrew Davidson and Humadeep Muppidi (Plymouth: Lexington, 2009), 189.

22. Orhan Pamuk, *Snow*, trans. Maureen Freely (London: Faber, 2004), 6.

23. Girard, *Deceit, Desire, and the Novel*, 84.

24. Pamuk, *Snow*, 98 and 99.

25. Pamuk, *Snow*, 331.

26. Pamuk, *Snow*, 328.

27. Pamuk, *Snow*, 359.

28. Pamuk, *Snow*, 388.

29. Pamuk, *Snow*, 18.

30. Irzık, "Orhan Pamuk's *Snow*," 195.

31. Pamuk, *Snow*, 284.

32. Girard, *Deceit, Desire, and the Novel*, 115.

33. Girard, *Deceit, Desire, and the Novel*, 138.

34. Pamuk, *Snow*, 99.

35. Pamuk, *Snow*, 299.

36. Pamuk, *My Father's Suitcase: Nobel Lecture*, 2006. www.nobelprize.org/nobel_prizes/literature/laureates/2006/pamuk-lecture_en.html.

Nobody's Fault

Dickens, René Girard, and the Novel

David Quint

ovels, according to René Girard, teach us that we would all like to be somebody else. Don Quixote sets out on his mad quest in order to be the knight-errant Amadis. Novels arose in the West at the moment when a nascent capitalism expanded the opportunities for men and women in fact to be other somebodies; on the road Don Quixote meets many fellow travelers, most of them headed for Seville, the commercial entrepôt and jumping off point to the New World. The first of these observations, Girard's locating in the novel his powerful universal, theory of mimetic desire, effectively minimizes or discounts the second, that novels have a history and came into being to depict and reflect upon a newfound social mobility. Girard's history of the novel, told in his chapter on Stendhal in *Deceit, Desire, and the Novel*, is reactionary—in the original sense of that word. Recounted in what passes as Stendhal's voice and point of view rather than that of the critic, it is a story about the fate of the postrevolutionary nobility, that is, of the few authentic nobles such as Stendhal's fictional M. de la Mole. They are spiritual survivors of the more halcyon period of the ancien régime when nobles were noble—not in competition with the bourgeoisie—and could act out of spontaneous passion with *unmediated* desire. Girard's is a top-down social view of the novel. The aristocracy, no longer authentic, becomes riddled with snobbery and cannot be distinguished from its bourgeois emulators. Top-down and trickle-down: in his defense of Proust's focus on the "summit of the social edifice," Girard writes that it is there that "the ontological sickness is most acute. The symptoms observed by the novelist will gradually spread to the lower layers of that society."[1] Girard makes this history of the genre possible by his jumping chronologically from Cervantes to Stendhal, leaving out the entire eighteenth-century novel and its various versions of the rise of a sometimes virtuous bourgeosie. It also leaves out Cervantes's debt, that is, the debt of the genre of the novel itself, to the picaresque, which makes the hidalgo Don Quixote's romance quest for a new identity obversely mirror the efforts of the picaro, the masterless man and member of the urban poor—such as the hero of *Lazarillo de Tormes* or Ginés de Pasamonte inside *Don Quixote* itself—to find any social identity at all: the novel, that is, began by viewing society from the bottom.

To put this another way, Girard's history of the novel that culminates in the Christian Dostoyevsky and in which "there is no gulf between the great novelists" universalizes his theory of mimetic desire, which Girard himself reduces, in Augustinian terms, to pride.[2] If the human vanity and snobbery exposed by the novel is the result of the Fall and Original Sin, there can indeed be little history to which the genre might respond: *Plus ça change*. There is little that a rearrangement of society and politics—such as a French Revolution—could do to alter an anthropology that is both fundamental and misanthropic. What is the use of reading the novel as an advocate or instrument of social change? Girard warns that "if we consider all the heroes individually we shall be tempted to take seriously the excuses they give for their desires. We run the risk of missing the metaphysical meaning of that desire."[3] Those excuses might have something to do with inequitable circumstances that would require social action, but such action can be deferred indefinitely in favor of metaphysics. In what could be a response to Lukacs's idea of the novel as the epic of a world that has been abandoned by God and of the consequent demonic quality of its hero's psychology, Girard finds in the novel a stark choice between returning to the Christian deity or defining ourselves on human models, who will, as the title of *The Possessed* suggests, turn into so many demons—"men become gods in the eyes of each other":[4] they will both take us over and disappoint us when they are revealed to be projections of our own infinite desire that only the infinite might satisfy. And yet, Girard also describes, via Stendhal, a different Fall within more recent history. Once upon a time in Europe, men and women knew their places, especially a few high nobles, real men and free men, whose pride was justifiable and did not need the aid of a human mediator: they were already, we might say, close to God. This second narrative inside *Deceit, Desire, and the Novel* suggests that novels, in particular the nineteenth-century novels that are its subject, do possess a history: a counterrevolutionary project in which Girard's criticism of them can appear to participate. In the *The Way of the World* (1987), Franco Moretti has openly identified such a novelistic project, carried out in the European bildungsroman, and characterized it as a weak, unheroic compromise, in the name of individual bourgeois normalcy, with the implications of incomplete popular revolutions.[5] Girard's version, admitting no compromise and especially critical of snobbery in "the intermediate and bourgeois regions of desire"[6] is far more *Ultra*, for all his equations of revolutionaries and reactionaries as two sides of the same coin.[7]

I propose to counter Girard's top-down reading of the novel with a reader from hell or, if you like, from the underground. Miss Wade is the most Girardian character in *Little Dorrit* (1855–57), the most Girardian and perhaps greatest of Dickens's novels.[8] It is his novel that, even more than *Great Expectations* (1861), takes snobbery and the quest for self-respect head-on. It declines its typically copious Dickensian cast of characters through the two sisters of the Dorrit family; the good characters of the novel are so many imperfect reflections of the Christian goodness and self-sacrifice of Amy, the bad characters so many worse versions of Fanny, the social climber who has "spirit." This is the novel's synonym for pride, most pathetically expressed by their father, William Dorrit, who keeps up the pretense of gentility while reduced to begging in the Marshalsea debtor's prison: he has preserved what he calls "Spirit. Becoming Spirit."[9] In Miss Wade's case, "spirit" also suggests something demonic: "You come to me like my own anger, my own malice" says Harriet (nicknamed Tattycoram), who in the next breath is said, under the attention of Miss Wade, to writhe "as if she were rent by the Demons of old" (I.2; 25); much later, Miss Wade defends herself from the accusation that she "has spirited away" (II.20; 637) the young Tattycoram from her benefactors and employers, the Meagles. The entire nine-hundred-page novel is framed in its second and penultimate chapters by the struggle of Tattycoram under this bad angel. The title of the illustration of the first of these scenes, "Under the Microscope," already casts Miss Wade as a reader, scientific and pitiless, and she later claims that she has "studied myself, and people about me" (II.20; 640). An illegitimate child, Miss Wade leads a life of homelessness and willed social alienation on both sides of the English Channel. Her scanty lodgings in dark, dead houses suggests "an Eastern caravanserai"—"a few articles of furniture that evidently did not belong to the room, and a disorder of trunks and travelling articles."[10] She both lives an unrooted picaresque experience and associates with Blandois, the novel's caricature of a picaresque criminal (who also bears the physiognomy of Napoleon III): Miss Wade reads up from the bottom of society. She offers a reading of this novel—and perhaps, as we shall see, of what Moretti sees as the compromised nineteenth-century novel itself—that is marked as perverse (she is a fallen woman and her relationship with Tattycoram is coded with lesbianism) and that goes against the grain of its Christian ethos.[11] But her reading and unhappy character challenge, none-theless, the substitution of metaphysical explanation for social solution. In what follows, I shall use Girard and demonstrate the power of his critical model for reading Dickens; Dickens and his Miss Wade, in particular, will, in turn, read and criticize *Deceit, Desire, and the Novel*.

Both Miss Wade and Tattycoram are jealous of "Pet" Meagles, although we do not find out about Miss Wade's jealousy until the end of the remark-able document, titled by the novel as the "The History of a Self-Tormenter," that she gives to its hero Arthur Clennam some seven hundred pages later well into its second part (II; 21). Pet, whose real name is Minnie, is the beautiful only surviving daughter, loved to the point of being spoiled, by her doting parents, the prototypically middle-class Meagles, who have cashed in Mr. Meagles banking wealth and retired to a suburban paradise in Pope's Twickenham. Pet plays the role of Girardian Other on whom others can project their desires and wish to be. Without the benefit of having read Girard, Dickens underscores the point when Mr. Meagles tells Arthur that Pet had a twin sister who died in infancy; he has just related how he and Mrs. Meagles chose to take the young girl Harriet out of the London Foundling Hospital to be a little maid to Pet, giving her the playful, affectionate name of Tattycoram, and taking full allowance for any defect in her temper due to her having "no parents, no child-brother or sister, no individuality of home, no Glass Slipper, or Fairy Godmother" (I.2; 18). Mr. and Mrs. Meagles, for all their benevolence, do not seem to connect Tattycoram to their dead daughter, to make her a real child-sister or twin to "Pet." In a subsequent scene at Twickenham, Clennam sees a portrait of the two twins:

> The picture happened to be near a looking-glass. As Arthur looked at it again, he saw, by the reflection of the mirror, Tattycoram stop in passing outside the door, listen to what was going on, and pass away with an angry and contemptuous frown upon her face, that changed its beauty into ugliness.[12]

Twins, a mirror image: Dickens depicts the primordial scene of mimetic, triangular desire. Tattycoram wishes to be included in the family portrait, as the missing twin, but, when she finds herself in the dependent position as servant, her love for Pet and the Meagles turns into envious hatred. Later Mr. Meagles reports the reproof that she flung at him as she ran away from their establishment to the protection of Miss Wade, "Who were we that we should have the right to name her like a dog or a cat?" (I.27; 315). She has been given a pet name, and treated like a family pet, but not as Pet, a real daughter, of which there can only be one, although there once, in fact, were two. Miss Wade tells Tattycoram that her function is precisely to mark and maintain the social difference between herself and her mistress: "You can be, again, a foil to his pretty daughter, a slave to her pleasant willfulness, and a toy in the house showing the goodness of the family. You can have your droll name again, playfully pointing you out and setting you apart, as it is right that you should be pointed out and set apart" (II.27; 319). In the ironic what-goes-around-comes-around world of *Little Dorrit*, the Meagles will, in turn, be condescended to by their in-law, the snobbish petit-noble Mrs. Gowan, who refuses to acknowledge their name and ridicules them as the "Miggles people." They will lose Pet in her marriage to Henry Gowan, who will treat her like Lion, his pet dog with a cat's name, whom on one occasion he beats and kicks (II.6; 479–80). But Mr. Meagles at least will console himself that Pet has married into a good family, for he is a snob. At the end of the novel, this loss seems symbolically made up when a repentant Tattycoram returns to her kind benefactors, bringing with her the box of papers that Miss Wade has refused, out of nothing but spite, to surrender; Pet has been replaced by the pet servant girl.

Miss Wade sees a singular likeness of her own case in the circumstances of Tattycoram, and the writing she bestows on Clennam, a history of self-torment, articulates the ressentiment of the social outsider.[13] Miss Wade's autobiographical account of herself is a textbook case and confirmation of Girard's model of mimetic desire, of identification with and hatred of the mediating Other, and it bears more than passing resemblance to Girard's own textbook case, the more pathological hero of *Notes from the Underground.* *Little Dorrit* dates from 1856–1857; a French translation was already available in 1858. We know that that his brother Michael urged Dostoyevesky to read *Little Dorrit* in 1859, and that he had a copy in his library at his death.[14] Perhaps Miss Wade and her narrative had come to his attention before *Notes from the Underground,* published in 1864. Miss Wade begins by stating that "I have the misfortune of not being a fool" (II.21; 644), a declaration of her superior intelligence and perception that finds its counterpart in the underground man's protestation that "I was guilty, first of all, because I was cleverer than all the people round me (I have always considered myself cleverer than any one else in the world, and sometimes, I assure you, I have been ashamed of it.)"[15] Her befriending of Tattycoram as a kindred spirit, in order, so Tattycoram will later say, to make her dependent and submissive to her in place of the Meagles (II.2; 643), corresponds to the underground man's one bid for friendship: "I was already a tyrant at heart. I wanted to exercise complete authority over him, I wanted to implant a contempt for his surroundings in his heart, I demanded that he should break away from these surroundings, scornfully and finally . . . I felt that he was completely in my power. I grew to hate him for the sake of gaining a victory over him, for the sake of exacting his complete submission to me" (*Notes* II.iii; 174–75). Their desires to dominate their relationships with others, their wanting to be loved and accepted and their aversion to such love and acceptance, stem in both cases from their low social status and material well-being—what Girard, who mispresents the underground man's condition as puniness and sickness, would call "excuses"—and both are rescued from indigence by small inheritances, in Miss Wade's case the money of which the false patriarch Casby is the trustee and which she will only touch when she has no choice, money that presumably comes from the father and family who will not acknowledge her. When a wavering Tattycoram seems to long for her old days of service to the kindhearted, parental Meagles in preference to dependence on Miss Wade's protection, Miss Wade peremptorily concludes: "My poverty will not bear competition with their money" (II.30; 643).

In Miss Wade's case, illegitimacy, as much as the powerlessness of poverty, conditions her rejection of admission into society: we can dismiss it as an excuse, but there may be some awkwardness in doing so when the box of papers Miss Wade happens to hold contains the secret of Clennam's illegitimacy that Amy Dorrrit works so hard and successfully to conceal from him: apparently this stigma of social exclusion does mean something after all.[16] Miss Wade's history narrates that as a young girl she took the kindness and consideration that others tried to show her because she was an orphan as "vanity and condescension," their way of showing their superiority over her and of further marking her difference. Her passionate love for her popular school companion classically illustrates Girard's explanation of the desire for "the Other, who seems to enjoy the divine inheritance,"[17] and Miss Wade projects upon this girl her own will to power and a deliberate plan directed at herself: "To be familiar and endearing with them all—and so make me mad with envying them." Her love-hate relationship to the friend expresses itself in the feeling that "I could so hold her in my arms and plunge to the bottom of a river—where I would still hold her after we were dead" (II.21; 645). The image will be subsequently realized in *Our Mutual Friend* and the fate of that other Dickensian hero of social resentment, the murderous Bradley Headstone.

Miss Wade's first posting as a governess comes to an end when the well-meaning mother of the family brings up the subject of her illegitimate birth, trying to reassure her by citing the case of her husband's dead dear sister,

> not in law his sister, but who was universally loved and respected—I saw directly that they had taken me in for the sake of the dead woman, whoever she was, and to have that boast of me and advantage of me . . . I left that house that night.[18]

Like the dead twin of Pet Meagles, this dead sister seems both to offer and not to offer a place in the family to the hired dependent: Miss Wade will not have anything to do with this kindness that is less than kin. Similarly, when, as governess in another household, Miss Wade is loved and offered marriage by a well-to-do nephew, only a year younger but younger-looking than she,

she is made jealous by seeing him in company with his cousin: "I have seen all the while, in people's eyes, that they thought the two looked nearer on an equality than he and I . . . his young appearance made me ridiculous" (II.21; 649). There will always be a mediator whose place Miss Wade both wants and does not want to take. There will always be for this outsider some reason that prevents her from entering into society, and that reason is finally the preservation of the vanity that she has invested in her abjection and resentment. She is offered marriage, material security, and a fresh start in colonial Indian society: "My pride rose against this barefaced way of pointing out the contrast my married life was to present to my then dependent and inferior position" (II.21; 649). At this point Miss Wade meets Henry Gowan, the novel's true villain, if an apparently feckless one, a disappointed artist who is "jaundiced and jealous" (I.17; 202) and who has "a supreme a contempt for the class that had thrown him off as for the class that had not taken him in" (II.26; 306). He is a match for Miss Wade, who, she says, understood her and with whose attentions she is now able, in her own turn, to drive her fiancé into jealousy. The marriage broken off, Gowan seduces and then leaves Miss Wade in order to turn his attentions to Pet Meagles. Hence Miss Wade's hatred for Pet, hence her presence, we only learn now, stalking the Meagles at the beginning of the novel: "as I hate her now; and naturally, therefore, could desire nothing better than that she should marry him" (II.21; 651). Why? we may ask in response to this astounding sentence. Because Miss Wade knows that Gowan will mistreat Pet, that he will treat her as a pet, not as an equal. But also because this marriage will make Miss Wade's own abjection the more complete: the man whom "I was once dupe enough, and false enough to myself, almost to love" (II.20; 640) is now definitively lost to her.

With its succession of mediators—the school friend, the dead sister, the young cousin, Pet Meagles—of loves repeatedly turned to hate, of the kindnesses of others interpreted as patronizing condescension and spurned, Miss Wade's testimony seems to bear out that she does, indeed, possess the "unhappy temper" (II.21; 645, 651) that she is infuriated to hear ascribed to her. It is a metaphysical condition, both Dickens and Girard appear to agree, rather than a social one, and, with the exception of the villainous Gowan, she has no one to blame for her social exclusion other than herself. From the very beginning of the novel, she has both spelled out the master carceral metaphor of the novel and refused its Christian solution: "Do you mean that a prisoner forgives his prison?" the prison, that is, of social circumstances in which we find ourselves. Well, that *is* the meaning or injunction of the novel, but Miss Wade would wish instead, she says, to burn the prison down: "If I had been shut up in any place to pine and suffer, I should always hate that place and burn it down, or raze it to the ground" (I.2; 22). By contrast to this unhappy temper, Tattyrcoram merely has a temper that she often loses and must count to five and twenty to regain. Her good angel winning out against the power of Miss Wade, she returns to the Meagles at the end of the novel, helping to resolve its convoluted plot with the box of documents, but more pointedly, spelling out its middle-class Christian ideology.

In a novel that begins at Marseilles, which, Mr. Meagles says, "sent the most insurrectionary tune into the world that ever was composed" (I.2; 15), the battle over the soul of the servant Tattycoram hinges on whether class resentment against their superiors can be instilled in the laboring class or whether the repenting Tattycoram can get over the idea that these social betters "triumphed above me, and that they wanted to make me envy them, when I know—when I even knew then, if I would—that they never thought of such a thing" (II.33; 787). Miss Wade has taken Tattycoram to France, the land of revolution, and Frenchified servants can be very dangerous, as Mr. Tulkinghorn learns to his peril in *Bleak House*, stabbed to death by the French maid Hortense, who hails from around Marseilles herself and seems to bring to the mind of Esther Summerson "some woman from the streets of Paris in the reign of terror."[19] Dickens's next novel after *Little Dorrit*, *A Tale of Two Cities*, would tell the story of that terror.[20] But Tattycoram returns to England to her bourgeois employers Father and Mother Meagles, "who never deserved their names better, than when they took the headstrong foundling-girl into their protection again" (II.33; 787). *La revolution française n'aura pas lieu.* Not in Twickenham anyway. In fact, Tattycoram's return follows and coincides with the novel's comic version of revolutionary action—when the agent Pancks cuts off the flowing locks of his own bourgeois employer Casby and exposes him as the bogus Patriarch he is (II.3232). Pancks is an "Incendiary" (II.34; 794) in the eyes of Casby's daughter, Flora Finching, and so the narrator winkingly calls him again in the novel's final paragraphs (II.34; 801), but this is as far as *Little Dorrit* imagines violence against the moneyed classes, burning the prison down.

Still, this unmasking of Casby as a "philanthropic sneak" (II.32; 77) does tell another side of the story, and we may wonder how wrong Miss Wade was to denounce, even in the well-meaning Meagles, a "swollen patronage and selfishness, calling themselves kindness, protection, benevolence" at the end of her history (II.21; 651). Tattycoram's return is part morality play and also part of what Moretti has characterized as the judicial "fairy-tale" model of the English novel.[21] But Mr. Meagles has reminded us from the beginning that Tattycoram does not have a glass slipper or fairy godmother, and at the end of the novel, she seems destined to return to the role of Cinderella in domestic service, minus the prince, whom the novel's heroine Amy Dorrit does attain, although in the somewhat dubious form of Arthur Clennam. Mr. Meagles holds up Amy as a model of "Duty" to Tattycoram (II.33; 788). But it is hard to separate this self-sacrificing ideal from the duties the employer asks from his worker: reproaching Pancks for not squeezing more out of his tenants, the odious Casby has told him a chapter earlier: "You are made to do your duty, but you don't do your duty" (II; 32; 775).

So if *Little Dorrit* suggests, as René Girard does, that we should not make excuses for Miss Wade, both her story and that of Tattycoram, nonetheless, offer some resistance to its fairy-tale structure and morality. To be fair to Dickens and in answer to Moretti, *Little Dorrit* quite openly acknowledges the fairy-tale nature of its story from rags and prison to riches and back to middle class respectability and industry in the tale that Amy tells to Maggy of the Princess and the tiny woman (I; 24), and by casting the perennial ten-year-old Maggy as its model reader, it asks us to read beyond it. Like most novels, like most literature worthy of the name, *Little Dorrit* has the advantage over the critic, Girard or Moretti, of offering more than one point of view. In the second chapter, a French gentleman, and it would be a French gentleman speaking in French, poses the rhetorical question to Miss Wade, "Mademoiselle doubts its being so easy to forgive?" (I.2; 22). These are doubts that the novel expresses about itself from the beginning, and they extend to other novels as well. Miss Wade's ten-page history is a knowing send-up of the Governess Novel, that Cinderella story of impoverished gentility—not quite a servant but a domestic dependent—rewarded with marriage.[22] But the conjunction of this history and the story of Tattycoram strikes deepest at Dickens's own oeuvre: it rewrites, again in miniature, the story of Esther Summerson in *Bleak House*, the novel that preceded *Little Dorrit* by four years.

Like Miss Wade and Tattycoram, Esther is an orphan and illegitimate child. But she takes the grim reference to her unfortunate birth by her aunt, whom she knows as her godmother, but hardly of the fairy variety, not as an occasion for resentment—her godmother has refused to give her a birthday party, and an ordinary child just might feel resentful—but rather as an incentive to "strive, as I grew up to be industrious, contented and kindhearted, and to do some good to some one, and win some love to myself if I could" (3; 18). Esther understands that she is being educated to be a governess, but that novelistic option is taken off the table when her guardian Mr. Jarndyce makes her the companion of the golden-haired Ada Clare and gives her the housekeeping keys to Bleak House. For a moment, Esther imagines that Jarndyce is her lost father, but puts that dream of family and inclusion aside: "It was not for me to muse over bygones, but to act with a cheerful spirit and a grateful heart. So I said to myself, 'Esther, Esther, Esther! Duty my dear!' and gave my little basket of housekeeping keys such a shake, that they sounded like bells, and rang me hopefully to bed" (6; 131). Plucky, dutiful Esther is rewarded with a husband and with a first-person narrative that dwarfs that of Miss Wade and makes her the central character of *Bleak House*. Her situation for much of the novel nonetheless boils down to a genteel version of the domestic drudgery that Tattycoram is encouraged to embrace; like Tattycoram she is given not just one playful pet name, but a handful: "Old Woman, and Little Old Woman, and Cobweb, and Mrs. Shipton, and Mother Hubbard, and Dame Durden, and so many names of that sort, that my own name soon became quite lost among them" (8; 148). And, like Tattycoram, she is put in the service of, and has to measure herself beside, a girl of extraordinary beauty and higher social expectation, Ada, the novel's apparent pet, a Girardian mediator, who is the mirror in which Esther sees herself before and after mirrors were removed from her room after her bout of smallpox.

But things as bad as smallpox happen to Ada and to other characters around Esther, her nearest and dearest, just as Henry Gowan happens to Pet Meagles. Alexander Welsh has wryly commented, "Summerson proves . . . [a] dangerous young person to be acquainted with," and shows how Dickens lets the plot fulfill secret wishes and aggression of which the character herself is unaware. These wishes make Esther's story a version of Dickens's autobiography, his reliving of his own father's neglect and his experience of working in the blacking factory, where he briefly fell out of gentility into the laboring class.[23] In *Little Dorrit*, he brings those sentiments into the open in the temper tantrums of Tattycoram and in the demonic temper of Miss Wade: they are how an Esther Summerson might plausibly feel in a social position that strips her of self-respect and therefore induces the response of pride and class anger. The minor characters of *Little Dorrit* suggest a palinode for *Bleak House*, an antidote to the fairy tales told by both Dickens novels, including the fairy tale of Christianity itself. Their class resentment expresses the bad conscience of the novel, but also its social conscience and realism.

It is not so easy to forgive, the French critic of *Little Dorrit* suggests, and this is René Girard's point as well when he insists in *Deceit, Desire, and the Novel* on the "metaphysical meaning" rather than the conditions, the mere "excuses," that cause social inferiors and outcasts to envy and hate their supposed betters. Read in Girard's Christian terms—and to a real extent, these are Dickens's terms, too—the unhappy pride of Miss Wade makes excuses instead for the social order and would justify the working title of *Little Dorrit*, "Nobody's Fault." That title is ironic enough in a novel whose social satire includes the Circumlocution Office, whose motto is "HOW NOT TO DO IT" (I.10; 100), run from the top by the noble Barnacle family. If mimetic desire is a purely metaphysical problem, then its metaphysical solution bypasses or absolves the social, and this may be the not so secret agenda of *Deceit, Desire, and the Novel*, which might make us think, too, that the novel as a genre cannot dispense with such aristocrats as the Barnacles.[24] Girard is an acute theorist of ressentiment, which he sees turning upon and poisoning the self in a kind of short circuit.[25] But ressentiment or a human response very much akin to it can go under the name of indignation, with a more altruistic valence and less blaming of society's victims. Indignation describes both the feelings of persons whose dignity has been taken away from them and the feelings that move others—readers of novels among them—on their behalf. It also contains the awareness that dignity, pride if you will, can be a human and social good. It is not easy to forgive society, but it is also too easy a way out. There is a middle ground between forgiving society and burning it down. It is the middle, muddled ground of a reformist, if compromised and hypocritical bourgeoisie—and it is the historical ground of the novel.

Notes

1. René Girard, *Deceit, Desire, and the Novel: Self and Other in Literary Structure*, trans. Yvonne Freccero (Baltimore: Johns Hopkins University Press, 1965), 227.

2. Girard, *Deceit, Desire, and the Novel*, 56–59, 69.

3. Girard, *Deceit, Desire, and the Novel*, 55.

4. Girard, *Deceit, Desire, and the Novel*, 61. Georg Lukács, *The Theory of the Novel* (1920), trans. Anna Bostock (Cambridge: MIT Press, 1971), 88–93.

5. Franco Moretti, *The Way of the World: The Bildungsroman in European Culture*, trans. Albert J. Sbragia (London: Verso, 1987).

6. Girard, *Deceit, Desire, and the Novel*, 71.

7. Girard, in the supposed voice of Tocqueville, writes: "The passion for equality is a madness unequalled except by the contrary and symmetrical passion for inequality, which is even more abstract and contributes even more directly to the unhappiness caused by freedom in those who are incapable of accepting it in a manly fashion" Girard, *Deceit, Desire, and the Novel*, 137.

8. Charles Dickens, *Little Dorrit*, ed. Harvey Peter Sucksmith (Oxford: Clarendon Press, 1979). Indications are to part, chapter, and page numbers in this edition.

9. Mr. Dorrit's remarks occur in a chapter titled "Spirit," (I.31; 362); earlier Fanny has reproached Amy, "Have you no spirit at all?" (I.20; 237).

10. Dickens, *Little Dorrit*, I.27; 318. It should be noted that these furnishings mirror those of the shabby genteel Mrs. Gowan, who with her fellow aristocrats, described one chapter earlier, lives in the cramped and shared quarters of Hampton Court, "encamped there like a sort of civilized gypsies" (II.26; 303): these are, to take up the novel's central figure, willing, if discontented, inmates of their prison.

11. Annamarie Jagose, "Remembering Miss Wade: *Little Dorrit* and the Historicizing of Female Perversity," *GLQ* 4 (1998): 425–51, reads Miss Wade as a lesbian, but not according to twentieth-century definitions of lesbianism; Janet Retseck, "Sexing Miss Wade," *Dickens Quarterly* 15 (1998): 217–25, makes a case against defining Miss Wade's sexuality.

12. Dickens, *Little Dorrit*, I.16; 189.

13. For similar remarks—minus the Girardian scheme—on Miss Wade and her role as critic of the ethos of beneficent paternalism in the *Little Dorrit*, see David Suchoff, *Critical Theory and the Novel* (Madison: University of Wisconsin Press, 1994), 79–83.

14. N. M. Lary, *Dostoevsky and Dickens* (London: Routledge and Kegan Paul, 1973), 89.

15. *The Best Short Stories of Dostoevsky*, trans. David Magarshack (New York: Modern Library, 1955), I.ii; 114. Indications are to part, chapter, and page number in this edition.

16. On the illegitimacy that links Miss Wade and Arthur Clennam, see Diane Sadoff, "Storytelling and the Figure of the Father in *Little Dorrit*," *PMLA* 95 (1980): 238.

17. Girard, *Deceit, Desire, and the Novel*, 58.

18. Dickens, *Little Dorrit*, II.21; 648.

19. Charles Dickens, *Bleak House* (New York: Oxford University Press, 1948), 12; 158, 21; 320. Indications are to chapters and page numbers in this edition.

20. "The bolts and bars of the old Bastille couldn't keep her," Mr. Meagles remarks of Tattycoram after she has left his household (I.27; 313). Barbara Black links Miss Wade to Madame Defarge in *A Tale of Two Cities* in "A Sisterhood of Rage and Beauty: Rosa Dartle, Miss Wade and Madam Defarge," *Dickens Studies Annual* 26 (1998): 91–106.

21. Moretti, *Way of the World*, 185–214.

22. For overviews, see Katharine Leaf West, *Chapter of Governesses* (London: Cohen and West, 1949); Cecilia Wadsö Lecaros, *The Victorian Governess Novel* (Lund: Lund University Press, 2001).

23. Alexander Welsh, *Dickens Redressed: The Art of* Bleak House *and* Hard Times (New Haven: Yale University Press, 2000), 35.

24. Girard, *Deceit, Desire, and the Novel*, 227–28.

25. Girard acknowledges his debt to Max Scheler's *Ressentiment* but, it seems to me, oversimplifies Scheler's description of the relationship of Christianity and ressentiment when he claims that Scheler "never succeeded in distinguishing *ressentiment* from Christian religious feeling" (Girard, *Deceit, Desire, and the Novel*, 59). Scheler does indeed oppose Christian love as the opposite of ressentiment, but argues nonetheless that the latter can masquerade as the former: "I realized that the root of Christian love is entirely *free* of *ressentiment*, but that *ressentiment* can very easily use it for its own purposes by simulating an emotion which corresponds to this idea. This simulation is often so perfect that even the sharpest observer can no longer distinguish real love from *ressentiment* which poses as love." M. Scheler, *Ressentiment*, ed. Lewis A. Coser, trans. William W. Holdheim (New York: Free Press, 1961), 88. In chapter 4 (114–36), Scheler also distinguishes Christian love from modern humanitarianism, which he takes, in agreement with Nietzsche, to be based on ressentiment. I will take humanitarianism any day.

"Let Us Carve Him as a Feast Fit for the Gods"

Girard and Unjust Execution in Nineteenth-Century Narrative

I n the final chapter of *Deceit, Desire, and the Novel*, René Girard identifies in the works of Cervantes, Dostoyevsky, Flaubert, Stendhal, and Proust a "unity in [their] novelistic conclusions": the destructive force of mimetic rivalry in each of his chosen texts is only negated by what he labels "conversion in death"—a "repudiat[ion of a protagonist's] will to power," a "break with the world which fascinated him," a "renunciation of metaphysical desire" (292–93). For Girard, the greatest moral exempla are "the wise man of old or the Christian saint" (272) and above all Christ, "that incomparable being," who models freedom from desire (275) and calls us to follow his example. Accordingly, Girard argues that the role of Christian thought in the formation of narrative conclusions has been undervalued:

> We are in the habit of never taking Christian symbolism seriously, perhaps because it is common to many works both mediocre and sublime. We attribute a purely decorative function to this symbolism when the author is not a Christian, and a purely apologetic function when he is a Christian. Truly "scientific" criticism would discard all these a priori judgments and would note the amazing points of similarity among all the different novelistic conclusions. . . . And we would at last realize that

Christian symbolism is universal for it alone is able to give form to the
experience of the novel.[1]

What Girard calls the "Christian symbolism" of narrative closure is a collection of textual features—biblical allusion, hints of resurrection and immortality, and a resultant "breadth and depth of vision" that he calls "vertical
transcendency." For Girard, the deployment of such features results in truly
dynamic narrative art that "merges with the great religious ethics and the
most elevated forms of humanism" (308).

In *The Scapegoat*, Girard locates Christ's "incomparable" value in his
status as a victim possessing a unique innocence that can be proclaimed and
recognised by all, "without any sentimental piety or suspect emotion."[2] The
New Testament narrative contains its own acknowledgment that the victim
to be sacrificed for the restoration of public order is innocent of any taint of
wrongdoing: in John 11:50–52, Caiaphus observes that "if we let him thus
alone . . . the Romans shall come and take away both our place and our people," hence "it is expedient that one man should die for the people, and that
the whole nation perish not" (KJV). Chief among the many criticisms that
can be directed against the Gospel narratives is what to do with the injustice
that is thus enshrined at the heart of the Christian redemptive scheme. In
a perceptive analysis of Girard's contributions to theology, Mark Johnston
asks what Girard felt the Passion of Christ achieved that his death by natural
causes could not.[3] For many orthodox Christians, the answer is substitutionary atonement—that Christ died to pay the penalty for the sins of others,
that the world might be redeemed—but as Johnston correctly concludes,
Girard rejects such a forensic approach:

> The real purpose of Christ's sacrifice and death is not to propitiate an angry
> or insulted Father-god, but to complete the movement begun in Yahweh's
> rejection of sacrifice, and finally bring sacrificial religion to an end. Christ
> comes, not to found a religion, but to unmask religion's origins in our most
> violent impulses, to render it no longer tenable as a solution to mimeti-
> cally generated acquisitive tension, and finally to present a new, definitive
> resolution of the recurrent crisis.[4]

The consequence is an ethical and literary sensitivity to the plight of the
innocent scapegoat: in Johnston's reading of Girard's work,

To thus assimilate the significance of Christ's suffering and death would mean that we can never look at victims, even the victims of so-called legitimate violence, including the juridical violence of the state, in the same way. After the Cross, the face of God incarnate looks back at us from the image of the victim. Victimization, sacrifice, and religious violence have been forever unmasked as illegitimate strategies by which our murderous envy of each other is temporarily discharged, and yet preserved as an ongoing psychological orientation.

This is the salvation that Christ offers: . . . a new resolution of the internecine mimetic tension, not by way of another temporary sacrificial discharge, but through the availability of a wholly new form of mimesis, the imitation of Christ's own self-sacrificing love.[5]

Girard is thus compelled to negotiate some difficult terrain: on the one hand, he emphasizes the irreplaceable singularity of Christ's sacrifice and proclaims its importance in literature that dwells on symbolic features of the Passion; on the other, he hopes the progress of civilization will eventually disavow the bloodthirstiness of founding murders, scapegoating, and expulsions, and finally attain a postsacrificial religious equilibrium. In *A Theater of Envy: William Shakespeare*, Girard reveals himself to be aware of the paradox: he notes, "as a dramatic strategist, Shakespeare deliberately resorts to the power of scapegoating," thus "channeling different segments of his audience toward two different interpretations of one and the same play: a sacrificial explanation for the groundlings . . . and a nonsacrificial, mimetic one for those in the galleries."[6] Something of this doubleness resides in the work of all the Victorian authors who found themselves compelled (by its sheer artistic potential) to deal in the currency of sacrifice, even as they wished to critique its brutality. As Girard observes, "The view of sacrificial violence as a precious but dangerously unstable substance endowed with paradoxical properties, is crucial to human culture" (214), and authors in every generation attempt to make sense of the traction exerted by its tragic appeal—a task rendered all the more urgent in times of epistemological crisis such as the mid-nineteenth century.

The Christian tradition attempts to deal with this central moral obstacle—the punishment of the innocent—by a clear assertion of Christ's voluntary submission and self-surrender to the forces marshalled against him. In this way, Christ is represented as simultaneously both priest and sacrifice, yielding himself to death out of love for his father's will (see for example, Hebrews 9:25–10:18). The rise of forensic Protestantism in the years after the publication of Joseph Butler's famous *Analogy of Religion, Natural and Revealed, to the Course and Constitution of Nature* (1736) tended to cast this act of self-sacrifice in penal terms, and although (as Johnston's argument shows) substitutionary atonement is by no means the only way in which the Passion might be understood, it was the Unitarian critique of vicarious punishment that brought these issues into focus in the first half of the nineteenth century. Orthodox defenses of the doctrine of atonement were compelled to assert that the act afforded the innocent substitute no permanent injury (by virtue of his immortality).[7]

In his comparative survey of the great European and English bildungsromans of the long nineteenth century, the literary critic Franco Moretti argued that it was precisely a preoccupation with innocence and passive submission that distinguished English novels from their more morally sophisticated European counterparts. If Girard was right to stress that conversion characterizes the ending of his chosen European texts, Moretti points out that so obsessed were the English with a model of goodness founded on Christian precedent that many Victorian protagonists had little to repent of at the point of narrative closure: while authors from Henry Fielding to George Eliot often resort to forensic models to try the protagonists's qualities, the accusations usually turn out to the wrongful, and the verdict is habitually an acquittal.[8] In this way, Moretti concludes, the wisdom of the English law is also dramatized and affirmed.[9] Many comic novels do indeed accord with this model, but there is also a fascination with martyrdom in Victorian writing, with the (temporally) undeserved death of those who are prepared to pay for their faith with their life. Novels including John Henry Newman's *Callista* (1853), Charles Kingsley's *Hypatia* (1856), George Eliot's *Romola* (1863), and Eliza Lynn Linton's *The True History of Joshua Davidson* (1872) all dwelt upon the interpretative difficulties experienced by saints or martyrs as they transmit their own testimony of God's existence to the wider community who waits to interpret the meaning of their sufferings. That sacrifice and martyrdom became such prominent motifs of nineteenth-century writing speaks to the ways in which martyrdom tests with compelling clarity the values for which a man is prepared to die—an epistemological crisis of particular relevance when a society is in urgent need of democratic reform but hopes to avoid the bloodshed of another French Revolution.[10]

In her magisterial study *The Science of Sacrifice: American Literature and Modern Social Theory*, Susan Mizruchi observes that the Christian discipline of self-sacrifice has little in common with the dynamics of sacrificial scape-goating: the former, she contends, is the metaphorical practice of "isolated individuals," while the latter is a "collective ritual, expressing a sense of group risks and benefits."[11] This is clearly true, and yet the cultural work of devotional writing in general and the Victorian realist novel in particular is precisely to align these two potentially distinct phenomena. On the one hand, the incentive for this is scriptural: while not everyone will be called to martyrdom in Christ's name, all can surrender their own desires and become his disciples in the service of their neighbors: this is the philosophy of Paul's epistles (see for example, Romans 12:1) and of literature that emphasizes self-abnegation as the template of true discipleship. But on the other hand, per-sonal belief in the value of martyrdom can legitimate the subjugation of the individual to the greater good of the community, thus ensuring that believers are prepared to consent to their own sacrifice should the need arise. And there were many reasons why the tension between the claims of the "one" and the "many" were felt with particular force in the nineteenth century:[12] a crucial stimulus was the rise of the laissez-faire system of economics in which each man asserts his own self-interest—in response many Victorian realist novels promoted a compensatory ethics of mutual dependence in which each man should ideally act as the Good Samaritan to his neighbor. Indeed, as I argued in *Atonement and Self-Sacrifice in Nineteenth-Century Narrative*, so great was the literary suspicion of self-interest—so great the preference for a culture of altruism in an age of economic competitiveness—that authors from Dick-ens to Eliot felt compelled to advocate an ethics of extreme self-sacrifice:[13] "better to be Abel than Cain," in Dickens's terms,[14] "more comfortable to be the calf than the butcher," in Eliot's.[15] At the same time, the expansion of the franchise, the impact of Benthamite utilitarianism, and the rise of the professions called for a clearer articulation of the theories of political and legal representation in the decades between the two Reform Bills of 1832 and 1867. Realist fiction with morally improving intentions thus placed itself in an awkward position, denouncing physical violence (particularly Chartist agitation), yet advocating self-sacrifice in the interests of a greater good that could, at its most extreme, demand consent to one's own immolation. Victorian fiction is extraordinarily attentive to the costs involved in such transactions, giving voice to the suffering individuals who will potentially be excluded from wider benefit, yet at the same time affirming that self-interest must be sacrificed to the greater good.

Nowhere was this tension felt more acutely than in literature that addressed the wrongful execution of the innocent, the specter that haunted the English legal system as campaigners worked tirelessly to reform it through the long nineteenth century. To give one example of a moving case that resonated throughout the Victorian period: in July 1815, national controversy erupted when a young woman in domestic service, Eliza Fenning, was executed for the attempted murder of the family who employed her—a conviction widely perceived as wrongful.[16] In the articulate letters she composed in prison prior to her execution, she protested that "it is a cruel thing to suffer for the guilty!" and she conceptualized her plight in terms of the language of self-sacrifice: "I trust to a merciful God, that knows the secret thoughts of all hearts, will grant me grace, and renew me with a new heart, that my past and present sufferings may prove an acceptable sacrifice for my past faults."[17] For the radical activists who agitated tirelessly on her behalf, Fenning was a scapegoat, and the savage treatment she received strengthened arguments for the amelioration of criminal trial procedure. Even as the Christian salvific scheme valorizes the suffering of the innocent substitute, law reformers from Jeremy Bentham to Samuel Romilly sought to calibrate punishment and culpability as they repudiated archaic models of sacrifice that scapegoated the guiltless. But the legal system of the early nineteenth century was in transition, from the procedural brutality that supported the Bloody Code (in which trials rarely lasted for more than thirty minutes and prisoners were unrepresented) to a more professionalized model in which defendants could obtain full legal representation if their financial means allowed.[18] Nineteenth-century literature both registered and catalyzed the ways in which the law's negotiation between individual rights and social order changed in this period.

In his *Commentaries on the Laws of England* (1765–69), William Blackstone provided one of the earliest statements of what has since become known as the golden thread of the English common law, that a man is to be presumed innocent of a charge brought against him until proven otherwise by the prosecution. In Blackstone's famous phrase, "It is better that ten guilty persons escape, than the one innocent suffer."[19] Yet upon its first articulation, this principle encountered great resistance, and the objection that most clearly tethers it to ideas of sacrifice of the one for the many was voiced by the Anglican clergyman William Paley in his *Principles of Moral and Political Philosophy* (1785):

> If by saying it is better be meant that it is more for the public advantage, the proposition, I think, cannot be maintained. . . . The misfortune of an individual, for such may the sufferings, or even the death, of an innocent person be called, when they are occasioned by no evil intention, cannot be placed in competition with [the security of civil life]. I do not contend that the life or safety of the meanest subject ought, in any case, to be knowingly sacrificed. No principle of judicature, no end of punishment, can ever require that. But when certain rules of adjudication must be pursued, when certain degrees of credibility must be accepted, in order to reach the crimes with which the public are infested; courts of justice should not be deterred from the application of those rules by every suspicion of danger, or by the mere possibility of confounding the innocent with the guilty. They ought rather to reflect that he, who falls by a mistaken sentence, may be considered as falling for his country; whilst he suffers under the operation of these rules, by the general effect and tendency of which, the welfare of the community is maintained and upheld.[20]

Lord Denman was one of many jurists to criticize this implicitly utilitarian tendency to see all individuals as commensurable units to be exchanged without due attention to their moral complexion: writing in the *Edinburgh Review* in 1824, Denman reminded his audience that "human beings are never to be run down, like beasts of prey, without respect to the laws of the chase":

> If society must make a sacrifice of any one of its members, let it proceed according to general rules, upon known principles, and with clear proof of necessity; "let us carve him as a feast fit for the gods, not hew him as a

carcase for the hounds" . . . we maintain that it is desirable that guilty men should sometimes escape, by the operation of those general rules, which form the only security for innocence.[21]

With its quotation from Shakespeare's *Julius Caesar* (act 2, scene 1, lines 173–4), this passage alludes to the political context of any decision to condemn one man to death in the apparent service of the many: as Girard notes in *A Theater of Envy*, when discussing Brutus's decision to kill Caesar in what he considers to be the interest of the Roman republic, sacrifice is—at first glance—to be distinguished from butchery, but on closer inspection the boundary is shifting and problematic:

> Sacrificers are always aware that, in their feeble hands, the difference between the two kinds of violence is perishable. Whenever it is lost, sacrifice reverts to the bad violence of the crisis from which it came in the first place; it makes the crisis worse than if no sacrifice had been attempted. . . . The carving metaphor is an island of classical harmony surrounded on all sides by the sound and the fury of wrath and envy. . . . If the sacrificers partake of the chaos outside, if they surrender to the tumultuous emotions of mimetic rivalry, their sacrifice will surely fail. . . . If the murder looks so ugly that the people are repelled, the would-be sacrifice will turn to bloody chaos. Brutus would like his "sacrifice" to be so beautiful that no confusion will be possible; it will be the absolute other of the crisis. The problem, however, is that violence has only one absolute other and that is nonviolence, total abstention from all violence.[22]

In *Julius Caesar*, the debate concerns a foundational murder that may or may not save the polis, but what is at stake in the defense of capital punishment—and its attendant risk of wrongful execution—is the acknowledgment that the criminal law, and the wider social order it is designed to enforce, are in turn predicated upon the atavistic memories and symbolic remnants of revenge and sacrifice. As Girard argues in *Violence and the Sacred*,

> The death of the individual has something of the quality of a tribute levied for the continued existence of the collectivity. A human being dies, and the solidarity of the survivors is enhanced by his death. The surrogate victim

dies so that the entire community, threatened by the same fate, can be reborn in a new or renewed cultural order.[23]

What the nineteenth-century reformers sought was a better fit between guilt and punishment—the replacement of exemplary or deterrent punishment with the "just deserts" that J. S. Mill, in his essay "Utilitarianism" (1861), defined as "the clearest and most emphatic form in which the idea of justice is conceived by the general mind"—the hope "that each person should obtain that (whether good or evil) which he deserves."[24] According to Debora Shuger, sacrifice became archaic for precisely this reason: penal substitution "violates the contours demarcating the autonomous individual." Liability to vicarious punishment depends upon the subordination of the individual to the group: "corporate identity" is its "ethical ground" and communal solidarity is the context in which "one member can substitute for another":

> To the extent that persons are regarded as parts of a whole, they may offer their lives for that whole, whereas insofar as a person is viewed as an autonomous moral subject, *coram Deo*, he has an obligation to preserve his life. . . . The modern individual . . . is thus defined in terms of alienation from sacrifice.[25]

The novel's history is coincident with the rise of individualism and what Joseph Slaughter has called "the birth pains of . . . democratic citizen-subjectivity":[26] the genre anticipates and represents the proper conditions for the work of individual self-development. Yet, culturally, the Victorians could not escape the traction of Evangelical self-sacrifice: as Paley reminds us, an acceptance of wrongful punishment is the narrative trajectory of the Passion and identification with Christ the strongest religious compulsion of the period. And, crucially, Victorian arguments in favor of the moral value of reading depended upon the mental labors of imaginative substitution—the requirement that we "change places in fancy with another" as Adam Smith expressed the idea of sympathy in his *Theory of Moral Sentiments* (1759)—was thus crucial to our ethical education.[27] Hence it is unsurprising that many mid-Victorian novels are characterized by a conflicted attitude to substitution and exchange, which may effect salvation but simultaneously expose us to risks of wrongful execution and vicarious punishment.

Victorian novels register and experiment creatively with these tensions between models of order based on revenge and sacrifice on the one hand, and personal responsibility and "just deserts" on the other. The same novels that align themselves most closely with legal order and the rules of evidence— Dickens's *Bleak House* (1852–53), for example, or Eliot's *Adam Bede* (1859)— often resort to sacrifice to effect narrative closure and to instigate those acts of moral reformation that are so important to Girard in *Deceit, Desire, and the Novel*. The representation of sacrifice clearly releases or enables some response on the part of the reader that more comic narrative arcs do not: in the words of Jonathan Kertzer, "Justice permits restoration; sacrifice promises transformation."[28] There is no better example of this dynamic than Charles Dickens's novel *A Tale of Two Cities* (1859). At the point of narrative closure, the dissolute lawyer Sidney Carton recovers from alcoholic despondency to assume the role of the sacrificial substitute, saving the life of his more successful rival in love, Charles Darnay. As he mounts the scaffold to the guillotine in Paris during the Reign of Terror, Carton takes comfort from Christ's promise: "I am the resurrection and the life, saith the Lord: he that believeth in me, though he were dead, yet shall he live: and whosoever liveth and believeth in me shall never die":[29] his biography, on the one hand, amplifies and illuminates the Gospel message—"greater love hath no man than this, that a man lay down his life for his friends"[30]—but on the other hand, the novel becomes the apocryphal fictional embroidery that circles insistently around the central dogma of New Testament teaching. In navigating between the rewards and the risks of Carton's self-sacrificial execution, Dickens must express revulsion at the arbitrary violence of the Revolution and simultaneously disavow the suggestion that Carton's end is an altruistic suicide, incited by erotic hopelessness or nihilistic despair.[31] Dickens cautiously observes that "if Carton had given an utterance to his thoughts on the scaffold, and if they had been prophetic, they would have been these"—but he then proceeds to demonstrate and dramatize the political and personal triumph effected by self-sacrifice:

> I see a beautiful city and a brilliant people rising from this abyss, and, in their struggles to be truly free, in their triumphs and defeats through long years to come, I see the evil of this time and of the previous time of which this is the natural birth, gradually making expiation for itself and wearing out.

> I see the lives for which I lay down my life, peaceful, useful, prosperous and happy in that England which I shall see no more. I see her with a child upon her bosom, who bears my name. . . . I see that I hold a sanctuary in their hearts, and in the hearts of their descendants, generations hence. . . . I see that child who lay upon her bosom and who bore my name, a man winning his way up in that path of life which once was mine . . . I see him, foremost of the just judges and honoured men, bringing a boy of my name, with a forehead that I know and golden hair, to this place—then fair to look upon, with not a trace of this day's disfigurement—and I hear him tell the child my story, with a tender and faltering voice.[32]

As John Glavin has suggested, there is a suggestion of narcissistic self-replication here (and Carton also gains virtual paternity of his rival's son, achieving in death what he had failed to do in life).[33] But this is to read against the grain. Much of the affective power of this resolution derives from its Christian precedent—the impression Dickens is prepared to create that Carton, as a narrating consciousness, "survives" his own death, to claim "a sanctuary" in the hearts of those who love him, and to prove the emotional truth of the Evangelical mantra that "the crown ever consummates the Cross."[34]

In his *Life of Charles Dickens* (1872), John Forster observed that Dickens himself was not prone to acts of self-sacrifice,[35] and critics have consequently seen Dickens's treatment of the biblical original on which he modeled his ending as rather predatory and parasitic: in Janet Larson's words,

> In a climate where the historical facticity of God's Word in all its parts is no longer assured, nor even deemed necessary . . . the novelist who wants the design of a vicarious atonement for a Sydney Carton can borrow it from the New Testament without having to believe the doctrine as rooted in fact or as necessary to salvation.[36]

There is truth in this, but we must not overlook Girard's acute insight into the power and function of Christian symbolism in the architecture of narrative conclusions: neither "purely decorative," nor "purely apologetic," the representation of Carton's triumph over death and self-interest gestures toward the crucial vector of "vertical transcendency" that Girard located in the great European narratives.[37] Clearly Dickens found in the ritual of violent sacrifice something compelling—what Michael Kirwan in *Girard and Theology* identifies as the way in which the ideology of sacrifice "makes possible an order that law alone is unable to provide."[38] For Dickens, the cultural work of literary sacrifice is to release a powerful affective response in his readers that he hopes will produce tears of repentance and stimulate a form of moral renewal. Politically, then, Dickens refuses to see sacrifice, forgiveness, mercy as purely private matters—Carton's example, like that of Christ, shows that such values, practiced by loving individuals, can survive the damage inflicted by the impersonal forces of history.

Notes

1. René Girard, *Deceit, Desire, and the Novel: Self and Other in Literary Structure*, trans. Yvonne Freccero (Baltimore: Johns Hopkins University Press, 1965), 310.

2. René Girard, *The Scapegoat*, trans. Yvonne Freccero (Baltimore: Johns Hopkins University Press, 1986), 126.

3. Mark Johnston, *Saving God: Religion after Idolatry* (Princeton: Princeton University Press, 2010), 166.

4. Johnston, *Saving God*, 163.

5. Johnston, *Saving God*, 164–65.

6. René Girard, *A Theater of Envy: William Shakespeare* (Oxford: Oxford University Press, 1991), 6.

7. See for example, Joseph Gilbert, *The Christian Atonement* (London: William Ball, 1836), 294.

8. See Jan-Melissa Schramm, *Testimony and Advocacy in Victorian Law, Literature, and Theology* (Cambridge: Cambridge University Press, 2000), 101–44.

9. Franco Moretti, *The Way of the World: The Bildungsroman in European Culture*, trans. Albert J. Sbragia (London: Verso, 1987), 182–95.

10. See David Carroll, *George Eliot and the Conflict of Interpretations* (Cambridge: Cambridge University Press), 170–95.

11. Susan Mizruchi, *The Science of Sacrifice: American Literature and Modern Social Theory* (Princeton: Princeton University Press, 1998), 29.

12. See Alex Woloch, *The One vs. the Many: Minor Characters and the Space of the Protagonist in the Novel* (Princeton: Princeton University Press, 2003).

13. Schramm, *Atonement and Self-Sacrifice*, 1–37. See also Ilana Blumberg, *Victorian Sacrifice: Ethics and Economics in Mid-Century Novels* (Athens: Ohio State University Press, 2013).

14. Charles Dickens, *Our Mutual Friend* (1864–65) (Harmondsworth: Penguin, 1985), 770.

15. George Eliot, *Daniel Deronda* (1876) (Harmondsworth: Penguin, 1986), 218.

16. For a detailed discussion of her trial and its place in the wider campaign for the abolition of capital punishment, see V. A. C. Gatrell, *The Hanging Tree: Execution and the English People, 1770–1868* (Oxford: Oxford University Press, 1994), 339–370.

17. Eliza Fenning's correspondence, printed in William Hone, *The Important Results of an Elaborate Investigation into the Mysterious Case of Eliza Fenning* (1815), cited in Ben Wilson, *The Laughter of Triumph: William Hone and the Fight for the Free Press* (London: Faber and Faber, 2005), 115–17.

18. See John Langbein, *The Origins of Adversary Criminal Trial* (Oxford: Oxford University Press, 2003).

19. William Blackstone, *Commentaries on the Laws of England*, 4 vols. (Oxford: Clarendon Press, 1765–69), 4:352.

20. William Paley, *The Principles of Moral and Political Philosophy* (London: Faulder, 1785), 552–53.

21. Lord Thomas Denman, "Law of Evidence—Criminal Procedure—Publicity," *Edinburgh Review* 79 (1824): 186.

22. Girard, *A Theater of Envy*, 214–16.

23. René Girard, *Violence and the Sacred*, trans. Patrick Gregory, (Baltimore: John Hopkins University Press, 1977), 269.

24. J. S. Mill, "Utilitarianism" (1861), in *Essays on Ethics, Religion, and Society*, ed. J. M. Robson (Toronto: University of Toronto Press, 1969), 255.

25. Debora Shuger, *The Renaissance Bible: Scholarship, Sacrifice and Subjectivity* (Berkeley: University of California Press, 1994), 72–73.

26. Joseph Slaughter, *Human Rights, Inc.: The World Novel, Narrative Form, and International Law* (New York: Fordham University Press, 2007), 57.

27. Adam Smith, *The Theory of Moral Sentiments* (1759, rev. 1790), ed. Knud Haakonssen (Cambridge: Cambridge University Press, 1992), 11.

28. Jonathan Kertzer, *Poetic Justice and Legal Fictions* (Cambridge: Cambridge University Press, 2010), 10.

29. John 11:25, KJV.

30. John 15:13, KJV.

31. See, for example, John Bowen, "Counting On: *A Tale of Two Cities*," in *Charles Dickens, A Tale of Two Cities and the French Revolution*, ed. Colin Jones, Josephine McDonagh, and Jon Mee (Basingstoke: Macmillan, 2009), 104–25; and Catherine Waters, *Dickens and the Politics of the Family* (Cambridge: Cambridge University Press, 1997), 144.

32. Charles Dickens, *A Tale of Two Cities* (1859) (Harmondsworth: Penguin, 1994), 366–67.

33. See John Glavin, *After Dickens: Reading, Adaptation, and Performance* (Cambridge: Cambridge University Press, 1999), 140–46.

34. Charles Williams, *The Sacrifice of Christ: An Inquiry into the Fact and the Doctrine of the Christian Atonement* (London: Simpkin, Marshall, 1858), 45.

35. John Forster, *The Life of Charles Dickens* (1872), 2 vols. (London: Dent, 1966), 2:194.

36. Janet Larson, *Dickens and the Broken Scripture* (Athens: University of Georgia Press, 1985), 16.

37. Girard, *Deceit, Desire, and the Novel*, 308.

38. Michael Kirwan, *Girard and Theology* (London: T. & T. Clarke, 2009), 75.

Dostoyevsky's Metaphysical Theater

The Underground Man and the Masochist in *Deceit, Desire, and the Novel* and *Resurrection from the Underground*

Yue Zhuo

Among the authors studied by René Girard in *Deceit, Desire, and the Novel*, Dostoyevsky represents the most "serious" case. In Dostoyevsky's universe, hatred is so intense that it explodes, leading to contradictory feelings that go beyond the conscious grasp of characters themselves. Everything seems to be contaminated, not only the public and political life as in the novels of Stendhal, the secret private life as in the world of Proust, but also family and the intimate circle of individuals. In Dostoyevsky, the "corrosive disease" of the internal mediation is more diffuse; it exerts its dissolving power at every level of existence, reaching a degree that is not seen in the French novelists. If Stendhal's and Proust's universes occupy what Girard calls the "upper regions of internal mediation," made somehow milder by bourgeois properties, Dostoyevsky's world "occupies its lowest,"[1] retaining traces of feudal cruelty and opening on to a world of darkness, chaos, and sickness.

Dostoyevsky's world is a world of "double mediation" pushed to extremes. By "double mediation" Girard means two identical and yet opposite mimetic triangles, the external and the internal,[2] begin to superimpose onto each other. If, according to him, "external mediation" involves imitation (in essence "spiritual"), distance, and model-choosing, while "internal mediation" entails envy, proximity, and rivalry, the "double mediation" is the conflation of these two mechanisms: the mediator becomes both the model and the rival. "We now have a subject-mediator and a mediator-subject, a model-disciple and a disciple-model. Each imitates the other while claiming that his own desire is prior and previous. Each looks on the other as an atrociously cruel persecutor."[3]

This essay will look at two of the most salient figures in Dostoyevsky's novels that show a particular inclination for the double mediation: the underground man and the masochist. What will happen when the two meet and begin a collaborative acrobatic descent toward nothingness? If, shortly after the original publication of *Deceit, Desire, and the Novel* in French, Girard moves further to the "underground" and devotes an entire book to Dostoyevsky, under the title of *Du double à l'unité* (*From the Double to Unity*),[4] can the underground man and the masochist, two narrative archetypes that he emphasized in *Deceit, Desire, and the Novel*, form a pair of splitting doubles that invite an eventual "unity," which Girard sees as achieved in Dostoyevsky's last novels? If so, what is the nature of this "splitting" (*dédoublement*) and how do the two dissolve into one? How do the doubles go lower and lower into the underground, reaching a point so abyssal that it will have no other solution but to point back to a vertical transcendence (resurrection)?

The Underground Man

When we enter the universe of Dostoyevsky, one figure immediately catches our attention by his behavioral oddities and his ontological agony. It is the figure of the underground man. Girard himself was intrigued by the question: why, while we can easily condemn vanity in Stendhal and snobbism in Proust, we do not usually despise Dostoyevsky's heroes? It is because, he answers readily, snobbism and vanity belong to our "normal" everyday world; we like to think of them as vices we ourselves have fortunately been spared, while seeing at the same time others less impervious to them. It is the vain "social self" we would not like ourselves to be tainted with. The underground man's obsession, on the other hand, seems "pathological" and "metaphysical" to us. "It belongs to the world of the psychiatrist or philosopher. We have not the heart to condemn one who is possessed."[5]

Girard quickly adds, however, that the underground man is as haunted by the fear of ridicule as Stendhal's *vaniteux* or Proust's snob, his obsessive desire unleashed often by the fear of exclusion. In fact, his existential uneasiness stems from a perpetual oscillation between self-celebration and fear of inferiority. "Needless to say, I hated all the office clerks from first to last and despised them all," writes the narrator in *Notes from the Underground*, "yet at the same time I was also somehow afraid of them. Sometimes, it happened that I would even rate them as superior to myself."[6] On the one hand, the underground man is eager to show that he has been living according to a romantic ideal, cultivating "the beautiful and the sublime" all his life, which gives him reasons to think he is above ordinary people and their mundane concerns; on the other hand, he seems to be tortured by the thought that there is no one like him and he is unlike anyone else: "I am one person and they are *everybody*."[7] The underground man's drama, compared to that of the snob, is purer and more "authentic," because it is a lonely metaphysical one freed from concerns of material gain and social advantage. His biggest problem is that he does not know if he truly wants his "uniqueness" or "pureness" or not, if he wants to keep the dream of his metaphysical autonomy or repudiate it.

In *Deceit, Desire, and the Novel*, Girard has not dismissed this underground psychology as categorically as he soon would in *Resurrection from the Underground*, but he is well aware of the problem this one-man theater can entail: the metaphysical theater simply cannot exist without an external prop. In his solitary dreams the underground man can elevate himself effortlessly up to the seventh heaven, but a moment always arrives when the dream no longer suffices for him. What he needs is an audience, and this Other can only fall back on a human mediator. The underground man would therefore throw himself into "humiliating" adventures, and he would fall as deeply down in reality as he ascended to the heights in his dreams. The underground people, as Girard further explains in *Resurrection from the Underground*, are imitators just like the *vaniteux* or the snobs, but they try to hide their imitation from others, and even from themselves. Those at the extreme of underground existence, leading an "addicted" or "sick" life, are "irresistibly attracted to those who spurn them and they irresistibly spurn those who are attracted to them."[8]

The more intense is the hatred the underground man feels for others (the everybody), the closer he will draw himself to his rivals. It is this principle of negative imitation that defines the very essence of the double (or reciprocal) mediation that Girard sees in so many modern novels. If obstruction to the rival's access to object is one of the chief characteristics of double media-tion,[9] in Dostoyevsky the mediator is further foregrounded and the object further neglected. What we now see is the desire circulating alone between the two rivals at an enhanced speed, and "with every cycle it increases in intensity like the electric current in a battery which is being charged."[10] It is this strange negative collaboration that flings the desire higher and further, making both parties chase after each other. The desiring subject, in fact, is no longer interested in taking possession of the object itself. Only negativity motivates him. Only the promise of a victorious resistance attracts him from now on, and the one who can acquire the next step of obstruction becomes the master. Girard compares this negative imitation to the working of the romantic passion defined by Denis de Rougemont in his famous *Love in the Western World*: "New obstacles have to be found in order to desire again and in order to exalt that desire to the proportions of a conscious, intense and continually interesting passion."[11] Alone, the underground man is doomed to disillusionment and boredom, feeling indifferent and blasé vis-à-vis his object of possession. He has to come nearer and near to slavery in order to shake off his boredom.

The Masochist

The masochist is the manifestation of the Romantic underground man in the modern world. Girard, who considers the "movement toward slavery (or 'fall')" a basic principle of novelistic structure, sees masochism establishing itself more decisively in Proust and in Dostoyevsky than in Stendhal, as if, just as slavery was, according to Hegel, the future of mastery, Proust and Dostoyevsky represent the "future" of Stendhal in that their novels reveal further debasement.[12] The masochist "may be originally a master who has become blasé. Continual success, or rather continual disappointment, makes him desire his own failure; only that failure will indicate an authentic deity, a mediator who is invulnerable to his own undertakings."[13] What differenti-ates the masochist from the underground man is that the former hastens the course of his destiny by telescoping all obstacles he can find: enslavement, derision, and shame. In other words, he gathers into a single moment various phases of the negative process that until now have been separated, in order to enhance its intensity. Contempt and obstruction only redouble the desire because they confirm the superiority of the mediator.

Unlike the underground man, the masochist perceives the necessary relation between unhappiness and metaphysical desire, but not only will he not relinquish that desire, he strikes right into the impossibility and chooses to see in shame, defeat, and enslavement signs of divinity and the preliminary condition of all metaphysical success. When he perceives his desire has hollowed out an abyss beneath his feet, he "voluntarily hurls himself into it, hoping against hope to discover in it what the less acute stages of metaphysical sickness have not brought him."[14] It is this "deviated" and "perverted intuition" of metaphysical truth that defines the very nature of the masochist, who absorbs in fact all the values of Christian morality, but in an inverted and tortured way. The masochist "bases thus his enterprise of autonomy on failure; he founds his project of being God on an abyss."[15]

Girard dismisses the conventional understanding of masochism as linked to sexual practice and insists that sexual masochism is nothing but a mirror image of the more important "existential masochism," spiritual in essence.[16] "Even in this pure sexual masochism," he writes, "it cannot be said that the subject desires suffering. What he desires is his mediator's presence, contact with the sacred."[17] Psychologists and psychiatrists, according to him, often missed this crucial point because they do not see that behind the masochist's shame, humiliation and suffering, it is the metaphysical desire that is insatiable. The masochist is someone who is lost as to whom he could imitate, he hopes that misery and suffering will reveal that truth to him. He essentially gets himself ready in the position of a torture victim, ready for self-sacrifice, for a substitute of divinity he finds in the human world.

The Eternal Husband

To understand this masochism, Girard claims that we should forget the medical terminology and simply read Dostoyevsky's *The Eternal Husband.*[18] Indeed, *The Eternal Husband* represents the most spectacular example of the negative imitation that Girard sees so prevalent in Dostoyevsky's novels, the final stage perhaps of a collaborative downward swirl before the fall into abyss, precisely because it is a life-and-death struggle between an underground man and a masochist.

Alexey Ivanovich Velchaninov, a rich bachelor and a middle-aged Don Juan, lives in a state of weariness and boredom. He suffers from hypochondria and depression, and dreams of some crime he had committed and concealed, which he thinks will be exposed one day should the people who know about it show up to confront him. For several days now he has been obsessed by the fleeting appearances of a stranger in his neighborhood, who seems to him both mysterious and familiar, disturbing and odd. This second person's identity is soon revealed. His name is Pavel Pavlovitch Trusotsky, whose wife, Natalya Vassiyevna, a former mistress of Velchaninov's, has just died. Velchaninov discovers that Trusotsky left his native town and traveled to St. Petersburg, not to chase after him, but to follow the funeral procession of one of Natalya Vassiyevna's other lovers, Bagautov, who had also just died. Since the accusation he awaits from his one-time rival/victim never came, Velchaninov becomes inexplicably drawn to Trusotsky and their relation becomes increasingly tangled, mainly around the latter's daughter, Liza, whom Velchaninov believes to be his own daughter with Natalya Vassiyevna. He also discovers that Trusotsky drinks heavily and torments Liza, and that he has a compulsion to hang himself. Velchaninov takes Liza away from Trusotsky and places her in a foster home, where she dies shortly after. Is he responsible for her death? The novel doesn't tell us. During the funeral, Trusotsky, drunk, unexpectedly delegates Liza's fatherhood to Velchaninov, which suggests he knew that the latter was the girl's biological father. Trusotsky wants to pursue happiness and decides to marry a second time. But the first thing he does is to present Velchaninov to his young fiancée Nadya and her family, only to find that he has become the object of ridicule and that Nadya has developed a liking for Velchaninov. Trusotsky then admits he loves Velchaninov and the two enter into a final master-slave physical and psychological duel, during which Trusotsky cuts Velchaninov with a razor knife.

The Eternal Husband is a master example of the "corrosive" double mediation, with both of its main characters confirming for the other the double illusion of grandeur and baseness. Velchaninov is the underground man and the "predatory type," but he shares masochistic tendencies since he spends his entire time waiting to be punished. The more that retribution fails to realize itself, the more he internalizes his own guilt and becomes drawn toward his future hangman. Trusotsky is the masochist, whose feeling of inexistence compels him to enslave himself repeatedly to women, but he accelerates the process by enslaving himself first to his rivals. He is the "eternal husband," or more precisely, the "eternal cuckold." Both Velchaninov and Trusotsky become "obstacle addicts," "unable to desire in the absence of an obstacle-who-is-also-a-model, a beloved enemy who has 'turned a heaven into a hell.'"[19] The object of their original rivalry, the wife, has long been dead. And the object of their true desire, death, symbolized here by the grave of Liza, stands as an abyss that neither one nor the other can reach. Yet each claims a greater share of it: "How do you know what that little grave here means . . . for me!" Trusotsky cries, desperately trying to overcome Velchaninov's voice: "We both stand at the side of that little grave, but on my side there is more than on yours, more."[20]

From Double to Unity

Toward the end of *Deceit, Desire, and the Novel*, Girard becomes increasingly insistent on an opposition that made his book famous; namely, the twofold novelistic world consists of "illusions" lived by the characters on the one hand, and the lucid unified vision of the novelist who exposes them on the other. He calls the former "romantic deception" (*mensonge romantique*) and the latter "novelistic truth" (*vérité romanesque*). Dostoyevsky, compared to Cervantes, Stendhal, Flaubert, and Proust, is the most paradoxical, because he both follows his characters to the baseness of their underground psyche and denounces at the same time the "falsity" of their existence most powerfully.[21] To understand Dostoyevsky is therefore to understand this incongruity between the unsatisfied metaphysical desire and the seemingly self-sufficient underground existence, to follow the logic of "illusions" to the extreme so one can be freed from it. "The underground is a caricature," Girard tells us, and the reader should see Dostoyevsky is laughing at his own hero.[22]

For Girard, the entire literary itinerary of Dostoyevsky can be seen as a movement from the double to unity, a process of gathering lost souls and the split self of the underground toward a new, fuller, resurrected existence. In *Resurrection from the Underground*, he argues that the best explanation of

Dostoyevsky's earlier fiction can be found in the novelist's later work, especially in *The Brothers Karamazov*, and that "Dostoyevsky himself attained a spiritual understanding and personal integration which is not completely exemplified in any one of his great characters, but which he found and developed through creating these very fictional characters."[23] Dostoyevsky himself, in other words, evolved from a self-divided, "underground," "romantic" young writer to become a mature, holistic, literary "genius." If One had always been his goal, "his research was double in its method."[24]

This telos of unity and light, however, cannot efface the reader's fascination with the split self and chaos so pervasive in Dostoyevsky. It is perhaps for this reason that Girard himself devoted an entire book to the "underground existence" shortly after *Desire, Deceit, and the Novel* in order to understand how the "deviated" double worked toward the resurrected unity. The underground man's grand illusion, as Girard reveals, lies in his blindness and pride. He believes he is "unique" but suffers intensely from not being able to distinguish himself concretely from the people around him. He believes he is one in his solitary dream, but in failure he divides in two and becomes a contemptible person and a contemptuous observer of the human scene, and this is why he constantly lives in a contradiction between a lamentable existence and a grandiose rhetoric. The underground man is in fact a romantic and antimodern person who rejects rationalist values such as pragmatism and utilitarianism. Just as Christianity, at the end of the eighteenth century, repudiated by the French philosophers, "reappeared in inverted form in the underground,"[25] the underground individuals, sickened by the ambient behavior of "enlightened self-interest," went secretive in order to keep his "ideal." In a secularized modern world, this unsatisfied desire for the divine will have to fall on a human mediator. The underground man's "fall," in a way, is inevitable.

What is most compelling in Girard's discovery of Dostoyevsky is when he tells us how the latter renders his novelistic "truth." Unlike what the narrator of Proust does in *Remembrance of Things Past*, there is never in Dostoyevsky an "existential," epiphanic moment during which the narrator appears to reveal the final novelistic verity.[26] Dostoyevsky's "truth" is always already folded back into the novelistic structure, precisely through the creation of the split self/selves. Dostoyevsky's novels, in other words, are not divided into a "time to tell" and a "moment to reveal"; all is intermittence and chaos, all is separated scenes and revelation at the same time. What other critics fail to see is that the "existentialist malady" of the underground characters "does not depend on the author but on the spread of ontological sickness, on the proximity and multiplication of the mediators."[27] Thus, Dostoyevsky's greatest novelistic invention could be considered a novelistic "conversion": his fundamental method is to spread out the temporal span of confrontations among mediators, exhausting all possible relationships between different characters in the novel.

The "romantic" lie—the doubling of the self—romantics themselves never recognize, Girard argues. They want to believe they are perfectly one. Novelists do recognize the lie, and that's why they transcribe it in the form of masochism and sadism.

> Theoretically no communication is possible between the two halves, but the masochism of the "good" and the sadism of the "bad" reveal the instability of the structure, the perpetual tendency of the two halves to pass into one another without ever achieving a complete merger.[28]

In the example of *The Eternal Husband*, the theme of sadism is less present; it is more about the race between the underground man and the masochist to see who can fall into the abyss first without becoming a sadist. It is a spectacle to watch oneself falling through the eyes of one's double. If the underground man already symbolizes the inverse image of metaphysical truth, the masochist represents the last stage of metaphysical desire before death and self-destruction. The underground man and the masochist are doubles and rivals of each other; in their rollercoaster ride toward the void, they need each other in order to start the negative motor force, and they hate each other because whoever reaches the deepest point of the inverted verticality will probably have a better chance to look back toward transcendence.

Conclusion

The basic hypothesis that Girard sets up both in *Deceit, Desire, and the Novel* and in *Resurrection from the Underground* is an opposition between two axes of desires, a metaphysical one pointing vertically toward an (divine) object, and a mimetic one pointing horizontally toward a (human) model. Ideally, Girard would like the desire to point directly to One; that is to say, true desire, for him, is the desire to be. It should not be dispersed to the (human) Other. It should refer to the Original model, and that Original is identical to itself; it is not lacking in itself. The experience of desire can be born from a lack, but the object of desire cannot be. It is supposed to be full and real, manifesting itself readily when the desiring subject aspires for it.

The problem arises when the Enlightenment values swept away the traditional religious and metaphysical structures. In the era of secularization, when individuals are motivated by self-interest and social flexibility, substituting consciously and unconsciously the social for the spiritual, the manifestation of that original copy becomes less and less evident. Man thinks he can become himself his God and master, but he falls inevitably on the Other. Even religious man may be forced to reorient his desire and make a difficult choice: "Christianity directs existence toward a vanishing point, either toward God or toward the Other. Choice always involves choosing a model, and the true freedom lies in the basic choice between a human or a divine model."[29]

The model that Girard spends most of his time describing in these two early works on literature is the desire moving on the horizontal level, the mimetic one within the human world. More precisely, how the desiring subject, even when he takes possession of his object, can lose interest in it, or have the feeling of grasping a void, as if desire is now defined solely in relation to the rival, and no longer in relation to the object. How should we reconcile this apparent contradiction that Girard leaves us: on the one hand, the premise of a primordial Object, original and replete, and on the other hand, the fading of all objects when the mimetic process begins—what the desire ultimately desires is the abandonment of all objects in the human world?

French philosopher Clément Rosset's explanation of the functioning of desire in the modern world may shed light on our understanding of Girard's two axes. Rosset situates Girard in a French tradition of modern writers and philosophers who have associated desire with lack: Baudelaire, Mallarmé, Bataille, Lacan, and Derrida. Desire manifests in these authors as something functioning outside the orbit of the real. It is this "discrepancy [*désaccord*] between the desire and the real" that constitutes the foundation of modern desire. From this perspective, an object cannot be attractive if it belongs to the real world. In fact, desire keeps such a negative rapport with the real—often characterized by "allergy" or "nontolerance"—that we can hardly speak of any "object of desire."[30]

Where Girard's theory is original is the intervention of the Other. If the object can still attract and have value, it is because it appears as the object of desire of another person. This relaying of desire makes the object even more abstract, because it is now not only disconnected from the real, but also it succumbs to the power of the imaginary. The desired object is always deferred, passed from one fascinating eye to the next, embarking on a circuit of movement that does not allow it to stop anywhere concrete. The desiring subject, on the other hand, suffers from not having a concrete object: "The object of desire is an object forever missing."[31]

Desire as a state of lack, Rosset continues, can be traced as far back as in Plato. Love, to summarize the last thesis of *The Symposium*, is nothing but a failure to be full (*manqué-à-etre*); it strives to find the second half that reconstitute its original unity. But while in ancient or classical theories, the object of desire can still be identified as complete and recognizable (such as unity of being), in modern theories, the way desire functions changes. It is still a lack-of-being, but the object the desire desires becomes itself lacking (*"objet lui-même manquant"*). Whereas the classical object of desire can still be conceived and described (whether it's God or the plenitude of eternal life), the modern one remains absolutely unconceivable and irrepresentable, except by the negative idea that it is other than reality. It cannot be thought of outside the very process of desiring, unless we "destroy at the same time the fragile edifice of the desire itself."[32]

Girard's theory of mimetic desire runs counter to some positive modern conceptions of desire as something beneficially connected to the real and "constructive" (Deleuze, Rosset). In *Deceit, Desire, and the Novel*, all imitation is seen as violent and destructive; hence, after having denounced this "lie" rigorously in *Resurrection from the Underground*, Girard calls for a final Resurrection. What I have tried to show is not that Girard's model is "reductionist" (a common critique of which Girard himself is aware), but how the desire moving on the horizontal level and the one agonizing on the vertical level collapse into each other, creating a paradox that is less explained to the readers. More specifically, I have wanted to show how, against the ultimate "impossible," the noumenal "metaphysical desire," or what Rosset calls the indescribable Other, Girard builds up an elaborate system entirely based on the functioning of negativity in the hope of thwarting that very impossibility. The underground man and the masochist are two main actors in this dark metaphysical theater, two mediators/models who eagerly run on the horizontal carpet, but who fuse into One to take the descending elevator toward the void. But even during the climax of their "negative collaboration," the Original model is still not revealed. What is revealed is an inversed image of the "transcendence," death, the grave, and nothingness.

Christian symbolism, Girard reminds us, is not incompatible with nihilism. Still, the Dostoyevskian journey to the end of the night ends with a promising Resurrection. Only a religious conversion can truly regain the transcendental original object of desire and unify split and alienated selves from the chaotic world of mimetic desire, even though we are not quite sure how the leap to God is suddenly achieved, since the last place we are left with was a hopeless pit in the ground. As Girard moves toward his final telos of interpretation of Dostoyevsky, the reader cannot help thinking he is repeating the very double process laid out in *Deceit, Desire, and the Novel*, that is, while heroes live blindly their romantic "lies," the novelist, motivated by a nondesiring point of view, tells the truth. The true novelist here is in fact Girard himself. While he shows us how Dostoyevsky the genius has finally found his way, uniting little by little elements of underground psychology that remain isolated and divided in his prior, "romantic" works, one feels Dostoyevsky has become a novelistic character himself. While we are certainly happy to find out the "truth" about his oeuvre, we are most drawn to the process of the "novelistic" unfolding, or conversion: how Dostoyevsky has become the double, triple, quadruple of himself, blending into his own characters, the underground man and masochist being the foremost.

Notes

1. René Girard, *Deceit, Desire, and the Novel: Self and Other in Literary Structure*, trans. Yvonne Freccero (Baltimore: Johns Hopkins University Press, 1965), 44.

2. All desire is triangular and mimetic according to Girard; it is a desire "according to the Other." The mediation is external when the object of desire is transcendental, or "metaphysical," when the world of subject and that of his model (which Girard also calls the mediator) do not affect each other. The mediation is internal when the desiring sphere of the subject and that of his mediator are in contact, both belonging to the human world, and when their distance is small enough to permit rivalries.

3. Girard, *Deceit, Desire, and the Novel*, 99.

4. René Girard, *Dostoïevski: Du double à l'unité* (Paris: Plon, 1963), translated into English under the title of *Resurrection from the Underground: Feodor Doestoevsky*, ed. and trans. James G. Williams (New York: Crossroad, 1997). A new edition of the English translation under the same title was published by Michigan State University Press (East Lansing, 2012).

5. Girard, *Deceit, Desire, and the Novel*, 67.

6. Fyodor Dostoyevsky, *Notes from the Underground* and *The Double*, trans. Ronald Wilks (London: Penguin Classics, 2009), 39.

7. Dostoyevsky, *Notes from the Underground*, 40.

8. Girard, *Resurrection from the Underground: Feodor Dostoevsky* (1997), 81.

9. According to Girard, the object becomes secondary in double mediation. It is less about one wanting the object than about one not wanting to see it in someone else's hands. Girard gives the example of M. de Rênal in *The Red and the Black*. To illustrate this mechanism, M. de Rênal, the mayor of a small village called Verrières, first copies his desire for a tutor from an imaginary desire of Valenod, his rival and assistant, the sub-prefect of the town. The reality is that Valenod never considered making Julien his children's tutor. But now upon hearing an offer has been made to Julien, he matches up his desire hastily by making the latter an offer as well. Girard, *Deceit, Desire, and the Novel*, 101.

10. Girard, *Deceit, Desire, and the Novel*, 99.

11. Denis de Rougemont, *Love in the Western World* (Princeton: Princeton University Press, 1983), 52; cited in Girard, *Deceit, Desire, and the Novel*, 165.

12. Girard, *Deceit, Desire, and the Novel*, 170.

13. Girard, *Deceit, Desire, and the Novel*, 177.

14. Girard, *Deceit, Desire, and the Novel*, 180.

15. Girard, *Deceit, Desire, and the Novel*, 177.

16. Girard, *Deceit, Desire, and the Novel*, 186.

17. Girard, *Deceit, Desire, and the Novel*, 184.

18. Girard, *Resurrection from the Underground*, 14.

19. Girard, *Resurrection from the Underground*, 77.

20. Feodor Dostoevsky, *The Short Novels of Dostoevsky*, trans. Constance Garnett (New York: Dial Press, 1958), 444.

21. Girard, *Deceit, Desire, and the Novel*, 269.

22. Girard, *Resurrection from the Underground*, 81; Girard, *Deceit, Desire, and the Novel*, 262.

23. See James G. Williams, "Foreword: René Girard," in Girard, *Resurrection from the Underground*, xvi.

24. Girard, *Resurrection from the Underground*, 42.

25. Girard, *Resurrection from the Underground*, 45.

26. Girard, *Deceit, Desire, and the Novel*, 248–49.

27. Girard, *Deceit, Desire, and the Novel*, 248.

28. Girard, *Resurrection from the Underground*, 24.

29. Girard, *Deceit, Desire, and the Novel*, 58.

30. Clément Rosset, *L'Objet singulier* (Paris: Les Éditions de minuit, 1979), 43.

31. Rosset, *L'Objet singulier*, 47.

32. Rosset, *L'Objet singulier*, 47.

Deceit, Desire, Violence, and Death in the Short Stories of Georges Bernanos

Brian Sudlow

efore he ceased writing on critical matters, René Girard never offered his readers an essay, let alone something more substantial, on the fictional work of French author, polemicist, and right-wing Catholic monarchist Georges Bernanos. Bernanos is mentioned in passing in several places in Girard's oeuvre but there is no extensive analysis or commentary on Bernanos's writings. Such a lacuna represents something of a lost opportunity. A priori, there can be few authors in the French literary canon who have explored as much as Bernanos the human capacity for deceit and how it intertwines with human desire. There are likewise few authors who have such a reputation for depicting the violence that those driven by desire can do to each other, as well as the liberation that awaits those who struggle free from the mimetic chains they forge for themselves.

Girardian theory has been used to great effect to illuminate the writings of other French Catholic authors of the same generation as Bernanos. Most recently, Timothy Williams has explored the work of François Mauriac from a Girardian perspective in *Desire and Persecution in* Thérèse Desqueyroux.[1] Could it be that Girard's mimetic theory can also unlock the dark and frequently violent fiction of Bernanos, much as Williams has used it to shed new light on the equally sombre work of Mauriac? Pierre-Paul Delvaux speculated as much in the 1980s, sketching out a tentative albeit somewhat labored Girardian analysis of Bernanos's last and most mysterious novel, *Monsieur Ouine*.[2] This novel was published in 1943 while Bernanos was in self-imposed exile in Brazil during the Second World War. Nonetheless, the fact that its composition dates back to 1931 invites inquiry into whether Girardian tendencies can be traced in Bernanos's earlier creative writing. While a survey of his novels from this earlier period—*Sous le Soleil de Satan* (1926), *L'Imposture* (1928), and *La Joie* (1929)—would require more space than I have at my disposal, we could ask to what extent Girardian tendencies can be found in Bernanos's three short stories that date from the 1920s, all of which are included at the beginning of the Pléiade edition of the *Oeuvres romanesques*. As Sabrinelle Bédrane has forcefully argued, their importance in the Bernanosian oeuvre is overshadowed by the much better known novels, and yet these stories–"Madame Dargent" (1922), "Une Nuit" (1928), and "Dialogue d'ombres" (1928)—powerfully rehearse some of Bernanos's greatest themes.[3]

If the question of genre arises here, it by no means hinders analysis from the perspective of mimetic theory. Girard himself later used the theoretical insights he had set forth about the novel to analyze works of drama in his book on Shakespeare, not to mention various genres found in the Judeo-Christian Scriptures in *Things Hidden Since the Foundation of the World*. Though they can lay claim to a long and distinguished pedigree, short stories in collected format first began to be published in the nineteenth century.[4] In other words, they emerged along with the novel in the age of democracy when, from the Girardian perspective, the sociological conditions of internal mediation intensified and urged themselves more forcefully upon the creative literary mind.[5] Bédrane has also argued that Bernanos is one of several interwar writers in France whose short stories operate as workshops for novelistic exploration and in which "everything is significant, no word is wasted."[6] From this perspective, Bernanos short stories might even be seen as novels in miniature.

In Bernanos's short stories, with their small number of characters and sometimes explosive action, the nature of mimetic desire and of imposture is consistently distilled with acuity. Likewise, the possibility of illuminating conversion and the hermeneutical power of death can be clearly discerned, demonstrating conclusively the great usefulness of bringing a Girardian analysis to bear on Bernanos's imaginative creation in its early stages.

Girardian Dynamics in the Three Short Stories

While these three stories are probably the least read of Bernanos's fictional work, they were written in one of his most creative periods. Moreover, while they were not planned as an integral triptych, the degree of convergence between their themes justifies our analyzing them together. The exact date of the composition of "Madame Dargent" is not known, but the story appears to have been written between 1919 and 1921.[7] It was published in 1922 in the *Revue hédomadaire*, in which publication "Une Nuit" also appeared six years later in 1928.[8] In the interim Bernanos had already published his first two novels, *Sous le Soleil de Satan* and *L'Imposture*, though the closeted death chamber scene in the earlier "Madame Dargent" is no less redolent of his mature novelistic work than the mud, rain, and tension of the jungle in the later "Une Nuit." The third of our stories, "Dialogue d'ombres," was likewise published in 1928, though this time in the *Nouvelle Revue française*, a significant publication indicative of Bernanos's growing reputation during the late 1920s.[9]

Their essential plot lines can be briefly outlined. "Madame Dargent" recounts the tale of a novelist's wife who throughout her life has imitated her husband's characters to win his affection, and who on her deathbed confesses to the murder of his mistresses and his love child. "Une Nuit" relates the story of a colonial adventurer in the South American jungle who returns a runaway native slave to her French-Creole master, who is dying of poison administered by the native. "Dialogue d'ombres" depicts the conversation of two lovers whose affection is but a hollow shell of self-harming cruelty or of neglect. On the face of it, these stories seem to rehearse many of the grand Bernanosian themes: death, conscience, solitude, anguish, grace, hope in a hopeless situation, and self-deception. It is in these and similar static categories that Bernanos's fiction is often read.[10] Yet when these stories are brought under a Girardian light, there emerges a range or even a coordinated ensemble of subtle preoccupations with mimesis and violence, deceit and imposture and, lastly, what we can call deliverance, as the event of death and the moment of revelation cross paths. Beyond their correlations with the standard Bernanosian themes, it is their role in structuring dramatic action that allows us deeper insight into the power of Bernanos's art in its early period, paving the way for the works of his maturity, such as *Journal d'un curé de campagne* (1936) and *Monsieur Ouine* (1943). Making reference in particular to Girard's *Deceit, Desire, and the Novel*, the following analysis will approach these preoccupations one by one rather than story by story, to trace more clearly the convergence of the mimetic elements underlying their inspiration.

Mimesis and Violence

The Girardian dynamics structuring "Madame Dargent" are quite tangible. The story benefits from the kind of mimetically driven structure that, says Girard, extends throughout all literature devoted to "novelistic truth."[11] Like Don Quixote, Madame Dargent has lived by imitation of fictional characters, a process that incurs few risks due to the external mediation of her desire. The discovery of her husband's infidelity, however, leads to a breach in the enclave of external mediation, and Madame Dargent succumbs to what Girard would call the "evil spell of vain rivalry."[12] The intensity of the clash between Madame Dargent's desires and those of her rivals is telescoped by Bernanos into Madame Dargent's deathbed confession, from which moment it rises to an apex in which Monsieur Dargent suffocates Madame Dargent in unconscious fulfillment of the Girardian contagion of violence. "Madame Dargent" then demonstrates Bernanos's apparently innate understanding of the dangers of mimetic desire.

If mimesis is more thematic in "Madame Dargent"—whose very name is for Bernanos redolent of immoderate desire—it is triangular violence and rivalry which predominate in "Une Nuit." The story's focus on death even lends it in fact something of the apocalyptic character that Girard locates in Dostoyevsky's writing.[13] Darnetal, a French adventurer, discovers the body of another Frenchman, Picard, near whose grave lurks Picard's former servant, the native Bisbillitta. Bisbillitta, who will be killed accidentally by Darnetal, is an object desired or controlled by three colonialists: by the deceased Picard, by Darnetal, who recaptures her, and by Alahowigh, the French-Creole master from whom Bisbillitta has run away.

In Girardian terms, Bisbillitta is an ambiguous character. At once a violent participant in the conflicted triangles of desire that objectify her (Bernanos explains for us that in her language the word for "lover" and "master" are the same), she is in other ways an innocent victim whose death, nevertheless, could in no way be described as sacrificial. The story is rocked by recurrent outbreaks of violence in which Bisbillitta is caught up: Alahowigh has killed Picard to possess Bisbillitta; she has poisoned Alahowigh in revenge; and now finally, in the dark hut, Darnetal unwittingly stabs Bisbillitta as they grapple, and she is killed. As in "Madame Dargent," the contagion of violence serves to establish or challenge domination or control, and yet none of the characters appear to understand what ills beset them. It is surely crucial that the action unfolds during "Une Nuit" when the things hidden from the foundation of the world remain obscure and unsuspected by both the perpetrators and victims of violence. Alahowigh alone appears tired of his rivalry with Bisbillitta.

Bernanos's third short story, the "Dialogue d'ombres," is just that: a dialogue, between Jacques, an aging romantic novelist, and Françoise, to whom he is offering a marriage of convenience. Françoise has been objectified by all her lovers, but she has desired to give herself up to objectification as a way of destroying her pride. Beneath this disturbing scenario lies Bernanos's portrayal of a relationship in which, to use the language of *Deceit, Desire, and the Novel*, Françoise and Jacques become gods in the eyes of each other.

The story parodies so many romantic scenes, as the couple sitting under the shadow of a tree discuss their relationship, surrounded by the rain and the sound of mournful crows cawing in the background. This parody is itself an act of artistic aggression on Bernanos's part; the lampooning of the standard romantic images expressing the "kaleidoscope of appearances" behind which lurk the *mensonge romantique*.[14] On the one hand, Jacques claims to find his whole meaning in Françoise, and yet he is only offering her a marriage of convenience. On the other hand, Françoise affirms that she too depends entirely on Jacques, but her protestations show that her love is entirely self-centered. From early on in the story, this is a relationship characterized not by communion but by an unconsciously hostile consumption of the other. It is a kind of mutual self-feeding in which Françoise more than Jacques appears to oscillate between the poles of pride and shame delineating the contours of what Girard calls the "underground consciousness."[15]

There are, however, two particular dynamics to the mimetic rivalry that their relationship sustains. On the one hand, Jacques, for whom love means the thrill of possessive domination, is caught in a double bind: it is only his lover's self-esteem that makes her desirable, but Françoise's commitment to self-humiliation threatens to rob him of that thrill. On the other hand, Françoise adopts the self-abasing, masochistic role that Girard and Oughourlian discuss in *Things Hidden Since the Foundation of the World* and according to which the defeat of the self signifies the success of the Other, who becomes in victory a new model for the self.[16] Françoise's action is thus highly paradoxical and theoretically schizophrenic; first, it appears to scapegoat Françoise's individuality and all her rivals so as to seal her union with Jacques in an act of self-destructive violence; second, as it feigns self-destruction (we might even say as a kind of metaphorical death), it starts on a path that leads to what we can call an *altergenesis*—the begetting of new rivals on whose desires Françoise aims to feast. The stifling atmosphere of this story is as it were the tranquil eye of a hurricane of self-serving desire that in Françoise is tending toward "the complete destruction of life and spirit."[17]

Casting a mimetic perspective on these stories brings to light certain aspects of Bernanos's art that deserve better attention and allows us to unlock Bernanos's understanding of the triangular nature of desire. The patterns of desire generated through imitation in "Madame Dargent" and "Dialogue d'ombres" are explicit; those in "Une Nuit" are implicit but indubitable. The link between imitated desire, rivalry, and violence is also a tangible plot device in these stories. The intestinal violence that Girard's later anthropological studies will relate to the generation of sacrificial rites is, for Bernanos, the inevitable result of the collision of competing desires, yet with this difference: Bernanos realizes that there are no rites left to evacuate conflict.[18] None of the death scenarios in these stories rehearse the catharsis that ritualization of hostility might afford. For that very reason, however, the passive hostility in "Dialogue d'ombres" and the active aggression in "Madame Dargent" illustrate most fully the moral attitudes and decisions of characters whose choices are unaccountable without a mimetic framing, and whose actions can only result in an inexorable march towards death (real in "Madame Dargent" and figurative in "Dialogue d'ombres"). In contrast, the constant waves of violence in "Une Nuit" lead us by an inductive process to the sources of conflict found in imitation. Mimetic devices and violence devoid of canalization thus play crucial roles in structuring these stories and bringing their characters to life.

Imposture, Deceit, and Myth

Given the prominence of imitation and violence in these three short stories, it is surely significant for a Girardian reading of Bernanos's early writings that they also contain many instances of myth, deceit, or—to use a Bernanosian term for these phenomena—*imposture*. Just as imitation and violence serve as structural features of the three stories, so too does the concealment of truth.

The deathbed confession of Madame Dargent only works dramatically because it draws back the veil that has concealed her erstwhile acts of murder. Madame Dargent is the author of the deceits that have hidden her violence from the world and particularly from her husband—acts arguably aimed at maintaining the harmony of the marital home but on the basis of deception. At a deeper level, however, the first deceit or myth of this story lies in how Monsieur Dargent's characters became in his wife's eyes the all-powerful beings whose command of her husband's affections Madame Dargent needed to acquire. Thus, even before Madame Dargent conceals her own desires or her acts of violence, she suffers what Girard calls the "illusion experienced at the moment of desire."[19]

Paradoxically, Monsieur Dargent believes the myths that his wife suffers from are of a totally different order. Throughout his married life, he has concealed all his infidelities from her and assumes that her passivity arises from her ignorance, little realizing that she has answered his concealed violence against their marriage vows by her own concealed act of violence against those he really loved. From beginning to end, therefore, deceit is as integral to the structure of this story as mimesis or violence.

"Une Nuit" likewise is placed from the beginning under the sign of deception. Its plot unfolds during the night, the moment in which deception, pretense, and imposture are most easily achieved, and a metaphor for the lack of self-knowledge that all the story's protagonists display. The story's use of deceit, however, can be seen in two curiously contrasting ways.

On the one hand, the lies of the story either conceal violence against, or serve as a prelude to, the victimization of Bisbillitta. As we have already noted, Bernanos knows instinctively there are no rites left to canalize violence. Nevertheless, he constantly foregrounds the actions of those who disguise violence with myth. As soon as he accidentally stabs Bisbillitta during their fight, Darnetal feels the urge to conceal what he has done from the dying Alahowigh. Alahowigh accuses Bisbillitta of constantly lying simply to act as a cover for her own hostility, while Bisbillitta accuses him of lying also. The concealing of the truth in this story has its correlations with Madame Dargent's attempts to veil her violence from her husband; it is always aimed at protecting the perpetrator of violence.

On the other hand, certain deceits in "Une Nuit" are unveiled to show the misunderstandings on which certain desires are based: those desires that serve as illusions "at the moment of desire."[20] Alahowigh claims his own father was a French lord, but his father's condemnation and exile in South America make it more likely he was no nobler than any other French convict sent into exile in the colonies. Alahowigh, though illiterate, has kept his father's favorite book and regards it as a great artifact of French culture, even a sacred object, which he would like to have buried with him. Yet when he finally expires and his treasure falls from his hands, Darnetal sees that the book, while innocent enough, is in fact about deceit and imposture: *A Thousand and One Jokes to Play in Society (Followed by One Hundred Ways of Getting Some Else to Buy You a Drink)*. For Bernanos the *dupe* is deceived not only by the myths that conceal violence, nor simply by the transformation induced by the illusion at the moment of desire. Rather, the *dupe* is the one whose perception of what is desirable has itself arisen by some mistake that is patently cretinous. For Bernanos, therefore, Alahowigh is the victim not merely of unregulated desire and illusion but also of culpable delusion. While Bernanos anticipates the Girardian understanding of desire by imitation, and of the deceit that desire can induce, he is also ruthless in depicting the ridiculousness of the illusions to which those driven by mimesis can fall. While this tendency is redolent of Flaubert's intolerance for *la bêtise*; it is the "supernatural pity" of Darnetal at the end of the story that prevents Bernanos's treatment of the *dupe* achieving a kind of Flaubertian ruthlessness.[21]

If imposture and deceit are deployed in "Dialogue d'ombres," it is primordially to depict this rise of desire through such *duperie*. The process of *altergenesis*, which we noted above in Françoise, manufactures psychologically the model whom she will subsequently esteem without apparently noticing that she has conjured up her own model in her imagination. Jacques has become a god to Françoise, as her illusion settles into a more deeply rooted delusion.

Nevertheless, in this story and in "Madame Dargent," another dimension of deceit and imposture shapes Bernanos's depiction of literature and literary authors. "Madame Dargent" and "Dialogue d'ombres" have central characters who are novelists but of two quite different kinds. On the one hand, Monsieur Dargent seems to have more confidence in his romantic lies than in any novelistic truth that Bernanos's stories can unveil. He is so convinced of the wonders of his own art that he finds it tragic that his wife cannot appreciate the poetic drama of her own death. In "Dialogue d'ombres," on the other hand, Jacques, who has hitherto been a romantic novelist, is now becoming aware of the deceits that have underpinned his writings and of the curious mimetism between his own life and theirs. With the illusion of his autonomy dawning on him, he experiences the first signs of a novelistic conversion, though his insights remain limited and without fruit. Thus, to Françoise, he admits:

> Between them and me there is a *monstrous resemblance*, which I have never realized and which you have made me see. [My writings] bear the secret of certain lies—the craftiest and the vilest—which have been useful to me.[22]

If this conversion does not necessarily evoke the realization that desire is triangular, it at least leads Jacques to the conclusion that his stories have acted as devices of imposture to conceal the secret driving force behind his literature. Jacques has realized that the art he once believed to be representational is in fact dependent on illusion.

Bernanos's mimetic credentials are further underlined by his handling of deceit and imposture in our three short stories. These devices serve as tools to structure the interaction of the protagonists of each story, contributing to the waves of tension and relief that propel these carefully crafted miniatures toward their goal. While Bernanos depicts the illusion that arises in the mimetically driven subject, he exposes with even greater force the delusion that drives the desires of the *dupe*. At this early period in Bernanos's creative output, therefore, the importance he accords to the Girardian dynamic of triangular desire is perfectly matched by his appreciation of the power and pervasiveness of deceit.

Conversion, Illumination, and Deliverance

Girard's novelistic conversion involves an awareness of the romantic lie, appreciating the real nature of desire as triangular, and acknowledging those things that must be renounced in the rediscovery to the true self.[23] If we can judge Bernanos on the basis of these stories, it would appear that, from the beginning, he was aware of triangulated desire, and considered the veiling and unveiling of desire and its illusions as key literary devices. Yet Bernanos was never devoted to literature for literature's sake; his interest in such literary tools was only a correlation of his most important concerns with the moral and spiritual destiny of the individual. In support of this observation, what is striking in these three short stories is the way in which Bernanos uses moments of conversion or illumination as a resolution for the crises evoked by the structural devices of mimesis, violence, and deceit. The three short stories under consideration in this chapter all depict characters who come to realize how deeply mediated their desires have been, or who long for deliverance from the mimetic slavery they are groping to understand.

Such illumination and deliverance are most distinct in "Madame Dargent." Monsieur Dargent, as we have noted, observes at the beginning of the story that his wife will not be an observer of her own passing. Yet the self-deceiving novelist is unprepared for what happens next. His dying wife begins to hallucinate and claims to see below her a great lake of water, before letting out a low, controlled groan more chilling than any scream. "I have seen myself in the water," she tells her husband, only moments before she begins her confession.[24] For Bernanos, this vision shows Madame Dargent confronting her conscience *in articulo mortis*, as a moment of illumination and, perhaps, divine grace.

Yet this hallucination also serves the purpose of novelistic truth, and invites Madame Dargent to make disclosure of her deceit and her violence before she dies. Bernanos leads us into Madame Dargent's conscience, showing the reader the true self of the dying woman, in whose reflected light the author and the reader are led to conclusions about their own selves.[25] In Madame Dargent's case, her "double"—her reflection in the water—is no rival but confronts her with who she really is. Furthermore, in realizing who she really is, she grasps the nature of the mimetic error that led her down this path of desire, deceit, and violence. Thus, she tells her husband:

"There is no such thing as unhappy love. Only love renounces and I did not renounce."[26]

Madame Dargent thus gives expression to arguably the most difficult cultural implication of Girardian theory: that abandoning the negative runaway of mimetic desire is a moral option revealed to us primordially in the supertranscendent love of Christ.[27] Even if "Madame Dargent" ends with her violent death, the story at least sees her acknowledge the fatal chain that links together desire, deceit, and violence. Madame Dargent is illuminated and in some ways delivered from the burdens of misplaced mimesis by a wisdom whose exemplar is found in Christ.

In "Une Nuit," deliverance through Christ is more pronounced, and yet the reader is tantalized by the prospect of an illumination *manqué* in Alahowigh that contrasts with Darnetal's deliverance from the horror of the "Nuit." As we noted above, the myth of Alahowigh's origins are revealed, at least to Darnetal and the reader, but Bernanos does not complete the cycle by bringing Alahowigh to a realization about love. Instead, his desperate desire to learn about Christ wilts in frustration before Darnetal's ignorance of Christianity. Throughout the final section of the story, Alahowigh begs Darnetal to tell him the secret of "white men." We learn that the native Bisbillitta, who has lain dead on the floor for some time, had been baptized and knew this secret. But Darnetal, overcome by the horror of the situation, finally admits that he cannot tell Alahowigh what he wants to hear:

> "I was taught those things when I was young . . . perhaps. If the girl had spoken of it, doubtless it would have come back to me. . . . It's true that the French have a religion, like the natives. Many have forgotten it, you know. . . . But listen, friend. I know at least that this God is just and good. He has pity on wicked men and died for them, nailed by the hands and feet, weeping. That's all I know."
>
> "Let me give you a final kiss," [said Darnetal].
>
> "No," replied [Alahowigh], I can't believe you have lost this amazing secret that would have restored me to the innocence of childhood!"[28]

Darnetal's failure to remember the catechism finds its dramatic commentary in his reading of the absurd contents of the book that Alahowigh has so treasured, and brings about for Darnetal a moment of illumination. Struck by his inability to offer no more consolation than a book of stupid pranks, he is overcome by what Bernanos calls a "supernatural pity" and feels that only in this extremity of hopelessness can the mercy of a god break through like lightning. If the emergence of mercy or of a loving God at the end of this story of deceit and violence is arguably a Girardian moment that dispels the extreme violence and horror of the tale, the attainment of illumination in such bleak circumstances is wholly Bernanosian.

"Dialogue d'ombres" presents us with yet another configuration of the possibility of illumination, but one in which the protagonist struggles against the light. Françoise, as we have noted, behaves self-destructively only in order to give birth to a new rival in *altergenesis*. Yet she stumbles against what she calls her pride, which tells her that she should not indulge in this trafficking of the self. Curiously, it is Jacques who offers a commentary on the strange mimetic character of Françoise in this moment in which she might almost be mistaken for a saint. Now, the saint destroys self-love so as to love God; Françoise, on the other hand, is trying to destroy something inside her that rejects her own self-objectification. Françoise fosters a self-hatred that at this time Bernanos held to be the common ground between the sinner and the saint, though later, in *Journal d'un curé de campagne*, he would insist that God's grace lay not in self-hatred but rather in self-forgetfulness.[29] What Françoise misses, however, is how very close her mimetic conduct brings her to a pattern of sainthood that, according to Bernanos, would have released her from self-destruction through the imitation of Christ.

There is arguably no classic Girardian conversion in any of these three short stories. Nevertheless, there are moments of awareness or illumination that suggest where deliverance is to be found: in the recognition of the disaster that imitative desire can lead to, or the acknowledgment of the Christian solution to the dilemmas that immoderate mimetic desire can produce. As bleak as Bernanos's imagination can be, he never leaves the map of hope undisclosed to those who are rent by the machinery of desire, rivalry, deceit, and violence.

Death as the Final Hermeneutic of Desire

A last corroboration of our argument that Bernanos understood the dynamics identified by mimetic theory is that these three stories are anchored in the great theme—both Bernanosian and Girardian—of death. Death is scattered throughout Bernanos's oeuvre, from the demise of the first Mouchette in *Sous le Soleil de Satan* (1926) to the death of Monsieur Ouine (1943) in the eponymous novel. Bernanos's greatest political pamphlet, *Les Grands Cimetières sous la lune* (1938), is a reflection on the death of the innocent victims of the nationalist political purgation of Majorca during the Spanish Civil War.[30] His final work, *Dialogues des Carmélites* (1949), dramatizes the execution of a convent of nuns during the Great Terror. For Bernanos, individual drama always borders on eschatology. Death is both the great rupture and a continuation. It is often a moment of confrontation with the conscience. In a culture shaped significantly by meliorism and progressivism, Bernanos's preoccupation with death is a sign of his conviction that what matters is not how one lives but how one dies. Without ever referencing Girard, Ann Stoffels has even called Bernanos the "French Dostoyevsky."[31] Ineluctably, Bernanos would have understood Girard's contention that the "truth of metaphysical desire is death."[32]

Death in these stories takes on three guises that provide a commentary on each story's mimetic dynamics. As we have seen, in "Madame Dargent" death occasions illumination and the destruction of the dying woman's deceits. At the same time, Monsieur Dargent's murder of Madame Dargent after her confession shows a Girardian contagion of violence at work. Death paradoxically continues the cycle of violence just as it presents us with the key to understanding the desires and deceits of the story's protagonists.

"Une Nuit" is a story littered with corpses, from the corpse of Picard, whose features ooze through the mud of the jungle floor when Darnetal slips and falls on his grave, to the corpses of Alahowigh and Bisbillitta. Death is everywhere in "Une Nuit," always fulfilling the iron laws of mimetic violence and deceit, but finally bringing about Darnetal's encounter with the mercy of a god, rather than with a god's hostility. If the "Nuit" is the moment of deceit and deception, as we observed above, it is also the classic symbol of the end of life, apparently a hopeless and bleak prospect alien to the refashioning of death by Christ in which the hero "dies to be reborn."[33] Just as for Girard the mimetic cycle is undermined by a salvific death, so in Bernanos's imagination one must go to death's door to find any hope of salvation.

"Dialogue d'ombres," the last of these three stories, appears to undermine this preoccupation with death. Two lovers talk beneath the shadows of a tree in what is, as we have already noted, a parody of the romantic scene. Yet the story is subtly all about death, and in this regard it arguably undermines Girard's observation that the closer one is to death, the more one withdraws from lying.[34] *Ombres* in French means *shadows*, not only in relation to light and dark but in the sense of ghosts or phantoms. There is no moment of death in "Dialogue d'ombres" because, in a sense, Françoise and Jacques are already dead: they are the *ombres*. Their existence is as it were a continual death in which they mimetically feed off each other's desires. In spite of his dawning realization of his mimetic behavior, Jacques is locked into the enduring habit of objectivizing his love interests, a practice that leaves him in a death-like isolation in which only the parody (the imitation) of living relationships is possible. In contrast, Françoise's desire for self-annihilation is like a mimetic parody of the scapegoat whose death is the catalyst of harmony. While it might be tempting to see Bernanos's treatment of Françoise, Jacques, and Alahowigh as a relic of hostility and pride in Bernanos's own moral imagination, this enduring death of Françoise and Jacques is redolent of the salvific drama that is written into all Bernanos's work. Christ's transcendent love would seem all the less decisive if it were not pitched against the possibility of damnation (eternal death). Moreover, if it were not possible to choose damnation, Christ's love would be as coercive as any act of mimetic violence.

It is clear, therefore, that these three stories of Bernanos adumbrate in resounding ways Girard's insights into the hermeneutical power of death. To perceive the metaphysical structure of desire, says Girard, is to foresee its catastrophic conclusion. To associate it with death is to acknowledge its ultimate meaning.[35] These three stories of Bernanos appear to accord perfectly with these conclusions. The fact that the three narratives are haunted by the prospect of the consequences of death indicates once more the close convergence we can point to between what Bernanos discovered as a creative artist and what Girard, the theorist of mimetic desire, set out in *Deceit, Desire, and the Novel*. There can be no doubt, in the final analysis, that Bernanos's short stories, dating from the first period of his novelistic career, clearly demonstrate his right to be considered alongside the other masters of the *vérité romanesque*.

Notes

1. Timothy Williams, *Desire and Persecution in "Thérèse Desqueyroux" and Other Selected Novels of François Mauriac* (New York: Edwin Mellen Press, 2007).

2. Pierre-Paul Delvaux, "Esquisse pour une lecture de *Monsieur Ouine* à la lumière de René Girard," in *Etudes bernanosiennes 19: confrontations (2)*, ed. Michel Estève (Paris: Minard, 1988), 209–28.

3. Sabrinelle Bédrane, "Nouvelles de l'entre-deux-guerres, récits brefs d'aujoud'hui: À l'ombre du récit à l'orée du récit?" *Révue d'histoire littéraire de la France* 109.2 (2009): 277–87.

4. Paul March-Russell, *The Short Story: An Introduction* (Edinburgh: Edinburgh University Press, 2009).

5. Michael Kirwan, *Discovering Girard* (London: Darton, Longman and Todd, 2004), 25–30.

6. Bédrane, "Nouvelles de l'entre-deux-guerres," 283.

7. Georges Bernanos, "Madame Dargent," in *Oeuvres romanesques, Dialogue des Carmélites*, ed. Albert Béguin and Michel Estève (1922; Paris: Gallimard, 1961), 1–14. All translations into English from Bernanos's works are mine.

8. Georges Bernanos, "Une Nuit," in *Oeuvres romanesques, Dialogue des Carmélites*, 15–38.

9. Georges Bernanos, "Dialogue d'ombres," in *Oeuvres romanesques, Dialogue des Carmélites*, 39–53. Jean-Loup Bernanos speculates as to whether the latter two stories date from the same period as the first, but even a gap of as many as eight or ten years between the composition of the first and the last story would appear to make little difference to the preoccupations they express in common. Cf. Jean-Loup Bernanos, "Préface," in Georges Bernanos, *Dialogue d'ombres: Nouvelles, premiers écrits* (Paris: Seuil, 1999), 9.

10. For example, Guy Gaucher, *Le Thème de la mort dans les romans de Bernanos* (Paris: Minard, 1967); Pierre Gilles, *Bernanos et l'angoise: Étude de l'oeuvre romanesque* (Nancy: Nancy University Press, 1984).

11. René Girard, *Deceit, Desire, and the Novel: Self and Other in Literary Structure*, trans. Yvonne Freccero (Baltimore: Johns Hopkins University Press, 1965), 95.

12. Girard, *Deceit, Desire, and the Novel*, 114.

13. Girard, *Deceit, Desire, and the Novel*, 288–89.

14. Girard, *Deceit, Desire, and the Novel*, 307.

15. Girard, *Deceit, Desire, and the Novel*, 277.

16. René Girard, *Things Hidden Since the Foundation of the World*, research undertaken in collaboration with Jean-Michel Oughourlian and Guy Lefort, trans. Stephen Nann and Michael Metteer (Stanford: Stanford University Press, 1987), 307.

17. Girard, *Deceit, Desire, and the Novel*, 283.

18. René Girard, *Violence and the Sacred*, trans. Patrick Gregory (Baltimore: John Hopkins University Press, 1977), 12.

19. Girard, *Deceit, Desire, and the Novel*, 82.

20. Girard, *Deceit, Desire, and the Novel*, 82.

21. Girard, *Deceit, Desire, and the Novel*, 151.

22. Bernanos, "Dialogue d'ombres," 45 (my emphasis).

23. Girard, *Deceit, Desire, and the Novel*, 298.

24. Bernanos, "Madame Dargent," 7.

25. Girard, *Deceit, Desire, and the Novel*, 298.

26. Bernanos, "Madame Dargent," 9.

27. Girard, *Things Hidden*, 317.

28. Bernanos, "Une Nuit," 36–37.

29. Bernanos, "Journal d'un curé de champagne," in *Oeuvres romanesques, Dialogue des Carmélites*, 1258.

30. For a Girardian reading of Bernanos's political works, see my chapter, "Rethinking the Modernity of Bernanos: A Girardian Perspective," in *God's Mirror: Renewal and Engagement in French Catholic Intellectual Culture in the Mid-Twentieth Century*, ed. by Katherine Davies and Toby Garfitt (New York: Oxford University Press, 2014).

31. "La relation Bernanos-Dostoïevski," in Estève, *Etudes bernanosiennes 19*, 40.

32. Girard, *Deceit, Desire, and the Novel*, 282.

33. Girard, *Deceit, Desire, and the Novel*, 304.

34. Girard, *Deceit, Desire, and the Novel*, 290.

35. Girard, *Deceit, Desire, and the Novel*, 288–90.

Mimetic Desire
in Otherworldly Narratives

Laura Wittman

I n Luigi Pirandello's 1929 play *Lazzaro*, the main character, Diego, a staunchly Catholic family patriarch, has temporarily died and then returned to life. Taking the silence of the biblical Lazarus a step further, Pirandello imagines his protagonist does not even remember nearly dying, let alone a vision of the beyond, until others inform him. In fact, much of the drama revolves around the competing claims of those who demand a particular story—the doctor, the priest, family members, and Diego himself—from a protagonist who has nothing to report. Pirandello's play speaks remarkably to present-day concerns about the nature of the self in relation to memory, and in particular to traumatic memories, which are increasingly known to be unreliable. Specifically, Diego undergoes what we would now call a near-death experience, and the play foregrounds a major issue in near-death studies: what to make of the psychological transformation—often positive—of people whose memories of near death are clearly the subject of substantial confabulation. As an expert in fiction, Pirandello is well aware that the extrapolation from later transformation to the putative event at its origin is the interpretation of a narrative, which includes moral assumptions about the purpose of narratives as well as philosophical claims about the nature of mimesis.[1]

Triangular Desire in *Lazzaro*

Pirandello's play opens with an apparently minor conflict that foreshadows
the central drama to come. Diego has been raising his two children, the ado-
lescent Lia and the older Lucio (away at seminary), according to his intran-
sigent Catholic faith. After acerbic comments by the nurse Deodata that the
young girl, who is sickly and paralyzed in the legs, needs country fresh air and
not asceticism,[2] doctor Gionni, who agrees with Deodata, appears, announcing "Back to life! Back to life!" (115). He is carrying a small white rabbit, Lia's
pet, who had died the previous evening: thanks to a shot of adrenaline at the
heart, he has brought her back to life. Lia exclaims with stupor, "And she's
resurrected?" (116). Her father then arrives with the Monsignore, Lelli, and
immediately rebuts, "quickly and hard" [*pronto e duro*], "It means she must
not have been dead" (117). The doctor, similarly "quickly and firmly" [*pronto
e fermo*], insists, "She did not seem, but was [dead]." As the argument continues, Diego asserts, "I know that only God can, through a miracle, bring one
back from death to life," whereas Gionni counters, "I can consider science to
be one of God's instruments" (118). In the end, Diego refuses to allow Lia to
keep the rabbit, while Deodata condemns him for his harshness.

This opening immediately presents Diego, the Catholic ascetic, and
Gionni, the progressive doctor, as rivals for the education and the heart of
the children. In Girard's theory, triangular desire is at the heart of rivalry,
and arises from the fact that secretly, even to himself, the subject emulates his
rival, desiring the very same things he desires, unconsciously imitating him.
Key to this triangular structure is the need for the "desiring subject" to "forget
the role of the Other in his vision of the world."[3] In view of this, it is remarkable how much the first act of the play insists on Diego's powerlessness: not
only has he been unable to heal his own children (Lucio is also depicted as
sickly and unfit for life), he has also been unable to keep his own wife, Sara.
We learn that conflict over how to raise the children led her to retreat to
her husband's farm, where after a two-year showdown when he refused to
send the children to her, she eventually took the peasant Arcadipane as her
partner, working the land and raising two more children with him. Deodata
condemns Sara for living in sin, incensed that Diego does not throw her out
in order to give the farm to his children; she finally accuses him, "It's obvious!
It's obvious! You still love her!"[4] Diego answers that he intends to give up all

his wealth and turn the farm into an almshouse, forcing his wife to leave, and imposing on himself and his children a life of "poor among the poor." At the end he concludes, "I pray to God every night that he call me back to himself, not because I want relief from these trials he wishes me to undergo, but to relieve them [Sara and Arcadipane] from the sin in which they live. For I know she has found a man, she has found a man."[5]

Diego here exhibits many of the characteristics of the Girardian desiring subject, who can never reach his goal because he cannot see that his goal has been determined by his rival, whom he is unconsciously emulating. Diego claims that he wants the best for his children, and wants to save them, and his wife, from sin. But in reality, it is the power of Gionni he wants, the power to regenerate life, the life he, Diego, has failed in so many ways to live. In founding an almshouse, he is willing to sacrifice his children and his wife in an attempt at self-sacrifice that is his last, paradoxical bid for power. This recalls Girard's comments on the descent into masochism of the subject caught in triangular desire: "only that failure will indicate an authentic deity, a mediator who is invulnerable to his own undertakings"; "he now chooses to see in shame, defeat, and enslavement not the inevitable results of an aimless faith and an absurd mode of behavior but rather the *signs* of [his mediator's] divinity."[6] As Sara later points out, Diego, his children, and the derelicts he proposes to house have no idea how to work the land and will be condemned to beg for food, whereas if he gives the farm to a good steward, he can give the proceeds not needed by him to the poor (128). Notably Sara and Arcadipane have for years been giving everything but what they need to subsist to the hospital.[7] Diego, in other words, does not genuinely wish to help people; rather he emulates Gionni, who works in a hospital, secretly admiring his power to the point of confirming it by his descent into abject poverty.

Were we to leave the play at this point, we might conclude that Pirandello, who was after all a committed skeptic in matters religious, wished to denounce bigotry as a form of envy for the certainties and successes of science. Diego's unwillingness to see the marvelous in Gionni's work, as Lia instead can, is a sign of his inauthenticity, for he wishes to appropriate the marvelous for himself, thereby killing it, rather that acknowledging his admiration for it. A Girardian analysis would push this interpretation a step further, seeing in Gionni a "deviated transcendency,"[8] a false replacement for the God Diego desires, but in bad faith, negating him because he is unwilling to renounce his "metaphysical autonomy."[9] From this Girardian perspective, to unmask the triangular structure of desire—to realize Diego is jealous of Gionni—goes hand in hand with realizing that the only true model for our desire, which will prevent further triangulations from happening, is God, and specifically the Christian God—Diego should have the courage of his faith, in other words, and stop worrying about Gionni:

> Choice always involves choosing a model, and true freedom lies in the basic choice between a human or a divine model. The impulse of the soul towards God is inseparable from a retreat into the Self. Inversely the turning in on itself of pride is inseparable from a movement of panic toward the Other. . . . [This vision] provides a coherent interpretation of the strict analogies and of the radical difference between Christianity and imitative desire. . . . "Passion is the change of address of a force awakened by Christianity and oriented toward God."[10]

As we will see in the next section, the rest of Pirandello's play questions this sort of reading by suggesting that human desire may indeed be constantly deviating (falling prey to false models) but that this does not necessarily tell us what it is deviating from (where to find a true model).

Unmasking Triangular Desire or Choosing Emulation?

Turning now to the second part of Pirandello's *Lazzaro*, we find that everything is poised for a dramatic revelation of the triangular structure that underlies Diego's bigotry. After we learn of Diego's plans to create an almshouse, his estranged wife Sara visits him to announce not only that she is leaving the farm of her own initiative, but that their son Lucio has abandoned the seminary and his plans to become a priest. He wishes instead to "be reborn from me, his mother" by embracing the pantheistic vitalism and chthonic divinity she represents.[11] Diego is so shocked at the news that he rushes out to find his son and is hit by a car. The scene ends as the doctor stands over his body and declares him dead.[12] Act Two opens at the farm, as Sara, Arcadipane, and their children prepare to leave. Lucio and Gionni are also there, arguing. We find out that Diego has been resurrected by Gionni's medical miracles, but that he has no recollection of this, nor of the fatal accident. Lucio is convinced that finding out the truth will open Diego to "his true resurrection,"[13] which would come from a "salutary upheaval in his spirit,"[14] in the direction of recognizing that God is unfathomable, and that dogmatic views are too narrow. For the doctor, telling Diego what happened "might kill him," not just spiritually but literally.[15] The rest of the act unfolds amidst conflicting interpretations of Diego's return to life. Sara intones a celebration of her rebirth through "the things of the country, life, real life," described as "savage" and "brutal," transforming her into "a creature just now emerged from the hands of God"[16]: the implication is that religion should not be about transcendence but about a very pagan, even Heraclitean, cycle of life and death. The beggar Cico, in contrast, is very upset because he will no longer be able to use threats of the afterlife to convince people to give alms; nor will he able to hope for a better life for himself: bitterly, he concludes, "Dead—he knows nothing. Where has he been?—He should know, and he doesn't. . . . it's a sign that, for the person who dies, over there, there is nothing at all—nothing. . . . Nothing . . . nothing at all."[17] Cico is a clear example of ressentiment: he cannot see how much focus on the other life's nothingness robs him of the reality of this one. Girard notes that ressentiment is tied to "internal mediation";[18] however, we resent not only our rivals in the pursuit of a common object of desire, but also all that which reveals the inauthenticity of our desire: Cico, it is implied, would do better to realize that a truer faith would not demand certainties about Paradise.

By the time act 2 ends, therefore, we have been set up to expect a clear alternative: either we side with Cico, whose views echo those of Diego at the rabbit's "resurrection" in act 1, and we remain caught in triangular desire and its false transcendence, or we side with Sara, whose vitalism has already begun to transform Lucio, and we thus find "true freedom" and the true object of our desire.[19] This is, however, precisely where Pirandello's play tests the limits of Girard's theory by coming so close to fulfilling it. Specifically, at the end of *Deceit, Desire, and the Novel*, Girard argues that, having explored to their full the mechanisms of triangulation, and the false deviations of desire, the narrator of Proust's *Recherche* can finally slip in the word "resurrection" with hope of its true meaning: "we can discern the outlines of the symbolism of vertical transcendency."[20] Leaving the issue of Proust interpretation aside, the point here is that for Girard, to see the triangular structure whereby I

desire what my rival desires is also, immediately, to intuit a completely different, vertical, and presumably authentic desire—or love—of God. In *Deceit,
Desire, and the Novel*, we are not told exactly how this happens, but I believe
we can infer from Girard's later work, particularly *Things Hidden Since the
Foundation of the World* and *Job: The Victim of his People*, that the violence
of triangular desire is undone by Christ's willingness to be an innocent, self-
conscious scapegoat, providing a model of authentic love. Christ is a model
we can imitate without falling into resentment because he gives over his
autonomy to the Father, just as we should give ours over to Christ: as Girard
insists repeatedly, our desire for metaphysical autonomy is what "gives rise to
slavery" of triangulation.[21]

Returning then to Pirandello, do we find that "vertical transcendence"
and the end of striving for metaphysical autonomy emerge from seeing
through the mechanism of triangular desire? What is in fact the effect of
Diego's "resurrection," which so ironically puts his dogmatic faith to the
test? Act 3 of *Lazzaro* brings us to a very unexpected conclusion. As already
suggested, we have been prepared for Diego's initial horror, when he finds
out by accident that a death certificate had been completed for him: his first
reaction is in fact just like Cico's, a resentful rage at the "nothing" of the
afterlife (169–70). We have also been prepared to see as its alternative a new
sort of faith, which is not the same as Sara's vitalism, but is rather Lucio's
reinterpretation of it:

> Do you see what happens? In order for our self not to end, we abolish
> life in the name of God, and we make God reign over there (who knows
> where) in a presumed realm of death, so that he might give us, over there,
> a prize or a punishment. . . . See, doctor? this should be for him [Diego] as
> it was for me, the true resurrection through death: denying it in God, and
> believing in this sole Immortality, not ours, not for us, not hope for a prize
> or fear of a punishment: believing in this eternal present of life that is God,
> and that's all.[22]

This faith is reminiscent of Catholic Modernism (especially of Maurice
Blondel's *L'Action* and Antonio Fogazzaro's *Il Santo*) because of its emphasis
on experience and action in the present, which draws on the historical rediscovery of early Christian notions that salvation lies in a radical transformation

of our relation to others (from "it" to "thou," to summarize it a bit simplistically) and not in any afterlife or religious dogma.[23] This is consistent with Pirandello's broader perspective in *Lazzaro*, which is the central play of his trilogy "of modern *myths*." All three forms of myth, religious, social, and artistic, were attempts to reconcile the irrational with modern rationality, by providing the chthonic and maternal "life" with "form" according to Pirandello's terminology. Lucio's version of religion, above, accepts that human forms are never equal to the eternity of God, and does so by accepting first of all that even the human soul may not be eternal as we know it. So far, we are still in Girardian territory, even if Lucio's Modernist Catholicism is not exactly the same transcendence evoked by Girard. In particular, as in Girard, the recognition, and abandonment, of the self's desire for autonomy ("in order for our self not to end") leads to a new faith that is personally felt from the heart, rather than dictated by the imitation of dogma.

In the last scene of the play, Lucio finally confronts his father, and the obvious question for us is whether he will be able to convert him to this new more sincere, more direct faith, as he has been asserting he is called to do. This is where the play comes to a sudden twist:

> Now I truly feel and understand the word of Christ: CHARITY! Since men cannot, each and every one and all the time, stand, God himself wants on earth his House, which promises true life over there; his Saintly House, where the tired and the miserable and the weak can kneel. . . . Monsignore, yes, now *he kneels* in front of you. I feel worthy of putting the habit back on, for the divine sacrifice of Christ and for the faith of others![24]

Lucio chooses to emulate his father and to embrace the church of fathers, which he clearly does not feel called to in his heart, rather than follow his mother's vitalism. This seems to be a terrible abdication of authenticity, whose overt justification, "for the faith of others," though it is an expression of charity, cannot undo the bad faith inherent in fulfilling the priestly office without believing in it. From a Girardian perspective, this makes no sense, because Lucio appears to be unlearning what he has learned throughout the play, falling into bigotry as his father did, failing to see, perhaps, how much he is actually giving in to resentment by doing what his father had wanted all along, but only now that it is too late. Pirandello here objects to Girard along lines that are voiced also by Gianni Vattimo, when he points out that knowing the structure of triangulation and mimetic violence does not necessarily produce the will to overcome it.[25] But the very end of the play raises a further, deeper objection. When Sara says, bitterly, "He is going back to die again in his habit" (*Va a rimorire nel suo abito*) the doctor responds, "He himself said that in God one cannot die," forcing her to recognize, "So it is true that there are saints upon the earth."[26] To confirm these words, at the very end of the play, Lucio says to his father, echoing the words of Jesus to Lazarus in the Bible, "Stand up and walk"; but he is also saying them to his sister, Lia, who suddenly gets up from her wheelchair and walks. The implication is of course that the father too will "walk" spiritually, and the play ends with the word "miracle."[27]

This ending has disappointed a number of critics, who see in it a return to the shallow religion of fathers, of (bad) faith for future benefit. However, I propose that Pirandello needs this miracle in order to confront us with a paradox: it is possible to be an actual, effective saint, while remaining in bad faith, as long as this bad faith is chosen consciously for the right reasons. Lucio does not so much unmask mimetic desire as choose to embrace it willingly. Crucially, his choice is motivated not by the notion that behind false mediators a true mediator might be found, but rather by the practical question of which mediation will be most effective in his current circumstances. He accepts the church, even though he clearly prefers a more Modernist, maternal faith, because this will have a genuine effect on his father, who needs it the most. In Pirandello's view, then, to see the triangular structure of desire leads beyond the self's attachment to authenticity, beyond the very possibility that there is a single model that will save us (for Girard, the Christian one). We see here the skeptic Pirandello recognizing that a religious myth that is familiar to people may be preferable to no myth at all: like the Modernists who wished to reform Catholicism from within, Pirandello recognizes the deep connections between Catholicism and Italian popular culture. Furthermore, *Lazzaro* was first performed, in England, in the summer of 1929, just as the Lateran pacts between Italy's Fascist government and the Catholic Church were being signed. In light of this, the play seems to be a plea for people not to reject Christianity, and Catholicism, piecemeal. Given Pirandello's adhesion to Fascism, considered opportunistic by some, which nonetheless lasted until his death in 1936, the play's end also reads like a plea for compromise to counter the near-civil war that resulted from weak liberal era governments and the devastation of World War I. Though I do not wish to defend this political message, what seems most productive about *Lazzaro* is its contention that there is no way out of emulation, only the choice of what or who to emulate.[28]

Conclusion: Making the Wrong Choice for the Right Reasons

In *Lazzaro*, Pirandello shows us that amid attempts to extrapolate a moral truth from conflicting memories, or to unmask an authentic origin to justify later transformations, our choice is not based on truth value but on the more pragmatic question of what is preferable as a way to live in the present. To put it bluntly, the systems we use to remember traumatic memories are constructed later, and Pirandello warns that we would do well to admit that. It is at this juncture that Girardian mimetic theory is most useful. As we have seen, it helps us to understand the specific dangers Pirandello sees in our refusal to admit that we construct the value of near-death experience—or any life-changing experience that defies "normal" memory—retrospectively. In *Lazzaro*, such a refusal yields a religious interpretation that is unaware of mimicking scientific models; but it can also yield its complementary opposite, a resentful, militantly secular view that is unaware of its metaphysical resentment. Both are forms of bad faith, or, in Girard's terms, of mimetic desire running rampant, and the play thus reveals that the polarization between the discourses of science and religion as regards near-death experience is an evasion of the genuinely difficult issue: what to do with a life-changing event that provides no road map for the direction of change.[29]

It is here that Pirandello parts ways with Girard. For the latter, at least in the embryonic formulation of mimetic theory present in *Deceit, Desire, and the Novel*, becoming aware of the mimetic structure and of the true source of rivalry would somehow produce an authentic religious experience, in which the individual relinquishes his or her claims to metaphysical autonomy. The road map would come, then, not from near-death experience itself, but from its unmasking the inauthenticity of our previous desires; faced with this, we should abandon all willful, ego-driven, jealous, and mimetic interpretations and become aware of the one, nonmimetic truth of the experience, namely, in Girard's view, our true longing for Christian transcendence. For Pirandello, by contrast, awareness of mimesis cannot project us beyond it; his play rejects any black-and-white dualism that may be traced in Girard's initial formulation of his theory by foregrounding a character, Lucio, who learns to accept and modulate mimetic desire. Notably, Pirandello agrees with Girard that focus on the ego's autonomy is a key problem, which blinds us to mimetic transformations. However, for him the issue is autonomy *tout court*, not metaphysical autonomy. In our construction of a road map for change after near-death experience, in other words, a key illusion to abandon is that we are free to construct that road map any way we like—not just as regards its religious implications, but insofar as it appeals to fundamental aspects of individual psychology and deeply held cultural values. The more we learn to play with our prejudices, to get to know them, and to accept them with some humor, the better off we will be. This notion of play is central to Pirandello's sense of "*umorismo*": in his treatise *L'umorismo* as well as his novel *Uno, Nessuno, e Centomila*, he depicts humor as the moment in which we discover that our identity is made of innumerable masks; crucially, there is no real face beneath them; rather we must learn to revel in the unstable nothingness of our identity.[30]

Ultimately, Pirandello challenges us to rethink individuality in relation to mimetic desire in two ways. First, he calls us to nuance always/never statements: if we no longer need to preserve one kind of self-conscious desire as qualitatively different from all the rest, as Girard wants, we can be open to understanding mimetic desire, or mirroring, as a range of possibilities. For Pirandello, the more polarized rivalry of science and religion is undercut by other types of imitation, such as Lucio's admiration for his mother's natural religiosity, or Gionni's respect for Lucio's Modernist faith. What this implies as regards the memories of life-changing events is key: for all that they appear to be so radical, and tend to be figured as conversions with a clear before and after, such transformations are not of an all-or-nothing sort. Lucio is displaced from where he started, but not turned into another person or born again. Second, letting go of self-conscious freedom and always/never choices does not condemn us to total relativism, as Girard fears. On the contrary, it constantly confronts with ethical choices in the absence of an overall system to determine them and in a contingent situation where complete free will is not possible (Pirandello's historical circumstances are here unavoidably relevant, but he would say that indeed none of us are free of historical circumstances). I would like to propose that this amounts to something like making the wrong choice for the right reasons: Lucio becomes a priest though his faith is not Catholic, but, most important, this decision stems from his recognition that he is not alone and must help others. His father's near-death experience could have led not only to more dramatic, but also to more morally lofty interpretations, or at least, to ones that had stronger claims to originality and authenticity: Lucio eschews this in favor of something that seems more mundane, more commonplace, but also more genuinely common. The choice he makes is not really wrong, so much as it is an admission that such a thing as the right choice, in an absolute sense, may not exist. In *Lazzaro*, then, Pirandello asks us to accept responsibility for the answers we choose, even if they are contingent and conditioned by others.

Notes

1. This essay draws from chapter 2 of a book project entitled *Lazarus' Silence: Near-Death Experiences in Fiction, Science, and Popular Culture*. What I give here is the portion of chapter 2 that focuses on Pirandello and on Girard's mimetic theory. For "life review" and the now canonical description of the elements of near-death experience, which launched the field, see Raymond A. Moody, *Life after Life* (Harrisburg, PA: Stackpole Books, 1976). Further refinements of characterization are found in Kenneth Ring, *Life at Death: A Scientific Investigation of the Near-Death Experience* (New York: Coward, McCann & Geoghegan, 1980); Michael B. Sabom, "The Near-Death Experience," *JAMA* 244 (1980): 29–30; B. Greyson, "A Typology of Near-Death Experiences," *American Journal of Psychiatry* 142 (1985): 967–69. On issues of self-reporting, and her attempt to interview a wide range of patients, see Penny Sartori and Paul Badham, *The Near-Death Experiences of Hospitalized Intensive Care Patients* (Lewiston, NY: Edwin Mellen Press, 2008). For an overview of work on veridical perception and the problem of *affabulation*, see Janice Miner Holden, "Veridical Perception in Near-Death Experiences," in *The Handbook of Near-Death Experiences: Thirty Years of Investigation*, ed. Janice Miner Holden et al. (Santa Barbara, CA: Praeger, 2009), 185–212. A thorough, and respectful, skeptical account is Susan Blackmore, *Dying to Live: Near-Death Experiences* (Buffalo, NY: Prometheus Books, 1993).

2. Luigi Pirandello, *La nuova colonia, Lazzaro, I giganti della montagna* (Milan: Garzanti, 2008). All translations are mine.

3. René Girard, *Deceit, Desire, and the Novel: Self and Other in Literary Structure*, trans. Yvonne Freccero (Baltimore: Johns Hopkins University Press, 1965), 39.

4. Pirandello, *La nuova colonia, Lazzaro*, 123.

5. "Prego Dio ogni sera che mi richiami a sé, non per avere io un sollievo da queste prove che ha voluto mandarmi, ma per levar loro [Sara and Arcadipane] dal peccato in cui vivono. Perché io so che lei ha trovato un uomo, ha trovato un uomo." Pirandello, *La nuova colonia, Lazzaro*, 125.

6. Girard, *Deceit, Desire, and the Novel*, 176, 177.

7. Pirandello, *La nuova colonia, Lazzaro*, 124.

8. Girard, *Deceit, Desire, and the Novel*, 192.

9. Girard, *Deceit, Desire, and the Novel*, 56.

10. Girard, *Deceit, Desire, and the Novel*, 58–59.

11. Pirandello, *La nuova colonia, Lazzaro*, 111, 130.

12. Pirandello, *La nuova colonia, Lazzaro*, 134.

13. Pirandello, *La nuova colonia, Lazzaro*, 138.

14. Pirandello, *La nuova colonia, Lazzaro*, 140.

15. Pirandello, *La nuova colonia, Lazzaro*, 141.

16. Pirandello, *La nuova colonia, Lazzaro*, 147.

17. "Morto—non sa nulla. Dov'è stato?—Dovrebbe saperlo, e non lo sa. . . . è segno che, per chi muore, di là non c'è più nulla—nulla . . . Nulla . . . più nulla." Pirandello, *La nuova colonia, Lazzaro*, 157–58.

18. Girard, *Deceit, Desire, and the Novel*, 11.

19. Girard, *Deceit, Desire, and the Novel*, 58.

20. Girard, *Deceit, Desire, and the Novel*, 313.

21. Girard, *Deceit, Desire, and the Novel*, 259.

22. "Vedi com'è? Per non finire noi, annulliamo in nome di Dio la vita, e facciamo regnare Dio anche di là (non si sa dove) in un presunto regno della morte, perché ci dia là, un premio o un castigo. . . . Ecco, vede, dottore? questo dovrebbe esser per lui, [Diego] com'è stato per me, il vero risorgere dalla morte: negarla in Dio, e credere in questa sola Immortalità, non nostra, non per noi, speranza di un premio o timore di castigo: credere in questo eterno presente della vita ch'è Dio, e basta." Pirandello, *La nuova colonia, Lazzaro*, 143.

23. See Maurice Blondel, *Action: Essai d'une critique de la vie et d'une science de la pratique* (Paris: Alcan, 1893); Antonio Fogazzaro, *Il Santo* (Milan: Mondadori, 1970). For the main tenets of religious Modernism, see Ernesto Buonaiuti, *The Programme of Modernism* (New York: G. P. Putnam's Sons, 1908). On Pirandello's trilogy, and the notions of "vita" and "forma," see Luigi Pirandello, *La nuova colonia, Lazzaro, I giganti della montagna* (Milan: Garzanti, 2008), lvi; Susan Bassnett-McGuire, "Pirandello's British Première: Lazzaro," *Yearbook of the British Pirandello Society* 2 (1982): 28–31; Lucia Massi, "Pirandello's Theory of 'Modern Myths,'" *Yearbook of the British Pirandello Society* 6 (1986): 1–18; Julie Dashwood, "Pirandello's Myth Plays," *Yearbook of the Society for Pirandello Studies* 12 (1992): 64–77; Anna Meda, "Lazzaro e la riscrittura pirandelliana del mito biblico," *Quaderni d'Italianistica: Official Journal of the Canadian Society for Italian Studies* 14.1 (1993): 41–56; Sergio Bullegas, *Pirandello e "Lazzaro": Il mito sulla scena* (Alessandria: Edizioni dell'orso, 1994); Fulvia Airoldi Namer and Julie Dashwood, "Pirandello's Myth Plays," in *Luigi Pirandello: The Theatre of Paradox* (Lewiston, NY: Mellen, 1996), 148–72; Umberto Mariani, "'A Will to Believe': Religion in Pirandello's Late Plays," *Forum Italicum* 33.2 (1999): 393–401.

24. "Ora intendo e sento veramente la parola di Cristo: CARITÀ! Perché gli uomini non possono star tutti e sempre in piedi, Dio stesso vuole in terra la sua Casa, che prometta la vera vita di là; la sua Santa Casa, dove gli stanchi e i miseri e i deboli si possano inginocchiare. . . . Ecco, Monsignore,

così, *s'inginocchia* davanti a Lei, ora che mi sento degno di nuovo di rindossar l'abito per il divino sacrificio di Cristo e per la fede degli altri! Pirandello, *La nuova colonia, Lazzaro*, 164.

25. Gianni Vattimo and René Girard, *Christianity, Truth, and Weakening Faith: A Dialogue*, trans. William McCuaig (New York: Columbia University Press, 2010), 71.

26. Pirandello, *La nuova colonia, Lazzaro*, 165.

27. Pirandello, *La nuova colonia, Lazzaro*, 171–72.

28. On Pirandello's plays and Fascism, see Maria Elena Santuccio, "Mito e antimito nell'Italia fascista: La trilogia pirandelliana dei miti e il teatro nazionalista e fascista di propaganda," *Italian Studies* 63.1 (2008): 85–104. More generally, on Pirandello's sense that there is no stable identity we can cling to, see Paolo Valesio, "A Remark on Silence and Listening," *Oral Tradition* 2.1 (1987): 286–300; Thomas Harrison, *Essayism: Conrad, Musil, and Pirandello* (Baltimore: Johns Hopkins University Press, 1992); Raffaele Cavalluzzi, "Pirandello: La soglia del nulla," *La nuova ricerca* 12.12 (2003): 205–15.

29. For the complementary opposite play to Pirandello's, in which a near-death experience spawns militantly secular interpretations that are later put into question, see Graham Greene, *The Potting Shed: A Play in Three Acts* (New York: Viking Press, 1957).

30. See Luigi Pirandello, *L'umorismo: saggio*, 2nd ed. (Florence: L. Battistelli, 1920); Luigi Pirandello, *Uno, nessuno e centomila: romanzo*, 3rd ed. (Milan: Mondadori, 1936).

Desire, Deceit, and Defeat in the Work of Roberto Arlt

The work of the Argentine writer Roberto Arlt (1900–1942), a contemporary of Jorge Luis Borges, and one of the pioneers of urban modernist fiction in Latin America, lends itself to a Girardian analysis—or, rather, a confrontation with the ideas of René Girard. For virtually all of Arlt's literary protagonists (both in prose and in drama) are portrayed as shaping their identity with the help of literary, novelistic, or theatrical models, a kind of performative mimesis that is strongly reminiscent of the disjunction between idealism and reality, as we find it most famously in *Don Quixote* and *Madame Bovary*. Fiction appears here as a measure to judge reality as deficient, yet also as a medium to transcend and "correct" prosaic reality and social alienation.

Arlt's own literary mimesis—which generally has to be distinguished from that of his characters—is influenced by an eclectic array of writers. As Beatriz Sarlo has written, Arlt's downtrodden antiheroes struggle to achieve an identity by appropriating different literary forms, both high and low, to compensate for their cultural deprivation: "The feuilleton, the Spanish translations of Russian writers, the sentimental novel, Ponson du Terrail, Dostoyevsky, and Andrejev, all entered into this gigantic process of cannibalization and deformation, of emulation and parody, which is Arlt's practice of writing."[1] In fact, the reading of the Russian classics in Spanish translation was decisive for Arlt's apprehension of the Spanish language, for he was the son of a German father and an Italian-speaking mother from Tirol.

The mediating function of literature, then, is a central aspect of Arlt's and his characters' integration into a desired world, a world of desire. In the urban context of Arlt's writing, namely the Buenos Aires of the 1920s, shaped by massive waves of European immigration and the fermentation of political radicalism, this inwardly projected world of the subject appears as the last residue of individual will in a world that is otherwise shaped by the signs of modernist alienation. As a matter of fact, Arlt, whose literary works are haunted by destitution, crime, madness, and prostitution, is one of the first Latin American writers who fell under the spell of Dostoyevsky—whose influence on Latin American letters generally during the first decades of the twentieth century can hardly be overstated. The reason for this affinity may perhaps be seen in the fact that Argentina's situation during the 1920s resembles the one of Russia at the end of the nineteenth century, when, as Girard mentions, it passed suddenly, without intermediary developments, "from traditional and feudal structures to the most *modern* society."[2] In Argentina, the economic crisis of the year 1929–30 led to a crisis of ideological consensus similar to the one Russia had experienced during the 1870s.[3]

Girard on Dostoyevsky

In *Deceit, Desire, and the Novel*, Girard values literary authors according to the degree to which they dismantle and expose the subject's belief in its own autonomy, the Promethean myth of modernity (259). Yet Girard deconstructs not only the spontaneity of desire, he also states that the novelistic recognition of mimetic desire leads ultimately to its abandonment and transcendence. Therefore, mimetic desire, the "mimetic fallacy," can apparently never be liberating or subversive, but rather it inevitably leads to disillusionment and failure, as Girard demonstrates with regard to paradigmatic novels of the nineteenth century (Stendhal, Flaubert). Even if the concept of psychological unity has long been abandoned among modernist writers, according to Girard they still cultivate a utopian idea of freedom, an individual autonomy that rejects any suggestion of imitation. As Girard writes, "Our contemporary heroes never imitate anyone. They are perfectly autonomous," and they always maintain their "precious freedom intact." [4]

In contrast to these contemporary self-delusions, Girard presents the case of Dostoyevsky as a model for a never-surpassed self-consciousness with regard to the manifestation of Romantic desire. The Russian writer, according to Girard, refutes the psychological unity of the novelistic character, as well as the "metaphysical illusion." [5] The contemporary misreading of Dostoyevsky, he maintains, is grounded in the identification of the protagonist of the *Notes from the Underground* (1864) with the author himself, who, says Girard, exposes and "satirizes" here his own prior Romantic self. [6] Again in contrast, contemporary "neo-Romanticism," by which Girard primarily appears to refer to the existentialist novel of Camus and Sartre, and their dependence on André Gide's reading of Dostoyevsky, centered on the so-called "acte gratuit," recognizes the principle of desire always and only in the other, never in oneself; it admits to the imitation of desire only to the degree that it is distinguished from "original," authentic desire. [7] Modernist demythification, then, leads to its own myth of detachment and autonomy, a subject of nondesire.

In his book on Dostoyevsky (1963) Girard has further elaborated on these ideas, contrasting the (neo-)Romantic idea of self-identity with the paradigmatic self-consciousness of the "double" subject in *Notes from the Underground*, which is marked precisely by his self-observing awareness of the fatal disjunction between grandiloquent aspirations and factual baseness (23). As Victor Brombert has observed in a similar vein: "Situating the adversarial other in himself, the underground man becomes more than the other: he becomes *the others.*" [8] In *Deceit, Desire, and the Novel* Girard writes that the rapprochement of subject and mediator in Dostoyevsky leads to an impulse of sadomasochism, and finally the "apocalyptic" wish of self-destruction: "The ultimate meaning of desire is death but death is not the novel's ultimate meaning" (290). Therefore, the Dostoyevskian protagonist's confrontation with death and nothingness leads to a final "conversion" (think especially of *Crime and Punishment*), similar to the one of Don Quixote. Girard then hypostatizes "the renunciation of metaphysical desire" as the "great conclusion" of the great anti-Romantic novels he analyzes. [9] This is the moment of truth and self-recognition that emerges at the final rupture with mediated desire, when the subject renounces his pride and hence is liberated from servitude to the principle of mimesis. In fact, from Dostoyevsky's viewpoint of an orthodox Christianity, his troubled antiheroes erect only an illusion of autonomy and liberty, and the divorce and contradiction between words and deeds is ultimately a sign of their imperfection, their failure to govern themselves. Thomas Pavel's characterization of the Dostoyevskian antihero is very suggestive in this regard: "The verbal exaltation that animates these beings and makes them hold forth, or ramble on, is in no way the mark of a free subjectivity that extends itself into discourse, as Bakhtin has maintained, but is simply the sign of a profound distress that prevents these beings from seeing into their own interiority and expressing their torments with simplicity."[10]

Arlt's Antiheroes and the Ambivalence of Mediated Desire

Arlt's literary works bear out Girard's belief that any author must be judged individually as to how the mimetic principle works in this particular case. Arlt's novels certainly appear close to Dostoyevsky not only in their auto-confessional structure, but in that they are opposed to the idea of "spontaneous" Romantic desire, as well as the neo-Romantic myth of detachment. Yet, in contrast to Dostoyevsky or Cervantes, they do not lead toward a "conversion," but end invariably and inevitably in defeat; and, as we will see, they are distinguished by a simultaneous critique and justification of the mimetic principle.

Arlt's novelistic and dramatic protagonists achieve presence to the extent that they perform a preconceived image or type. Just like Arlt himself, his literary antiheroes are distinguished by their eclectic reading habits. This is true especially for Silvio Astier, the young protagonist of Arlt's first novel, *El juguete rabioso* (*The Rabid Toy*, 1926), one of the first urban novels in Latin America. Silvio's reading typically mixes the high and the popular: Dostoyevsky, Baudelaire, Nietzsche, Pio Baroja, Victor Hugo, Carolina Invernizio, and especially Ponson du Terrail.[11] Desire in Arlt is always mimetic and eclectic by nature, yet characteristically—and, say, in contrast to Don Quixote—it is often deliberately directed at and attracted to models from the low, marginal edge of the social scale, the criminal, the plebeian, the popular. This inversion of values is not exclusive to Arlt, but may in fact be compared with other examples of contemporary Argentine literature that similarly conceive antiheroes that are popular outlaws, most famously, of course, by way of the myth of the gaucho.[12] Arlt's texts portray dis-integrated subjects, or rather character-masks, who appear as victims of modernization. These figures, typically situated in the lower bourgeoisie, escape from sordid, alienated reality into imaginary counterworlds, which offer them the illusory possibility of self-empowerment.

In *El juguete rabioso*, fifteen-year-old Silvio, together with a group of friends, dreams of becoming a "famous bandolero," after having devoured numerous texts of "literatura bandoleresca."[13] He now recounts to us, in a retrospective, confessional account of his life, his literature-induced dream "to be a bandit and to strangle libidinous magistrates; to right wrongs and to protect the widows."[14] This essentially Romantic conception of the *bandolero*, however, cannot really be enacted in reality, because the state of advanced urbanization in Buenos Aires and the centralization of the police force turns the bandit into a perpetrator of crime pure and simple, deprived of all Romantic associations.[15] This example shows that Arlt's novel adheres, despite its stylization of a marginal outlaw protagonist, to the formal features of the bildungsroman, presenting a simultaneous initiation into literature and crime, whereby the moments of "disillusion" are often located in the reader's realization of the obvious mismatch between dream and reality. For instance, Silvio's wish to become a new Napoleon or Edison, a sort of "superior being," confronted with his modest chemical and technical inventions, evidently demonstrates the failure of imitating such outsized models.

The Arltian individual forever strives to transcend its low social standing, and Silvio's highest wish is not so much money or material well-being, but "the desire for distinction" [*ese anhelo de distinción*].[16] We may recognize here a variation of the psychology of the underground man, who, as Girard writes in his study on Dostoyevsky, compensates his "actual baseness" with an "imaginary grandeur": "But the dream is frenzied and its realization is impossible. The underground hero throws himself into humiliating adventures, and he falls as deeply down in reality as he ascended to the heights in his dream."[17] In fact, early in the novel, when Silvio assembles a "bomb" from discarded technical bits and pieces, this counts for him as supreme evidence of his "intellectual superiority."[18] However, in order to survive he has to enter into the sphere of more prosaic work, and the humbling experiences he undergoes lead Silvio to the retrospective insight into the megalomania of his aspirations: "Oh, how ironic! I who had dreamed of being a great bandit like Rocambole and an ingenious poet like Baudelaire."[19] As this passage shows, the projected act of mimesis conflates programmatically art and crime, in a spirit of calculated transgression that resonates with the contemporary poetics of the avant-garde.[20]

In the last chapter of *El juguete rabioso*, Silvio yet again follows his revered model of Rocambole (the outcast hero of the multivolume adventure novel by Ponsol du Terrail) by imitating his (and Judas's) act of betrayal, namely by giving away the name of a companion, Rengo, with whom he had planned to commit a robbery in the house of a wealthy engineer. This act of betrayal, although it constitutes an instance of imitation, marks the ultimate failure of Silvio. The engineer Arsenio Vitri—to whose social standing Silvio has aspired—reproves him for being a traitor to his friend. Thus neither his dream to succeed socially as an engineer, nor his plan to become a *bandolero*, become true. With regard both to Vitri, the representative of the social elite, and to his companion Rengo, Silvio's stance is distinguished by both admiration and hatred. In the course of the novel, Silvio had repeatedly allied himself with other miserable figures of the city, yet the subject's hatred is ultimately less directed at the socially superior, and much more at these fellow characters, thus revealing a sort of self-hatred at the core of his identity. Girard's comments on the implied social context of Dostoyevsky's underground man apply here: "Underground pride, strange thing that it is, is [collective] pride. The most intense suffering proceeds from the fact that the speaker does not succeed in *distinguishing himself* concretely from the persons that surround him.... All underground individuals believe they are all the more 'unique' to the extent that they are, in fact, alike."[21]

While Silvio himself might believe in the spontaneity of his desire, the novel's retrospective, autobiographical perspective, that is, the difference between Silvio-protagonist and Silvio-narrator (a feature derived from the model of the picaresque, as well as Dostoyevsky), throws a partially ironic light on his aspirations. The repeated attempts and failures to achieve social integration, as well as the collage-like nature of his bizarre technical inventions, and, of course, the collage-like structure of the novel itself, underscore the dispersal of any notion of organic unity and subjectivity, as well as any "romantic" notion of individual artistic originality—and it thus exposes and comments upon traditional principles of literary realism, but it also might be said to implicitly comment on the paradoxes of the aesthetics of the avant-garde.[22] In this sense, the novel demonstrates the constructedness, and hence the nonspontaneity, of desire and art, as well as the inevitable failure of the attempt to construct a solid self from consecrated models of heroism. Yet, in contrast to Girard's examples, namely the "classic" novels of disillusion (Cervantes, Stendhal), in Arlt artifice and deception are ultimately not renounced, but, from the perspective of the narrating self, rather consciously adopted in the service of an ultimately anti-Romantic, explicitly theatrical conception of personhood, as it is quite typical for the vanguard cultural context of the 1920s, as well as Arlt's own experiments with Pirandellian metatheater during the early 1930s.[23]

Such ideas are further developed in Arlt's most famous novel, *Los Siete Locos* (*The Seven Madmen*, 1929), where the protagonist Remo Erdosain's subjectivity is similarly shaped by the ideas of melodrama and popular culture. Yet, in contrast to the parody of the bildungsroman in *El juguete rabioso*, this later novel, as the title already indicates, stresses more the collective dimension of metaphysical desire, which, according to Girard, presupposes a greater proximity of the mediator to the subject, and leads, in Dostoyevsky, as well as in Arlt, to a "vertigo of nothingness" and "orgy of destruction."[24]

As in Dostoyevsky's *The Double* (1846), the protagonist of *Los Siete Locos* is a low-standing, "depersonalized" employee,[25] whose humiliating social position is compensated by the seductions of adventure. Erdosain is an impoverished bill collector for a sugar company, who is fired after he has stolen some money from the company, and eventually also left by his wife. He joins a motley group of pseudo-revolutionaries, a secret society that plans to finance a social revolution on a global scale with a chain of brothels, and who are led by the charismatic figure of the Astrologer, "the *manager* of madmen" [*el* manager *de locos*]. The eponymous "madmen," who are "characterized" precisely in terms of embodying a certain role or type, are more often referred to with their epithets than with their personal names (Buscador del Oro, La Coja, el Rufián Melancólico, el Hombre que vio a la Partera, la Bizca).[26] Although Erdosain is also assigned a specific role by the Astrologer, namely the function of constructing chemical industries for the production of toxic substances, the novel dedicates considerable space to the exploration of his tormented psyche, and hence combines typification and "masked" roles with a sustained, yet incoherent, analysis of an individual consciousness.

Also in *Los Siete Locos*, then, the characters are frequently shown to be "imitators" in the vein of literary models, and consequently reality appears less wonderful or "interesting" than what they have apprehended themselves from their reading of novels.[27] Even when in some cases the opposite is suggested—that is, that reality is as "novelistic" as a novel[28]—there still remains the idea of the novel as embodying a principle of wonder and suspension of logic, distinct from pedestrian reality. In yet another variation of this theme, a character may appeal to a truth as distinct from the lies, distortions, stereotypes, or absurdities of novels.[29] In one striking instance, Erdosain, dreaming of scientific experiments with beta rays, invokes the "absurd character in an English novel"[30] who forever preserves his youth (an allusion to *The Picture of Dorian Gray*, a model for the link between duplicity, art, and crime), thus reinforcing the reader's sense that the character's search for self-identity is bound up with a kind of metaliterary and metatheatrical chain, in which every mask hides yet another mask. Or, when Erdosain demonstrates impassiveness (in front of a fellow madman's wife), he sees himself as enacting a comic performance, "like one of those bankers in the novels of Xavier de Montepin . . . with the inward happiness of being able to represent the comedy of the unemotional man."[31] Significantly, this impassiveness surprises Erdosain himself, since it appears as an altogether sudden manifestation, discontinuous with his previous behavior.[32] When he dreams of a millionaire who would finance and hence realize his technical inventions, the narrator lets us know that Erdosain's imagination is conceived as a kind of theatrical scene.[33] Yet even this dream-fantasy, the imagined conversation with the millionaire, becomes somehow too tedious for Erdosain, who is always impatient with the practical details that stand in the way of sudden transformation.[34] Another of the madmen, the pharmacist Ergueta, is "mad" insofar as he sees his life modeled on the narratives of the Bible, to the extent that he justifies his marriage with a prostitute on these grounds, and he sees the idea of revolution as an imminent form of spiritual redemption.[35] Similarly, the sudden emergence of Ergueta's wife, her asking Erdosain for help, while confronting him with her life story and an account of Ergueta's madness, makes Erdosain think that this "drama" is to be treasured like a "novelistic element."[36] In general, Erdosain actively strives for the achievement of something unexpected that would reveal him as radically different from himself, and which would simultaneously be a release from his "incoherence" and "madness."[37] The truth pursued by the various characters is generally rooted in fictions and the desire for self-realization.[38]

As a matter of fact, for these "mad" characters "reality" constantly shows itself as deficient. As soon as Erdosain has conceived the plan to kill his personal enemy Barsut—a criminal act that would constitute for him a singular, Dostoyevskian, and "gratuitous" act of self-affirmation "'to be' by way of a crime"[39]—it is already revealed as betraying this very hope: "Erdosain already complained that the 'plan' was so simple and so little like a novel. He would have appreciated a more dangerous, less geometric adventure."[40] Erdosain's feeling of hatred toward Gregorio Barsut, the cousin of his wife Elsa, who has betrayed Erdosain's theft of his employer, and had later slapped him in the face, marks the latter as a sort of scapegoat, as well as his double, whereby the position of enacting and suffering humiliation are constantly reversed—the "plot" of the novel revolves around the plan to kidnap and kill Barsut (which later turns out be only "staged" for Erdosain by the Astrologer). Barsut is repeatedly referred to as the figure of the "other,"[41] and their mutual relation is described as a form of triangular desire, marked by mutual "envy"[42] and hatred: "Between them existed an undefined, obscure situation. One of those situations, which two men who despise each other, tolerate for reasons independent of their will."[43]

The existential angst of Erdosain, then, is countered by the idea of a fundamentally discontinuous notion of subjectivity, where identity can always abruptly and marvelously re-invent itself, "as in the plots of North American movies, where yesterday's beggar is today the director of a secret society, and the gold-digging secretary turns out to be a multimillionairess in disguise."[44] This utopian perspective might be seen as the counterpart to the urban alienation of Erdosain, the shaky ground of his identity. Yet Arlt's antihero has a distinctively ambivalent view of the cinema, since it embodies not only the desire for wish-fulfillment and heroic transformation, the desire to become the Other,[45] but also, and in contrast to the medium of the novel, the threat of alienation, the fear that the simulated movements are ultimately devoid of life. In the chapter that explicates Erdosain's plan for self-affirmation by way of committing murder, the cinema, alongside other technological media, serves as a metaphor for his sense that the real life is situated outside the limits of his own being/body, that he is, as it were, the distanced spectator of himself.[46]

As we have seen, Arlt's characters are generally defined by the discourse of their desire. Yet to a certain extent the characters are also their own narrators, insofar as they choose and model their own invented self-representation in front of others, and generally try to escape from their sad reality by way of narrations in front of a public. The individual failure of figures such as Erdosain and Barsut contrasts with the literary fame they achieve by having become characters of the novel we are reading (Erdosain shortly before his death tells his life story to the marginal homodiegetic narrator)—or indeed the representation of their life in a Hollywood film that is anticipated at the end of the novel's sequel, *Los Lanzallamas* (*The Flame Throwers*, 1931), with Barsut as the main protagonist.[47]

While the antihero Erdosain is introverted and essentially incapable to act (similar to other novelistic antiheroes in the modernist novel, as in Kafka or Svevo), the counterfigure of the Astrologer is a person of power who actively fabricates and disseminates fantasies, lies, and dreams. The Astrologer is conceived as a cynical authoritarian figure, a prophet and manipulator, who is ultimately quite indifferent to the various ideologies (fascism, communism) he invokes. The power of the Astrologer derives precisely from his capacity to appropriate media, and thus to instigate a mimetic desire and to exert control over the individual.[48] The supposed movement of social revolution is indeed defined as a manipulation and reenactment of established, yet radically divergent ideas; it is explicitly referred to as an "imitation" of previous movements of social transformation: "we will be Bolshevists, fascists, atheists, militarists, in diverse states of initiation."[49] In other words, the revolution is a "farce," and this is precisely the word used at the first meeting of the group members in the den of the Astrologer. The participants are all defined in terms of a specific role they assume in order to hide their true identity and their egoistic motives. In fact, the conceit of the staging of the "revolution" is the novel's most complex expression of theatricality and the uses of fiction. Characteristically, in the long discourse in which the Astrologer lays out his program of mystic-spectacular power ("Discurso del Astrólogo"), he stresses how he aims to invent a new image of a god for the masses hungry for miracles, making use of the sensationalist press, photography, and cinematography,[50] thus creating the image of a pseudo-Christ figure whose physiognomy would be a cross "between Krishnamurti and Rudolph Valentino."[51]

The creation of such manipulative fictions is thus portrayed as both a life-sustaining force and as an essential part of the modern mechanics of power. Significantly, for Erdosain the mirage of the "strong man" is less an ideological temptation, but it is instilled in him through mediatic representation; the longing for presence is informed by mediated images of the figure of the dictator. While it is of course well known that figures such as Hitler and Mussolini built their power to a large extent on the manipulation of their media images, the fascination of these images for Erdosain, and, by extension perhaps, for the Argentina of the 1930s, lies in the fact that their exclusive presence by way of media heightens their phantasmagoric status, just as *Los Siete Locos* is generally distinguished by a geopolitical imaginary that links the concrete city space of an anonymous Buenos Aires with references to Hollywood, Brazil, and a host of other imagined, or exotic locations.[52] As Fernando Rosenberg has pointed out in this regard, the modernity of *Los Siete Locos* resides to a large extent in the disembodied, mediated presence of "globalized" names and references.[53] In this context, then, the mechanical reproduction of images does not diminish their "aura," as Walter Benjamin would have it, but rather heightens their auratic, fantasy-inducing role. In *Los Siete Locos*, both subjective self-affirmation and quasi-political interpellation are conditioned by the appropriation of certain culturally mediated models.

In Arlt, the romantic-utopian impulse is primarily located on the level of the protagonist, not on the level of the author, who, on the contrary, is intent upon showing how the desire for presence is the result of social and cultural conventions, as shaped by different media. This introduces, by way of ideological critique, the element of critical self-consciousness and revision appreciated by Girard in Dostoyevsky. Arlt's lowly individuals have no other choice but to fabricate and "invent" their identity by stealing and reassembling the bits and pieces they can find, to transform their lives by art high and low, and, in the process, to infuse art with new life.[54] Arlt's work in general oscillates between this desire for liberation and the failure following from the constraints of literary and social conventions. One of Arlt's favorite authors was Cervantes, and he was similarly interested in protagonists who are misguided by the false consciousness of literary mimesis. Both authors denounced the mimetic credulity of their protagonists, but they recognized the vital attractions of "popular literature," from the romance to the feuilleton, as ultimately legitimate media to voice a dissatisfaction with reality. In this sense, Arlt's paradoxical staging of mimetic desire demonstrates the aporias of a specifically modernist situation in which the false romanticism of desire is dramatically heightened, and it can no longer be renounced, as Girard would have it, but rather is the collective sign of a social and psychological utopia.[55]

Notes

1. Beatriz Sarlo, *Una modernidad periférica: Buenos Aires 1929 y 1930* (Buenos Aires: Nueva Visión, 1988), 53. All translations are my own. On Arlt's reading, see also Rita Gnutzmann, "Introducción," in Roberto Arlt, *El juguete rabioso* (Madrid: Cátedra, 2011), 24–29.

2. René Girard, *Deceit, Desire, and the Novel: Self and Other in Literary Structure*, trans. Yvonne Freccero (Baltimore: Johns Hopkins University Press, 1965), 44.

3. On the parallel Russia/Argentina, cf. José Amicola, "Elógio de la razón y la locura," in Roberto Arlt, *Los siete locos. Los lanzallamas*, ed. Mario Goloboff (Madrid: Colección Archivos, 2000), 679; cf. also the suggestive remarks in Ernesto Sabato, *El escritor y sus fantasmas* (Barcelona: Seix Barral, 2011), 14–15.

4. Girard, *Deceit, Desire, and the Novel*, 258.

5. Girard, *Deceit, Desire, and the Novel*, 259.

6. Girard, *Deceit, Desire, and the Novel*, 260.

7. Girard, *Deceit, Desire, and the Novel*, 269.

8. Victor Brombert, *In Praise of Antiheroes: Figures and Themes in Modern European Literature, 1830–1980* (Chicago: University of Chicago Press, 2001), 41.

9. Girard, *Deceit, Desire, and the Novel*, 291, 293–94.

10. Thomas Pavel, *La Pensée du Roman* (Paris: Gallimard, 2003), 339.

11. Arlt, *El juguete rabioso*, 93.

12. José Morales Saraiva, "Semántica de la desilusión en *El juguete rabioso* de Roberto Arlt," in *Roberto Arlt: Una modernidad argentina*, ed. José Morales Saraiva and Barbara Schuchard (Frankfurt am Main: Vervuert, 2001), 31.

13. Arlt, *El juguete rabioso*, 87.

14. Arlt, *El juguete rabioso*, 89.

15. Saraiva, "Semántica de la desilusión," 32.

16. Arlt, *El juguete rabioso*, 173.

17. René Girard, *Resurrection from the Underground: Feodor Dostoevsky*, ed. and trans. James G. Williams (New York: Crossroad Publishing Company, 1997), 18.

18. Arlt, *El juguete rabioso*, 93.

19. Arlt, *El juguete rabioso*, 135.

20. See Vicky Unruh, *Latin American Vanguards: The Art of Contentious Encounters* (Berkeley: University of California Press, 1994), 84–94; Josefina Ludmer, *The Corpus Delicti: A Manual of Argentine Fictions*, trans. Glen S. Close (Pittsburgh: University of Pittsburgh Press, 2004), esp. 113–16.

21. Girard, *Resurrection from the Underground*, 21.

22. Unruh, *Latin American Vanguards*, 91.

23. Arlt's most sophisticated play, *Saverio el cruel* (1935), in which the characters perform an elaborate fiction for the credulous protagonist, recalls the staging of fictions in *Don Quixote*, as well as Pirandello's *Henry IV* (1922).

24. Girard, *Deceit, Desire, and the Novel*, 282.

25. Girard, *Resurrection from the Underground*, 21.

26. As Paul Jordan writes: "Although characters are present in the sense that names are associated with attributes, there are in this novel no characters in the sense of discrete representations of individual beings"; *Roberto Arlt: A Narrative Journey* (London: King's College London, Department of Spanish and Spanish-American Studies, 2000), 43. Óscar Masota speaks of "the unnovelistic quality of the characters"; *Sexo y traición en Roberto Arlt* (Buenos Aires: Jorge Alvarez, 1982), 18.

27. Roberto Arlt, *Los Siete Locos*, ed. Flora Guzmán (Madrid: Cátedra, 1992), 288.

28. Arlt, *Los Siete Locos*, 115, 120.

29. Arlt, *Los Siete Locos*, 118, 163, 263.

30. Arlt, *Los Siete Locos*, 106.

31. Arlt, *Los Siete Locos*, 243–44.

32. Arlt, *Los Siete Locos*, 244.

33. Arlt, *Los Siete Locos* 104.

34. Arlt, *Los Siete Locos* 205.

35. Arlt, *Los Siete Locos*, 93, 261.

36. Arlt, *Los Siete Locos*, 247.

37. Arlt, *Los Siete Locos*, 189.

38. Loris Tassi, *Variazioni sul tema della letteratura: L'opera di Roberto Arlt* (Rome: Aracne, 2007).

39. Arlt, *Los Siete Locos*, 153.

40. Arlt, *Los Siete Locos*, 163.

41. Arlt, *Los Siete Locos*, 98.

42. Arlt, *Los Siete Locos*, 98.

43. Arlt, *Los Siete Locos*, 100.

44. Arlt, *Los Siete Locos*, 86.

45. Arlt, *Los Siete Locos*, 198.

46. Arlt, *Los Siete Locos*, 135.

47. Arlt, *Los Siete Locos. Los Lanzallamas*, ed. Goloboff, 598.

48. On the relation between mimesis, power, and social control, see the perceptive remarks in Gunter Gebauer and Christoph Wulf, *Mimesis: Kultur, Kunst, Gesellschaft* (Hamburg: Rowohlt, 1992), 332–34.

49. Arlt, *Los Siete Locos*, 214.

50. Arlt, *Los Siete Locos*, 308.

51. Arlt, *Los Siete Locos*, 213.

52. Arlt, *Los Siete Locos*, 90.

53. Fernando J. Rosenberg, *The Avantgarde and Geopolitics in Latin America* (Pittsburgh: University of Pittsburgh Press, 2006), 49–62.

54. See Unruh, *Latin American Vanguards*, 183.

55. It seems to me that Girard, less in *Deceit, Desire, and the Novel* than in *Evolution and Conversion*, is more willing to recognize the liberating potential of mimetic desire, its participation in the process of building an individual identity (failed or not), where one's own culture is seen as a copy, not a *creatio ex nihilo*. René Girard, *Evolution and Conversion: Dialogues on the Origin of Culture*, with Pierpaolo Antonello and João Cezar de Castro Rocha (New York: Continuum, 2007), 58.

Recantation without Conversion

Desire, Mimesis, and the Paradox of Engagement in Pier Paolo Pasolini's *Petrolio*

Christoph F. E. Holzhey

At the end of his life, Pier Paolo Pasolini famously recants. Published a week after his death and dated five months earlier, his "Abiura dalla *Trilogia della vita*" reiterates his diagnosis of a devastating cultural and anthropological transformation brought about by mass media and consumerist power, and highlights the "trauma" inflicted on private sexual lives such as his own, with the result that "what in sexual fantasies was pain and joy has become suicidal disappointment, shapeless torpor."[1] Pasolini explains that the films comprising the *Trilogy of Life—The Decameron* (1971), *The Canterbury Tales* (1972), and *Arabian Nights* (1974)—were based on the idea of presenting "'innocent' bodies with the archaic, dark, vital violence of their sexual organs" as the "last bulwark of reality" against the triumphant "unreality" imposed by the models of mass media.[2] While he had previously thought that such bodies could still be found, their subsequent transformation not only turned desire into repulsion, but also retroactively—and therefore indeed traumatically—revealed to him his past illusions. He can now only say that "for some years I have been able to delude myself."[3]

Such disillusionment and recantation are the material for great novels according to René Girard's *Deceit, Desire, and the Novel*. Against the "Romantic" assumption of desire spontaneously originating from a substantial self,

233

Girard insists that all desire is based on imitation and may engage in dynamics of degradation. Girard speaks of a "dynamic structure in the form of a descending spiral" and proclaims that the "individual and collective history of secondhand desire always moves toward nothingness and death,"[4] thereby formalizing the pattern of degradation analyzed in *Deceit, Desire, and the Novel* both within individual novels and in their totality. Among the late "degraded forms of mediated desire" toward which "every metaphysical desire . . . tends" is masochism, which in turn "clearly reveals the contradiction which forms the basis of metaphysical desire."[5] Insisting on the priority of existential masochism before both sexual masochism and sadism, Girard emphasizes that even in sexual masochism, it is not suffering that is desired, but the "mediator's presence, contact with the sacred."[6] Girard rejects the reassuring view of "restricting the deplorable consequences of metaphysical desire" to the masochist conceived as "a monster whose sentiments have nothing in common with those of 'normal' people" and thereby universalizes his understanding of masochism while keeping its stigma as something to be deplored and avoided. The only escape appears to be to convert and renounce desire, which is precisely what Girard maintains happens in the conclusion of all novels at the moment of the hero's death: "All novelistic conclusions are conversions" and "All the heroes, in the conclusion, utter words which *clearly contradict their former ideas*."[7]

Girard relates the hero's tragic conversion in death in an intriguing way to the author. He maintains that "the title of hero of a novel must be reserved for the character who triumphs over metaphysical desire in a tragic conclusion and thus becomes capable of writing the novel. The hero and his creator are separated throughout the novel but come together in the conclusion."[8] Novels, in Girard's account, are thus postconversion narratives about the trials and tribulations of preconversion lives. In the case of Proust, this also applies to the narrator, who is cured in death and comes to life again as novelist, reappearing "in person in the body of this novel."[9]

Pasolini was indeed working on a novel while formulating his recantation and speaking of a cessation of desire. In early 1975, Pasolini writes: "my feeling in fact is a 'ceasing to love.'"[10] Unfinished when he was murdered in 1975, *Petrolio* was described by Pasolini as a "kind of 'summa' of all my experiences, all my memories," to be "presented in the form of a critical edition of an unpublished text (considered a monumental work, a modern *Satyricon*)."[11]

The novel resonates in many ways with Girard's framework, as it reflects extensively on the nature of desire, highlights the important role of imitation in its "degradation," and includes also, for instance, extensive scenes of (sexual) masochism linked to a sense of the sacred. It even includes Pasolini's recantation and attributes it to the novel's protagonist, Carlo.[12] What is more, Pasolini also insists, in a letter to Alberto Moravia now included in the novel, that he is addressing the readers not as a conventional narrator but "as myself, in flesh and bone."[13] Often read as Pasolini's final blow against everything in which he had believed in the past and even as his testamentary act of self-destruction, the novel could thus appear as a postconversion novel, which in its representation of past desires contrasted with their postconversion absence could be placed in continuation of the descending line Girard traces from Cervantes via Stendhal and Proust to the "Dostoyevskian Apocalypse."

At the same time, everything in *Petrolio* seems to oppose this kind of conversion narrative. Interested in a meditation on the form itself, it is a text that "does not begin,"[14] proceeds as an accumulation of fragments, and resists completion and linearity. "Mine is a / novel / not 'on a spit' [*a schidionata*] but 'in a swarm' [*a brulichio*], and so it's understandable if the reader remains a little < ... > disoriented,"[15] writes the narrator in one of his many metanarrative comments. Such a busily swarming and deliberately confusing form not only signals an absence of conversion but arguably also satisfies a desire resisting conversion. While the novel is centrally concerned with mimetic desire and exhibits many of the vicissitudes analyzed by Girard, it is also more attuned to the ambivalence of mimetic desire and allows for alternative developments. *Petrolio* thereby questions the tragic "necessity" of conversion-in-death, on which *Deceit, Desire, and the Novel* insists as the "normative" telos of novels and, by doing so, makes space for a however paradoxical form of ongoing political engagement.

The part on which I will focus is the account of a vision in which Carlo, the novel's protagonist, observes a young man named "The Shit" (*Il Merda*) and his girlfriend Cinzia go through a sort of contemporary hell on the outskirts of Rome. It is an ironic rewriting of Dante's *Inferno* in the shape of fifteen "Gironi," where the sins of Dante's Hell are replaced by what Pasolini deems to be the sins of contemporary society with its consumerism and bourgeois aspirations: sins like conformism, bourgeois respectability and dignity, ugliness, cowardice, false tolerance, vulgarity. Each Girone is constructed in a double way: first, what the text calls the "Real Scene" or "Reality" is presented,[16] namely the condition of the subproletariat in the mid-1960s before the so-called Italian "Economic Miracle" and the advent of neocapitalism, and then its current corrupted version, which the text calls "Vision." The structure highlights the importance of imitation for what Pasolini describes in drastic terms as an "anthropological mutation" and even "genocide,"[17] that is, the destruction of nonbourgeois classes through consumerist power.[18] Almost every infernal Girone is characterized by the presence of a "Model," which lies buried in the heart of the Girone within a small tomb. On the tomb a little statue is placed that reproduces the features of the Model, and its power to induce mimesis is so strong that the inhabitants of the Girone are fully absorbed in imitating it: "Imitation . . . is the 'formal' basis of their code of existence."[19]

The several Gironi form a "museum of horrors" that culminates, in the final Girone, with the display of the new heterosexual couple. This new format of relationship is portrayed pitilessly as the embodiment of pride, self-righteousness, and exhibitionist self-absorption:

> The couples are of all types; but they all behave in exactly the same way, observing the following rules: 1) They expect the admiration of the bystanders, though they manage, smiling and serene for the most part, not to look at anyone even for an instant; 2) They manifest in the most unequivocal way their utter self-sufficiency and total lack of interest in anything that doesn't have to do with their xxx relationship.[20]

The narrator comments on the insincerity of the love displayed and links it to ugliness, which he keeps emphasizing as the central feature in The Shit's vision:

> The ostentatiousness of the love that binds the couples . . . clearly reveals that these relationships \loves\ are deeply insincere. . . . And this is the reason that even in this Girone, where there are also Women, the spirit of Ugliness and Repulsiveness prevails.[21]

Given the strong resonances with mimetic theory, one might be tempted to interpret the critique of insincerity to be equivalent to a critique of desires grounded in imitation. While this would mean holding onto the ideal of a true, spontaneous desire—even if such desire should eventually be recognized impossible, in which case all desire gets rejected—the wider context imposes a different reading, namely that what is denounced is a love so insincere that it is unreal, devoid of any desire or interest whatsoever and therefore incapable of eliciting desire or interest.

Nearing the end of The Shit's vision, the narrator comments on the painful process of writing the vision:

> How much trouble and anguish it has cost me to describe it, I do not wish to tell the reader; it will be enough for me to remind him that it is terrible to inhabit and know a world where eyes are no longer able to give a look—I do not say of love, but even of curiosity or sympathy.[22]

This painful anguish over a dying desire indicates that the conversion Girard demands of true novelists has not (yet) fully occurred, that is, that the narrator has not (yet) fully renounced desire. Although Girard also emphasizes the pain in conversion, he describes the result of a "genuine conversion" as pure bliss.[23] This is not to say that *Deceit, Desire, and the Novel* does not have a place for a cessation of desire without conversion. However, it reads all appearances of nondesire as a strategy or pose (what Girard calls "coquetry" or "pseudo-narcissism"),[24] which only aggravate the degradation of desire and thereby confirm the necessity of renouncing desire through conversion. Girard continues to hold onto the necessity of conversion even when desire seems to exhaust itself. In his essay "Conversion in Literature and Christianity," for instance, the cycles of frustration to which mimetic desire is said necessarily to lead—because it is either hindered from reaching its objects or disappointed by them—involves the search for ever new models up to the point "when we are totally disenchanted and cannot find any new model. This is the worst kind of frustration, the one the experts call post-modern or post-Christian desire; perhaps one could even call it post-mimetic desire."[25] He proceeds by calling the "mortality of desire . . . the real problem in our world," but then quickly returns to conversion as the only way out of the circularity of desire. He does not stop to conceptualize the remarkable suggestion of "post-mimetic desire," which would seem to contradict his usual insistence that mimetic desire is sufficient to account for all vicissitudes of desire.

However, if mimetic desire takes on a central role in Girard's frame-work, it is because it does not have any ontological grounding per se (only imitation and appetites do) but it is an expression of a particular historical configuration. In *Deceit, Desire, and the Novel* the analytical starting point is a notion of desire called "Romantic," according to which desire is an expres-sion of the being of a substantial, autonomous, self-sufficient self. The admi-rably resourceful and persevering demonstration that imitation is involved in all cases where a subject of literature appears to exhibit such a desire derived from, or induced by, an external principle or being, lends plausi-bility to the conclusion that all desire is based on imitation. Yet this does not lead Girard to abandon a "Romantic" conception of desire in terms of "being." Instead, he effectively performs a reversal, turning desire's assumed origin into desire's aim: desire from being (i.e., emerged as imitation from other's desires) becomes desire for being. At times, it seems as if mimetic desire is to explain the necessary emergence of a metaphysical desire, but if object and model can and must eventually disappear in the unfolding of mimetic desire, it is only because desire is assumed to be metaphysical from the start. In *Violence and the Sacred*, Girard in fact explicitly derives mimetic desire from a desire for being.[26] Desire here is somehow "spontane-ous" rather than mimetic, after all: lacking being, it has being as its aim. In Freudian terms, one would have to say that if Girardian desire is doomed to continuous failure and frustration it is because satisfaction is exclusively defined in terms of narcissistic pleasures, which Girard also foregrounds in masochism when he insists that the "masochist desires exactly what we ourselves desire: autonomy and a god-like self-control, his own self-esteem and the esteem of others."[27]

It is hard to contradict such a view on desire as essentially metaphysical, which is as pervasive as it is persuasive, given that it is self-consistent and can absorb all apparent exceptions. If desire is metaphysical and has death as its truth and inevitable end, all attempts at fulfillment are bound to turn out in vain. Girard speaks of an "extreme weakness"[28] where Lacanians would invoke an essential lack. In either case, no one—however privileged—is spared from it. Desire, in this picture, would only be fulfilled by achieving godlike autonomy, the impossibility of which makes even masters become slaves. In this way, even masochism and the submission to socially or intel-lectually inferior others,[29] which would seem the opposite of seeking to prevail in the game of internal mediation and rivalry, can be understood as a consequence of metaphysical desire.

A theory that takes desire to be fully mimetic is less stable than this: it is thoroughly paradoxical.[30] What makes paradoxes interesting here is that rather than resisting sense, they allow for self-consistent solutions that reinforce themselves through positive feedback. This mechanism is central in Girard's argumentation and works well to make plausible the spiraling, escalating, and catastrophic dynamics on which he keeps insisting.[31] However, the self-confirming runaway solutions make it all too easy to forget that systems with positive feedback, precisely because of the paradoxical instability underlying them, can generally be expected to have several self-consistent but also incommensurable solutions.[32] This is one way to understand the debates on whether to ground desire in lack or excess, or also to privilege desire or pleasure as a theoretical category[33]—debates that became prominent just around the time when *Petrolio* was written and a larger interest in literature's mobilization of paradoxical desires and pleasures developed.[34]

Such a multistable structure of paradox is also to be expected in a fully mimetic theory of desire that has no fixed ground to which it can reduce all manifestations of desire by symptomatically reading experiences of pain and pleasure respectively as confirmation for the futility of desire and for the subject's delusion. In Girard's sophisticated analysis of desire, pleasure and pain play in fact an important role that is surprisingly undertheorized. Frustration of desire, for instance, is portrayed as painful, and it would seem that such pain motivates the multiple transformations of desire and ultimately provides the condition for conversion, but there seems to be no place in his framework for a desire to alleviate pain or to repeat pleasure.[35] While Girard rejects the mistake of making suffering the actual object of desire in masochism, he does not allow for the possibility that pleasure may be the object of the masochist's desire and that this desire may be fulfilled, albeit by more paradoxical than exclusively narcissistic forms of pleasure.

Petrolio narrates several masochistic scenes of Carlo enjoying submission to subproletarian boys and men. For instance, in a long note he pays some twenty boys to allow him to service them in a field, and while the encounters are no doubt humiliating and painful, they also fulfill Carlo's desire, which halfway through "had finally become the desire for depravity, for obscenity, for excess."[36] And another long note describes Carlo's relationship with the Sicilian waiter Carmelo and speaks of a "kind of comic satisfaction" coexisting in Carlo with the "marvelous giddiness and the . . . overpowering contrition" of an "obedient slave," of "marvelous martyrdom," and of there "no longer [being] anything that divided Carlo from his desire, which until now he had always considered unrealizable."[37]

It does not seem implausible that Carlo's—like Pasolini's earlier—fascination with—and desire for—"others" is imbued with fantasies of their divine autonomy and participation in the sacred, of their insensitivity to the world of the self-hating bourgeois, and of their refusal to reciprocate. Nor that he loses interest, becomes disinterested, and even disgusted once he recognizes in these others the mimetic desire of entering his bourgeois world. At the same time, one can also take seriously the satisfaction that the narrator attributes to masochistic encounters with others in the past and the horror he attributes to the vision of being without any form of desire. What is more, one can also take seriously the explanation that the vision suggests for the loss of desire and that involves neither conversion nor some worry about the imitative nature of desire, but on the contrary the acknowledgment of a mimetic relationship to others. Mimetic desire is indeed taken for granted here, and what is deplored is the absence of desires capable of eliciting desire, as the text underlines by repeating a couple of pages later almost verbatim the striking formulation about love, curiosity and sympathy:

> /he thought/ < . . . > that in all the crowds of young men and boys who populated the Gironi and Bolge of Torpignattara THERE WAS NOT A SINGLE ONE who had had toward someone or something a look, I will not say of love or sympathy, but simply of curiosity.[38]

Rather than mourning the impossibility of spontaneous desire, *Petrolio* embraces the way desire feeds upon itself through imitation, indicates that this can work both to increase or decrease it, and thereby breaks up teleological structures.

The third Girone, for instance, makes it clear that the past also was ruled by models, which are therefore not considered as negative per se but rather as necessary for a happiness anchored in what Pasolini calls "Reality" and endows with a sense of the sacred:[39]

the attitude that is isolated and revealed in this Girone does not have a Model ... that can be held up /concretely/ as an object of Imitation, replacing the old one, which preceded it in earlier centuries and was valid, in fact, until a few years ago. A glance at the "double," the profound scene of the original reality that remains in the < ... > of the Vision—and already yellowed, like an old photograph—leaves no doubt about what the earlier Imitation /and Value / < ... > consisted of: which have now, apparently, been overtaken by history. There is a holiday atmosphere, one of happiness: sun and poverty. The ordinary time is precisely that of the dream. A late spring, I repeat, or a warm winter. There is no reference point. But everything is suspended as if it were eternal.[40]

In the Vision of the contemporary situation, "Everything is the opposite" and it is the "absence of a Model" that is presented as the cause of painful disorientation:

the young suffer /atrociously/ from this deprivation; they don't know whom they should resemble, that is, what Model to follow. They have some models ... but this Model, which represents certainty in the eternal values of existence, that is, in health, doesn't exist.[41]

Pasolini's critical contrast of the present with the past resonates in some ways with the conservative history of decline from external to internal and mutual mediation that Girard narrates in *Deceit, Desire, and the Novel* and links to processes of democratization and increasing equality, leading to the fragmentation and decomposition of the self as mediators multiply and become unstable.[42] However, while Girard and Pasolini are similarly worried about the dissolution not only of stable models but also of class differences, there are notable differences. In Girard, the preferred mode of external mediation depends foremost on a social stratification that is hierarchical and ultimately secured through "vertical transcendency" and the divine right of the supreme ruler. An aristocratic perspective informs the view on the degradation toward internal mediation, for which the French Revolution provides a paradigm.[43] Pasolini, by contrast, focuses on the poor and on their transformation through contemporary consumerism. The scorn heaped on the conformism that makes the people populating The Shit's vision assimilate not only to each other but also to the bourgeoisie may be unsettling and Pasolini's critique of the "intermingling of classes" (*interclassismo*) is understandably controversial. However, it should be noted that in the second Girone, which isolates the model of "dress codes and conformity to them" and concludes that "it's a humiliating and deplorable phenomenon, the intermingling of classes," the point is that "social equality," which here only concerns wearing the same clothes, was not reached because the poor struggled for it, but in a patronizing way, namely "because it has been conceded to them."[44] Rather than the maintenance of a vertical social hierarchy sustained by a unique model for all, the issue here is a horizontal structuring sustained by a unique model for each. In the third Girone of the lost model, the positive description of the past indeed asserts:

> What is common to all is the consciousness that they are following a unique Model: that of their street, their neighborhood, their universe. A unique Model that, although it entails poverty, is the best and most sympathetic Model in the world. That ensures for them, I repeat, inner strength, consistency, and therefore health.[45]

Rather than an undifferentiated mass with desires stabilized through the vertical remoteness of their models, the poor are here regarded as culturally diversified, each grounded by a stable and unique model because they lived in distinct, regionally separate universes. This is what makes for their reality in Pasolini's emphatic sense, indicated, for instance, in the later passage: "Distinct (from region to region, from city to city, from center to periphery). Singular, particular. Therefore *real*."[46] While this notion of reality is also infused with a sense of the sacred, it does not rely on vertical transcendency. It corresponds rather to the dreamlike "holiday atmosphere," where "everything is suspended as if it were eternal," while being opposed to the deplored historical process of homologizing irrealization where reality is only present as a memory or "yellowed" image.[47]

Pasolini's fascination with the poor as reality—be it the Friulian peasants, Roman or Neapolitan subproletariat, the non-European other in the so-called Third World, or the archaic others of antique myths—can thus be seen to rely not on a hierarchical relationship, but on incommensurability, that is, on a nonrelational difference both to and among them. One could say that it depends on the relative autonomy, completeness, and closure of alternative, nonbourgeois universes, provided that one remembers that these do not consist of spontaneously desiring "Romantic" individuals, but of different classes or distinct, singular and particular groups, each with their own models and traditions.

In terms of Girard's explanation of masochism, it seems necessary to distinguish here: Carlo—like Pasolini—might be fascinated by subproletarian others who could not care less about him, his position and erudition, who despise him and have sex with him only against payment, but what is painful in The Shit's vision is that they don't even desire each other rather than they are not individually self-sufficient. Pasolini's *abiura* thus signals a conversion not of himself but rather of those who were (thought to be) others to the bourgeois-capitalist order. Pasolini's desire does not change in its aim, but it can no longer find objects.[48] It may be frustrated, but far from renouncing it, Pasolini insists on it and seeks to adapt to the changed situation by adopting different forms of engagement and intervention: no longer a celebration of sexuality, for instance—which he recognizes to be all too easily instrumentalized by integrating power[49]—but a ruthless satire on the conformist, corrupted behavior of the formerly cherished others.

What sustains and enables such a critique is ultimately a different concept of desire, one that is not premised upon a fundamental metaphysical desire or an essential lack (of being) and that can never be fulfilled by definition, but one that is incapable of finding appropriate objects only at this particular sociohistorical moment. The pain and dismay expressed in Pasolini over the absence of love, sympathy, or even just curiosity points in this direction, seeing that curiosity expresses an openness toward novelty, change, and difference rather than a desire based on lack. Ultimately, however, the choice between different theories of desire and pleasure is arguably undecidable. For any observable action, it is always possible to posit a disavowed lack as the cause and interpret the continuation of actions as an indication that the lack is never filled, but one can also posit that any action is motivated by a pursuit of pleasure, use this to define the subject's pleasure—which may appear counterintuitive to external observers—and thereby allow for the possibility of a pleasure in submission and humiliation, for instance, or indeed in desire itself. Nevertheless, the choice of theories has aesthetic and ethical consequences. Girard thus privileges a teleological narrative leading to the renunciation of desire in the tragic mode of the hero's repudiation of his life in the moment of death. Resisting conversion, Pasolini, by contrast, holds onto desire in a thoroughly fragmented, confusing, self-splitting, and self-shattering text. Such textuality could actually be considered to fulfill desire if one follows Leo Bersani's notion of aesthetics based on the argument with and against Freud that "sublimation is coextensive with sexuality" and "sexuality is ontologically grounded in masochism."[50] From this perspective, *Petrolio* could be seen to be not principally concerned with representing desires in order to tell the truth about them, nor with repressing, compensating, or transcending them, but rather with their sublimation understood as the replication of the paradoxical pleasures of self-shattering experiences.[51] While Bersani speaks of an "ironic self-reflection," into which art "transmutes biological masochism," and reads in Pasolini's *Salò* an "ironic repetition" through which "Pasolini de-narrativizes Sade,"[52] I would like to conclude by juxtaposing the paradoxical pleasures contained in and by the novel's teleological narrative according to Girard's normative reading with Pasolini's mobilization of a paradoxical laughter through which he maintains a political engagement with the world.

The Vision ends with The Shit's exhaustion through the effort to embody the Model of the domineering man in the new heterosexual couple:

> The pain in the arm with which he embraces his woman and supports her like a sack must be unbearable by now. He tries to smile with a patient and indifferent air; but then, instead, /abruptly/, he yields. . . . and The Shit, fainting, "falls as a dead body falls."[53]

The quotation from the last line of *Inferno* 5 of Dante's *Divine Comedy* contributes to making the Vision end in ridicule and at the same time provides an interesting intertext with Girard's theorizing of conversion and the novel. Girard indeed refers to the famous canto of Paolo and Francesca to contradict its Romantic reading as prime example of triumphant passion and link it instead to the "archetype for the novel form"—a form that is both teleological and retrospective: "The final revelation illuminates, retrospectively, the path traversed," and the work, which is "itself retrospective," is the narrative of a "spiritual metamorphosis," in the light of which "worldly existence, the spiral descent, appears as a *descent into Hell*, that is, as a necessary ordeal on the way to final revelation."[54] What is remarkable here is that while the spiritual metamorphosis appears as the goal justifying the "ordeal" of a descent into hell, it is itself in need of compensation, which is provided precisely by the work narrating the "ordeal" of a descent to hell: The work is "at the same time narrative of and the recompense for spiritual metamorphosis."[55] The startling suggestion that narratives of hell form a reward for conversion rather than a fear-inducing deterrent questions the teleological premise while restoring paradoxes of desire and pleasure. The implications are quite dizzying, but this is precisely what is evoked by the falling body at the end of the Francesca canto. The body is that of Dante-the-pilgrim, whose fainting can indeed be interpreted as the result of being seduced by Francesca's prose while beginning to realize his own, earlier implication in the courtly, highly literary tradition that she reproduces.[56] While the pilgrim continues his journey to experience hell, purgatory, and paradise, and can well be imagined to return purged and converted like a Girardian novelist, the work he writes reproduces in retrospect a model of desire that will continue to fascinate its readers and reward them for their spiritual metamorphosis.

Pasolini's rewriting of Dante's *Inferno* performs a double reversal: The Shit and Cinzia are the new Paolo and Francesca, but while they seek to elicit desire, admiration, and envy by imitating and projecting in an exhibitionist manner the model of a fully absorbing, self-sufficient, unique love, the mechanism and strategies of internal mediation break down. There is nothing seductive about them and it is not their beholder Carlo who loses consciousness, overpowered by a sublime *mise en abîme* of desire, but it is The Shit who falls like a dead body out of sheer physical exhaustion. The Shit's Vision dramatizes what Girard much later acknowledges he "used to believe could never happen," namely that "contemporary individuals aren't strong enough to have mimetic desire" because consumption society has "created these socially indifferent human beings" trapped in a "self-defeating and self-exhausting" "solipsism."[57] However, whereas Girard seems to "welcome" this development in desire, which appears as a previously inconceivable variation of conversion,[58] *Petrolio* finds it terrifying—but also ridiculous, laughable.

After The Shit's collapse, "snickering" Gods lead Carlo to a bird's-eye view of Rome seen as composed of sexual organs—all the cupolas, squares, and bell towers are, respectively, seen as breasts, vaginas, and penises—in the shape of "an immense Swastika." However, the vision does not quite end here and the narrator highlights that "what's left of the Vision also has a metalinguistic significance" and a meaning that is "also valid for the general plan of the author's intentions":[59] Carlo sees an "enormous tabernacle" containing a large simulacrum of a "monstrous woman" [*mostro muliebre*] consisting of "two stocky legs," a "huge woman's head" in place of the groin between them, and in her right hand a long stick, which turns out to be a penis. The image bears the inscription: "I have erected this statue in order to laugh."[60] The first-person narrator glosses this "Last flash of the Vision" by indicating that the inscription

> A) predicts or prefigures a "mystical" act that will occur at the end of this novel: which will be a resolving, vital, completely positive and orgiastic act, and will reestablish the serenity of life and make the course of history resume; B) is placed as an epigraph for this entire work (the "monumentum" par excellence); but its meaning here is diametrically opposed to the one noted above: it is in fact mocking, sarcastic, delusory (but no less sacred on that account!).[61]

The laughter as described here in pagan, sexual, and life-affirming terms and subsequently explained in reference to a "long tradition of mystery cults"[62] has a rather different character from the conversions-in-death Girard analyzed.[63] Nevertheless, one might be tempted to see a parallel to Girard's insistence on finding the novels' meaning and truth in their end, which also implies reading the whole work in view of the final experience as a delusory, perhaps even mocking account. However, while this approach presupposes that the opposite interpretations of the inscription apply to different parts of the work—interpretation (A) to the conclusion and interpretation (B) to the remaining, "preconversion"/"preorgiastic" narrative—*Petrolio* resists such a distribution with the result that laughter becomes thoroughly paradoxical: at once delusory and completely positive, at once mocking and mocked.

In his essay "Perilous Balance: A Comic Hypothesis," Girard also comes close to suggesting that his monumental theory is made for laughter.[64] Deconstructing the apparent opposition of tragedy and comedy, he argues that tragedy becomes comedy once one focuses on the "recurrence [of patterns] and other structural effects," which is precisely what Girard insists on doing with literature. Indeed, he notes that "good literary criticism is often a little comic, because only half-visible patterns become fully visible in it."[65] Significantly, the essay also contains a rare instance of interrogating pleasure: "If laughter is really the slippery affair I describe . . . why is it pleasurable?" This question, which could also be asked of desire, is answered by the indication that "everything we call our 'self,' our 'ego,' our 'identity,' our 'superiority'"—that is, what Girard otherwise persistently presumes to be the first and final object of desire—is seen in an ambivalent, paradoxical way, namely as "both the ultimate prize we are trying to win . . . and a most frightful burden."[66] Interestingly, the question of pleasure was prompted by opposing the "well-protected illusion of superiority" characteristic of most laughter to Baudelaire's recognition of "a truly superior laughter, the one that welcomes its own downfall."[67] However, Girard quickly unfolds the paradox of pleasure through hierarchization and temporalization by considering the phenomenon of pleasurable laughter not as contradicting an essentially metaphysical desire, but as stabilizing it through a merely "temporary release."

While Girard here follows in effect the familiar interpretation of carnival as a stabilizing supplement of order, *Petrolio*'s laughter welcomes its own downfall. Having indicated that also the whole work was "erected . . . in order to laugh," the text highlights the paradox of such laughter in a note entitled "The game" [*Il gioco*]. It begins by distinguishing between those who have never believed in anything and those who had "the vice of believing" but at some point—"perhaps gradually, because of a logical, or even illogical series of disappointments"[68]—stop believing. For the latter, the "discovery of 'nothingness'"—which "for others has always been so natural"—is a novelty that entails the "exhilarating sensation that all this is only a game." As if to clarify the difference to Girard's conversion and renunciation, the narrator introduces a further distinction among the former believers:

> It's clear that I don't mean those who discover philosophical, cosmic "nothingness." In that case it would be a matter of conversion, entirely consistent with their preceding illusions and beliefs, and would cause a cutting off from everything; withdrawal from the word; asceticism.[69]

Instead, he is speaking of those who after discovering "social 'nothingness'" (*il nulla sociale*) "participate more intensely" and are "interested in the social world reduced to nothing and rebuilt on pragmatism."

Whereas belief in values and ascetic conversion equally divide up the world to reject parts of it, the narrator insists on a mockery that is all-encompassing and that paradoxically implies an equally all-encompassing reacceptance:

> Someone who mocks a part of the social world—let's say the conformist bourgeoisie . . .—cannot help at the same time mocking /those who know/ this. Mockery can involve only the whole, entire reality.
>
> And in fact it is the whole, entire reality that—the very moment it is mocked—is accepted again. Reality is not divided. . . . The mocking view of it succeeds in reconciling the /integration/ inevitable in order and, at the same time, the most radical and revolutionary criticism.[70]

The reconciliation and acceptance of the entire reality is no doubt paradoxical, not only on a logical level, but also on that of desire and pleasure. It implies, "fatally, a regression, a conservative or moderate reacceptance of society," and leads, as Pasolini writes terrified in his *abiura*, to a "process of adaptation": "adapting to degradation and accepting the unacceptable."[71] At the same time, not only is there pleasure in abandoning hope for the future, but disenchantment also allows for the return of a deep interest in others:

> Every preconceived idea of the future . . . succumbs to derision; in fact, if there is one thing that causes us to smile inside with greater pleasure, it is precisely the future. The idea of hope for the future becomes irresistibly comic. The resulting lucidity strips the world of fascination. But the return to it is a form of rebirth; the eye of irony sparkles as it looks at events, at men, at the old imbeciles in power, the young men who believe they are beginning heaven knows what. The terrible wound they have inflicted has healed and formed a scar; now they have among them a new collaborator and friend, who is deeply, and with strange lucidity, interested in their problems and helps solve them without too much fuss.[72]

There are elements of conversion here—such as the figure of rebirth and the reconciliation of self, other and the world—but the all-encompassing laughter makes it appear under a different aspect. If Pasolini recants his *Trilogy of Life* but does "not regret having made it,"[73] his monument erected in order to laugh is built upon a paradox that does not implode or self-destruct. On the contrary, his aesthetics of laughter resists tempting reductions to essential nothingness or its correlative, a projection of vertical transcendency through sublime tragedy, and retains instead the full spectrum, from painful suffering without prospect of redemption to a sense of gratuitous engagement with and curiosity about others.

Notes

This article is based on a talk given together with Manuele Gragnolati and is the result of a continuous conversation with Manuele, for which I am very grateful.

1. Pier Paolo Pasolini, *Lutheran Letters*, trans. Stuart Hood (Manchester: Carcanet New Press, 1983), 50.

2. Pasolini, *Lutheran Letters*, 49.

3. Pasolini, *Lutheran Letters*, 50; translation corrected.

4. René Girard, *"To Double Business Bound": Essays on Literature, Mimesis, and Anthropology* (Baltimore: Johns Hopkins University Press, 1978), 4.

5. René Girard, *Deceit, Desire, and the Novel: Self and Other in Literary Structure*, trans. Yvonne Freccero (Baltimore: Johns Hopkins University Press, 1965), 180, 181–82.

6. Girard, *Deceit, Desire, and the Novel*, 184, 186.

7. Girard, *Deceit, Desire, and the Novel*, 293, 294; emphasis in the original.

8. Girard, *Deceit, Desire, and the Novel*, 296; emphasis in the original.

9. Girard, *Deceit, Desire, and the Novel*, 233.

10. Pasolini, *Lutheran Letters*, 11.

11. Pier Paolo Pasolini, *Petrolio*, trans. Ann Goldstein (New York: Pantheon Books, 1997), v, ix. While this translation is based on the volume edited by Maria Careri, Graziella Chiarcossi, and Aurelio Roncaglia (Turin: Einaudi, 1992), I also consulted the newer edition contained in Pier Paolo Pasolini, *Romanzi e racconti*, ed. Walter Siti and Silvia De Laude (Milan: Mondadori, 1998), vol. 2:1159–830. References to *Petrolio* include the note number followed by a colon and the page number of the English translation.

12. Pasolini, *Petrolio*, 73:330.

13. Pasolini, *Petrolio*, ix. In the more recent Meridiani edition, the letter with the sentence "ho parlato al lettore in quanto io stesso, in carne e ossa" concludes the novel; Pasolini, *Romanzi e racconti*, vol. 2:1827.

14. Pasolini, *Petrolio*, 1:3.

15. Pasolini, *Petrolio*, 22A:82.

16. Pasolini, *Petrolio*, 71B:285.

17. Pasolini, *Petrolio*, 72A:320–21, 72F:327.

18. For a recent discussion of Pasolini's insistence on a "cultural apocalypse," see Alessia Ricciardi,

"Pasolini for the Future," *California Italian Studies Journal* 2.1 (2011), http://escholarship.org/uc/item/8v81z3sg.

19. Pasolini, *Petrolio*, 71E:290.

20. Pasolini, *Petrolio*, 71V:311.

21. Pasolini, *Petrolio*, 71V:313.

22. Pasolini, *Petrolio*, 72F:327.

23. Girard, *Deceit, Desire, and the Novel*, 294.

24. Girard, *Deceit, Desire, and the Novel*, 105–6; René Girard, *Things Hidden Since the Foundation of the World*, research undertaken in collaboration with Jean-Michel Oughourlian and Guy Lefort, trans. Stephen Nann and Michael Metteer (Stanford: Stanford University Press, 1987), 370–71.

25. René Girard, *Mimesis and Theory: Essays on Literature and Criticism, 1953–2005*, ed. R. Doran (Stanford: Stanford University Press, 2008), 264.

26. René Girard, *Violence and the Sacred*, trans. Patrick Gregory (Baltimore: John Hopkins University Press, 1977), 155.

27. Girard, *Deceit, Desire, and the Novel*, 183. It would lead here too far to engage with Girard's vehement critique of Freud's essay on narcissism, e.g., in "Narcissism: The Freudian Myth Demythified by Proust" (Girard, *Mimesis and Theory*, 293–311) or Girard, *Things Hidden*, 367–82. For an early, incisive analysis, see Sara Kofman, "The Narcissistic Woman: Freud and Girard," *Diacritics* 10.3 (1980): 36–45, who observes: "What Girard does not forgive Freud . . . is in a general way his dualism, but in particular his irreducible maintenance of a stress upon sexual difference" (44). I agree that differences of focus and terminology aside, what is fundamentally at stake in Girard's critique of Freud is his rejection of Freud's insistent—albeit always shifting—drive dualism to account for the complex plurality of human subjectivity in favor of a monistic model of desire.

28. Girard, *Deceit, Desire, and the Novel*, 282.

29. Girard, *Deceit, Desire, and the Novel*, 283.

30. In *Evolution and Conversion*, Girard discusses the intrinsically paradoxical nature of his theory based on double-bind features. René Girard, *Evolution and Conversion: Dialogues on the Origin of Culture*, with Pierpaolo Antonello and João Cezar de Castro Rocha (New York: Continuum, 2007), 178.

31. See, e.g., Girard, *Things Hidden*, where Girard relates Gregory Bateson's double bind mechanism to information theory, cybernetics, and positive feedback mechanisms, making the system tend toward "runaway" (292, 358). If he suggests here that "mimetic crisis can be seen as a kind of runaway," the whole first chapter of *Battling to the End* is devoted to "The Escalation to Extremes"; René Girard, *Battling to the End: Conversations with Benoît Chantre*, trans. Mary Baker (East Lansing: Michigan State University Press, 2010), 1–26. However, already in *Deceit, Desire, and the Novel*, the "structure of metaphysical desire" is compared with an object falling at an increasing speed and defined in terms of its "catastrophic conclusion" as an "apocalypse" (288).

32. See, e.g., William Rasch, "In Search of the Lyotard Archipelago: Or, How to Live with Paradox and Learn to Like It," *New German Critique* 61 (1994): 55–75.

33. See especially Deleuze and Guattari, *L'Anti-Œdipe* (Paris: Les éditions de Minuit, 1972) and Gilles Deleuze, "Plaisir et désir," *Magazine littéraire*, 325 (1994): 57–65 (letter to Foucault dated 1977).

34. Cf. Gilles Deleuze, *Présentation de Sacher-Masoch* (Paris: Les éditions de Minuit, 1967) and Roland Barthes, *Le plaisir du texte* (Paris: Éditions du Seuil, 1973).

35. If Girard spends considerable effort in showing that his theory of mimetic desire can do without Freud's ad hoc introduction of the death drive in *Beyond the Pleasure Principle*, one could argue that this is because his framework only knows of the death drive, leaving something of the order of the pleasure principle an open question to be introduced ad hoc or unreflected as common sense. See, e.g., the section "The Death Instinct and Modern Culture" (Girard, *Things Hidden*, 409–15).

36. Pasolini, *Petrolio*, 55:178.

37. Pasolini, *Petrolio*, 62:248.

38. Pasolini, *Petrolio*, 73:330.

39. For recent discussions of Pasolini's notion of "Reality" in relation to the sacred, see René de Ceccatty, "Pasolini: Dialoghi con la realtà," in *Corpus XXX: Pasolini, Petrolio, Salò*, ed. Davide Messina (Bologna: CLUEB, 2012), 96–108; and Filippo La Porta, *Pasolini* (Bologna: Il Mulino, 2012).

40. Pasolini, *Petrolio*, 71G:296.

41. Pasolini, *Petrolio*, 71G:297.

42. Girard, *Deceit, Desire, and the Novel*, 91.

43. Girard, *Deceit, Desire, and the Novel*, 118–19.

44. Pasolini, *Petrolio*, 71F:295.

45. Pasolini, *Petrolio*, 71G:296–97.

46. Pasolini, *Petrolio*, 126:430.

47. Pasolini, *Petrolio*, 71G:296. Cf. also the "Iconografia ingiallita" that Pasolini inserted into his *La Divina Mimesis* at the last moment while writing *Petrolio*. See Manuele Gragnolati, "Pier Paolo Pasolini's Queer Performance: *La Divina Mimesis* between Dante and *Petrolio*," in Messina, *Corpus XXX*, 134–64.

48. Cf. Deborah Amberson, "Masochism and Its Discontents: From Franciscan Orgies to Schreberian Unmannings of Putrescence in Pasolini's *Petrolio*," *The Italianist* 30 (2010): 374–94. While I agree with Amberson that Pasolini sees the "strategy" of masochistic relationships with others failing by the time of writing *Petrolio*, I argue that he continues to invest in the conjunction of masochism and resistance, but this time on the level of the aesthetics of texts.

49. Pasolini, *Lutheran Letters*, 49.

50. Leo Bersani, *The Freudian Body: Psychoanalysis and Art* (New York: Columbia University Press, 1986), 45 and 39.

51. Cf. Bersani, *The Freudian Body*, 111. For a reading of *Petrolio* with Bersani, see Manuele Gragnolati, "Pier Paolo Pasolini's Queer Performance" and Manuele Gragnolati, "*Amor che move*": *Linguaggio del corpo e forma del desiderio in Dante, Pasolini e Morante* (Milan: Il Saggiatore, 2013), 55–67.

52. Bersani, *The Freudian Body*, 111 and 53.

53. Pasolini, *Petrolio*, 72G:329.

54. Girard, *"To Double Business Bound,"* 5.

55. Girard, *"To Double Business Bound,"* 5.

56. See Gragnolati and Webb in this volume, as well as Heather Webb, "Deceit, Desire, and Conversion in Girard and Dante," *Religion and Literature*, special issue, *"Deceit, Desire and the Novel* 50 Years Later: The Religious Dimension," ed. Ann W. Astell and Justin Jackson, 43.3 (2011): 200–207.

57. René Girard, *Evolution and Conversion*, 251–52.

58. In chapter 7 of *Evolution and Conversion*, titled "Modernity, Postmodernity and Beyond," Girard resists the suggestion that contemporary Western society is becoming dysfunctional through a domination of internal mediation or that it is sustained by a "ruthlessness of free market and neo-liberal thinking" (245). Instead, he sees the West as having arrived at "something special"—at a "society that can be stable without strict internal hierarchical structure" (240)—and globalization as "primarily an economic development that produces wealth and helps in stabilizing society" and as meaning mainly the "abolition . . . of the entire sacrificial order" through an "encompassing spread of Christian ethics and epistemology," which enabled "economy itself, as it has developed" (245).

59. Pasolini, *Petrolio*, 74:331.

60. Pasolini, *Petrolio*, 74/74A:334.

61. Pasolini, *Petrolio*, 74A:334.

62. Pasolini, *Petrolio*, 74A:334.

63. For recent discussions of laughter and the comic in *Petrolio*, see Francesca Cadel, "Politics and Sexuality in Pasolini's *Petrolio*," in *The Power of Disturbance*, ed. Manuele Gragnolati and Sara Fortuna (London: Legenda, 2009), 107–17; and Marco Antonio Bazzocchi, "Baubò: La scena comica dell'ultimo Pasolini," in Mesina, *Corpus XXX*, 13–28.

64. Girard, *"To Double Business Bound,"* 121–35.

65. Girard, *"To Double Business Bound,"* 125.

66. Girard, *"To Double Business Bound,"* 130.

67. Girard, *"To Double Business Bound,"* 130.

68. Pasolini, *Petrolio*, 84:341.

69. Pasolini, *Petrolio*, 84:342.

70. Pasolini, *Petrolio*, 84:342–43.

71. Pasolini, *Lutheran Letters*, 52. Cf. Deborah Amberson, "Neo-capitalism, *Acedia* and Non-style in Pier Paolo Pasolini's *Petrolio*," *Quaderni d'italianistica* 29.2 (2008): 53–72, which, focusing on Pasolini's self-attribution of "acedia" in the *Abiura*, goes so far as to suggest parallels to The Shit's torpor and Pasolini's stylistic choices. However, it should be noted that by projecting a "flat, objective, colorless, etc. style" for the author of the "critical edition" that was to be Petrolio, Pasolini is not attributing this style to the novel as such, which, as Amberson also notes, does not reflect "stated ambitions to transparency" (63).

72. Pasolini, *Petrolio*, 84:343.

73. Pasolini, *Lutheran Letters*, 49.

Jonathan Franzen's Novelistic Conversion

Trevor Cribben Merrill

Jonathan Franzen's first two books, *The Twenty-Seventh City* (1988) and *Strong Motion* (1992), are a lot better than most contemporary works of fiction, but they are a lot worse than his third novel, *The Corrections* (2001), a family drama that vaulted Franzen to fame and established him as arguably the best American novelist of his generation. The modest critical success enjoyed by the first two novels, which were published within four years of each other, their similarly sprawling, postmodern plots, and their often cumbersome attempts to weave broader social issues into the narrative fabric, lead me to regard them as belonging to a single group, a sort of early Franzen diptych. Meanwhile, the relatively long period—nearly ten years—separating the publication of *Strong Motion* and *The Corrections*, the latter novel's immense critical and popular success, and its more seamless melding of public and private themes, distinguish it from those earlier books, suggesting that it belongs to a new period in Franzen's life as an author.

How did Franzen go from being a merely promising young author with a couple of books to his credit to writing a novel hailed by the public and critics alike as a masterpiece, one that seems likely to remain lodged in American collective memory for some time to come? What happened in the ten years between *Strong Motion* and *The Corrections*?

One way of beginning to understand Franzen's metamorphosis is to examine the weaknesses of the second (and better) of his early novels, so as to pinpoint what differentiates it from the later work. Like *The Corrections*, this second novel is a multicharacter drama of family dysfunction set against a backdrop of social upheaval and corporate greed. *Strong Motion* displays obvious flaws, noted by practically all the reviewers: its plot is contrived, many of its characters are flat and cartoonish, and its bitterly anticapitalist bent is likely to irritate even those who agree with the author's views. Nonetheless, it is, on the whole, an ambitious effort that testifies to the young Franzen's gift for constructing and furnishing an imaginary world. The book's shortcomings are neither technical nor imaginative; rather, they are human and existential. The novel embodies a disaffected, slightly paranoid postmodern worldview that *The Corrections* manages to transcend.

A comparison between *Strong Motion*'s protagonist, Louis Holland, and his counterpart in *The Corrections*, Chip Lambert, reveals profound structural and existential divergences. In the former novel, the central male character, who can plausibly be seen as an authorial alter ego, remains in the eye of the hurricane as buildings topple and lives collapse around him; in the latter book, on the other hand, Chip is himself caught up in the storm. Where the first novel tries and fails to provide a persuasive fall-and-redemption pattern, the second one enmeshes its protagonist in a personal disaster that mirrors the novel's larger trajectory and opens a window onto Franzen's creative process.

A "not entirely untroubled person," *Strong Motion*'s Louis Holland is a twenty-three-year-old, prematurely balding hipster who works at a Boston area radio station and rarely loses his cool. Indeed, he does not seem to feel much of anything—not even the 4.7 earthquake that strikes nearby Cape Ann and sets the plot rolling—but the reader is not fooled: beneath the detached surface lurks a sensitive, perceptive intelligence. When, on their first meeting, his sister's boyfriend sees fit to give him career advice, Louis plays dumb:

> "Whatever you do, don't let 'em involve you in any kind of ownership scheme—"
>
> "Oh I won't," Louis said, so earnestly it would have made an observant person wary.[1]

He then gets the best of the exchange, turning the tables on his interlocutor with a cutting question, which he delivers with endearing grammatical awkwardness ("Do you know how to listen when you've asked somebody a question about themself?"). There is in these passages an unmistakable flash of authorial wish fulfillment, as if the scene had been constructed to repair some real-life slight or defeat. The novel later brings Louis and his adversary to friendship and mutual respect, but this doesn't change the fact that Franzen overplays his hand in this early scene, arranging things so that the boyfriend comes off as arrogant and overbearing. Meanwhile, the main character emerges from the confrontation looking quite rosy (even his rudeness can be excused as the result of a brother's protective instincts). As the novel progresses, Louis experiences an occasional burst of anger or pang of desire, but it is mostly the people around him who fly off the handle or lose control of themselves. Meanwhile, he sees what they do not (his sister is blind to her boyfriend's flaws; Louis takes it upon himself to disabuse her).

It would be going too far to say that Louis Holland is a flattering authorial self-portrayal, a romantic double of the novelist. In *Strong Motion*, Franzen is already far too strong a writer to indulge openly in vicarious score settling. It cannot be an accident, though, that Louis remains mostly the master of situations, even where love is concerned. Though initially he pines after Lauren, an attachment from his college days, and Renée, a Harvard seismologist several years his elder, he soon becomes the apple of discord, arousing passionate jealousies and hatreds. Louis is far from immune to such ugly emotions, but when he does get jealous, the experience is described as mostly positive: "It was a great thing, jealousy. It was a drug that charged up the nerve endings and delivered a first-class rush."[2] No sooner has he allowed Renée to gain the upper hand in their relationship than he recovers his advantage in a moment of postcoital disenchantment. He turns on the bedroom light, exposing "the fetal mashedness of a tired face" and transforming the imagined, idealized angel "floating on thermals high above him" into a "feathered and lumpy piece of meat."[3] When Lauren reenters the novel, proclaiming her love for him, Louis the heartbreaker allows the new competitor for his affections back into his life, ditching Renée until the novel's touching but uneasy finale, which both provides and withholds closure.

With its crowded plot, which includes a family inheritance, unprecedented (and unexplained) seismic activity on the East Coast, antiabortion activists, and a cross-country love triangle, *Strong Motion* seems to be attempting a synthesis between the explicitly postmodern approach of *The Twenty-Seventh City* and the more conventional realist aesthetic that Franzen manages to bring off convincingly only in his third novel. The result is an uneasy compromise, a novel too antic to work as realist fiction and too realistic to work as Pynchonesque postmodernism. Louis's realization that he loves Renée signals a move away from ironic detachment toward greater seriousness and sincerity. Yet the novel never quite builds up the momentum to finish on a satisfying note. Its last lines are an evasion as much as they are an ending: "I just have to walk now. Walk with me, come on. We have to keep walking."[4]

One explanation for this lack of resolution is that catastrophe strikes the protagonist only indirectly. Though emotionally vulnerable, Louis Holland avoids the kind of devastation that befalls other characters (to take but the most obvious example: Renée is hospitalized and almost dies of gunshot wounds). At the end of the story, he is reunited with the woman he loves, but his inner transformation lacks a strong external correlative. And since we experience Louis as a central character, and since much of our understanding of what transpires in the book is filtered through him, we don't quite live the novel's tragedies from the inside. To get something, you have to give something up. In *Strong Motion*, one has the impression that Franzen wanted to achieve a transformative ending without really putting his main character's life or ego in danger.

Louis's story can be contrasted with Chip Lambert's in *The Corrections*. The two characters have much in common. Both are Midwesterners living on the East Coast, slackers with messy love lives, dysfunctional families, and poor career prospects. Both are sharp-eyed observers of the popular culture, hip, intelligent, and sensitive, and good-hearted despite their failings. There are, of course, many differences between them, as well. Some of these differences are superficial (Louis is brown-haired and prematurely balding; Chip is blond); others, such as their respective ages, are less so (Louis is a recent college graduate with a passion for radio; Chip is a disgraced college professor with literary ambitions who is described near the novel's beginning as "a little too old for the leather he was wearing").[5] But the real dissimilarity lies not in physical traits or even in some personality quirk but in the way the two protagonists are respectively portrayed. Where Louis gets the upper hand, Chip is defeated. Louis wins his duel of wits with his sister's boyfriend at the beginning of *Strong Motion*; Chip loses his with his student Melissa near the beginning of *The Corrections*. A professor in the "Textual Artifacts" department of a Northeastern liberal arts college, he has spent a semester teaching his class how to critique the capitalist status quo, furnishing them with arguments gleaned from texts on semiology and structuralism by the likes of Baudrillard and Foucault. Pointing out that Chip seems as motivated by his hatred for capitalism and corporate culture as by the positive desire for intellectual insight, Melissa unleashes a devastating critique of the critic:

> "Excuse me," Melissa said, "but that is just such bullshit."
>
> "What is bullshit?" Chip said.
>
> "This whole class," she said. "It's just bullshit every week. It's one critic after another wringing their hands about the state of criticism. Nobody can ever quite say what's wrong exactly. But they all know it's evil. They all know 'corporate' is a dirty word. And if somebody's having fun or getting rich—disgusting! Evil! . . . it's evil to be rich and evil to work for a corporation, and yes, I know the bell rang." She closed her notebook.
>
> "OK," Chip said. "On that note. You've now satisfied your Cultural Studies core requirement. Have a great summer."
>
> He was powerless to keep the bitterness out of his voice. He bent over the video player. . . . He sensed a few students lingering behind him, as if they wanted to thank him for teaching his heart out or to tell they'd enjoyed the class, but he didn't look up from the video player until the room was empty.[6]

The terms of this debate are in many ways identical to the face-off between Louis and his sister's boyfriend in *Strong Motion*—the slick defender of the corporate vision versus the indie cultural critic and his skepticism bordering on paranoia. Except that where Louis's inscrutable poses and lofty mock innocence carry the day, Chip loses the battle. Though some of the students may be on his side, and though the larger point his adversary makes is no doubt too harsh, we feel that she has touched a nerve and spoken his truth. From that moment, Melissa's ascendancy over him grows until his obsession for her condemns him to a hell of shame and guilt. Her self-absorption draws him like an irresistible magnetic field and at the same time increases his self-loathing. He wants

> to make her pay for liking herself in a way he couldn't like himself. How he hated and how he loved the lilt in her voice, the bounce in her step, the serenity of her amour propre! She got to be her and he didn't. And he could see that he was ruined—that he didn't like her but would miss her disastrously.[7]

Beautiful women fight for Louis; Chip is dumped twice in succession (first by Melissa, then by his next girlfriend, Julia). And where *Strong Motion* takes Louis and his outsider's mystique more or less at face value, *The Corrections* makes Chip a comic character, his sneering deconstructions of American capitalism, like the metal stud in his ear, part and parcel of an inauthentic pose. There is perhaps nothing inherently valuable about creating a character who fails, and if Chip were merely a loser his story wouldn't be as interesting as it is. But Chip is more than just the victim of his own undisciplined impulses and depressive tendencies. He is also a hero who matures into an adult by the novel's conclusion, and who does so by overcoming inner obstacles more daunting than those faced by Louis Holland in *Strong Motion*.

Chip's tragicomic arc, which forms a *Künstlerroman* within the wider family saga, points to a personal transformation in the author's life. This is where René Girard's ideas can help us. According to Girard's conception of how great novels are written, the novelist has to write his (or her) novel twice: the first time around, the outcome of his creative efforts is fundamentally self-serving. Then comes the recognition that the first version of the novel is an aesthetic failure, followed by a period of transition during which the author gradually begins to realize that he has been living a lie, and that this lie—the "*mensonge romantique*," or "romantic lie," as Girard put it in *Deceit, Desire, and the Novel*—was the thing holding him back as a creator of literature.

The second version of his book is born of that eye-opening realization, which leads to his handing over some version of his own delusion to the protagonist. The character in turn becomes the bearer of and believer in the lie, even as he marches slowly through the narrative toward truth. At the conclusion of the novel, the character then experiences what Girard calls a "novelistic conversion," in which he wakes up from his fantasy and, like Don Quixote repudiating his quest at the end of Cervantes's novel, comes to see that he has been chasing a mirage.

For Girard, this moment is the trace of the author's own conversion, which gave him the power to write (or to start writing) the successful novel. The trace can be explicit (the character decides to write a novel, for example, as at the end of Proust's *In Search of Lost Time*) or it can be an implicit translation of the author's personal experience in the form of some tragic happening, like death or a life-threatening illness.

I see the ending of Chip's story as a "novelistic conversion." The return of the prodigal son to Midwestern St. Jude marks the birth of an authentic writer capable for the first time of seeing far beyond the narrow limits of his resentment. The key moment in the transformation, however, occurs abroad. After his hopes of selling his overwrought screenplay are dashed, Chip sets off to Lithuania with a dubious character named Gitanas to put his anti-American ideology into action, hoping to fleece overseas investors into pouring money into the collapsing Lithuanian economy. The scheme succeeds at first. Then it fails spectacularly as civil unrest engulfs the country. Waylaid and surrounded by masked thugs in police uniforms as he and his accomplice try to make off with the remains of their ill-gotten loot, Chip is ordered to strip at gunpoint: "Death, that overseas relation, that foul-breathed remittance man, had suddenly appeared in the immediate neighborhood. Chip was quite afraid of the gun. His hands shook and lost feeling. . . . The 'police' examined his wallet as well but didn't steal his litai or his credit cards. Dollars were all they wanted."[8] The thugs let them go, and Chip heads for the border alone. It is as he walks through the night that he has his "great revelation":[9]

> He was straining to hear whether any of the homicidal farm dogs in the surrounding darkness might be unleashed, he had his arms outstretched, he was feeling more than a little ridiculous, when he remembered Gitanas's remark: *tragedy rewritten as farce.* All of a sudden he understood why nobody, including himself, had ever liked his screenplay: he'd written a thriller when he should have written a farce.
>
> Faint morning twilight was overtaking him. In New York he'd honed and polished the first thirty pages of "The Academy Purple" until his

memory of them was nearly eidetic, and now, as the Baltic sky brightened, he bore down with a mental red pencil on his mental reconstruction of those pages, made a little trim here, added emphasis or hyperbole there, and in his mind the scenes became what they'd wanted to be all along: ridiculous. The tragic BILL QUAINTENCE became a comic fool.

. . .

He spoke out loud: Make it *ridiculous*. Make it *ridiculous*.[10]

Franzen's novel is about the way children try to "correct" the mistakes their parents made. It is also (in a tame though prescient way) about "corrections" in the financial markets. But this passage suggests that the "corrections" referred to in the title are also literary, revisions made to correct and reorient the "strong motion" of earlier works in a more fruitful direction. The thriller in question is Chip's laughably bad screenplay, but one might also read his moment of revelation as a more direct commentary on Franzen's own oeuvre. *Strong Motion*, with its sleuthing and shooting, and *The Twenty-Seventh City*, with its political conspiracy and intrigue, are serious "thrillers" that aim for earthshaking high tragedy and miss, while *The Corrections* is both the funniest of the author's novels and the first to explore the dysfunction of family life with sincere compassion.

In 2012, Jonathan Franzen published a book of essays, *Farther Away*, that includes a 2009 lecture entitled "On Autobiographical Fiction." Here he recounts the long, painful gestation of *The Corrections*. His subject is ostensibly the conflict between wanting, as an artist, to delve into the secrets of family life, and fearing the damage that one might do by using friends and family members as subject matter—the "conflicting demands of good art and good personhood," as Franzen puts it.[11] It seems to me, however, that the deeper dilemma Franzen faced in writing *The Corrections* was of a different order. It wasn't, in other words, simply his fear of giving offense or being disloyal to spouse and family that prevented him at first from delving into autobiographical issues, but rather what he calls his "wish to be all intellect, all worldly expertise, so as to avoid the messy business of my private life" (134). This wish to hold private life at arm's length—to repress shame, the word that occurs again and again in the novel's early passages about Chip— was incarnated in the character who was originally to have played the central role in the novel. Andy Aberant was "creepy and self-conscious and remote and depressing,"[12] and after many unsuccessful attempts to work him into the novel Franzen finally jettisoned him: "I drew a little tombstone for him in my notes and gave him an epitaph from *Faust II: 'Den können wir erlösen.'* I honestly don't think I understood what I meant then in saying, 'Him we can redeem.' But it makes sense to me now."[13] Aberant is "redeemed" as Chip Lambert, via whom Franzen, "ashamed of being a bleeding and undefended person instead of a tower of remoteness and command and intellect like DeLillo or Pynchon," manages to "isolate and quarantine shame as an object, ideally as an object of comedy."[14]

Everything is here in this short text: the turn away from postmodern influences and the conscious rejection of the intellectual mode as embodied by the remote, self-conscious hero, Andy Aberant (the very name suggests the aberrance of the Romantic outsider), who is laid to rest only to be resurrected in the form of a comic character. "On Autobiographical Fiction" is the confessional equivalent of the passages cited above from the denouement of *The Corrections*. The long struggle that culminated in Franzen's surpassing himself is condensed in Chip Lambert's fall from grace, in his "failure," as the novel's second part is entitled, but especially in his brush with death and his subsequent realization that by making plot and character ridiculous instead of tragic he can redeem his screenplay. Franzen's confession adds support to the hypothesis that *The Corrections* came into being through an act of retrospective self-demystification. Take this admission about *Strong Motion*: "Looking back, although I'm still proud of that novel, I can now see the ways in which its ending was deformed by my wishful thinking about my marriage."[15] There is no such distortion at the end of *The Corrections*. To the contrary, the return of the prodigal son does away with all distortions, replacing the misty lenses of Louis Holland's glasses in the first pages of *Strong Motion* ("his glasses were white with fog") with the crystal clear vision of Chip Lambert as he approaches his family home. I do not think it would be amiss, here, to speak of a resurrection:

A holly wreath was on the door. The front walk was edged with snow and evenly spaced broom marks. . . . The old street with its oak smoke and snowy flat-topped hedges and icicled eaves seemed precarious. It seemed mirage-like. It seemed like an exceptionally vivid memory of something beloved and dead.[16]

Not until the novel's coda, however, does the redemptive pattern of Chip's life become truly apparent. Chip meets and falls in love with Alison, the female doctor who has been taking care of his ailing father. He later moves in with her, and, tellingly, removes the stud in his ear, a sort of initiation in reverse that symbolizes the end of adolescence and the beginning of a new life. In *Strong Motion*, Louis and his girlfriend Renée can't decide whether to have children. Their hesitation infuses the final scenes of the novel, making closure impossible. *The Corrections* has achieved a vision of family life and responsibility that leaps effortlessly over such hesitation: as the novel closes, we learn that Chip and Alison will be the parents of twins.

What *The Corrections* suggests is that the path to aesthetic achievement is so often a long and agonizing one not only because of external hardships but also, and above all, because writing a great, or even a good, work of literature means first wrestling with inner demons. As Franzen noted in "On Autobiographical Fiction," writing his best novel was first and foremost a matter of personal transformation: "Much of the struggle consisted—as I think it always will for writers fully engaged with the problem of the novel—in overcoming shame, guilt, and depression."[17] The idea that authentic writing is impossible without such a transformation is not a new one. Perhaps it goes back as far as St. Augustine and Dante, whose works both chronicle and mirror structurally the transformation that preceded their creation. It is apparent in any case that the novel, more so even than the formally codified screen or the stage play, is only partly about technique. In his essay on Dostoevsky, René Girard observes: "One should not compare the author's successive works to the musical exercises by which musicians gradually increase their virtuosity. What is essential lies elsewhere."[18] Though refining one's technique is no doubt important, the kind of savoir faire that can be learned by imitating capable models or reading a creative writing manual is not enough. Great literature, writes Girard, "requires a victory over pride itself."[19] Between the lines of Chip's failure and subsequent redemption we can read the story of Franzen's struggle to achieve that hard-won victory.

Notes

1. Jonathan Franzen, *Strong Motion* (New York: Farrar, Straus and Giroux, 1992), 7.

2. Franzen, *Strong Motion*, 196.

3. Franzen, *Strong Motion*, 208.

4. Franzen, *Strong Motion*, 526.

5. Jonathan Franzen, *The Corrections* (New York: Farrar, Straus and Giroux, 2001), 15.

6. Franzen, *The Corrections*, 44.

7. Franzen, *The Corrections*, 61.

8. Franzen, *The Corrections*, 532.

9. Franzen, *The Corrections*, 534.

10. Franzen, *The Corrections*, 534.

11. Jonathan Franzen, "On Autobiographical Fiction," in *Farther Away* (New York: Farrar, Straus and Giroux, 2012), 133.

12. Franzen, "On Autobiographical Fiction," 135.

13. Franzen, "On Autobiographical Fiction," 135.

14. Franzen, "On Autobiographical Fiction," 136.

15. Franzen, "On Autobiographical Fiction," 132.

16. Franzen, *The Corrections*, 536.

17. Franzen, "On Autobiographical Fiction," 131.

18. René Girard, *Deceit, Desire, and the Novel: Self and Other in Literary Structure*, trans. Yvonne Freccero (Baltimore: Johns Hopkins University Press, 1965), 3.

19. Girard, *Deceit, Desire, and the Novel*, 72.

Mimetic Desire and Monstrous Doubles in Jonathan Littell's *The Kindly Ones*

Robert Buch

"A Russian novel—written in French—by a young American." This is how *The Kindly Ones* was characterized by one of the author's first interlocutors, the eminent French historian Pierre Nora.[1] A novel hence at once Russian, French, American, and—we might add—Greek, its title, *Les Bienveillantes* in the original, borrowed from the third part of Aeschylus's *Oresteia*, *The Eumenides*, that is, the Furies of vengeance appeased and invited to settle in the polis. Given its principal settings, sites, and action Littell's work might also be regarded as a German novel: the mass killings on the Eastern Front; Stalingrad; the death camps; and so on, in short, a book about "the terror from Germany," to quote a well-known line by Edgar Allan Poe. Nora's phrase nicely captures the novel's astonishing range and hybrid character. It also reflects the puzzlement of its readers: their fascination and frustration in view of the book's unwieldiness.

Implicit in the novel's multinational and multilingual affiliations are four generic paradigms. (1) It is "Russian" in its epic scope and its aspirations to a certain realism. The *Nouvel Observateur* hailed it as the new *War and Peace*, and in his conversation with Nora, Littell himself has acknowledged his indebtedness to *Life and Fate*, Vasily Grossman's magnum opus on World War II, the siege of Stalingrad, and German labor and death camps.[2] (2) It is written in French because the author wanted to situate his work in the lineage of the great nineteenth-century novel à la Flaubert. But what has struck readers no less is another connection, namely to what is called *la littérature du mal*, the authors celebrating excess, transgression, and violence, from Sade to Baudelaire, from Lautréamont to Bataille and Genet.[3] (3) I am reluctant to label what might be specifically American about the novel or to suggest which proto-American genre it might bring to mind. The reviewers, however, have cited two titles that point the way: *The Talented Mr. Ripley* and *American Psycho*.[4] Like these works, *The Kindly Ones* offers the portrait of a deranged and yet exceedingly lucid subject, featuring the psychotic polarity between an educated, sensitive, and melancholy character and the bouts of mindless violence to which this same character succumbs time and again. It is also the memoir of the protagonist's itinerary over the killing fields and through the death camps, his memories of war and genocide, and the unabashed admission of his engagement on behalf of these causes. The third paradigm on which Littell draws, though clearly more difficult to assign to a specific national tradition, is that of confessional writing, but with a twist, namely, that the subject scrutinizing his past is anticipating and seeks to parry posterity's negative judgment. (4) The fourth paradigm invoked explicitly by the title and at work implicitly throughout the novel is that of Attic tragedy, above all the *Oresteia* already mentioned.[5]

Both the appeal and the incongruence of the novel are due to its attempt to imitate and fuse these different paradigms, a doubling and crossing, if the wordplay is permitted, that has resulted in a most peculiar crossbreed, a work of truly monstrous proportions. This monstrosity has proven highly discomforting, appalling even, to some, notably among the book's German audience, while fascinating to others, especially in France and Italy, where the novel became a bestseller and received prestigious literary awards, winning both the Prix Goncourt and the Prix de l'Académie Française.[6]

Rather than analyzing how these different paradigms collude and collide in Littell's novel, the present essay, taking its cues from René Girard, focuses on mimetic desire and the figure of the double in *The Kindly Ones*. Both go a long way in accounting for the extraordinary character of this book, its audacity and its burden. There are no indications that Littell was familiar with Girard's work. In view of his own French-American background and his avowed interest in writers like Bataille, it seems unlikely, however, that the novelist would have had no exposure to Girard's thought at all. Be that as it may, the point of the following discussion is not genetic, but rather structural. The two Girardian tropes are prominently at work in the novel and cast light on some of its most intractable enigmas. At the same time, there are significant departures from the way these tropes work in Girard.

Aue, Lecteur

Like the characters in Cervantes, Stendhal, Flaubert, and Proust at the center of *Deceit, Desire, and the Novel*, the narrator and main protagonist of *The Kindly Ones*, one Maximilian Aue, is an avid reader. As a matter of fact, he discusses Stendhal—on the thrill and distinction a death sentence can confer—with a Soviet officer about to be executed; he reads Flaubert—in Stalingrad, of all places—and quotes passages from Proust's *Jean Santeuil* from memory. But while these readings are often correlated to Aue's circumstances, they do not shape his imagination nor his understanding of his own experiences. There are some exceptions, to be sure. Aue once played Electra in a school production, a foreboding of the matricide he will commit later on; and while stationed in the Caucasus, to cite another example, he challenges a fellow officer to a duel after reading Lermontov's *A Hero of Our Time*. Still, even though *Les Bienveillantes* is replete with literary references and even though Aue's perceptions and discussions are clearly marked by his *Bildung*, his desire is not—or at least not in the way one might expect with Girard in mind. The principal purpose of the novel's encyclopedic scope and its narrator's literary range and sensibility is to serve as a foil for the unending series of atrocities the reader has to stomach. Literature figures less as a paradigm by which to take the measure of the shortcomings of reality (and transfigure it) than a means of reflecting, and refracting, experiences too excessive to countenance.

Although Aue is depicted as *lecteur* and *littérateur*, his occasional allusions to literature and the musings of an evidently highly cultivated mind are counterbalanced by what must be regarded as the predominant discursive register of his narrative, namely the report: statistics, figures, organizational charts, the *furor bureaucraticus* of genocide administration (interspersed now and then with melancholy meditations on his strange fate in it all).

It is a passion for facticity and accuracy that seems to drive (and at times inundate) this narration: painstaking reconstruction of the sites and the logistics of the genocidal operations; elaborate accounts of the bizarre and byzantine ramifications of the Nazi organizations and their hierarchies, and the turns and twists a career in them could take; but also of the ideological debates within the interwar right-wing and Nazi intelligentsia. The narrator himself, embarked on such a career and—implausibly, it is true—moving from the Eastern Front to the Caucasus, to Stalingrad, to Paris, to Berlin, to Auschwitz, and back to Berlin, is charged with writing reports and taking stock of the war effort, and later with assessing the organization and logistics of the concentration camps, hence the "panoramic" or epic view the novel affords its readers. As if to outdo the realist tradition in the name of hyper-realism, the book is filled to the brim with details, often mundane, of the everyday life in the midlevel and upper ranks of the Nazi war and genocide administration. It is as though Littell sought to give color to the gray of the "banality of evil." But for all the matter-of-factness with which the organization and organizational problems of the genocide are recorded in the book, such excessive banality is countered in turn with its opposite: hair-raising scenes of transgression and sadomasochistic acts that have no obvious connection to the political setting but seem to spring from the cold-blooded cruelty of an "Aryan Mr. Ripley" running amuck on a private killing spree.

The literary archive surely provides the touchstone and gamut for Littell's writing: from the character's literary culture to his own detached writings of reports and strategy papers to the tangled and "tragic" plot of his family romance. However, on the intradiegetic level the protagonist's putative models or mediators, the others whose imitation might help to understand his conflicted desires and allegiances, are difficult to discern.

Mimetic Desire: Una

Although the question of mediation, so crucial in *Deceit, Desire, and the Novel*, does not seem to pertain in the case of Littell's main protagonist, Aue's desire is nonetheless mimetic, if in a rather literal sense. For it is not triangular, but dyadic, and ultimately narcissistic, fueling an agonistic struggle with respect, not so much to an Other, emulated, envied, resented, and rivaled, as with being in the world. Indeed, Aue's peculiar investment in the cause of Nazism is presented as being rooted in a primal and impossible longing for a oneness irretrievably lost. Aue's desire springs from a painful and violent cut: The separation from his twin sister Una with whom he had an incestuous relationship that was brought to an abrupt stop shortly after the two adolescents were caught by their parents. Aue's main fantasy is to recover this blissful sense of wholeness. It's an oceanic desire of fusing, of undoing the separation, the split, of revoking, as it were, the process of individuation. It is, in other words, the desire to become one with the other—again: indistinguishable and inseparable, a condition captured by the image of the twins' childlike bodies, still barely distinguishable in terms of gender, intertwined, locked together in an erotic embrace like two snakes coiled around one another.[7] At the height of one of his delirious bouts, Aue fantasizes about being united again with his sister in his mother's womb, the French mother he hates as much for the perceived betrayal of his German father as for having given birth to them and thus separated the two. Aue's desire is infantile and regressive, testimony to a constitutive deficiency in the order of things, a kind of ontological malaise. It is the desire, *au fond*, not to have been born; the wisdom of Silenus meeting Aristophanes's myth of the two halves yearning for reunion (in Plato's *Symposium*). Since the primal fantasy—mimesis in the sense of becoming one with the other, turning into the other—is barred from realization, Aue resorts to a different, lesser solution: he seeks to experience sexual pleasure like a woman, like his sister. His homosexuality is thus a strange form of mimicry. He lets himself be penetrated and crushed by randomly picked men so as to achieve a brief spell of self-loss. In one particularly crucial episode, he watches himself in the mirror as he is penetrated and sees his sister's face, a brief glimpse of the primordial unity, the originary indistinction of the twins—an image quickly supplanted, though, by another face, that of his mother.

To sum up this rather peculiar libidinal profile and the painfully unrealizable ideal that sustains it: at the core of Aue's "mimetic desire" is, in a sense, the fantasy of breaking the boundaries of selfhood, becoming indistinguishable from the other, the fantasy of being his sister, and since that is not possible, he tries to approximate her in his sexual experience. It is not a process of undifferentiation, a leveling of difference that triggers violence, as in Girard's model, but on the contrary the introduction of difference within sameness, the original cut, that unleashes Aue's violence against those around him and that fuels his futile attempts to restore the original oneness or, short of that, revenge himself for his irrecuperable loss. In other words, Aue's quasi-metaphysical yearning for lost wholeness is not modeled on someone else's desire. Rather, it is a desire for change, for metamorphosis. The "ontological sickness" afflicting Aue is not the desire to be Godlike,[8] the dream of supreme autonomy and self-sufficiency, ultimately, the desire to be without desire. The prelapsarian condition he mourns is one in which the difference between subject and object, subject and other did not exist, or did not matter. It is a fantasy not of divine, unperturbed detachment from the world, but one of being reabsorbed into the world, returning to a state before consciousness.

Monstrous Doubles

Doubles abound in the novel. Aside from Una and Max, there are the two criminal police officers, Clemens and Weser, personifications of the Erinyes, that hound the narrator. Another important double are Leland and Mandelbrod, *éminences grises* of the Nazi party who are pulling the strings of Aue's fate from behind the scenes. Surrounded by a team of blond Amazon look-alikes, the two are reminiscent of the evil geniuses in James Bond movies. A long conversation with a captured Soviet officer about the similarities between a socialism based on race and one based on class provides another example of the novel's proliferation of doubles, though it remains somewhat underdeveloped. The most striking and disturbing doubling, however, occurs in several discussions of the relationship between Germans and Jews, featuring two complementary views. The first is expounded by Mandelbrod, himself a figure in which the Nazi bigwig assumes the traits of anti-Semitic caricature. According to Mandelbrod, the particular zeal with which the Germans implement their genocidal policies vis-à-vis the Jews reflects a deep-seated similarity in outlook and ambition. Hitler's grandiose vision of the special mission of Germany takes its cue from the idea of the chosen people, a distinction that obviously can only be conferred on one group. In other words, the Nazi fantasy of racial supremacy is in essence a replication of Jewish exceptionalism. In Girardian terms, the subject succumbs to its envy and resentment against its secret model, adopting the latter's ideal—to be the chosen people—and seeking to eliminate it as a rival. Mandelbrod calls the Jews "our privileged enemy," for "they resembled us too much."⁹

The point is echoed and expanded in a later conversation with Aue's sister and brother-in-law. Here the argument is that the Jews serve not only as the model to be emulated but also as a vehicle for externalizing German self-hatred, the sense of inferiority and ressentiment, features mirrored back to them by the anti-Semitic topos of Jewish mimicry.

> By killing the Jews . . . we wanted to kill ourselves, kill the Jew within us, kill that which in us resembles the idea we have of the Jew. . . . For we've never understood that these qualities that we attribute to the Jews . . . are fundamentally German qualities, and that if the Jews show these qualities, it's because they imitate us obsequiously like the very image of all that is fine and good in High Bourgeoisie, the Golden Calf of those who flee the harshness of the desert and the Law. . . . And we, on the other hand, our German dream, was to be Jews, pure, indestructible, faithful to a Law, different from everyone else and under the hand of God.¹⁰

The monstrous double gives rise to conflicting urges of appropriation/absorption, on the one hand, destruction/expulsion, on the other, encompassing as it does the idealized other and the disavowed aspects of the self, the violent and egoistic impulses, projected outward.¹¹

The elements of the familiar Girardian logic of the double, its transfiguration and expulsion, are complemented and completed in an earlier outburst of the narrator that few critics of the novel fail to quote.

> The murder of the Jews doesn't serve any real purpose. . . . It has no economic or political usefulness, it has no finality of a practical order. On the contrary, it's a break with the world of economics and politics. It's a waste, pure loss. That's all it is. So it can have only one meaning: an irrevocable sacrifice, which binds us once and for all, prevents us from ever turning back.¹²

The Bataillean overtones of the passage are unmistakable: the genocide is a sacrifice with no finality, an act of expenditure without any return, "a break with the world of economy and politics," a kind of celebration of irrational excess, unleashed for its own sake.[13] But the connection to Girard is no less obvious: it's a sacrifice "which *binds* us once and for all," forging a new community whose potential for internal conflict is thus averted. Once its self-destructive impulses have found an outlet, it is reunified; its bond reconfirmed; its spirit reinvigorated. There is an implication, however, that brings me to the last instantiation of doubling so crucial for the novel's narrative strategies. The irrevocable sacrifice not only binds and elevates those involved in a community of fate, it will also doom them. It will bring the desired distinction, allegedly modeled on the biblical ideal of the chosen people. But this distinction is double-edged. For with this "sacrifice" the German people will be forever marked, irredeemably compromised, like Cain bearing the stigma of their crime, set apart from the rest of humanity: the chosen people, and the accursed. Aue himself is one of them, perpetrator and—as he would have us believe, rather brazenly—scapegoat.

Hypocrite lecteur!

The last figure of the double I wish to examine is the reader, a reader addressed and constructed, from the outset, in two different keys: "Oh, my human brothers, let me tell you how it happened. I am not your brother, you'll retort, and I don't want to know" (3). This incipit contains two oblique references: François Villon's *Ballade des pendus* and the famous prefatory lines to Baudelaire's *Les Fleurs du mal*. With the first, Aue is appealing to the reader's compassion, whereas by way of the second he is haughtily snubbing his silent interlocutor: "Hypocrite lecteur, mon semblable, mon frère." The strategy of the beginning and subsequent instances of reader address is twofold: aggressively antagonizing the audience while by the same token insisting on the shared humanity of reader and narrator, the shared reservoir of ambition and anxiety, pettiness and magnanimity, cruelty and compassion. Aue taunts and coaxes the reader, unsettling his presumed complacency, chastising him for the presumptuousness of his judgment, while at the same time insisting that he, the narrator, is just as human as the reader. At once unlike anybody and like everybody, Aue is perversely and wickedly presenting himself as an everyman. And the concluding sentence of the prologue—"I am a man like you" (24)—suggests that the reader, conversely, might turn out to be not unlike the monstrous other exposing himself before him. Aue repeatedly insists on the humanity of the perpetrators, recalling his own quasi-reflexive murders as acts of compassion, "monstrous pity" (147) triggered by the persistence of the human that the perpetrators are incapable of destroying in their victims.[14]

> Those who kill are humans, just like those who are killed, that's what's terrible. You can never say: I shall never kill, that's impossible; the most you can say is: I hope I shall never kill. I too hoped so.[15]

To make matters worse, he is presenting himself in the image of the man of sorrows. In the wake of Villon's hanged men and the sinners of Dante's *Inferno*, he asks those passing by not only for their pity and prayers, but promises them absolution in return. "Human brothers who live after us / Do not have your hearts hardened against us / For, if you take pity on us poor fellows / God will sooner have mercy on you."[16] The criminals appeal for compassion and forgiveness even though they were killed "Par Justice," with justice, as they acknowledge themselves. It is a reversal of roles in which the murderers assume the position of the victim and in which the passers-by are promised God's mercy if only they are willing to stop and show some pity for the dead men. This is a truly perverse twist, then, on the scene of confession. At the same time, Littell's cynical and unsentimental narrator will proudly and stubbornly reject any verdict from the reader, whether negative or positive, his tacit appeals giving way to disavowal. The motifs of shared humanity and detachment sounded in "Toccata" (thus the title of the prologue), his attempt to "touch" and rebuff the reader, recur throughout the novel, especially in Aue's confrontations with real victims of the genocide. So does the pattern of self-righteous affirmation of his ideological commitments and its opposite, disbelief and confusion in light of where these commitments have taken him.

The conversion of the henchman into the sacrificial victim imparting forgiveness on the persecutors is at play not only in Aue's cynical comparisons between perpetrators and victims, but also in one of the novel's most explicit intertextual references. Alongside the horrors of the camps and of war, Aue himself is succumbing to increasingly violent and delirious breakdowns. It is as though his body was revolting against, but also replicating and inflicting on itself, the very horrors he witnesses. It becomes the site of ravaging forces, wearing him down, battering him, but also spurring him on, it seems, to his most egregious acts, the gratuitous murders first of his mother and stepfather, then of a lover, and in the end of his own best friend Thomas (also a double of sorts). This story within the story, obviously part of Littell's homage to the aesthetics of transgression, is rendered with a morbid attention to unsavory detail, zeroing in on the physical and mental disintegration of Max Aue, especially his inability to keep his food in his stomach and later on his chronic diarrhea. He is swept up in a sea of excrement and vomit.[17] These spells and attacks—somatic and fantasmatic, it is difficult to tell the line between—are nothing other than the persecuting furies of the novel's title. Aue is an abject figure, an outcast, a kind of *homo sacer*, or in Girard's parlance, a scapegoat, bearer of the accursed share.

The flip side to the character's ambiguity, the odd coincidence between his own mental and physical disintegration and the destruction he attends and administers, is his continual insistence on the exchangeability of judge and accused, the reader and himself. In a malicious thought-experiment he seeks to claim the reader for a different kind of community, not the community of those who suffer, but the community of those obliged to kill.

> If you were born in a country or at a time not only when nobody comes to kill your wife and your children, but also nobody comes to ask you to kill the wives and children of others, then render thanks to God and go in peace. But always keep this thought in mind: you might be luckier than I, but you're not a better person.[18]

The reader as monstrous double, and the perpetrator the inverted image of his victims—this is, in short, the play of doubling, continual mutations, and transfigurations to which this "monstrous" book owes its disturbing impact.

I alluded to the novel's many debts and borrowings in the beginning, its creative revision and fusion of various models, genres, and registers. The result is a hybrid work that seeks to marry factual fastidiousness with oneiric fantasies of transgression, straddling the divide between high and low culture: from Greek tragedy to James Bond. Given the range of allusions and references of this unwieldy, encyclopedic novel, finding echoes of Girard does not come as a surprise. What is perhaps more remarkable and telling are the departures from the Girardian "script": The main protagonist's mimetic desire, for instance, having much more to do with the theatrical notion of taking on another's form, of transforming oneself into the other rather than with imitating another's desire and deadly rivalry with the model. The latter appears to be at stake in the dubious complex of German-Jewish symbiosis and mimicry, which crops up repeatedly in the characters' attempts to make sense of the genocide. The novel features two types of mimicry then, and, as in Girard, in both instances extreme violence ensues. What has puzzled readers of the novel, perhaps more than anything else, is precisely the relationship between the two kinds of violent excess staged with such relentless insistence throughout the book. The one an effect of the narrator's extraordinary psychosexual makeup, in other words, essentially "private," subjective; the other at the center of the genocidal machine he is serving and seeks to justify and "rationalize" in spite of his own revulsion and doubts. It is as though Littell sought to capture both the "pathology" and the "banality" of evil, the madness and bureaucracy of the Nazi regime without quite accounting for their correlation. The paradoxical alliance between the two is perhaps nowhere as evident as in Aue's ironic task to optimize (i.e., rationalize) the operations of the camps whose wasteful, uneconomical production is actually at odds with the war effort, as he points out in report after report.

Without resolving this tension, Girard's theory of mimetic desire and sacrificial violence helps bring into focus the novel's countervailing tendencies and skewed symmetries. Aue is haunted by the memory of primal unity, the indistinction of subject and other; his fantasies revolve around self-loss and dissolution, whereas the project in whose service he is enlisted is about the opposite: asserting difference in the face of sameness. With Girard, Nazi anti-Semitism in *The Kindly Ones* seems predicated on the threatening similarity between Germans and Jews, giving rise to the lethal mix of desire and ressentiment that needs to be discharged so as to prevent self-destruction. In a curious twist, however, the crisis triggered by the perceived indistinction between the secret "twins," Germans and Jews, is not resolved at all by unleashing the pent-up violence against the monstrous double. According to the narrator's defiant apologia, the attempt to obliterate sameness and to restore and consolidate difference compounds the issue, resulting in more likeness rather than less, endowing the Germans with a monstrous singularity. For they have brought on themselves the very destiny they had reserved for their "enemy brothers." This is how in what is perhaps the most scandalous turn in the twisted argument of the prologue Aue can present himself in the guise of the ultimate scapegoat, the supreme victim: *Ecce homo*.

Notes

1. "Conversation sur l'histoire et le roman," *Le Débat*, special issue "*Les Bienveillantes* de Jonathan Littell," 144 (2007): 25–44 (2). For an updated bibliography see http://auteurs.contemporain. info/oeuvre.php?oeuvre=Les+Bienveillantes&no=847. The most comprehensive treatment of the novel thus far is a collection of essays in French: Murielle Lucie Clément, ed., "*Les Bienveillantes*" *de Jonathan Littell* (Cambridge: Open Book Publishers, 2010).

2. See Georges Nivat, "*Les Bienveillantes* et les classiques russes," *Le Débat* 144 (2007): 56–65. *The Nouvel Observateur* is quoted on the back cover of the first American edition (New York: HarperCollins, 2009).

3. On the novel's realism see Jürgen Link, "'Wiederkehr des Realismus'—aber welches? Mit besonderem Bezug auf Jonathan Littell," *KulturRevolution* 54.1 (2008): 6–21. On the connection to the literature of transgression and evil see Daniel Mendelsohn, "Transgression: *The Kindly Ones* by Jonathan Littell," *New York Review of Books* 56 (2009): http://www.nybooks.com/ articles/archives/2009/mar/26/transgression; Liran Razinsky, "History, Excess and Testimony in Jonathan Littell's *Les Bienveillantes*," *French Forum* 33.3 (2008): 69–87; Julia Kristeva, "À propos des Bienveillantes (De l'abjection à la banalité du mal)," *L'Infini* 99 (2007): 22–35; Peter-André Alt, Ästhetik *des Bösen* (Munich: Beck, 2010), 496–511.

4. See Peter Schöttler, "Tom Ripley au pays de la Shoah," *Le Monde*, October 14, 2006, 19; Stefan Mesch, "Aryan Psycho: Zur literaturkritischen Rezeption von Jonathan Littells 'Die Wohlgesinnten,'" *Literaturkritik.de* 5 (2008), http://www.literaturkritik.de/public/rezension. php?rez_id=11900.

5. Jonas Grethlein, *Littells Orestie: Mythos, Macht und Moral in Les Bienveillantes* (Freiburg: Rombach, 2009).

6. See Klaus Theweleit, "On the German Reaction to Jonathan Littell's *Les Bienveillantes*," *New German Critique* 36.1 (2009): 21–34.

7. "It was the age of pure innocence, superb, magnificent. Freedom possessed our narrow little bodies, thin and tanned; we swam like seals, dashed through the wood like foxes, rolled and twisted together in the dust, our naked bodies indissociable, neither one nor the other specifically girl or boy, but a couple of snakes intertwined." Jonathan Littell, *The Kindly Ones*, trans. Charlotte Mandell (London: Vintage, 2010), 405.

8. René Girard, *Deceit, Desire, and the Novel: Self and Other in Literary Structure*, trans. Yvonne Freccero (Baltimore: Johns Hopkins University Press, 1965), 53ff.

9. Littell, *The Kindly Ones*, 102.

10. Littell, *The Kindly Ones*, 874–75.

11. "Le *double monstrueux* . . . se substitue à tout ce que chacun désire à la fois absorber et détruire, incarner et expulser." René Girard, *La Violence et le sacré* (Paris: Hachette, 2008), 244.

12. Littell, *The Kindly Ones*, 142.

13. See, for instance, Georges Bataille, *The Accursed Share: An Essay on General Economy*, trans. Robert Hurley (New York: Zone Books, 1991). For an interesting comparison of Bataille and

Girard see Tiina Arppe, "Sacred Violence: Girard, Bataille and the Vicissitudes of Human Desire," *Distinktion* 19 (2009): 31–58.

14. The notion of the persistence of the human is indebted to two of the first accounts by camp survivors: Robert Antelme's *L'Espèce humaine* (1947) and Primo Levi's *Se questo è un uomo* (1947). See Debarati Sanyal, "Reading Nazi Memory in Jonathan Littell's *Les Bienveillantes*," *L'Esprit Créateur* 50.4 (2010): 47–66.

15. Littell, *The Kindly Ones*, 24.

16. François Villon, *Complete Poems*, ed. and trans. Barbara Sargent-Baur (Toronto: Toronto University Press), 264–65 (translation modified). "Freres humains qui aprés nous vivez / N'ayez le cueurs contre nous endurciz / Car se pitié de nous povres avez, / Dieu en avra plus tost de vous mercis." On the narrative strategies vis-à-vis the reader see Martin von Koppenfels, "*Captatio malevolentiae*: Infame Erzähler bei Céline und Littell," *Lendemains* 134–35 (2009): 252–67.

17. See Sabine van Wesemael, "Apropos des corps liquids," in Clément, *"Les Bienveillantes" de Jonathan Littell*, 317–30.

18. Littell, *The Kindly Ones*, 20.

Literature and Christianity

A Personal View

René Girard

We are supposed to be living in the so-called postmodern era, which is also labeled post-Christian. The modern era was anti-Christian but now we are post-Christian. This label means that Christianity is so outmoded, at long last, so completely passé that its enemies no longer have to worry. Vigilance is no longer needed. Christianity is on its way to being completely forgotten.

Is this so certain, however? You will observe that, in the expression "post-Christian," the more evocative word is the second one, Christian. Our time seems unable to define itself independently of what it regards as hopelessly outmoded. A remarkable thing about us is our excessive use, in the labeling of our intellectual fads and fashions, of that Latin word that cannot be used independently in English, "post." There seems to be a great scarcity of labels in our world and the same ones have to be used again and again. "Post" is the fashionable Latin preposition, or rather "postposition," right now and it seems indispensable.

In the old days it was mechanical contraptions that were used again and again. They were repaired and renovated endlessly because they were scarce and expensive. Many people had to buy everything secondhand. They bought used typewriters and used washing machines as well as used cars.

Nowadays there is so much technical stuff around that to repair a broken gadget is usually more expensive than to buy a new one. The same is true of intellectual fads and fashions. They are countless. The only things that seem in short supply are labels for these intellectual fads and fashions. We cannot afford to throw them away any more; they are scarce; they must be carefully stored away because they have to be used several times.

The period before ours was still able to invent new labels such as impressionism, expressionism, cubism, and surrealism. They all ended in "ism" of course; they all resembled each other and that was not a good sign. It was a warning that our labeling creativity was under pressure and about to run out. After World War II, indeed, it became impossible to invent a truly successful new label. As a result, now, old labels have to be saved and recycled almost as much as taxicabs in Cairo.

How do we recycle our stock of old labels? So far there have been two principal techniques. The first consists in using the adjective "new" in front of an old label and the second in using the Latin preposition "post." The first technique was used a great deal immediately after World War II. There was a *new criticism* and a *new novel*; there were several *new theaters*. One good thing about "new" is that it could be translated into French, or borrowed from French and then it became entirely *nouveau*. Thanks to this clever device, the recycling was recycled and its life span considerably increased. It was a great feat of literary engineering. The first great success was *art nouveau*, way back in almost prehistorical times, and then there was a *nouveau roman*, a *nouvelle critique*, and a *nouvelle musique* and so forth until the whole thing became an excessively microwaved *nouvelle cuisine*.

The problem with words such as "new" and *nouveau* is that they are only adjectives and their very devotion to novelty naively proclaims our dependence upon the past. The past is the substantive part of the recycled label, the hated referent which stubbornly reasserts an independent existence we seem to have lost. In order to solve this problem, we have replaced "new" by "post," and that is why the *postmodern* and *post-Christian* era is upon us. It came along with the poststructuralist era which is also postmetaphysical, postphilosophical, post-everything in sight. Everything is so "post" that we are rapidly becoming post-post.

One problem with "post" however, is that it cannot be translated into French. The French word for "post" is always already "post." Since the word cannot be laundered through any other language, its possibilities are somewhat limited and it is already running out of steam. Another problem with "post" is that, hard as it tries to detach itself from the past, it cannot succeed any better than "new" or "nouveau." The substantive part of the recycled label is still the old word, the hated referent. In the expression post-Christian, the only real content is Christian.

A discussion on Christianity and literature should be defined perhaps as the official remnant of Christianity in the post-Christian era allegedly we are living in. Like all remnants, it could turn out to be a seed. A good biblical metaphor for this session is Noah's Ark. We may be at this interesting juncture when Noah is wondering if the waters are still going up or if they are beginning to recede, and if he will soon be able to let loose the dove.

As far as I am concerned the subject of literature and Christianity is literally the story of my whole intellectual and spiritual existence. Many years ago, I started with literature and myth and then moved to the study of the Bible and Christian Scripture. Great literature literally led me to Christianity. This itinerary is not original. It still happens every day and has been happening since the beginning of Christianity. It happened to Augustine, of course. It happened to many great saints such as Saint Francis of Assisi and Saint Theresa of Avila who, like Don Quixote, were fascinated by novels of chivalry.

One of the greatest examples of literature leading to Christianity is Dante. The experience is expressed symbolically by the role of Virgil in Dante's *Divine Comedy*. There are many reasons why Dante chose Virgil. In the *Aeneid*, Virgil makes his hero Aeneas visit hell. More important was the fact that in the Middle Ages Virgil was regarded as a prophet of Christ and, most important of all, was the fact that Virgil was greatly appreciated by Dante and had really played a role, I believe, in leading the author to Christianity.

What role? In order to understand, you have to take literally the idea of guiding someone through hell. The world of *The Aeneid* is really a world of hellish violence and, according to Dante, the function of profane literature is to guide us through Hell and Purgatory. This is what Virgil did for Dante and it was a great help to Dante because hell is not a very nice place to live. It is not even a nice place to visit. If you still have even two cents worth of common sense when you are in hell, you want to get out, for very selfish reasons.

Common sense and selfishness can be good things up to a point. This fact is acknowledged in the parable of the prodigal son. Why does the prodigal son return to his father? Not because of some great mystical reason, not even because he is sorry. He decides to go back to his father when he realizes that even the lowest servant in his father's house is better off than he is now that he has left that house. He still has enough common sense and selfishness to recognize hell when he finds himself in it and he wants to escape.

In my case it was not Virgil or even Dante who guided me through hell but the five novelists I discussed in my first book: Cervantes, Stendhal, Flaubert, Dostoyevsky, and Proust. The more modern the novel becomes, the more you descend down the circles of a hell which can still be defined in theological terms as it is in Dante, but can also now be defined in nonreligious terms—in terms of what happens to us when our relations with others are dominated exclusively by our desires and theirs, and their relationships dominated by their desires and ours. Because our desires are always mimetic or imitative, even and especially when we dream of being completely autonomous and self-sufficient, they always make us into rivals of our models and then the models of our rivals, thus turning our relations into an inextricable entanglement of identical and antagonistic desires which result in endless frustration.

Frustration is the law of the genre but it can be of two kinds. If we are prevented by our model from acquiring the object we both desire, our desire keeps intensifying painfully as a result of the deprivation. If, on the contrary, we acquire the object we desire, the prestige of our model collapses and our desire weakens and dies as a result of being fulfilled. This is the second kind of frustration and it is worse than the first. When it happens, we look for another model for our desire but the moment may come, after many such experiences, when we are totally disenchanted and cannot find any new model. This is the worst kind of frustration, the one the experts call postmodern and post-Christian, perhaps even post-mimetic desire.

The mortality of desire, its finitude, is the real problem in our world since it destabilizes even the most fundamental institutions, beginning with the family. Our psychological and psychoanalytical theories do not even acknowledge the reality of this problem. Desire according to Freud is immortal, eternal, since human beings desire only substitutes for their parents and cannot cease to desire them. Freud is silent about the death of desire. Only great literature has a lot to say about that subject.

The individualism of our time is really an effort to deny the failure of desire. Those who claim to be governed by the pleasure principle, as a rule, are enslaved to models and rivals, which makes their lives a constant frustration. But they are too vain to acknowledge their own enslavement. Mimetic desire makes us believe we are always on the verge of becoming self-sufficient through our own transformation into someone else. Our would-be transformation into a God, as Shakespeare says, turns us into an ass. In Pascal's terms, it becomes "Qui veut faire l'ange fait la bête"—"Whoever tries to act like an angel turns into a beast."

Understanding the real failure of desire leads to wisdom and ultimately to religion. Many philosophies and all religions share in that wisdom which modern trendiness denies. Great literature shares in that wisdom because it does not cheat with desire. It shows the necessary failure of undisciplined desire. The greatest literature shows the impossibility of self-fulfillment through desire. Mimetic obsessions are dreadful because they cannot vanquish their own circularity, even when they know about it. They are the mother of all addictions such as drugs, alcohol, obsessive sexuality, etc. One cannot get out of the circle even as its radius becomes smaller and smaller and our world becomes more narrowly obsessive.

Unlike most philosophies which are fundamentally stoic or epicurean, Judaism and Christianity preach no kind of self-fulfillment or self-absorption. Nor do they preach self-annihilation in the manner of Oriental mysticism. Christianity acknowledges the ultimate goodness of imitation as well as the goodness and reality of the human person. It teaches that instead of surrendering to mimetic desire, by following the newest fashion and worshipping the latest idol, we should imitate only Christ or Christ-like noncompetitive models.

If one is badly caught up in this circularity and wants to get out of it, one must undergo an experience of radical change which religious people call a *conversion*. In the classical view of conversion, it is not something of our own doing but the personal intervention of God in our lives. The greatest experience for Christians is the experience of becoming religious under a compulsion that they feel cannot come from themselves but from God alone. What makes conversion fascinating to those who have this experience (but also to those who do not) is the feeling that at no time in the lives of human beings is God closer to us and actually intervening in our lives.

This experience is not necessarily identical with the Christian experience. Many good Christians never experience it, either because, as far back as they can remember, they have always believed, or because even though they became Christians in their adult life, they never experienced anything dramatic enough to be labeled a conversion. The religious experience of these people is not necessarily less profound or even less intense than the experience of those who benefited from a dramatic conversion.

Nevertheless the idea of conversion enjoys great prestige with all people religiously inclined because there is no doubt that the Gospels emphasize conversion. The Pauline idea of the new man, and Paul's theme of salvation through faith, can be interpreted in terms of radical conversion. Almost everything in Paul can be so interpreted.

There is a problem with the word we use to describe that experience, the word conversion itself, or the Greek word *metanoia*. According to my dictionaries, the Latin word *conversio* was used for the first time in the Christian sense by Augustine. But Augustine, curiously, did not use it in his *Confessions*, which are the story of his own conversion. He used it for the first and last time in *The City of God* (VII, 33) in a phrase which refers to Satan's efforts to prevent us from achieving our conversion to the true God.

The problem with the Latin word *conversio* is that it does not really mean what we all mean by a Christian conversion and what Augustine himself undoubtedly meant. It means turning around in a circle; it refers to a full circular revolution that ultimately brings you back to your point of departure. This is not what a Christian conversion is. A Christian conversion is not circular; it never returns to its point of origin. It is open-ended; it is moving toward a totally unpredictable future. It seems to me that the real Latin significance of the word is characteristically pagan in the sense that it reflects the pagan conception of history and time itself, which is circular and repetitive. This conception is always reminiscent of that Eternal Return which can be found in the *Puranas* and elsewhere in the East. Various versions of it are also present in some of the pre-Socratic philosophers in Greece, especially Anaximander, Heraclitus, and Empedocles.

The Latin word *conversio* refers to reversible actions and processes, such as the translation of a text into another language, and also to mythical metamorphoses. When Christians adopt the word, they change its connotation from a circular to a linear phenomenon which is open-ended. It now means a change that takes place once and for all, with no conceivable return to the starting point. Therefore it should be irreversible.

The Greek *metanoia* was first used in Greek language churches to designate a certain type of penance. It does not designate a circular motion but it is not very good either at signifying Christian conversion. It is too weak a word.

Meta-noeo means to change one's mind about something; to have second thoughts regarding something that seemed settled; to perceive a mistake too late, when it can no longer be changed. It can mean therefore regret, but nothing as strong as Christian repentance when the convert hears the question that Paul heard on the road to Damascus, "Why do you persecute me?"

The Christian conversion is a transformation that reaches so deep it changes us once and for all and gives us a new being so to speak. The result is so superior that it is not possible to cancel that change, either by moving back or going around in a circle. To us Westerners, moving in a circle is a fate worse than death. It is hell. The idea of conversion is much more than reform, repentance, re-energizing, repair, regeneration, revolution, or any other word beginning with "re" which suggests a return to something that was there before and which therefore limits us to a circular view of life and experience. In the Christian conversion, a positive change is connoted which is not caught inside a circle.

Christians give the notion of conversion a depth and a seriousness that must be recognized in order to appreciate the significance of an important episode in the history of early Christianity, the *Donatist* heresy. The Donatists were fourth-century Christians in North Africa who took Christian conversion so seriously that, after periods of persecution, they refused to reintegrate into the church those people who had not been heroic enough to accept martyrdom and had recanted. They regarded Christian conversion as something so momentous that it could occur only once in a lifetime. One didn't have a second chance. The Donatists felt that people who did not have enough courage to face the lions in the Roman circus and die gladly for their faith were not good enough to be Christians at all.

These people had such an exalted view of the Christian conversion that the idea of its happening twice was blasphemous. In their eyes, it debased the whole process and made a mockery of the Christian faith. The Donatists were condemned by the Church and were certainly wrong from an evangelical viewpoint. If their absolutist principle had applied to Peter on the night of Jesus's arrest, after his triple denial of Christ, he would not have been reintegrated. He would never have become the leader of the Church. The Donatists were wrong. To condemn their intransigence was certainly the right thing to do for the early Church, but their appeal to such great Christians as Tertullian gives us a clue as to how seriously the notion of conversion was taken in early Christianity.

The aspect of literature that corresponds to that view, to that absolute view of conversion, is the belief which I hold, that the most outstanding forms of literary creation are not, as a rule, the product merely of native talent, the pure gift of literary creation, even though that gift exists. Nor are they the product of an acquired skill or technique even though no writer can be really good unless he has sufficient skill as a writer.

The writers that seem the greatest to me do not consider what we call their genius a natural gift with which they were born. They view it as a belated acquisition, the result of a personal transformation not of their own doing, which resembles a conversion. As far as the relationship of literature and Christianity is concerned, my main interest has been the relatedness of a certain form of creation to this notion of religious and especially Christian conversion.

The novelist who made me interested in this relationship was Marcel Proust. In Proust, of course, the hero and the writer are one but not simultaneously. The hero comes first and then the writer takes over at the end of the novel. Thanks to a break, a rupture which the novelist experiences, the hero becomes the novelist. But it is not the novelist's achievement. He feels he had little to do with the event that turned him into a novelist.

When I was writing about Proust, it was already fashionable to say that Marcel the narrator is a pure invention of the novelist, that the art of a writer has nothing to do with his life. This is not true, of course. The novel, even though it is not Christian at all, is, in its beliefs, morals, and metaphysics, an aesthetic and even spiritual autobiography which claims to be rooted in a personal experience, a personal transformation structured exactly like the experience Christians call a conversion.

At the beginning of the last volume, *Time Recaptured*, the hero suffers a great illness and finds himself in a state of profound depression. He no longer hopes that, someday, he will become a great writer. Then, at the moment of complete discouragement, even depression, some trivial incidents happen to him, like walking on the uneven pavement of the Guermantes courtyard and being reminded of the same experience in the past. This kind of remembrance triggers in him an aesthetic and spiritual illumination that transforms him completely. This tiny event provides him with his whole subject matter, the dedication needed to write the book and, above all, the right perspective, a perspective totally free for the first time of the compulsion of desire, of the hope of fulfilling himself through desire.

The titles chosen by Proust for the novel as a whole and for the last volume of his novel, which is the first, of course, in the sense that it recounts the creative experience, are highly significant. The whole novel is entitled *À la recherche du temps perdu*, which literally means "searching for lost time," for the time the hero has wasted and frittered away until the moment of conversion. The title of the last volume, which was truly the first to be conceived and written at least in its main outline, is *Time Recaptured*. It is the story of that spiritual death and rebirth to which I just alluded. It is really the beginning of the great creative period in Proust's life.

Thus we have two perspectives in Proust and other great novels of novelistic conversion. The *first perspective* is the deceptive perspective of desire, which is full of illusions regarding the possibility of the hero to fulfill himself through desire. It is the perspective that imprisoned him in a sterile process of jumping from one frustrated desire to the next over a period of many years. Everything the narrator could not acquire, he desired; everything he acquired, he immediately ceased to desire, until he fell into a state of ennui that could be called a state of post-mimetic desire.

The *second perspective* is one that comes from the end of the novel, from the omega point of conversion, which is a liberation from desire. This perspective enables the novelist to rectify the illusions of the hero and provides him with the creative energy he needs to write his novel. The second perspective is highly critical of the first but it is not resentful. Even though Proust never resorts to the vocabulary of sin, the reality of sin is present. The exploration of the past very much resembles a discovery of one's own sinfulness in Christianity. The time wasted away is full of idolatry, jealousy, envy, and snobbery; it all ends in a feeling of complete futility.

The word *conversion* is indispensable because Proust is describing, on the whole truthfully, the personal upheaval in his life and the great surge of creativity that enabled him to become the great novelist he could not have been earlier. Everything in the life and legend of Marcel Proust fits the conversion pattern. He enters great literature just as, earlier, he might have entered the religious life. There is something quasi-monastic about the partly mythical but nevertheless authentic account of his spending the rest of his life isolated from the world, in his cork-lined bedroom, waking up in the middle of the night to write his novel, just as monks wake up to sing their prayers.

There are many indications of a great change in Proust. The people who have worked in the Proustian archives say that one can distinguish at a single glance the post-conversion writing from the pre-conversion writing. His great novel is entirely written in the converted handwriting. The interpretation of the great Proustian creation as conversion was propounded by some of the first interpreters of his work, especially Jacques Rivière. All I did was go back to that theory armed with more biographical facts, with *Jean Santeuil* and, of course, with the mass of writing Proust produced at that time and then discarded. The major difference between *Jean Santeuil* and the later masterpiece is the author's unawareness of his own mimetic desire.

I do not claim that Proust became a saint after his conversion or even that he had a religious conversion. He did not. It is unquestionable, however, that at that time and for the only time in his life, he became interested in Christianity. He felt it could be relevant to his transformation. He sought some advice and being totally ignorant about the subject, he had the curious idea of consulting, of all people, André Gide, a lapsed Protestant. André Gide discouraged him from investigating the matter any further.

What I really claim is that the creative experience of Proust is truly comparable in most respects to a religious conversion which cannot be said to have failed but which bore only aesthetic fruits and never resulted in a religious conversion. It functions like a religious conversion and certainly there is no reason to disregard the voice of the novelist himself, especially in the mass of now published manuscripts which he wrote during the *Time Recaptured* period.

Before his great change, Proust was a talented amateur. His conversion turned him into a genius. When André Gide read the manuscript of Proust's first volume for his publishing house, he rejected it out of hand. The author, in his eyes, was an intellectually insignificant social butterfly who had not turned into a major writer overnight. This sort of metamorphosis is very rare indeed, and Gide was statistically correct in choosing not to believe it. He was a busy editor; but in this case he was wrong.

My insistence on the word *conversion* is like a red flag to a bull. In my first book, I did not wave one red flag at the bull but five, since I applied this notion not only to Proust, but to the four other novelists I was studying, Cervantes, Stendhal, Flaubert, and Dostoyevsky. Take Don Quixote, for instance. On his deathbed he repents and says he wishes he had time to read good books instead of the novels of chivalry that had turned him into a lunatic, a puppet whose strings were pulled by a puppeteer who did not even exist, Amadis of Gaul. Take Julien Sorel about to be guillotined in *The Red and the Black*. Take Madame Bovary when she eats the arsenic which is about to kill her. Flaubert is already Proustian enough not only to say: "Madame Bovary, c'est moi" but to add that during the creation of the death of his heroine he had the taste of arsenic in his mouth. In other words, he shared the creative death of his heroine. It is the same thing with the Siberian exile of Raskolnikov in Dostoyevsky's *Crime and Punishment*.

In all these writers, I felt, there was a central work which is the conversion novel, *The Red and the Black* for Stendhal, *Madame Bovary* for Flaubert, *Crime and Punishment* for Dostoyevsky. In all these writers, I found the same two perspectives as in the great Proust, the pre-conversion and the post-conversion perspective that rectifies the pre-conversion perspective, which is always some kind of self-deception.

I was guided by Proust when I coined the notion of a novelistic conversion. In the great mass of manuscripts associated with *Time Recaptured*, there is a text which compares the still-to-be-written last and first volume of the great novel to the conclusions of many great novels in the past, and of some works that are not novels. Cervantes is there, and Stendhal, Flaubert as well. There are also other novelists I have not mentioned, such as George Eliot.

The notion of conversion provides the work with a past and a future, with its "human time," its temporal depth that unconverted novels do not have. The second perspective distances the writer from the experience he recounts. Great novels are written from both ends at the same time. We might say, there is first the perspective of the unenlightened hero, and then the omega perspective, the all-knowing perspective that comes from the end.

When I published my first book, my good friend John Freccero was quick to point out that my last chapter did not mention the most important work in connection with its thesis, the work that invented the spiritual autobiography and is based on a great experience of conversion, Augustine's *Confessions*. This work is the first and greatest example of the dual perspective in a work. It must be regarded as the first great literary autobiography in a sense that the ancient world did not really know.

Before all these examples and their ultimate model come the Gospels themselves and, if we look at them closely, we will see that we have the dual perspective in them also. In the three synoptic Gospels, but especially in Mark, the disciples are represented as unable to understand the teaching of Jesus at the time they hear it from his own mouth. They are not really converted—even Peter—though he is able to recognize Jesus as the Messiah.

The apostles do not understand much while they are listening to Jesus. They misunderstand everything. They believe in the triumphant Messiah after the Davidic model rather than the suffering Messiah after the Servant of Yahweh in Second Isaiah. Only after the death and resurrection of Jesus are they able to understand what they first heard without understanding. The resurrection to them is a conversion experience, which is the same as the descent of the Holy Spirit and Pentecost when they were filled with a grace which was not theirs when Jesus was still alive. The real definition of grace is that Jesus died for us and even though his own people, as a people, did not receive him, he made those who did receive him able to become children of God.

Note

This paper was originally delivered in December 1998 at the "Christianity and Literature" session of the Modern Language Association's national convention in San Francisco. It was first published in *Philosophy and Literature* 23.1 (1999): 32–43.

Contributors

PIERPAOLO ANTONELLO is Reader in Modern Italian Literature and Culture at the University of Cambridge and Fellow of St John's College. He published widely on contemporary Italian literature, film, intellectual history, and visual art. He has also worked extensively on René Girard's mimetic theory. With João Cezar de Castro Rocha, he published a long interview with Girard: *Evolution and Conversion: Dialogues on the Origins of Culture* (2007), which has been translated into nine languages. He also edited several collections of essays and books by Girard, including *Miti d'origine: Persecuzioni e ordine culturale*, with Giuseppe Fornari (2005); *O Sacrifício* (2011); and the dialogues between Girard and Gianni Vattimo, *Christianity, Truth, and Weakening Faith* (2010). He is member of the Research and Publications committees of Imitatio: Integrating the Human Sciences.

ROBERT BUCH is Senior Lecturer in German and European Studies at the University of New South Wales, Sydney. His research areas includes nineteenth- and twentieth-century French and German literature and intellectual history. He is the author of *The Pathos of the Real: On the Aesthetics of Violence in the Twentieth Century* (2010); he coedited *Blumenberg lesen* (2014) with D. Weidner.

BILL BURGWINKLE is Professor of Medieval French and Occitan Literature at the University of Cambridge and Fellow of King's College. He is a specialist in gender and sexuality, and critical theory. He is the author of *Sodomy, Masculinity and Law in Medieval Literature, 1050–1230* (2004), *Love for Sale: Materialist Readings of the Troubadour Razo Corpus* (1997), and *Razos and Troubadour Songs* (1990), coauthor of *Sanctity and Pornography: On the Verge* (2010) and coeditor of *The Cambridge History of French Literature* (2011) and *Significant Others: Gender and Culture in Film and Literature, East and West* (1992). He is currently working on Occitan para-poetic texts, the fictional Crusades, and a research project on medieval French literary cultures outside France.

MARIA DIBATTISTA, Professor of English and Comparative Literature at Princeton University, has written extensively on modern literature and film. Her most recent books are *Fast Talking Dames*, a study of American film comedy of the thirties and forties, *Imagining Virginia Woolf: An Experiment in Critical Biography*, and *Novel Characters: A Genealogy*. She is the editor of *Cambridge Companion to Autobiography* and a more specialized volume, *Modernist Autobiography*.

LUCA DI BLASI is University Lecturer in Philosophy at the Universität Bern, Switzerland. He has published widely on the topic of philosophy of religion, including *Der Geist in der Revolte: Der Gnostizismus und seine Wiederkehr in der Postmoderne* (2002). His last publications include Wendy Brown and Rainer Forst, *The Power of Tolerance. A Debate*, coedited with C. F. Holzhey (2014), *Der weiße Mann: Ein Anti-Manifest* (2013), *The Scandal of Self-Contradiction: Pasolini's Multistable Geographies, Subjectivities, and Traditions*, coedited with M. Gragnolati and C. F. E. Holzhey (2012), and Boris Groys and Vittorio Hösle, *Die Vernunft an die Macht: Ein Streitgespräch*, coedited with Marc Jongen (2011).

KAREN S. FELDMAN is Associate Professor of German at University of California, Berkeley. Her publications include *Binding Words: Conscience and Rhetoric in Hobbes, Hegel and Heidegger* (2006) and articles in *MLN*, *Germanic Review*, *Philosophy and Rhetoric*, and other journals and volumes.

MARCO FORMISANO is Professor of Latin Literature at Ghent University, Belgium. He is an expert in Latin literature and focuses in particularly on late antique literary aesthetics and poetics as well as on literary aspects of didactic treatises, especially about the art of war. His publications include *Tecnica e scrittura* (2001) and editions of Vegetius's *Epitoma rei militaris* and the *Passio Perpetuae et Felicitatis* (2003 and 2008); he coedited the collected volumes *War in Words* (with H. Böhme, 2011), *Perpetua's Passions* (with J. Bremmer, 2012), and *Décadence: "Decline and Fall" or "Other Antiquity"?* (with T. Fuhrer, 2014).

MANUELE GRAGNOLATI is Professor of Italian Literature at Oxford University and Fellow of Somerville College. He has published widely on the significance of embodiment in Dante and medieval culture, as well as on the relationship between subjectivity and language in Italian literature throughout the centuries. His publications include *Experiencing the Afterlife: Soul and Body in Dante and Medieval Culture* (2005), *The Power of Disturbance: Elsa Morante's "Aracoeli"* (2009; ed. with S. Fortuna); *Aspects of the Performative in Medieval Culture* (2010; ed. with A. Suerbaum), *Dante's Plurilingualism: Authority, Knowledge, Subjectivity* (2010, ed. with S. Fortuna and J. Trabant), *Metamorphosing Dante: Appropriations, Manipulations, and Rewritings in the Twentieth and Twenty-First Centuries* (2010; ed. with F. Camilletti and F. Lampart), *The Scandal of Self-Contradiction: Pasolini's Multistable Subjectivities, Traditions, Geographies* (2012; ed. with L. Di Blasi and C. Holzhey), *Amor che move: Linguaggio del corpo e forma del desiderio in Dante, Pasolini e Morante* (2013). He lives between Oxford and Berlin, where he serves as Associate Director of the ICI Berlin Institute for Cultural Inquiry.

CHRISTOPH F. E. HOLZHEY is the founding director of the ICI Berlin Institute for Cultural Inquiry and led the core project Tension/Spannung with its recent foci on *Multistable Figures* and *Complementarity*. He has edited several volumes in the series *Cultural Inquiry* with Turia + Kant in Vienna: *Tension/Spannung* (2011), *The Scandal of Self-Contradiction: Pasolini's Multistable Subjectivities, Traditions, Geographies* (with L. Di Blasi and M. Gragnolati, 2012), *Situiertes Wissen und regionale Epistemologie: Zur Aktualität Georges Canguilhems und Donna J. Haraways* (with A.

Deuber-Mankowsky, 2013), *Multistable Figures: On the Critical Potentials of Ir/Reversible Aspect-Seeing* (2014), and Wendy Brown and Rainer Forst, *The Power of Tolerance: A Debate* (with L. Di Blasi, 2014).

TREVOR CRIBBEN MERRILL is Lecturer in French at the California Institute of Technology. He is the author of *The Book of Imitation and Desire* (2013), a study of mimetic desire in the novels of Milan Kundera.

ROSA MUCIGNAT is Lecturer in Comparative Literature at King's College London. She is the author of *Realism and Space in the Novel, 1795–1869* (2013). Her current research interests are twofold: representations of Italianness in European philosophy and literature of the Romantic period; and the experience of modernity in literatures in "minor" languages. She has written on Pier Paolo Pasolini and Friuli, and has edited the collection of essays *Friulian Language: Identity, Migration, Culture* (2014).

WOLFGANG PALAVER is Professor of Catholic Social Thought and Dean of the Faculty of Catholic Theology at the University of Innsbruck, Austria. He has published books and articles on religion and violence, Thomas Hobbes, Carl Schmitt, and René Girard. His most recent book is *René Girard's Mimetic Theory* (2013).

DAVID QUINT is Sterling Professor of Comparative Literature and English at Yale University. His books include *Epic and Empire* (1993), *Montaigne and the Quality of Mercy* (1998), *Cervantes's Novel of Modern Times* (2003), and *Inside Paradise Lost* (2014).

ALESSIA RICCIARDI is Associate Professor in Italian at Northwestern University's Department of French and Italian and Comparative Literature Program. Her main areas of interest are French and Italian contemporary literature, cinema, political philosophy, psychoanalysis, and gender studies. Her books include *The Ends of Mourning*, which won the Modern Language Association's 2004 Scaglione Prize for Comparative Literature, and *After La Dolce Vita: A Cultural Prehistory of Berlusconi's Italy*, which won the 2012 Scaglione Prize for Italian Studies.

JAN-MELISSA SCHRAMM is a Fellow at Trinity Hall, and a University Lecturer in the Faculty of English at the University of Cambridge, where she teaches Victorian literature. She is the author of *Testimony and Advocacy in Victorian Law, Literature, and Theology* (2000), and *Atonement and Self-Sacrifice in Nineteenth-Century Narrative* (2012) as well as a number of articles and book chapters on legal thought and nineteenth-century literature. She is also coeditor (with Yota Batsaki and Subha Mukherji) of *Fictions of Knowledge: Fact, Evidence, Doubt* (2011). In 2012–13, she held a Leverhulme Research Fellowship to work on a monograph provisionally entitled "Censorship, Dramatic Form, and the Representation of the Sacred in Nineteenth-Century England."

BRIAN SUDLOW is Lecturer of French and Translation Studies at Aston University, UK. He has published several articles on Girard, as well as on Georges Bernanos, Charles Maurras, Règis Debray, Dietrich Von Hildebrand, Giorgio Agamben, Adolphe Retté, and G. K. Chesterton. He is the author of *Catholic Literature and Secularisation in France and England 1880–1914* (2011).

HEATHER WEBB is Lecturer in Italian at the University of Cambridge and Fellow of Selwyn College. She specializes in medieval literature and culture with a particular interest in Dante. She is the author of *The Medieval Heart* (2010) and a number of articles on Catherine of Siena, Dante, and Giovanni da San Gimignano. She has organized, with George Corbett, the Cambridge Vertical Readings in Dante's *Comedy*.

JOBST WELGE is Visiting Professor for Romance Studies/Cultural Studies at the University of Konstanz, Germany. His wrote *Genealogical Fictions: Cultural Periphery and Historical Change in the Modern Novel* (2014). His current work focuses on spatiotemporal constellations in the late nineteenth- and early twentieth-century novel in Italy, Spain, and Latin America.

LAURA WITTMAN is Associate Professor of French and Italian at Stanford University. She primarily works on nineteenth- and twentieth-century Italian and French literature from a comparative perspective. She is interested in connections between modernity, religion, and politics. Much of her work explores the role of the ineffable, the mystical, and the body in modern poetry, philosophy, and culture. Her book *The Tomb of the Unknown Soldier, Modern Mourning, and the Reinvention of the Mystical Body* (2011) was awarded the Marraro Award of the Society for Italian Historical Studies for 2012.

YUE ZHUO is Assistant Professor of French at Yale University. She specializes in twentieth-century French literature, literary theory, and intellectual history, and her research focuses on cross-discipline and cross-genre writings in modern French literature and philosophy. She has published articles and book chapters on authors such as Georges Bataille, Maurice Blanchot, Roland Barthes, and Pascal Quignard.

Index